Classics

From the Renaissance to the nineteenth century, Latin and Greek were compulsory subjects in almost all European universities, and most early modern scholars published their research and conducted international correspondence in Latin. Latin had continued in use in Western Europe long after the fall of the Roman empire as the lingua franca of the educated classes and of law, diplomacy, religion and university teaching. The flight of Greek scholars to the West after the fall of Constantinople in 1453 gave impetus to the study of ancient Greek literature and the Greek New Testament. Eventually, just as nineteenth-century reforms of university curricula were beginning to erode this ascendancy, developments in textual criticism and linguistic analysis, and new ways of studying ancient societies, especially archaeology, led to renewed enthusiasm for the Classics. This collection offers works of criticism, interpretation and synthesis by the outstanding scholars of the nineteenth century.

The Golden Bough: The Third Edition

This work by Sir James Frazer (1854–1941) is widely considered to be one of the most important early texts in the fields of psychology and anthropology. At the same time, by applying modern methods of comparative ethnography to the classical world, and revealing the superstition and irrationality beneath the surface of the classical culture which had for so long been a model for Western civilisation, it was extremely controversial. Frazer was greatly influenced by E.B. Tylor's *Primitive Culture* (also reissued in this series), and by the work of the biblical scholar William Robertson Smith, to whom the first edition is dedicated. The twelve-volume third edition, reissued here, was greatly revised and enlarged, and published between 1911 and 1915; the two-volume first edition (1890) is also available in this series. Volumes 7 and 8 (1912) discuss the relationship of human sacrifice to the fertility of crops.

The Golden Bough
The Third Edition

VOLUME 7:
SPIRITS OF THE CORN
AND OF THE WILD 1

J.G. FRAZER

CAMBRIDGE
UNIVERSITY PRESS

CAMBRIDGE UNIVERSITY PRESS

Cambridge, New York, Melbourne, Madrid, Cape Town,
Singapore, São Paolo, Delhi, Mexico City

Published in the United States of America by Cambridge University Press, New York

www.cambridge.org
Information on this title: www.cambridge.org/9781108047364

© in this compilation Cambridge University Press 2012

This edition first published 1912
This digitally printed version 2012

ISBN 978-1-108-04736-4 Paperback

THE GOLDEN BOUGH

A STUDY IN MAGIC AND RELIGION

THIRD EDITION

PART V

SPIRITS OF THE CORN
AND OF THE WILD

VOL. I

MACMILLAN AND CO., Limited
LONDON · BOMBAY · CALCUTTA
MELBOURNE

THE MACMILLAN COMPANY
NEW YORK · BOSTON · CHICAGO
DALLAS · SAN FRANCISCO

THE MACMILLAN CO. OF CANADA, Ltd.
TORONTO

SPIRITS OF THE CORN

AND OF THE WILD

J. G. FRAZER, D.C.L., LL.D., Litt.D.

FELLOW OF TRINITY COLLEGE, CAMBRIDGE
PROFESSOR OF SOCIAL ANTHROPOLOGY IN THE UNIVERSITY OF LIVERPOOL

IN TWO VOLUMES

VOL. I

MACMILLAN AND CO., LIMITED
ST. MARTIN'S STREET, LONDON

1912

COPYRIGHT

PREFACE

In the last part of this work we examined the figure of the Dying and Reviving God as it appears in the Oriental religions of classical antiquity. With the present instalment of *The Golden Bough* we pursue the same theme in other religions and among other races. Passing from the East to Europe we begin with the religion of ancient Greece, which embodies the now familiar conception in two typical examples, the vine-god Dionysus and the corn-goddess Persephone, with her mother and duplicate Demeter. Both of these Greek divinities are personifications of cultivated plants, and a consideration of them naturally leads us on to investigate similar personifications elsewhere. Now of all the plants which men have artificially reared for the sake of food the cereals are on the whole the most important; therefore it is natural that the religion of primitive agricultural communities should be deeply coloured by the principal occupation of their lives, the care of the corn. Hence the frequency with which the figures of the Corn-mother and Corn-maiden, answering to the Demeter and Persephone of ancient Greece, meet us in other parts of the world, and not least of all on the harvest-fields of modern Europe. But edible roots as well as cereals have been cultivated by many races, especially in the tropical regions, as a subsidiary or even as a principal means of subsistence; and accordingly they too enter largely into the religious ideas of the peoples who live by them. Yet in the case of the roots, such as yams, taro, and potatoes, the conception of the Dying and Reviving God appears to figure less prominently than in the case of the cereals, perhaps for the simple reason that while the growth and decay of the one sort of fruit go on above ground for all to see, the similar processes of the other are hidden under ground and therefore strike the popular imagination less forcibly.

Having surveyed the variations of our main theme among the agricultural races of mankind, we prosecute the enquiry among savages who remain more or less completely in the hunting, fishing, and pastoral stages of society. The same motive which leads the primitive husbandman to adore the corn or the roots, induces the primitive hunter, fowler, fisher, or herdsman to adore the beasts, birds, or fishes which furnish him with the means of subsistence. To him the conception of the death of these worshipful beings is naturally presented with singular force and distinctness; since it is no figurative or allegorical death, no poetical embroidery thrown over the skeleton, but the real death, the naked skeleton, that constantly thrusts itself importunately on his attention. And strange as it may seem to us civilised men, the notion of the immortality and even of the resurrection of the lower animals appears to be almost as familiar to the savage and to be accepted by him with nearly as unwavering a faith as the obvious fact of their death and destruction. For the most part he assumes as a matter of course that the souls of dead animals survive their decease; hence much of the thought of the savage hunter is devoted to the problem of how he can best appease the naturally incensed ghosts of his victims so as to prevent them from doing him a mischief. This refusal of the savage to recognise in death a final cessation of the vital process, this unquestioning faith in the unbroken continuity of all life, is a fact that has not yet received the attention which it seems to merit from enquirers into the constitution of the human mind as well as into the history of religion. In the following pages I have collected examples of this curious faith; I must leave it to others to appraise them.

Thus on the whole we are concerned in these volumes with the reverence or worship paid by men to the natural resources from which they draw their nutriment, both vegetable and animal. That they should invest these resources with an atmosphere of wonder and awe, often indeed with a halo of divinity, is no matter for surprise. The circle of human knowledge, illuminated by the pale cold light of reason, is so infinitesimally small, the dark regions of human ignorance which lie beyond that luminous ring are so immeasurably vast, that imagination is fain to step up to the border line and send the warm, richly coloured beams of her fairy lantern streaming out into the darkness; and so, peering into the gloom, she is apt to mistake the shadowy reflections of her own figure for real beings moving in the abyss. In short, few men are sensible of the sharp line that divides the known from the unknown; to most men it is a hazy borderland where perception and conception melt indissolubly into one. Hence to the savage the ghosts of dead animals and men, with which his imagination peoples the void, are hardly less real than the solid shapes which the living animals and men present to his senses; and his thoughts and activities are nearly as much absorbed by the one as by the other. Of him it may be said with perhaps even greater truth than of his civilised brother, "What shadows we are, and what shadows we pursue!"

But having said so much in this book of the misty glory which the human imagination sheds round the hard material realities of the food supply, I am unwilling to leave my readers under the impression, natural but erroneous, that man has created most of his gods out of his belly. That is not so, at least that is not my reading of the history of religion. Among the visible, tangible, perceptible elements by which he is surrounded—and it is only of these that I presume to speak—there are others than the merely nutritious which have exerted a powerful influence in touching his imagination and stimulating his energies, and so have contributed to build up the complex fabric of religion.   To the preservation of the species the reproductive faculties are no less essential than the nutritive ; and with them we enter on a very different sphere of thought and feeling, to wit, the relation of the sexes to each other, with all the depths of tenderness and all the intricate problems which that mysterious relation involves.   The study of the various forms, some gross and palpable, some subtle and elusive, in which the sexual instinct has moulded the religious consciousness of our race, is one of the most interesting, as it is one of the most difficult and delicate tasks, which await the future historian of religion.

But the influence which the sexes exert on each other, intimate and profound as it has been and must always be, is far indeed from exhausting the forces of attraction by which mankind are bound together in society.   The need of mutual protection, the economic advantages of co-operation, the contagion of example, the communication of knowledge, the great ideas that radiate from great minds, like shafts of light from high towers,—these and many other things combine to draw men into communities, to drill them into regiments, and to set them marching on the road of progress with a concentrated force to which the loose skirmishers of mere anarchy and individualism can never hope to oppose a permanent resistance.   Hence when we consider how intimately humanity depends on society for many of the boons which it prizes most highly, we shall probably admit that of all the forces open to our observation which have shaped human destiny the influence of man on man is by far the greatest.   If that is so, it seems to follow that among the beings, real or imaginary, which the religious imagination has clothed with the attributes of divinity, human spirits are likely to play a more important part than the spirits of plants, animals, or inanimate objects. I believe that a careful examination of the evidence, which has still to be undertaken, will confirm this conclusion ; and that if we could strictly interrogate the phantoms which the human mind has conjured up out of the depths of its bottomless ignorance and enshrined as deities in the dim light of temples, we should find that the majority of them have been nothing but the ghosts of dead men. However, to say this is necessarily to anticipate the result of future research ; and if in saying it I have ventured to make a prediction, which like all predictions is liable to be falsified by the event, I have done so only from a fear lest, without some such warning, the numerous facts recorded in these volumes might lend themselves to an exaggerated estimate of their own importance and hence to a misinterpretation and distortion of history.

J. G. FRAZER.

CAMBRIDGE, 4*th May* 1912.

CONTENTS

xi

Chapter III.—Magical Significance of

Games in Primitive Agriculture   Pp. 92-112

Chapter VIII.—The Corn-spirit as an Animal . . . . . Pp. 270-305

CHAPTER I

DIONYSUS

IN the preceding part of this work we saw that in antiquity the civilised nations of western Asia and Egypt
pictured to themselves the changes of the seasons, and
particularly the annual growth and decay of vegetation,
as episodes in the life of gods, whose mournful death
and happy resurrection they celebrated with dramatic
rites of alternate lamentation and rejoicing. But if the
celebration was in form dramatic, it was in substance
magical ; that is to say, it was intended, on the principles
of sympathetic magic, to ensure the vernal regeneration of
plants and the multiplication of animals, which had seemed
to be menaced by the inroads of winter. In the ancient
world, however, such ideas and such rites were by no means
confined to the Oriental peoples of Babylon and Syria,
of Phrygia and Egypt ; they were not a product peculiar to
the religious mysticism of the dreamy East, but were shared
by the races of livelier fancy and more mercurial temperament who inhabited the shores and islands of the Aegean.
We need not, with some enquirers in ancient and modern
times, suppose that these Western peoples borrowed from
the older civilisation of the Orient the conception of the
Dying and Reviving God, together with the solemn ritual,
in which that conception was dramatically set forth before
the eyes of the worshippers. More probably the resemblance
which may be traced in this respect between the religions of
the East and the West is no more than what we commonly,
though incorrectly, call a fortuitous coincidence, the effect of

Death and resurrection of Oriental gods of vegetation.

The Dying and Reviving god of vegetation in ancient Greece.

similar causes acting alike on the similar constitution of the human mind in different countries and under different skies. The Greek had no need to journey into far countries to learn the vicissitudes of the seasons, to mark the fleeting beauty of the damask rose, the transient glory of the golden corn, the passing splendour of the purple grapes. Year by year in his own beautiful land he beheld, with natural regret, the bright pomp of summer fading into the gloom and stagnation of winter, and year by year he hailed with natural delight the outburst of fresh life in spring. Accustomed to personify the forces of nature, to tinge her cold abstractions with the warm hues of imagination, to clothe her naked realities with the gorgeous drapery of a mythic fancy, he fashioned for himself a train of gods and goddesses, of spirits and elves, out of the shifting panorama of the seasons, and followed the annual fluctuations of their fortunes with alternate emotions of cheerfulness and dejection, of gladness and sorrow, which found their natural expression in alternate rites of rejoicing and lamentation, of revelry and mourning. A consideration of some of the Greek divinities who thus died and rose again from the dead may furnish us with a series of companion pictures to set side by side with the sad figures of Adonis, Attis, and Osiris. We begin with Dionysus.

Dionysus, the god of the vine, originally a Thracian deity.

The god Dionysus or Bacchus is best known to us as a personification of the vine and of the exhilaration produced by the juice of the grape.[1] His ecstatic worship, characterised by wild dances, thrilling music, and tipsy excess, appears to

---

[1] On Dionysus in general, see L. Preller, *Griechische Mythologie*,[4] i. 659 *sqq.* ; Fr. Lenormant, *s.v.* "Bacchus," in Daremberg and Saglio's *Dictionnaire des Antiquités Grecques et Romaines*, i. 591 *sqq.* ; Voigt and Thraemer, *s.v.* "Dionysus," in W. H. Roscher's *Lexikon der griech. u. röm. Mythologie*, i. 1029 *sqq.* ; E. Rohde, *Psyche*[3] (Tübingen and Leipsic, 1903), ii. 1 *sqq.* ; Miss J. E. Harrison, *Prolegomena to the Study of Greek Religion*, Second Edition (Cambridge, 1908), pp. 363 *sqq.* ; Kern, *s.v.* "Dionysus," in Pauly-Wissowa's *Real-Encyclopädie der classischen Altertumswissenschaft*, v. 1010 *sqq.*; M. P. Nilsson, *Griechische Feste von religiöser Bedeutung* (Leipsic, 1906), pp. 258 *sqq.* ; L. R. Farnell, *The Cults of the Greek States*, v. (Oxford, 1909) pp. 85 *sqq.* The epithet *Bromios* bestowed on Dionysus, and his identification with the Thracian and Phrygian deity Sabazius, have been adduced as evidence that Dionysus was a god of beer or of other cereal intoxicants before he became a god of wine. See W. Headlam, in *Classical Review*, xv. (1901) p. 23 ; Miss J. E. Harrison, *Prolegomena to the Study of Greek Religion*, pp. 414-426.

have originated among the rude tribes of Thrace, who were notoriously addicted to drunkenness.[1]   Its mystic doctrines and extravagant rites were essentially foreign to the clear intelligence and sober temperament of the Greek race.   Yet appealing as it did to that love of mystery and that proneness to revert to savagery which seem to be innate in most men, the religion spread like wildfire through Greece until the god whom Homer hardly deigned to notice had become the most popular figure of the pantheon.   The resemblance which his story and his ceremonies present to those of Osiris have led some enquirers both in ancient and modern times to hold that Dionysus was merely a disguised Osiris, imported directly from Egypt into Greece.[2]   But the great preponderance of evidence points to his Thracian origin, and the similarity of the two worships is sufficiently explained by the similarity of the ideas and customs on which they were founded.

While the vine with its clusters was the most character-istic manifestation of Dionysus, he was also a god of trees in general.   Thus we are told that almost all the Greeks sacrificed to " Dionysus of the tree." [3]   In Boeotia one of his titles was " Dionysus in the tree." [4]   His image was often merely an upright post, without arms, but draped in a mantle, with a bearded mask to represent the head, and with leafy boughs projecting from the head or body to shew the nature of the deity.[5]   On a vase his rude effigy is depicted appearing out of a low tree or bush.[6]   At Magnesia on the Maeander an image of Dionysus is said to have been found in a plane-tree, which had been broken by the

Dionysus a god of trees, especially of fruit-trees.

---

[1] Plato, *Laws*, i. p. 637 E ; Theopompus, cited by Athenaeus, x. 60, p. 442 E F ; Suidas, *s.v.* κατασκεδάζειν ; compare Xenophon, *Anabasis*, vii. 3. 32.   For the evidence of the Thracian origin of Dionysus, see the writers cited in the preceding note, especially Dr. L. R. Farnell, *op. cit.* v. 85 *sqq.*   Compare W. Ridgeway, *The Origin of Tragedy* (Cambridge, 1910), pp. 10 *sqq.*

[2] Herodotus, ii. 49 ; Diodorus Siculus, i. 97. 4 ; P. Foucart, *Le Culte de Dionyse en Attique* (Paris, 1904), pp. 9 *sqq.*, 159 *sqq.* (*Mémoires de*

l'Académie des Inscriptions et Belles-lettres, xxxvii.).

[3] Plutarch, *Quaest. Conviv.* v. 3 : Διονύσῳ δὲ δενδρίτῃ πάντες, ὡς ἔπος εἰπεῖν, Ἕλληνες θύουσιν.

[4] Hesychius, *s.v.* Ἔνδενδρος.

[5] See the pictures of his images, drawn from ancient vases, in C. Bötticher's *Baumkultus der Hellenen* (Berlin, 1856), plates 42, 43, 43 A, 43 B, 44 ; Daremberg et Saglio, *Dictionnaire des Antiquités Grecques et Romaines,* i. 361, 626 *sq.*

[6] Daremberg et Saglio, *op. cit.* i. 626.

wind.[1]   He was the patron of cultivated trees ;[2] prayers were
offered to him that he would make the trees grow ;[3] and he
was especially honoured by husbandmen, chiefly fruit-growers,
who set up an image of him, in the shape of a natural tree-
stump, in their orchards.[4]   He was said to have discovered
all tree-fruits, amongst which apples and figs are particularly
mentioned ;[5] and he was referred to as "well-fruited,"
"he of the green fruit," and "making the fruit to grow."[6]
One of his titles was "teeming" or "bursting" (as of sap
or blossoms) ;[7] and there was a Flowery Dionysus in Attica
and at Patrae in Achaia.[8]   The Athenians sacrificed to him
for the prosperity of the fruits of the land.[9]   Amongst the
trees particularly sacred to him, in addition to the vine,
was the pine-tree.[10]   The Delphic oracle commanded the
Corinthians to worship a particular pine-tree "equally with
the god," so they made two images of Dionysus out of it,
with red faces and gilt bodies.[11]   In art a wand, tipped with
a pine-cone, is commonly carried by the god or his
worshippers.[12]   Again, the ivy and the fig-tree were especially
associated with him.   In the Attic township of Acharnae
there was a Dionysus Ivy ;[13] at Lacedaemon there was a
Fig Dionysus ; and in Naxos, where figs were called *meilicha*,
there was a Dionysus Meilichios, the face of whose image
was made of fig-wood.[14]

[1] P. Wendland und O. Kern,
*Beiträge zur Geschichte der griechischen
Philosophie und Religion* (Berlin,
1895), pp. 79 *sqq.* ; Ch. Michel, *Recueil d'Inscriptions Grecques* (Brussels,
1900), No. 856.

[2] Cornutus, *Theologiae Graecae Compendium*, 30.

[3] Pindar, quoted by Plutarch, *Isis
et Osiris*, 35.

[4] Maximus Tyrius, *Dissertat.* viii. 1.

[5] Athenaeus, iii. chs. 14 and 23,
pp. 78 C, 82 D.

[6] *Orphica*, Hymn l. 4. liii. 8.

[7] Aelian, *Var. Hist.* iii. 41 ;
Hesychius, *s.v.* Φλέω[s]. Compare
Plutarch, *Quaest. Conviv.* v. 8. 3.

[8] Pausanias, i. 31. 4 ; *id.* vii. 21.
6.

[9] Dittenberger, *Sylloge Inscriptionum Graecarum*,[2] No. 636, vol.
ii. p. 435, τῶν καρπῶν τῶν ἐν τῇ χώρᾳ.

However, the words may equally well
refer to the cereal crops.

[10] Plutarch, *Quaest. Conviv.* v. 3.

[11] Pausanias, ii. 2. 6 *sq.*   Pausanias
does not mention the kind of tree ;
but from Euripides, *Bacchae*, 1064
sqq., and Philostratus, *Imag.* i. 17
(18), we may infer that it was a pine,
though Theocritus (xxvi. 11) speaks of
it as a mastich-tree.

[12] Müller-Wieseler, *Denkmäler der
alten Kunst*, ii. pll. xxxii. *sqq.* ; A.
Baumeister, *Denkmäler des klassischen
Altertums*, i. figures 489, 491, 492,
495.   Compare F. Lenormant, in
Daremberg et Saglio, *Dictionnaire des
Antiquités Grecques et Romaines*, i.
623 ; Ch. F. Lobeck, *Aglaophamus*
(Königsberg, 1829), p. 700.

[13] Pausanias, i. 31. 6.

[14] Athenaeus, iii. 14, p. 78 C.

Further, there are indications, few but significant, that Dionysus was conceived as a deity of agriculture and the corn. He is spoken of as himself doing the work of a husbandman : [1] he is reported to have been the first to yoke oxen to the plough, which before had been dragged by hand alone ; and some people found in this tradition the clue to the bovine shape in which, as we shall see, the god was often supposed to present himself to his worshippers. Thus guiding the ploughshare and scattering the seed as he went, Dionysus is said to have eased the labour of the husband-man.[2] Further, we are told that in the land of the Bisaltae, a Thracian tribe, there was a great and fair sanctuary of Dionysus, where at his festival a bright light shone forth at night as a token of an abundant harvest vouch-safed by the deity ; but if the crops were to fail that year, the mystic light was not seen, darkness brooded over the sanctuary as at other times.[3] Moreover, among the emblems of Dionysus was the winnowing-fan, that is the large open shovel-shaped basket, which down to modern times has been used by farmers to separate the grain from the chaff by tossing the corn in the air. This simple agricultural instru-ment figured in the mystic rites of Dionysus ; indeed the god is traditionally said to have been placed at birth in a winnowing-fan as in a cradle : in art he is represented as an infant so cradled ; and from these traditions and representa-tions he derived the epithet of *Liknites*, that is, " He of the Winnowing-fan." [4]

At first sight this symbolism might be explained very simply and naturally by supposing that the divine

Dionysus as a god of agriculture and the corn.

The win-nowing-fan as an em-blem of Dionysus.

Use of the winnow-ing-fan to cradle infants.

---

[1] Himerius, *Orat.* i. 10, Διονυσος γεωργεῖ.

[2] Diodorus Siculus, iii. 64. 1-3, iv. 4. 1 *sq.* On the agricultural aspect of Dionysus, see L. R. Farnell, *The Cults of the Greek States*, v. (Oxford, 1909) pp. 123 *sq.*

[3] [Aristotle,] *Mirab. Auscult.* 122 (p. 842 A, ed. Im. Bekker, Berlin edition).

[4] Servius on Virgil, *Georg.* i. 166 ; Plutarch, *Isis et Osiris*, 35. The literary and monumental evidence as to the winnowing-fan in the myth and ritual of Dionysus has been collected

and admirably interpreted by Miss J. E. Harrison in her article " Mystica Vannus Iacchi," *Journal of Hellenic Studies*, xxiii. (1903) pp. 292-324. Compare her *Prolegomena to the Study of Greek Religion* [2] (Cambridge, 1908), pp. 517 *sqq.* I must refer the reader to these works for full details on the subject. In the passage of Servius referred to the reading is somewhat uncertain ; in his critical edition G. Thilo reads λικμητὴν and λικμὸς instead of the usual λικνιτὴν and λικνόν. But the variation does not affect the mean-ing.

infant cradled in the winnowing-fan was identified with the corn which it is the function of the instrument to winnow and sift. Yet against this identification it may be urged with reason that the use of a winnowing-fan as a cradle was not peculiar to Dionysus ; it was a regular practice with the ancient Greeks to place their infants in winnowing-fans as an omen of wealth and fertility for the future life of the children.[1] Customs of the same sort have been observed, apparently for similar reasons, by other peoples in other lands. For example, in Java it is or used to be customary to place every child at birth in a bamboo basket like the sieve or winnowing-basket which Javanese farmers use for separating the rice from the chaff.[2] It is the midwife who places the child in the basket, and as she does so she suddenly knocks with the palms of both hands on the basket in order that the child may not be timid and fearful. Then she addresses the child thus : " Cry not, for Njaï-among and Kaki-among " (two spirits) " are watching over you." Next she addresses these two spirits, saying, " Bring not your grandchild to the road, lest he be trampled by a horse ; bring him not to the bank of the river, lest he fall into the river." The object of the ceremony is said to be that these two spirits should always and everywhere guard the child.[3] On the first anniversary of a child's birthday the Chinese of Foo-Chow set the little one in a large bamboo sieve, such as farmers employ in winnowing grain, and in the sieve they place along with the child a variety of articles, such as fruits, gold or silver ornaments, a set of money-scales, books, a pencil, pen, ink, paper, and so on, and they draw omens of the child's future career from the object which it first handles and plays with. Thus, if the infant first grasps the money-scale, he will be wealthy ; if he seizes on a book, he will be learned, and so forth.[4] In the Bilaspore district

[1] Ἐν γὰρ λείκνοις τὸ παλαιὸν κατεκοίμιζον τὰ βρέφη πλοῦτον καὶ καρποὺς οἰωνιζόμενοι, Scholiast on Callimachus, i. 48 (*Callimachea*, edidit O. Schneider, Leipsic, 1870-1873, vol. i. p. 109).

[2] T. S. Raffles, *History of Java* (London, 1817), i. 323 ; C. F. Winter, "Instellingen, Gewoonten en Gebruiken der Javanen te Soerakarta," *Tijdschrift voor Neêrlands Indie*, Vijfde Jaargang, Eerste Deel (1843), p. 695 ; P. J. Veth, *Java* (Haarlem, 1875-1884), i. 639.

[3] C. Poensen, "Iets over de kleeding der Javanen," *Mededeelingen van wege het Nederlandsche Zendelinggenootschap*, xx. (1876) pp. 279 *sq.*

[4] Rev. J. Doolittle, *Social Life of the Chinese*, edited and revised by the Rev. Paxton Hood (London, 1868), pp. 90 *sq.*

of India it is customary for well-to-do people to place a new-born infant in a winnowing-fan filled with rice and after-wards to give the grain to the nurse in attendance.[1]   In Upper Egypt a newly-born babe is immediately laid upon a corn-sieve and corn is scattered around it ; moreover, on the seventh day after birth the infant is carried on a sieve through the whole house, while the midwife scatters wheat, barley, pease and salt.   The intention of these ceremonies is said to be to avert evil spirits from the child,[2] and a like motive is assigned by other peoples for the practice of placing newborn infants in a winnowing-basket or corn-sieve. For example, in the Punjaub, when several children of a family have died in succession, a new baby will sometimes be put at birth into an old winnowing-basket (*chhaj*) along with the sweepings of the house, and so dragged out into the yard ; such a child may, like Dionysus, in after life be known by the name of Winnowing-basket (*Chhajju*) or Dragged (*Ghasitâ*).[3]   The object of treating the child in this way seems to be to save its life by deceiving the spirits, who are supposed to have carried off its elder brothers and sisters ; these malevolent beings are on the look-out for the new baby, but they will never think of raking for it in the dust-bin, that being the last place where they would expect to find the hope of the family.   The same may perhaps be the intention of a ceremony observed by the Gaolis of the Deccan.   As soon as a child is born, it is bathed and then placed on a sieve for a few minutes.   On the fifth day the sieve, with a lime and *pan* leaves on it, is removed outside the house and then, after the worship of Chetti has been performed, the sieve is thrown away on the

The win-nowing-fan sometimes intended to avert evil spirits from children.

[1] Rev. E. M. Gordon, "Some Notes concerning the People of Mungēli Tahsīl, Bilaspur District," *Journal of the Asiatic Society of Bengal*, lxxi., Part iii. (Calcutta, 1903) p. 74 ; *id.*, *Indian Folk Tales* (London, 1908), p. 41.

[2] C. B. Klunzinger, *Bilder aus Oberägypten* (Stuttgart, 1877), pp. 181, 182 ; *id.*, *Upper Egypt, its People and Products* (London, 1878), pp. 185, 186.

[3] R. C. Temple, " Opprobrious Names," *Indian Antiquary*, x. (1881) pp. 331 *sq.*   Compare H. A. Rose, " Hindu Birth Observances in the Punjab," *Journal of the Royal Anthropo-logical Institute*, xxxvii. (1907) p. 234. See also *Panjab Notes and Queries*, vol. iii. August 1886, § 768, pp. 184 *sq.* : " The winnowing fan in which a newly-born child is laid, is used on the fifth day for the worship of Satwáí.   This makes it impure, and it is henceforward used only for the house-sweepings."

road.[1] Again, the same notion of rescuing the child from dangerous spirits comes out very clearly in a similar custom observed by the natives of Laos, a province of Siam. These people "believe that an infant is the child, not of its parents, but of the spirits, and in this belief they go through the following formalities. As soon as an infant is born it is bathed and dressed, laid upon a rice-sieve, and placed—by the grandmother if present, if not, by the next near female relative—at the head of the stairs or of the ladder leading to the house. The person performing this duty calls out in a loud tone to the spirits to come and take the child away to-day, or for ever after to let it alone; at the same moment she stamps violently on the floor to frighten the child, or give it a jerk, and make it cry. If it does not cry this is regarded as an evil omen. If, on the other hand, it follows the ordinary laws of nature and begins to exercise its vocal organs, it is supposed to have a happy and prosperous life before it. Sometimes the spirits do come and take the infant away, *i.e.* it dies before it is twenty-four hours old, but, to prevent such a calamity, strings are tied round its wrists on the first night after its birth, and if it sickens or is feeble the spirit-doctors are called in to prescribe certain offerings to be made to keep away the very spirits who, only a few hours previously, were ceremoniously called upon to come and carry the child off. On the day after its birth the child is regarded as being the property no longer of the spirits, who could have taken it if they had wanted it, but of the parents, who forthwith sell it to some relation for a nominal sum—an eighth or a quarter of a rupee perhaps. This again is a further guarantee against molestation by the spirits, who apparently are regarded as honest folk that would not stoop to take what has been bought and paid for."[2]

Use of the winnowing-fan to avert evil from children in India, Madagascar, and China.

A like intention of averting evil in some shape from a child is assigned in other cases of the same custom. Thus in Travancore, "if an infant is observed to distort its limbs as if in pain, it is supposed to be under the pressure of some one who has stooped over it, to relieve which the mother

[1] Lieut.-Colonel Gunthorpe, "On the Ghosí or Gaddí Gaolís of the Deccan," *Journal of the Anthropological Society of Bombay,* i. 45.

[2] C. Bock, *Temples and Elephants* (London, 1884), pp. 258 *sq.*

places it with a nut-cracker on a winnowing fan and shakes it three or four times." [1]   Again, among the Tanala people of Madagascar almost all children born in the unlucky month of Faosa are buried alive in the forest.   But if the parents resolve to let the child live, they must call in the aid of a diviner, who performs a ceremony for averting the threatened ill-luck.   The child is placed in a winnowing-fan along with certain herbs.   Further, the diviner takes herbs of the same sort, a worn-out spade, and an axe, fastens them to the father's spear, and sets the spear up in the ground.   Then the child is bathed in water which has been medicated with some of the same herbs.   Finally the diviner says : " The worn-out spade to the grandchild ; may it (the child) not despoil its father, may it not despoil its mother, may it not despoil the children ; let it be good."   This ceremony, we are told, " puts an end to the child's evil days, and the father gets the spear to put away all evil.   The child then joins its father and mother ; its evil days are averted, and the water and the other things are buried, for they account them evil." [2] Similarly the ancient Greeks used to bury, or throw into the sea, or deposit at cross-roads, the things that had been used in ceremonies of purification, no doubt because the things were supposed to be tainted by the evil which had been transferred to them in the rites.[3]   Another example of the use of a winnowing-fan in what may be called a purificatory ceremony is furnished by the practice of the Chinese of Foo-Chow.   A lad who is suffering from small-pox is made to squat in a large winnowing sieve.   On his head is placed a piece of red cloth, and on the cloth are laid some parched beans, which are then allowed to roll off.   As the name for beans, pronounced in the local dialect, is identical with the common name for small-pox, and as moreover the scars left by the pustules are thought to resemble beans, it appears to be imagined that just as the beans roll off the boy's head, so will the pustules vanish from his body without leaving a

[1] S. Mateer, *Native Life in Travancore* (London, 1883), p. 213.

[2] J. Richardson, "Tanala Customs, Superstitions, and Beliefs," *Antananarivo Annual and Madagascar Magazine,*

Reprint of the First Four Numbers (Antananarivo, 1885), pp. 226 *sq.*

[3] Pausanias, ii. 31. 8 ; K. F. Hermann, *Lehrbuch der gottesdienstlichen Alterthümer der Griechen* [2] (Heidelberg, 1858), pp. 132 *sq.*, § 23, 25.

trace behind.[1]   Thus the cure depends on the principle
of homoeopathic magic.   Perhaps on the same principle a
winnowing-fan is employed in the 'ceremony from a notion
that it will help to waft or fan away the disease like chaff
Karen from the grain.   We may compare a purificatory ceremony
ceremony observed by the Karens of Burma at the naming of a new-
of fanning
away evils born child.   Amongst these people "children are supposed
from to come into the world defiled, and unless that defilement is
children. removed, they will be unfortunate, and unsuccessful in their
undertakings.   An Elder takes a thin splint of bamboo,
and, tying a noose at one end, he fans it down the child's
arm, saying :

'*Fan away ill luck, fan away ill success :*
Fan away inability, fan away unskilfulness :
Fan away slow growth, fan away difficulty of growth :
Fan away stuntedness, fan away puniness :
Fan away drowsiness, fan away stupidity :
Fan away debasedness, fan away wretchedness :
Fan away the whole completely.'

"The Elder now changes his motion and fans up the child's
arm, saying :

'*Fan on power, fan on influence :*
Fan on the paddy bin, fan on the paddy barn :
Fan on followers, fan on dependants :
Fan on good things, fan on appropriate things.'"[2]

Among the Thus in some of the foregoing instances the employment
reasons for
the use of of the winnowing-fan may have been suggested by the proper
the win- use of the implement as a means of separating the corn from
nowing-fan
in birth- the chaff, the same operation being extended by analogy to
rites may rid men of evils of various sorts which would otherwise adhere
have been
the wish to them like husks to the grain.   It was in this way that
to avert the ancients explained the use of the winnowing-fan in the
evils and
to promote mysteries.[3]   But one motive, and perhaps the original one,
fertility and
growth.

[1] Rev. J. Doolittle, *Social Life of the Chinese*, edited and revised by the Rev. Paxton Hood (London, 1868), pp. 114 *sq.*   The beans used in the ceremony had previously been placed before an image of the goddess of small-pox.

[2] Rev. F. Mason, D.D., "Physical Character of the Karens," *Journal of the Asiatic Society of Bengal*, New Series, No. cxxxi. (Calcutta, 1866), pp. 9 *sq.*

[3] Servius on Virgil, *Georg.* i. 166 : "*Et vannus Iacchi . . . Mystica autem Bacchi ideo ait, quod Liberi patris sacra ad purgationem animae pertinebant : et sic homines ejus mysteriis purgabantur, sicut vannis frumenta purgantur.*'

for setting a newborn child in a winnowing-fan and surround-
ing it with corn was probably the wish to communicate to
the infant, on the principle of sympathetic magic, the fertility
and especially the power of growth possessed by the grain.
This was in substance the explanation which W. Mannhardt
gave of the custom.[1] He rightly insisted on the analogy
which many peoples, and in particular the ancient Greeks,
have traced between the sowing of seed and the begetting
of children,[2] and he confirmed his view of the function of
the winnowing-fan in these ceremonies by aptly comparing
a German custom of sowing barley or flax seed over weakly
and stunted children in the belief that this will make them
grow with the growth of the barley or the flax.[3] An
Esthonian mode of accomplishing the same object is to set
the child in the middle of a plot of ground where a sower is
sowing hemp and to leave the little one there till the sowing
is finished ; after that they imagine that the child will shoot
up in stature like the hemp which has just been sown.[4]

With the foregoing evidence before us of a widespread
custom of placing newborn children in winnowing-fans we
clearly cannot argue that Dionysus must necessarily have
been a god of the corn because Greek tradition and Greek
art represent him as an infant cradled in a winnowing-fan.
The argument would prove too much, for it would apply
equally to all the infants that have been so cradled in all
parts of the world. We cannot even press the argument
drawn from the surname " He of the Winnowing-fan " which
was borne by Dionysus, since we have seen that similar
names are borne for similar reasons in India by persons who
have no claim whatever to be regarded as deities of the corn.
Yet when all necessary deductions have been made on this
score, the association of Dionysus with the winnowing-fan
appears to be too intimate to be explained away as a mere
reminiscence of a practice to which every Greek baby, whether

Use of the winnow-ing-fan in the rites of Dionysus.

[1] W. Mannhardt, "Kind und Korn,"
Mythologische Forschungen (Strasburg,
1884), pp. 351-374.
[2] W. Mannhardt, *op. cit.* pp. 351
sqq.
[3] W. Mannhardt, *op. cit.* p. 372,
citing A. Wuttke, *Der deutsche Volksaberglaube*[2](Berlin, 1869), p. 339, § 543;

L. Strackerjan, *Aberglaube und Sagen
aus dem Herzogthum Oldenburg* (Oldenburg, 1867), i. 81.

[4] Boecler-Kreutzwald, *Der Ehsten
abergläubische Gebräuche* (St. Petersburg, 1854), p. 61. This custom is
also cited by Mannhardt (*l.c.*).

human or divine, had to submit. That practice would hardly account either for the use of the winnowing-fan in the mysteries or for the appearance of the implement, filled with fruitage of various kinds, on the monuments which set forth the ritual of Dionysus.[1]   This last emblem points plainly to a conception of the god as a personification of the fruits of the earth in general ; and as if to emphasise the idea of fecundity conveyed by such a symbol there sometimes appears among the fruits in the winnowing-fan an effigy of the male organ of generation.   The prominent place which that effigy occupied in the worship of Dionysus[2] hints broadly, if it does not strictly prove, that to the Greek mind the god stood for the powers of fertility in general, animal as well as vegetable.   In the thought of the ancients no sharp line of distinction divided the fertility of animals from the fertility of plants ; rather the two ideas met and blended in a nebulous haze.   We need not wonder, therefore, that the same coarse but expressive emblem figured conspicuously in the ritual of Father Liber, the Italian counterpart of Dionysus, who in return for the homage paid to the symbol of his creative energy was believed to foster the growth of the crops and to guard the fields against the powers of evil.[3]

Myth of the death and resurrection of Dionysus.

Like the other gods of vegetation whom we considered in the last volume, Dionysus was believed to have died a violent death, but to have been brought to life again ; and his sufferings, death, and resurrection were enacted in his sacred rites. His tragic story is thus told by the poet Nonnus.   Zeus in the form of a serpent visited Persephone, and she bore him Zagreus, that is, Dionysus, a horned infant.   Scarcely was he born, when the babe mounted the throne of his father Zeus and mimicked the great god by brandishing the lightning in his tiny hand.   But he did not occupy the throne long ; for the treacherous Titans, their faces whitened with chalk, attacked him with knives while he was looking

[1] Miss J. E. Harrison, " Mystica Vannus Iacchi," *Journal of Hellenic Studies*, xxiii. (1903) pp. 296 *sqq.* ; id., *Prolegomena to the Study of Greek Religion*,[2] pp. 518 *sqq.* ; L. R. Farnell, *The Cults of the Greek States*, v. (Oxford, 1909) p. 243.

[2] Herodotus, ii. 48, 49 ; Clement of Alexandria, *Protrept.* ii. 34, pp. 29-30, ed. Potter ; Dittenberger, *Sylloge Inscriptionum Graecarum*,[2] No. 19, vol. i. p. 32 ; M. P. Nilsson, *Studia de Dionysiis Atticis* (Lund, 1900), pp. 90 *sqq.* ; L. R. Farnell, *The Cults of the Greek States*, v. 125, 195, 205.

[3] Augustine, *De civitate Dei*, vii. 21.

at himself in a mirror. For a time he evaded their assaults
by turning himself into various shapes, assuming the likeness
successively of Zeus and Cronus, of a young man, of a lion,
a horse, and a serpent. Finally, in the form of a bull, he
was cut to pieces by the murderous knives of his enemies.[1]
His Cretan myth, as related by Firmicus Maternus, ran thus.
He was said to have been the bastard son of Jupiter, a
Cretan king. Going abroad, Jupiter transferred the throne and
sceptre to the youthful Dionysus, but, knowing that his wife
Juno cherished a jealous dislike of the child, he entrusted
Dionysus to the care of guards upon whose fidelity he
believed he could rely. Juno, however, bribed the guards,
and amusing the child with rattles and a cunningly-wrought
looking-glass lured him into an ambush, where her satellites,
the Titans, rushed upon him, cut him limb from limb, boiled
his body with various herbs, and ate it. But his sister
Minerva, who had shared in the deed, kept his heart and
gave it to Jupiter on his return, revealing to him the whole
history of the crime. In his rage, Jupiter put the Titans to
death by torture, and, to soothe his grief for the loss of his
son, made an image in which he enclosed the child's heart,
and then built a temple in his honour.[2] In this version a
Euhemeristic turn has been given to the myth by representing Jupiter and Juno (Zeus and Hera) as a king and
queen of Crete. The guards referred to are the mythical
Curetes who danced a war-dance round the infant Dionysus,
as they are said to have done round the infant Zeus.[3]
Very noteworthy is the legend, recorded both by Nonnus
and Firmicus, that in his infancy Dionysus occupied for a
short time the throne of his father Zeus. So Proclus tells
us that "Dionysus was the last king of the gods appointed
by Zeus. For his father set him on the kingly throne, and
placed in his hand the sceptre, and made him king of all the
gods of the world."[4] Such traditions point to a custom of
temporarily investing the king's son with the royal dignity
as a preliminary to sacrificing him instead of his father.

Legend
that the
infant
Dionysus
occupied
for a short
time the
throne of
his father
Zeus.

---

[1] Nonnus, *Dionys.* vi. 155-205.   *Aglaophamus*, pp. 1111 *sqq.*
[2] Firmicus Maternus, *De errore pro-*   [4] Proclus on Plato, *Cratylus*, p. 59,
fanarum religionum, 6.   quoted by E. Abel, *Orphica*, p. 228.
[3] Clement of Alexandria, *Protrept.*   Compare Chr. A. Lobeck, *Aglao-*
ii. 17. Compare Ch. A. Lobeck,   *phamus*, pp. 552 *sq.*

Pomegranates were supposed to have sprung from the blood of Dionysus, as anemones from the blood of Adonis and violets from the blood of Attis : hence women refrained from eating seeds of pomegranates at the festival of the Thesmophoria.[1]   According to some, the severed limbs of Dionysus were pieced together, at the command of Zeus, by Apollo, who buried them on Parnassus.[2]   The grave of Dionysus was shewn in the Delphic temple beside a golden statue of Apollo.[3]   However, according to another account, the grave of Dionysus was at Thebes, where he is said to have been torn in pieces.[4]   Thus far the resurrection of the slain god is not mentioned, but in other versions of the myth it is variously related.   According to one version, which represented Dionysus as a son of Zeus and Demeter, his mother pieced together his mangled limbs and made him young again.[5]   In others it is simply said that shortly after his burial he rose from the dead and ascended up to heaven;[6] or that Zeus raised him up as he lay mortally wounded ;[7] or that Zeus swallowed the heart of Dionysus and then begat him afresh by Semele,[8] who in the common legend figures as mother of Dionysus.   Or, again, the heart was pounded up and given in a portion to Semele, who thereby conceived him.[9]

Turning from the myth to the ritual, we find that the Cretans celebrated a biennial[10] festival at which the passion

[1] Clement of Alexandria, *Protrept.* ii. 19.   Compare *id.* ii. 22 ; Scholiast on Lucian, *Dial. Meretr.* vii. p. 280, ed. H. Rabe.

[2] Clement of Alexandria, *Protrept.* ii. 18 ; Proclus on Plato's *Timaeus*, iii. p. 200 D, quoted by Lobeck, *Aglaophamus*, p. 562, and by Abel, *Orphica*, p. 234.   Others said that the mangled body was pieced together, not by Apollo but by Rhea (Cornutus, *Theologiae Graecae Compendium*, 30).

[3] Ch. A. Lobeck, *Aglaophamus*, pp. 572 *sqq.* See *The Dying God*, p. 3.   For a conjectural restoration of the temple, based on ancient authorities and an examination of the scanty remains, see an article by J. H. Middleton, in *Journal of Hellenic Studies*, ix. (1888) pp. 282 *sqq.*   The ruins of the temple have now been completely excavated

by the French.

[4] S. Clemens Romanus, *Recognitiones*, x. 24 (Migne's *Patrologia Graeca*, i. col. 1434).

[5] Diodorus Siculus, iii. 62.

[6] Macrobius, *Comment. in Somn. Scip.* i. 12. 12 ; *Scriptores rerum mythicarum Latini tres Romae nuper reperti* (commonly referred to as *Mythographi Vaticani*), ed. G. H. Bode (Cellis, 1834), iii. 12. 5, p. 246 ; Origen, *Contra Celsum*, iv. 17 (vol. i. p. 286, ed. P. Koetschau).

[7] Himerius, *Orat.* ix. 4.

[8] Proclus, *Hymn to Minerva*, quoted by Ch. A. Lobeck, *Aglaophamus*, p. 561 ; *Orphica*, ed. E. Abel, p. 235.

[9] Hyginus, *Fabulae*, 167.

[10] The festivals of Dionysus were biennial in many places.   See G. F.

of Dionysus was represented in every detail. All that he had done or suffered in his last moments was enacted before the eyes of his worshippers, who tore a live bull to pieces with their teeth and roamed the woods with frantic shouts. In front of them was carried a casket supposed to contain the sacred heart of Dionysus, and to the wild music of flutes and cymbals they mimicked the rattles by which the infant god had been lured to his doom.[1]   Where the resurrection formed part of the myth, it also was acted at the rites,[2] and it even appears that a general doctrine of resurrection, or at least of immortality, was inculcated on the worshippers ; for Plutarch, writing to console his wife on the death of their infant daughter, comforts her with the thought of the immortality of the soul as taught by tradition and revealed in the mysteries of Dionysus.[3]   A different form of the myth of the death and resurrection of Dionysus is that he descended into Hades to bring up his mother Semele from the dead.[4]   The local Argive tradition was that he went down through the Alcyonian lake ; and his return from the lower world, in other words his resurrection, was annually celebrated on the spot by the Argives, who summoned him from the water by trumpet blasts, while they threw a lamb into the lake as an offering to the warder of the dead.[5]   Whether this was a spring festival does not appear, but the Lydians certainly celebrated the advent of Dionysus in spring ; the god was supposed to bring the season with him.[6]   Deities of vegetation, who are

Death and resurrection of Dionysus represented in his rites.

Schömann, *Griechische Alterthümer*,[4] ii. 524 *sqq.* (The terms for the festival were τριετηρίς, τριετηρικός, both terms of the series being included in the numeration, in accordance with the ancient mode of reckoning.) Perhaps the festivals were formerly annual and the period was afterwards lengthened, as has happened with other festivals. See W. Mannhardt, *Baumkultus*, pp. 172, 175, 491, 533 *sq.*, 598. Some of the festivals of Dionysus, however, were annual. Dr. Farnell has conjectured that the biennial period in many Greek festivals is to be explained by "the original shifting of land-cultivation which is frequent in early society owing to the backwardness of

the agricultural processes ; and which would certainly be consecrated by a special ritual attached to the god of the soil." See L. R. Farnell, *The Cults of the Greek States*, v. 180 *sq.*

[1] Firmicus Maternus, *De errore profanarum religionum*, 6.

[2] *Mythographi Vaticani*, ed. G. H. Bode, iii. 12. 5, p. 246.

[3] Plutarch, *Consol. ad uxor.* 10. Compare *id.*, *Isis et Osiris*, 35 ; *id.*, *De E Delphico*, 9 ; *id.*, *De esu carnium*, i. 7.

[4] Pausanias, ii. 31. 2 and 37. 5 ; Apollodorus, *Bibliotheca*, iii. 5. 3.

[5] Pausanias, ii. 37. 5 *sq.* ; Plutarch, *Isis et Osiris*, 35 ; *id.*, *Quaest. Conviv.* iv. 6. 2.

[6] Himerius, *Orat.* iii. 6, xiv. 7.

supposed to pass a certain portion of each year under ground, naturally come to be regarded as gods of the lower world or of the dead. Both Dionysus and Osiris were so conceived.[1]

Dionysus repre-sented in the form of a bull.   A feature in the mythical character of Dionysus, which at first sight appears inconsistent with his nature as a deity of vegetation, is that he was often conceived and represented in animal shape, especially in the form, or at least with the horns, of a bull. Thus he is spoken of as "cow‑born," "bull," "bull-shaped," "bull-faced," "bull-browed," "bull-horned," "horn-bearing," "two-horned," "horned."[2]   He was believed to appear, at least occasionally, as a bull.[3]   His images were often, as at Cyzicus, made in bull shape,[4] or with bull horns;[5] and he was painted with horns.[6]   Types of the horned Dionysus are found amongst the surviving monuments of antiquity.[7]   On one statuette he appears clad in a bull's hide, the head, horns, and hoofs hanging down behind.[8]   Again, he is represented as a child with clusters of grapes round his brow, and a calf's head, with sprouting horns, attached to the back of his head.[9]   On a red-figured vase the god is portrayed as a calf-headed child seated on a woman's lap.[10]   The people of Cynaetha in north-western Arcadia held a festival of Dionysus in winter, when men,

---

[1] For Dionysus in this capacity see F. Lenormant in Daremberg et Saglio, *Dictionnaire des Antiquités Grecques et Romaines*, i. 632. For Osiris, see *Adonis, Attis, Osiris*, Second Edition, pp. 344 *sq.*

[2] Plutarch, *Isis et Osiris*, 35; *id.*, *Quaest. Graec.* 36; Athenaeus, xi. 51, p. 476 A; Clement of Alexandria, *Protrept.* ii. 16; *Orphica*, Hymn xxx. *vv.* 3, 4, xlv. 1, lii. 2, liii. 8; Euripides, *Bacchae*, 99; Scholiast on Aristophanes, *Frogs*, 357; Nicander, *Alexipharmaca*, 31; Lucian, *Bacchus*, 2. The title Εἰραφιώτης applied to Dionysus (*Homeric Hymns*, xxxiv. 2; Porphyry, *De abstinentia*, iii. 17; Dionysius, *Perieg.* 576; *Etymologicum Magnum*, p. 371. 57) is etymologically equivalent to the Sanscrit *varsabha*, "a bull," as I was informed by my lamented friend the late R. A. Neil of Pembroke College, Cambridge.

[3] Euripides, *Bacchae*, 920 *sqq.*, 1017; Nonnus, *Dionys.* vi. 197 *sqq.*

[4] Plutarch, *Isis et Osiris*, 35; Athenaeus, xi. 51, p. 476 A.

[5] Diodorus Siculus, iii. 64. 2, iv. 4. 2; Cornutus, *Theologiae Graecae Compendium*, 30.

[6] Diodorus Siculus, iii. 64. 2; J. Tzetzes, *Schol. on Lycophron*, 209, 1236; Philostratus, *Imagines*, i. 14 (15).

[7] Müller-Wieseler, *Denkmäler der alten Kunst*, ii. pl. xxxiii. ; Daremberg et Saglio, *Dictionnaire des Antiquités Grecques et Romaines*, i. 619 *sq.*, 631 ; W. H. Roscher, *Lexikon d. griech. u. röm. Mythologie*, i. 1149 *sqq.*; F. Imhoof-Blumer, "Coin-types of some Kilikian Cities," *Journal of Hellenic Studies*, xviii. (1898) p. 165.

[8] F. G. Welcker, *Alte Denkmäler* (Göttingen, 1849-1864), v. taf. 2.

[9] *Archaeologische Zeitung*, ix. (1851) pl. xxxiii., with Gerhard's remarks, pp. 371-373.

[10] *Gazette Archéologique*, v. (1879) pl. 3.

who had greased their bodies with oil for the occasion, used to pick out a bull from the herd and carry it to the sanctuary of the god. Dionysus was supposed to inspire their choice of the particular bull,[1] which probably represented the deity himself; for at his festivals he was believed to appear in bull form. The women of Elis hailed him as a bull, and prayed him to come with his bull's foot. They sang, " Come hither, Dionysus, to thy holy temple by the sea ; come with the Graces to thy temple, rushing with thy bull's foot, O goodly bull, O goodly bull ! " [2]   The Bacchanals of Thrace wore horns in imitation of their god.[3]   According to the myth, it was in the shape of a bull that he was torn to pieces by the Titans ; [4] and the Cretans, when they acted the sufferings and death of Dionysus, tore a live bull to pieces with their teeth.[5]   Indeed, the rending and devouring of live bulls and calves appear to have been a regular feature of the Dionysiac rites.[6]   When we consider the practice of portraying the god as a bull or with some of the features of the animal, the belief that he appeared in bull form to his worshippers at the sacred rites, and the legend that in bull form he had been torn in pieces, we cannot doubt that in rending and devouring a live bull at his festival the worshippers of Dionysus believed themselves to be killing the god, eating his flesh, and drinking his blood.

Another animal whose form Dionysus assumed was the goat.   One of his names was " Kid." [7]   At Athens and at Hermion he was worshipped under the title of " the one of the Black Goatskin," and a legend ran that on a certain occasion he had appeared clad in the skin from which he took the title.[8]   In the wine-growing district of Phlius, where in autumn the plain is still thickly mantled with the red and

Dionysus as a goat.

---

[1] Pausanias, viii. 19. 2.

[2] Plutarch, *Quaestiones Graecae*, 36 ; *id.*, *Isis et Osiris*, 35.

[3] J. Tzetzes, *Schol. on Lycophron*, 1236.

[4] Nonnus, *Dionys.* vi. 205.

[5] Firmicus Maternus, *De errore profanarum religionum*, 6.

[6] Euripides, *Bacchae*, 735 *sqq.* ; Scholiast on Aristophanes, *Frogs*, 357.

[7] Hesychius, *s.v.* Ἔριφος ὁ Διόνυσος,

on which there is a marginal gloss ὁ μικρὸς αἴξ, ὁ ἐν τῷ ἔαρι φαινόμενος, ἤγουν ὁ πρώϊμος ; Stephanus Byzantius, *s.v.* Ἀκρώρεια.

[8] Pausanias, ii. 35. 1 ; Scholiast on Aristophanes, *Acharn.* 146 ; *Etymologicum Magnum, s.v.* Ἀπατούρια, p. 118. 54 *sqq.* ; Suidas, *s.vv.* Ἀπατούρια and μελαναίγιδα Διόνυσον ; Nonnus, *Dionys.* xxvii. 302. Compare Conon, *Narrat.* 39, where for Μελανθίδη we should perhaps read Μελαναίγιδι.

golden foliage of the fading vines, there stood of old a
bronze image of a goat, which the husbandmen plastered
with gold-leaf as a means of protecting their vines against
blight.[1]   The image probably represented the vine-god
himself.   To save him from the wrath of Hera, his father
Zeus changed the youthful Dionysus into a kid ;[2] and when
the gods fled to Egypt to escape the fury of Typhon,

Live goats
rent and
devoured
by his wor-
shippers.

Dionysus was turned into a goat.[3]   Hence when his
worshippers rent in pieces a live goat and devoured it raw,[4]
they must have believed that they were eating the body and
blood of the god.

Custom of
rending
and
devouring
animals
and men
as a re-
ligious rite.
Ceremonial
cannibal-
ism among
the Indians
of British
Columbia.

The custom of tearing in pieces the bodies of animals
and of men and then devouring them raw has been practised
as a religious rite by savages in modern times.   We need
not therefore dismiss as a fable the testimony of antiquity
to the observance of similar rites among the frenzied
worshippers of Bacchus.   An English missionary to the Coast
Indians of British Columbia has thus described a scene like
the cannibal orgies of the Bacchanals.   After mentioning that
an old chief had ordered a female slave to be dragged to
the beach, murdered, and thrown into the water, he proceeds
as follows: "I did not see the murder, but, immediately
after, I saw crowds of people running out of those houses
near to where the corpse was thrown, and forming themselves into groups at a good distance away.   This I learnt
was from fear of what was to follow   Presently two bands
of furious wretches appeared, each headed by a man in a
state of nudity.   They gave vent to the most unearthly
sounds, and the two naked men made themselves look as
unearthly as possible, proceeding in a creeping kind of
stoop, and stepping like two proud horses, at the same time

[1] Pausanias, ii. 13. 6.   On their
return from Troy the Greeks are said
to have found goats and an image of
Dionysus in a cave of Euboea (Pausanias,
i. 23. 1).

[2] Apollodorus, *Bibliotheca*, iii. 4. 3.

[3] Ovid, *Metam.* v. 329 ; Antoninus
Liberalis, *Transform.* 28 ; *Mythographi
Vaticani*, ed. G. H. Bode, i. 86, p.
29.

[4] Arnobius, *Adversus nationes*, v.
19.   Compare Suidas, *s.v.* αἰγίζειν.

As fawns appear to have been also torn
in pieces at the rites of Dionysus
(Photius, *Lexicon*, *s.v.* νεβρίζειν ;
Harpocration, *s.v.* νεβρίζων), it is
probable that the fawn was another of
the god's embodiments.   But of this
there seems no direct evidence.   Fawnskins were worn both by the god and
his worshippers (Cornutus, *Theologiae
Graecae Compendium*, 30).   Similarly
the female Bacchanals wore goat-skins
(Hesychius, *s.v.* τραγηφόροι).

shooting forward each arm alternately, which they held out
at full length for a little time in the most defiant manner.
Besides this, the continual jerking their heads back, causing
their long black hair to twist about, added much to their
savage appearance. For some time they pretended to be
seeking the body, and the instant they came where it lay
they commenced screaming and rushing round it like so
many angry wolves. Finally they seized it, dragged it out
of the water, and laid it on the beach, where I was told the
naked men would commence tearing it to pieces with their
teeth. The two bands of men immediately surrounded
them, and so hid their horrid work. In a few minutes
the crowd broke into two, when each of the naked cannibals
appeared with half of the body in his hands. Separating
a few yards, they commenced, amid horrid yells, their still
more horrid feast. The sight was too terrible to behold.
I left the gallery with a depressed heart. I may mention
that the two bands of savages just alluded to belong to that
class which the whites term 'medicine-men.'" The same
writer informs us that at the winter ceremonials of these
Indians "the cannibal, on such occasions, is generally
supplied with two, three, or four human bodies, which he
tears to pieces before his audience. Several persons, either
from bravado or as a charm, present their arms for him
to bite. I have seen several whom he has bitten, and I hear
two have died from the effects." And when corpses were
not forthcoming, these cannibals apparently seized and
devoured living people. Mr. Duncan has seen hundreds of
the Tsimshian Indians sitting in their canoes which they
had just pushed off from the shore in order to escape being
torn to pieces by a party of prowling cannibals. Others
of these Indians contented themselves with tearing dogs
to pieces, while their attendants kept up a growling noise,
or a whoop, "which was seconded by a screeching noise
made from an instrument which they believe to be the abode
of a spirit."[1]

[1] Mr. Duncan, quoted by Commander R. C. Mayne, *Four Years in British Columbia and Vancouver Island* (London, 1862), pp. 284-288. The instrument which made the screeching sound was no doubt a bull-roarer, a flat piece of stick whirled at the end of a string so as to produce a droning or screaming note according to the speed of revolution. Such instruments are used by

Religious
societies of
Cannibals
and Dog-
eaters
among the
Indians of
British
Columbia.
Mr. Duncan's account of these savage rites has been fully borne out by later observation. Among the Kwakiutl Indians the Cannibals (*Hamatsas*) are the highest in rank of the Secret Societies. They devour corpses, bite pieces out of living people, and formerly ate slaves who had been killed for the purpose. But when their fury has subsided, they are obliged to pay compensation to the persons whom they have bitten and to the owners of slaves whom they have killed. The indemnity consists sometimes of blankets, sometimes of canoes. In the latter case the tariff is fixed : one bite, one canoe. For some time after eating human flesh the cannibal has to observe a great many rules, which regulate his eating and drinking, his going out and his coming in, his clothing and his intercourse with his wife.[1] Similar customs prevail among other tribes of the same coast, such as the Bella Coola, the Tsimshian, the Niska, and the Nootka. In the Nootka tribe members of the Panther Society tear dogs to pieces and devour them. They wear masks armed with canine teeth.[2] So among the Haida Indians of the Queen Charlotte Islands there is one religion of cannibalism and another of dog-eating. The cannibals in a state of frenzy, real or pretended, bite flesh out of the extended arms of their fellow villagers. When they issue forth with cries of *Hop-pop* to observe this solemn rite, all who are of a different religious persuasion make haste to get out of their way ; but men of the cannibal creed and of stout hearts will resolutely hold out their arms to be

the Koskimo Indians of the same region at their cannibal and other rites. See Fr. Boas, "The Social Organization and the Secret Societies of the Kwakiutl Indians," *Report of the U.S. National Museum for 1895* (Washington, 1897), pp. 610, 611.

[1] Fr. Boas, *op. cit.* pp. 437-443, 527 *sq.*, 536, 537 *sq.*, 579, 664 ; *id.*, in "Fifth Report on the North-western Tribes of Canada," *Report of the British Association for 1889,* pp. 54-56 (separate reprint) ; *id.*, in "Sixth Report on the North - western Tribes of Canada," *Report of the British Association for 1890*, pp. 62, 65 *sq.* (separate reprint). As to the rules observed after the

eating of human flesh, see *Taboo and the Perils of the Soul*, pp. 188-190.

[2] Fr. Boas, "The Social Organization and the Secret Societies of the Kwakiutl Indians," *Report of the U.S. National Museum for 1895* (Washington, 1897), pp. 649 *sq.*, 658 *sq.*; *id.*, in "Sixth Report on the North-western Tribes of Canada," *Report of the British Association for 1890*, p. 51; (separate reprint); *id.*, "Seventh Report on the North-western Tribes of Canada," *Report of the British Association for 1891*, pp. 10 *sq.* (separate reprint); *id.*, "Tenth Report on the North-western Tribes of Canada," *Report of the British Association for 1895*, p. 58 (separate reprint).

bitten. The sect of dog-eaters cut or tear dogs to pieces
and devour some of the flesh ; but they have to pay for the
dogs which they consume in their religious enthusiasm.[1]
In the performance of these savage rites the frenzied actors
are believed to be inspired by a Cannibal Spirit and a
Dog-eating Spirit respectively.[2] Again, in Morocco there is
an order of saints known as Isowa or Aïsawa, followers of
Mohammed ben Isa or Aïsa of Mequinez, whose tomb is at
Fez. Every year on their founder's birthday they assemble
at his shrine or elsewhere and holding each other's hands
dance a frantic dance round a fire. "While the mad dance
is still proceeding, a sudden rush is made from the sanctuary,
and the dancers, like men delirious, speed away to a place
where live goats are tethered in readiness. At sight of these
animals the fury of the savage and excited crowd reaches its
height. In a few minutes the wretched animals are cut, or
rather torn to pieces, and an orgy takes place over the raw
and quivering flesh. When they seem satiated, the
Emkaddim, who is generally on horseback, and carries a
long stick, forms a sort of procession, preceded by wild
music, if such discordant sounds will bear the name.
Words can do no justice to the frightful scene which now
ensues. The naked savages — for on these occasions a
scanty piece of cotton is all their clothing—with their long
black hair, ordinarily worn in plaits, tossed about by the
rapid to-and-fro movements of the head, with faces and
hands reeking with blood, and uttering loud cries resembling
the bleating of goats, again enter the town. The place is
now at their mercy, and the people avoid them as much as
possible by shutting themselves up in their houses. A
Christian or a Jew would run great risk of losing his life if
either were found in the street. Goats are pushed out from
the doors, and these the fanatics tear immediately to pieces
with their hands, and then dispute over the morsels of

Live goats rent in pieces and devoured by fanatics in Morocco.

[1] G. M. Dawson, *Report on the Queen Charlotte Islands, 1878* (Montreal, 1880), pp. 125 B, 128 B.
[2] J. R. Swanton, *Contributions to the Ethnology of the Haida* (Leyden and New York, 1905), pp. 156, 160 *sq.*, 170 *sq.*, 181 (*The Jesup North Pacific Expedition, Memoir of the American*

Museum of Natural History). For details as to the practice of these savage rites among the Indian coast tribes of British Columbia, see my *Totemism and Exogamy* (London, 1910), iii. pp. 501, 511 *sq.*, 515 *sq.*, 519, 521, 526, 535 *sq.*, 537, 539 *sq.*, 542 *sq.*, 544, 545.

bleeding flesh, as though they were ravenous wolves instead of men. Snakes also are thrown to them as tests of their divine frenzy, and these share the fate of the goats. Sometimes a luckless dog, straying as dogs will stray in a tumult, is seized on. Then the laymen, should any be at hand, will try to prevent the desecration of pious mouths. But the fanatics sometimes prevail, and the unclean animal, abhorred by the mussulman, is torn in pieces and devoured, or pretended to be devoured, with indiscriminating rage." [1]

Later mis-interpreta-tions of the custom of killing a god in animal form.

The custom of killing a god in animal form, which we shall examine more in detail further on, belongs to a very early stage of human culture, and is apt in later times to be misunderstood. The advance of thought tends to strip the old animal and plant gods of their bestial and vegetable husk, and to leave their human attributes (which are always the kernel of the conception) as the final and sole residuum. In other words, animal and plant gods tend to become purely anthropomorphic. When they have become wholly or nearly so, the animals and plants which were at first the deities themselves, still retain a vague and ill-understood connexion with the anthropomorphic gods who have been developed out of them. The origin of the relationship between the deity and the animal or plant having been forgotten, various stories are invented to explain it. These explanations may follow one of two lines according as they are based on the habitual or on the exceptional treatment of the sacred animal or plant. The sacred animal was habitually spared, and only exceptionally slain ; and accordingly the myth might be devised to explain either why it was spared or why it was killed. Devised for the former purpose, the myth would tell of some service rendered to the deity by the animal ; devised for the latter purpose, the myth would tell of some injury inflicted by the animal on the god. The reason given for sacrificing goats to Dionysus exemplifies a myth of the latter sort. They were sacri-

[1] A. Leared, *Morocco and the Moors* (London, 1876), pp. 267-269. Compare Budgett Meakin, *The Moors* (London, 1902), pp. 331 *sq.* The same order of fanatics also exists and holds similar orgies in Algeria, especially at the town of Tlemcen. See E. Doutté, *Les Aïssâoua à Tlemcen* (Châlons-sur-Marne, 1900), p. 13.

ficed to him, it was said, because they injured the vine.[1]
Now the goat, as we have seen, was originally an embodiment of the god himself. But when the god had divested
himself of his animal character and had become essentially
anthropomorphic, the killing of the goat in his worship came
to be regarded no longer as a slaying of the deity himself,
but as a sacrifice offered to him ; and since some reason had
to be assigned why the goat in particular should be sacrificed,
it was alleged that this was a punishment inflicted on the
goat for injuring the vine, the object of the god's especial
care. Thus we have the strange spectacle of a god sacrificed
to himself on the ground that he is his own enemy. And
as the deity is supposed to partake of the victim offered to
him, it follows that, when the victim is the god's old self, the
god eats of his own flesh. Hence the goat-god Dionysus is
represented as eating raw goat's blood ;[2] and the bull-god
Dionysus is called "eater of bulls."[3] On the analogy of
these instances we may conjecture that wherever a deity is
described as the eater of a particular animal, the animal in
question was originally nothing but the deity himself.[4]
Later on we shall find that some savages propitiate dead bears
and whales by offering them portions of their own bodies.[5]

All this, however, does not explain why a deity of Human
vegetation should appear in animal form. But the con- in the
sideration of that point had better be deferred till we have worship of Dionysus.

---

[1] Varro, *Rerum rusticarum*, i. 2. 19;
Virgil, *Georg.* ii. 376-381, with the
comments of Servius on the passage
and on *Aen.* iii. 118 ; Ovid, *Fasti*, i.
353 *sqq.*; *id.*, *Metamorph.* xv. 114 *sq.*;
Cornutus, *Theologiae Graecae Compendium*, 30.

[2] Euripides, *Bacchae*, 138 *sq.* : ἀγρεύων
αἷμα τραγοκτόνον, ὠμοφάγον χάριν.

[3] Schol. on Aristophanes, *Frogs*, 357.

[4] Hera αἰγοφάγος at Sparta, Pausanias, iii. 15. 9 ; Hesychius, *s.v.*
αἰγοφάγος (compare the representation
of Hera clad in a goat's skin, with the
animal's head and horns over her head,
Müller-Wieseler, *Denkmäler der alten
Kunst*, i. No. 229 B ; and the similar
representation of the Lanuvinian Juno,
W. H. Roscher, *Lexikon d. griech. u.
röm. Mythologie*, ii. 605 *sqq.*) ; Zeus

αἰγοφάγος, *Etymologicum Magnum, s.v.*
αἰγοφάγος, p. 27. 52 (compare Scholiast
on Oppianus, *Halieut.* iii. 10 ; L.
Stephani, in *Compte-Rendu de la Com-
mission Impériale Archéologique pour
l'année 1869* (St. Petersburg, 1870),
pp. 16-18) ; Apollo ὀψοφάγος at Elis,
Athenaeus, viii. 36, p. 346 B ; Artemis
καπροφάγος in Samos, Hesychius, *s.v.*
καπροφάγος; compare *id.*, *s.v.* κριοφάγος.
Divine titles derived from killing
animals are probably to be similarly
explained, as Dionysus αἰγόβολος (Pausanias, ix. 8. 2) ; Rhea or Hecate
κυνοσφαγής (J. Tzetzes, *Scholia on
Lycophron*, 77) ; Apollo λυκοκτόνος
(Sophocles, *Electra*, 6) ; Apollo σαυρο-
κτόνος (Pliny, *Nat. Hist.* xxxiv. 70).

[5] See below, vol. ii. pp. 184, 194,
196, 197 *sq.*, 233.

discussed the character and attributes of Demeter. Meantime it remains to mention that in some places, instead of an animal, a human being was torn in pieces at the rites of Dionysus. This was the practice in Chios and Tenedos ;[1] and at Potniae in Boeotia the tradition ran that it had been formerly the custom to sacrifice to the goat-smiting Dionysus a child, for whom a goat was afterwards substituted.[2] At Orchomenus, as we have seen, the human victim was taken from the women of an old royal family.[3] As the slain bull or goat represented the slain god, so, we may suppose, the human victim also represented him.

The legendary deaths of Pentheus and Lycurgus may be reminiscences of a custom of sacrificing divine kings in the character of Dionysus.
The legends of the deaths of Pentheus and Lycurgus, two kings who are said to have been torn to pieces, the one by Bacchanals, the other by horses, for their opposition to the rites of Dionysus, may be, as I have already suggested,[4] distorted reminiscences of a custom of sacrificing divine kings in the character of Dionysus and of dispersing the fragments of their broken bodies over the fields for the purpose of fertilising them. In regard to Lycurgus, king of the Thracian tribe of the Edonians, it is expressly said that his subjects at the bidding of an oracle caused him to be rent in pieces by horses for the purpose of restoring the fertility of the ground after a period of barrenness and dearth.[5] There is no improbability in the tradition. We have seen that in Africa and other parts of the world kings or chiefs have often been put to death by their people for similar reasons.[6] Further, it is significant that King Lycurgus is said to have slain his own son Dryas with an axe in a fit of madness, mistaking him for a vine-branch.[7] Have we not in this tradition a reminiscence of a custom of sacrificing the king's son in place of the father? Similarly Athamas, a King of Thessaly or Boeotia, is said to have been doomed by an oracle to be sacrificed at the altar in order to remove the curse of barrenness which afflicted his country; however, he contrived to evade the sentence and in a fit of madness killed his own son Learchus, mistaking him for a wild beast.

[1] Porphyry, *De abstinentia*, ii. 55.
[2] Pausanias, ix. 8. 2.
[3] See *The Dying God*, pp. 163 *sq.*
[4] *Adonis, Attis, Osiris*, Second Edition, pp. 332 *sq.*

[5] Apollodorus, *Bibliotheca*, iii. 5. 1.
[6] *The Magic Art and the Evolution of Kings*, i. 344, 345, 346, 352, 354, 366 *sq.*
[7] Apollodorus, *Bibliotheca*, iii. 5. 1.

That this legend was not a mere myth is made probable by a custom observed at Alus down to historical times: the eldest male scion of the royal house was regularly sacrificed in due form to Laphystian Zeus if he ever set foot within the town-hall.[1] The close resemblance between the legends of King Athamas and King Lycurgus furnishes a ground for believing both legends to be based on a real custom of sacrificing either the king himself or one of his sons for the good of the country; and the story that the king's son Dryas perished because his frenzied father mistook him for a vine-branch fits in well with the theory that the victim in these sacrifices represented the vine-god Dionysus. It is probably no mere coincidence that Dionysus himself is said to have been torn in pieces at Thebes,[2] the very place where according to legend the same fate befell king Pentheus at the hands of the frenzied votaries of the vine-god.[3]

The theory that in prehistoric times Greek and Thracian kings or their sons may have been dismembered in the character of the vine-god or the corn-god for the purpose of fertilising the earth or quickening the vines has received of late years some confirmation from the discovery that down to the present time in Thrace, the original home of Dionysus, a drama is still annually performed which reproduces with remarkable fidelity some of the most striking traits in the Dionysiac myth and ritual.[4] In a former part of this work I have already called attention to this interesting survival of paganism among a Christian peasantry;[5] but it seems desirable and appropriate in this place to draw out somewhat

Survival of Dionysiac rites among the modern Thracian peasantry.

---

[1] Herodotus, vii. 197; Apollodorus, *Bibliotheca*, i. 9. 1 *sq.* ; Scholiast on Aristophanes, *Clouds*, 257 ; J. Tzetzes, *Schol. on Lycophron*, 21; Hyginus, *Fabulae*, 1-5. See *The Dying God*, pp. 161-163.

[2] Clemens Romanus, *Recognitiones*, x. 24 (Migne's *Patrologia Graeca*, i. col. 1434).

[3] Euripides, *Bacchae*, 43 *sqq.*, 1043 *sqq.*; Theocritus, *Idyl.* xxvi. ; Pausanias, ii. 2. 7. Strictly speaking, the murder of Pentheus is said to have been perpetrated not at Thebes, of which he was king, but on Mount Cithaeron.

[4] See Mr. R. M. Dawkins, "The Modern Carnival in Thrace and the Cult of Dionysus," *Journal of Hellenic Studies*, xxvi. (1906) pp. 191-206. Mr. Dawkins describes the ceremonies partly from his own observation, partly from an account of them published by Mr. G. M. Vizyenos in a Greek periodical Θρακικὴ 'Επετηρίς, of which only one number was published at Athens in 1897. From his personal observations Mr. Dawkins was able to confirm the accuracy of Mr. Vizyenos's account.

[5] *Adonis, Attis, Osiris*, Second Edition, pp. 333 *sq.*

more fully the parallelism between the modern drama and the ancient worship.

Drama annually performed at the Carnival in the villages round Viza, an old Thracian capital. The drama, which may reasonably be regarded as a direct descendant of the Dionysiac rites, is annually performed at the Carnival in all the Christian villages which cluster round Viza, the ancient Bizya, a town of Thrace situated about midway between Adrianople and Constantinople. In antiquity the city was the capital of the Thracian tribe of the Asti; the kings had their palace there,[1] probably in the acropolis, of which some fine walls are still standing. Inscriptions preserved in the modern town record the names of some of these old kings.[2] The date of the celebration is Cheese Monday, as it is locally called, which is the Monday of the last week of Carnival. At Viza itself the mummery has been shorn of some of its ancient features, but these have been kept up at the villages and have been particularly observed and recorded at the village of St. George (Haghios Gheorgios). It is to the drama as acted at that village that The actors in the drama. the following description specially applies. The principal parts in the drama are taken by two men disguised in goatskins. Each of them wears a headdress made of a complete goatskin, which is stuffed so as to rise a foot or more like a shako over his head, while the skin falls over the face, forming a mask with holes cut for the eyes and mouth. Their shoulders are thickly padded with hay to protect them from the blows which used to be rained very liberally on their backs. Fawnskins on their shoulders and goatskins on their legs are or used to be part of their equipment, and another indispensable part of it is a number of sheep-bells tied round their waists. One of the two skin-clad actors carries a bow and the other a wooden effigy of the male organ of generation. Both these actors must be married men. According to Mr. Vizyenos, they are chosen for periods of four years. Two unmarried boys dressed as girls and sometimes called brides also take part in the play; and a man disguised as an old woman in rags carries a mock baby in a basket; the brat is supposed to be a seven-months' child born out of wedlock and begotten by an unknown

[1] Strabo, vii. frag. 48; Stephanus Byzantius, *s.v.* Βιζύη.
[2] R. M. Dawkins, *op. cit.* p. 192.

father. The basket in which the hopeful infant is paraded bears the ancient name of the winnowing-fan (*likni*, contracted from *liknon*) and the babe itself receives the very title " He of the Winnowing-fan " (*Liknites*) which in antiquity was applied to Dionysus. Two other actors, clad in rags with blackened faces and armed with stout saplings, play the parts of a gypsy-man and his wife; others personate policemen armed with swords and whips; and the troupe is completed by a man who discourses music on a bagpipe.

Such are the masqueraders. The morning of the day on which they perform their little drama is spent by them going from door to door collecting bread, eggs, or money. At every door the two skin-clad maskers knock, the boys disguised as girls dance, and the gypsy man and wife enact an obscene pantomime on the straw-heap before the house. When every house in the village has been thus visited, the troop takes up position on the open space before the village church, where the whole population has already mustered to witness the performance. After a dance hand in hand, in which all the actors take part, the two skin-clad maskers withdraw and leave the field to the gypsies, who now pretend to forge a ploughshare, the man making believe to hammer the share and his wife to work the bellows. At this point the old woman's baby is supposed to grow up at a great pace, to develop a huge appetite for meat and drink, and to clamour for a wife. One of the skin-clad men now pursues one of the two pretended brides, and a mock marriage is celebrated between the couple. After these nuptials have been performed with a parody of a real wedding, the mock bridegroom is shot by his comrade with the bow and falls down on his face like dead. His slayer thereupon feigns to skin him with a knife; but the dead man's wife laments over her deceased husband with loud cries, throwing herself across his prostrate body. In this lamentation the slayer himself and all the other actors join in: a Christian funeral service is burlesqued; and the pretended corpse is lifted up as if to be carried to the grave. At this point, however, the dead man disconcerts the preparations for his burial by suddenly coming to life

The ceremonies include the forging of a plough-share, a mock marriage, and a pretence of death and resurrection.

again and getting up. So ends the drama of death and resurrection.

The next act opens with a repetition of the pretence of forging a ploughshare, but this time the gypsy man hammers on a real share. When the implement is supposed to have been fashioned, a real plough is brought forward, the mockery appears to cease, the two boys dressed as girls are yoked to the plough and drag it twice round the village square contrary to the way of the sun. One of the two skin-clad men walks at the tail of the plough, the other guides it in front, and a third man follows in the rear scattering seed from a basket. After the two rounds have been completed, the gypsy and his wife are yoked to the plough, and drag it a third time round the square, the two skin-clad men still playing the part of ploughmen. At Viza the plough is drawn by the skin-clad men themselves. While the plough is going its rounds, followed by the sower sowing the seed, the people pray aloud, saying, " May wheat be ten piastres the bushel ! Rye five piastres the bushel ! Amen, O God, that the poor may eat ! Yea, O God, that poor folk be filled ! " This ends the performance. The evening is spent in feasting on the proceeds of the house-to-house visitation which took place in the morning.[1]

A kindred festival is observed on the same day of the Carnival at Kosti, a place in the extreme north of Thrace, near the Black Sea. There a man dressed in sheepskins or goatskins, with a mask on his face, bells round his neck, and a broom in his hand, goes round the village collecting food and presents. He is addressed as a king and escorted with music. With him go boys dressed as girls, and another boy, not so disguised, who carries wine in a wooden bottle and gives of it to every householder to drink in a cup, receiving a gift in return. The king then mounts a two-wheeled cart and is drawn to the church. He carries seed in his hand, and at the church two bands of men, one of married men and the other of unmarried men, try each in turn to induce the king to throw the seed on them. Finally he casts it on the ground in front of the church. The ceremony ends with

The ceremonies also include a simulation of ploughing and sowing by skin-clad men, accompanied by prayers for good crops.

Kindred ceremony performed by a masked and skin-clad man who is called a king.

---

[1] R. M. Dawkins, " The Modern Carnival in Thrace and the Cult of Dionysus," *Journal of Hellenic Studies,* xxvi. (1906) pp. 193-201.

stripping the king of his clothes and flinging him into the
river, after which he resumes his usual dress.[1]

In these ceremonies, still annually held at and near an
old capital of Thracian kings, the points of similarity to the
ritual of the ancient Thracian deity Dionysus are sufficiently
obvious.[2]   The goatskins in which the principal actors are
disguised remind us of the identification of Dionysus with a
goat: the infant, cradled in a winnowing-fan and taking
its name from the implement, answers exactly to the
traditions and the monuments which represent the infant
Dionysus as similarly cradled and similarly named : the
pretence that the baby is a seven-months' child born out
of wedlock and begotten by an unknown father tallies
precisely with the legend that Dionysus was born prematurely
in the seventh month as the offspring of an intrigue between
a mortal woman and a mysterious divine father :[3] the same
coarse symbol of reproductive energy which characterised
the ancient ritual of Dionysus figures conspicuously in the
modern drama : the annual mock marriage of the goatskin-
clad mummer with the pretended bride may be compared
with the annual pretence of marrying Dionysus to the
Queen of Athens : and the simulated slaughter and resurrection of the same goatskin-clad actor may be compared with
the traditional slaughter and resurrection of the god himself.
Further, the ceremony of ploughing, in which after his
resurrection the goatskin-clad mummer takes a prominent
part, fits in well not only with the legend that Dionysus was
the first to yoke oxen to the plough, but also with the
symbolism of the winnowing-fan in his worship; while the
prayers for plentiful crops which accompany the ploughing
accord with the omens of an abundant harvest which were
drawn of old from the mystic light seen to illumine by night
one of his ancient sanctuaries in Thrace.   Lastly, in the
ceremony as observed at Kosti the giving of wine by the king's

Analogy of these modern Thracian ceremonies to the ancient rites of Dionysus.

[1] R. M. Dawkins, *op. cit.* pp.
201 *sq.*

[2] They have been clearly indicated
by Mr. R. M. Dawkins, *op. cit.* pp.
203 *sqq.* Compare W. Ridgeway, *The
Origin of Tragedy* (Cambridge, 1910),
pp. 15 *sqq.*, who fully recognises the

connexion of the modern Thracian
ceremonies with the ancient rites of
Dionysus.

[3] Lucian, *Dialogi Deorum*, ix. 2 ;
Apollodorus, *Bibliotheca*, iii. 4. 4.
According to the latter writer Dionysus
was born in the sixth month.

attendant is an act worthy of the wine-god : the throwing of seed by the king can only be interpreted, like the plough-ing, as a charm to promote the fertility of the ground ; and the royal title borne by the principal masker harmonises well with the theory that the part of the god of the corn and the wine was of old sustained by the Thracian kings who reigned at Bisya.

The modern Thracian celebration seems to correspond most closely to the ancient Athenian festival of the An-thesteria.　　If we ask, To what ancient festival of Dionysus does the modern celebration of the Carnival in Thrace most nearly correspond ? the answer can be hardly doubtful.　The Thracian drama of the mock marriage of the goatskin-clad mummer, his mimic death and resurrection, and his sub-sequent ploughing, corresponds both in date and in character most nearly to the Athenian festival of the Anthesteria, which was celebrated at Athens during three days in early spring, towards the end of February or the beginning of March.　Thus the date of the Anthesteria could not fall far from, and it might sometimes actually coincide with, the last week of the Carnival, the date of the Thracian cele-bration.　While the details of the festival of the Anthesteria are obscure, its general character is well known.　It was a festival both of wine-drinking and of the dead, whose souls were supposed to revisit the city and to go about the streets, just as in modern Europe and in many other parts of the world the ghosts of the departed are still believed to return to their old homes on one day of the year and to be entertained by their relatives at a solemn Feast of All Souls.[1]　But the Dionysiac nature of the festival was revealed not merely by the opening of the wine-vats and the wassailing which went on throughout the city among freemen and slaves alike ; on the second day of the festival the marriage of Dionysus with the Queen of Athens was celebrated with great solemnity at the Bucolium or Ox-stall.[2]

---

[1] As to such festivals of All Souls see *Adonis, Attis, Osiris,* Second Edition, pp. 301-318.

[2] The passages of ancient authors which refer to the Anthesteria are collected by Professor Martin P. Nilsson, *Studia de Dionysiis Atticis* (Lund, 1900), pp. 148 *sqq.* As to the festival, which has been much discussed of late years, see

August Mommsen, *Heortologie* (Leipsic, 1864), pp. 345 *sqq.* ; *id., Feste der Stadt Athen im Altertum* (Leipsic, 1898), pp. 384 *sqq.*; G. F. Schoemann, *Griechische Alterthümer*[4] (Berlin, 1902), ii. 516 *sqq.* ; E. Rohde, *Psyche*[3] (Tübingen and Leipsic, 1903), i. 236 *sqq.* ; Martin P. Nilsson, *op. cit.* pp. 115 *sqq.* ; P. Foucart, *Le Culte de*

It has been suggested with much probability[1] that at this sacred marriage in the Ox-stall the god was represented wholly or partly in bovine shape, whether by an image or by an actor dressed in the hide and wearing the horns of a bull; for, as we have seen, Dionysus was often supposed to assume the form of a bull and to present himself in that guise to his worshippers. If this conjecture should prove to be correct—though a demonstration of it can hardly be expected—the sacred marriage of the Queen to the Bull-god at Athens would be parallel to the sacred marriage of the Queen to the Bull-god at Cnossus, according to the interpretation which I have suggested of the myth of Pasiphae and the Minotaur;[2] only whereas the bull-god at Cnossus, if I am right, stood for the Sun, the bull-god at Athens stood for the powers of vegetation, especially the corn and the vines. It would not be surprising that among a cattle-breeding people in early days the bull, regarded as a type of strength and reproductive energy, should be employed to symbolise and represent more than one of the great powers of nature. If Dionysus did indeed figure as a bull at his marriage, it is not improbable that on that occasion his representative, whether a real bull or a man dressed in a bull's hide, took part in a ceremony of ploughing; for we have seen that the invention of yoking oxen to the plough was ascribed to Dionysus, and we know that the Athenians performed a sacred ceremony of ploughing, which went by the name of the Ox-yoked Ploughing and took place in a field or other open piece of ground at the foot of the Acropolis.[3] It is a reasonable conjecture that the field of the Ox-yoked Ploughing may have adjoined the building called the Ox-stall in which the marriage of Dionysus with the Queen was solemnised;[4] for

Dionysos en Attique (Paris, 1904), pp. 107 *sqq.*; Miss J. E. Harrison, *Prolegomena to the Study of Greek Religion*[2] (Cambridge, 1908), pp. 32 *sqq.*; L. R. Farnell, *The Cults of the Greek States*, v. (Oxford, 1909) pp. 214 *sqq.* As to the marriage of Dionysus to the Queen of Athens, see *The Magic Art and the Evolution of Kings*, i. 136 *sq.*

[1] By Professor U. von Wilamowitz-

Moellendorff, *Aristoteles und Athen* (Berlin, 1893), ii. 42 ; and afterwards by Miss J. E. Harrison, *Prolegomena to the Study of Greek Religion*,[2] p. 536.

[2] *The Dying God*, p. 71.

[3] Plutarch, *Conjugalia Praecepta*, 42.

[4] Miss J. E. Harrison, *Mythology and Monuments of Ancient Athens* (London, 1890), pp. 166 *sq.*

that building is known to have been near the Prytaneum or Town-Hall on the northern slope of the Acropolis.[1]

Thus on the whole the ancient festival of the Anthesteria, so far as its features are preserved by tradition or can be restored by the use of reasonable conjecture, presents several important analogies to the modern Thracian Carnival in respect of wine-drinking, a mock marriage of disguised actors, and a ceremony of ploughing. The resemblance between the ancient and the modern ritual would be still closer if some eminent modern scholars, who wrote before the discovery of the Thracian Carnival, and whose judgment was therefore not biassed by its analogy to the Athenian festival, are right in holding that another important feature of the Anthesteria was the dramatic death and resurrection of Dionysus.[2] They point out that at the marriage of Dionysus fourteen Sacred Women officiated at fourteen altars ;[3] that the number of the Titans, who tore Dionysus in pieces, was fourteen, namely seven male and seven female ;[4] and that Osiris, a god who in some respects corresponded closely to Dionysus, is said to have been rent by Typhon into fourteen fragments.[5] Hence they conjecture that at Athens the body of Dionysus was dramatically broken into fourteen fragments, one for each of the fourteen altars, and that it was afterwards dramatically pieced together and restored to life by the fourteen Sacred Women, just as the broken body of Osiris was pieced together by a company of gods and goddesses and restored to life by his sister Isis.[6] The conjecture is ingenious and plausible, but with our existing sources of information it must remain a conjecture and

[1] Aristotle, *Constitution of Athens*, 3. As to the situation of the Prytaneum see my note on Pausanias, i. 18. 3 (vol. ii. p. 172).

[2] August Mommsen, *Heortologie*, pp. 371 *sqq.* ; *id.*, *Feste der Stadt Athen im Altertum*, pp. 398 *sqq.* ; P. Foucart, *Le Culte de Dionysos en Attique*, pp. 138 *sqq.*

[3] Demosthenes, *Contra Neaer.* 73, pp. 1369 *sq.* ; Julius Pollux, viii. 108 ; *Etymologicum Magnum*, p. 227, *s.v.* γεραῖραι ; Hesychius, *s.v.* γεραραί.

[4] Chr. A. Lobeck, *Aglaophamus*,

p. 505.

[5] Plutarch, *Isis et Osiris*, 18, 42.

[6] The resurrection of Osiris is not described by Plutarch in his treatise *Isis et Osiris*, which is still our principal source for the myth of the god ; but it is fortunately recorded in native Egyptian writings. See *Adonis, Attis, Osiris*, Second Edition, p. 274. P. Foucart supposes that the resurrection of Dionysus was enacted at the Anthesteria ; August Mommsen prefers to suppose that it was enacted in the following month at the Lesser Mysteries.

nothing more. Could it be established, it would forge another strong link in the chain of evidence which binds the modern Thracian Carnival to the ancient Athenian Anthesteria; for in that case the drama of the divine death and resurrection would have to be added to the other features which these two festivals of spring possess in common, and we should have to confess that Greece had what we may call its Good Friday and its Easter Sunday long before the events took place in Judaea which diffused these two annual commemorations of the Dying and Reviving God over a great part of the civilised world. From so simple a beginning may flow consequences so far-reaching and impressive; for in the light of the rude Thracian ceremony we may surmise that the high tragedy of the death and resurrection of Dionysus originated in a rustic mummers' play acted by ploughmen for the purpose of fertilising the brown earth which they turned up with the gleaming share in sunshiny days of spring, as they followed the slow-paced oxen down the long furrows in the fallow field. Later on we shall see that a play of the same sort is still acted, or was acted down to recent years, by English yokels on Plough Monday.

But before we pass from the tragic myth and ritual of Dionysus to the sweeter story and milder worship of Demeter and Persephone, the true Greek deities of the corn, it is fair to admit that the legends of human sacrifice, which have left so dark a stain on the memory of the old Thracian god, may have been nothing more than mere misinterpretations of a sacrificial ritual in which an animal victim was treated as a human being. For example, at Tenedos the new-born calf sacrificed to Dionysus was shod in buskins, and the mother cow was tended like a woman in child-bed.[1] At Rome a she-goat was sacrificed to Vedijovis as if it were a human victim.[2] Yet on the other hand it is equally possible, and perhaps more probable, that these curious rites were themselves mitigations of an older and ruder custom of sacrificing human beings, and that the later pretence of

Legends of human sacrifice in the worship of Dionysus may be mere misinterpretations of ritual.

---

[1] Aelian, *De Natura Animalium*, xii. 34. Compare W. Robertson Smith, *Religion of the Semites*[2] (London, 1894), pp. 300 *sqq.*

[2] Aulus Gellius, v. 12. 12.

treating the sacrificial victims as if they were human beings was merely part of a pious and merciful fraud, which palmed off on the deity less precious victims than living men and women. This interpretation is supported by the undoubted cases in which animals have been substituted for human victims.[1] On the whole we may conclude that neither the polished manners of a later age, nor the glamour which Greek poetry and art threw over the figure of Dionysus, sufficed to conceal or erase the deep lines of savagery and cruelty imprinted on the features of this barbarous deity.

[1] See *The Dying God*, p. 166 note [1], and below, p. 249.

CHAPTER II

DEMETER AND PERSEPHONE

DIONYSUS was not the only Greek deity whose tragic story and ritual appear to reflect the decay and revival of vegetation. In another form and with a different application the old tale reappears in the myth of Demeter and Persephone. Substantially their myth is identical with the Syrian one of Aphrodite (Astarte) and Adonis, the Phrygian one of Cybele and Attis, and the Egyptian one of Isis and Osiris. In the Greek fable, as in its Asiatic and Egyptian counterparts, a goddess mourns the loss of a loved one, who personifies the vegetation, more especially the corn, which dies in winter to revive in spring; only whereas the Oriental imagination figured the loved and lost one as a dead lover or a dead husband lamented by his leman or his wife, Greek fancy embodied the same idea in the tenderer and purer form of a dead daughter bewailed by her sorrowing mother. Demeter and Persephone as Greek personifications of the decay and revival of vegetation.

The oldest literary document which narrates the myth of Demeter and Persephone is the beautiful Homeric *Hymn to Demeter*, which critics assign to the seventh century before our era.[1] The object of the poem is to explain the origin of the Eleusinian mysteries, and the complete silence of the poet as to Athens and the Athenians, who in after ages took a conspicuous part in the festival, renders it probable that the hymn was composed in the far off time when Eleusis was still a petty independent state, and before the stately procession of the Mysteries had begun to defile, in The Homeric Hymn to Demeter.

[1] R. Foerster, *Der Raub und die Rückkehr der Persophone* (Stuttgart, 1874), pp. 37-39; *The Homeric Hymns*, edited by T. W. Allen and E. E. Sikes (London, 1904), pp. 10 *sq.* A later date—the age of the Pisistratids—is assigned to the hymn by A. Baumeister (*Hymni Homerici*, Leipsic, 1860, p. 280).

bright September days, over the low chain of barren rocky hills which divides the flat Eleusinian cornland from the more spacious olive-clad expanse of the Athenian plain. Be that as it may, the hymn reveals to us the conception which the writer entertained of the character and functions of the two goddesses : their natural shapes stand out sharply enough

The rape of Persephone. under the thin veil of poetical imagery. The youthful Persephone, so runs the tale, was gathering roses and lilies, crocuses and violets, hyacinths and narcissuses in a lush meadow, when the earth gaped and Pluto, lord of the Dead, issuing from the abyss carried her off on his golden car to be his bride and queen in the gloomy subterranean world. Her sorrowing mother Demeter, with her yellow tresses veiled in a dark mourning mantle, sought her over land and sea, and learning from the Sun her daughter's fate she withdrew in high dudgeon from the gods and took up her abode at Eleusis, where she presented herself to the king's daughters in the guise of an old woman, sitting sadly under the shadow of an olive tree beside the Maiden's Well, to which the damsels had come to draw water in bronze pitchers

The wrath of Demeter. for their father's house. In her wrath at her bereavement the goddess suffered not the seed to grow in the earth but kept it hidden under ground, and she vowed that never would she set foot on Olympus and never would she let the corn sprout till her lost daughter should be restored to her. Vainly the oxen dragged the ploughs to and fro in the fields ; vainly the sower dropped the barley seed in the brown furrows ; nothing came up from the parched and crumbling soil. Even the Rarian plain near Eleusis, which was wont to wave with yellow harvests, lay bare and fallow.[1] Mankind would have perished of hunger and the gods would have been robbed of the sacrifices which were their due, if Zeus in alarm had not commanded Pluto to disgorge his prey, to restore his bride Persephone to her mother Demeter. The grim lord of the Dead smiled and obeyed, but before he sent back his queen to the upper air on a golden car, he gave her the seed of a pomegranate to eat, which ensured that she would return to him. But Zeus stipulated that henceforth Persephone should spend two thirds of every

[1] *Hymn to Demeter*, 1 *sqq.*, 302 *sqq.*, 330 *sqq.*, 349 *sqq.*, 414 *sqq.*, 450 *sqq.*

year with her mother and the gods in the upper world and one third of the year with her husband in the nether world, from which she was to return year by year when the earth was gay with spring flowers.   Gladly the daughter then returned to the sunshine, gladly her mother received her and fell upon her neck ; and in her joy at recovering the lost one Demeter made the corn to sprout from the clods of the ploughed fields and all the broad earth to be heavy with leaves and blossoms.   And straightway she went and shewed this happy sight to the princes of Eleusis, to Triptolemus, Eumolpus, Diocles, and to the king Celeus himself, and moreover she revealed to them her sacred rites and mysteries.   Blessed, says the poet, is the mortal man who has seen these things, but he who has had no share of them in life will never be happy in death when he has descended into the darkness of the grave.   So the two goddesses departed to dwell in bliss with the gods on Olympus ; and the bard ends the hymn with a pious prayer to Demeter and Persephone that they would be pleased to grant him a livelihood in return for his song.[1]

The return of Persephone.

It has been generally recognised, and indeed it seems scarcely open to doubt, that the main theme which the poet set before himself in composing this hymn was to describe the traditional foundation of the Eleusinian mysteries by the goddess Demeter.   The whole poem leads up to the transformation scene in which the bare leafless expanse of the Eleusinian plain is suddenly turned, at the will of the goddess, into a vast sheet of ruddy corn ; the beneficent deity takes the princes of Eleusis, shews them what she has done, teaches them her mystic rites, and vanishes with her daughter to heaven.   The revelation of the mysteries is the triumphal close of the piece.   This conclusion is confirmed by a more minute examination of the poem, which proves that the poet has given, not merely a general account of the foundation of the mysteries, but also in more or less veiled language mythical explanations of the origin of particular rites which we have good reason to believe formed essential

The aim of the Homeric *Hymn to Demeter* is to explain the traditional foundation of the Eleusinian mysteries by Demeter.

---

[1] *Hymn to Demeter*, 310 *sqq*.   With the myth as set forth in the Homeric hymn may be compared the accounts of Apollodorus (*Bibliotheca*, i. 5) and Ovid (*Fasti*, iv. 425-618 ; *Metamorphoses*, v. 385 *sqq*.).

features of the festival.   Amongst the rites as to which the
poet thus drops significant hints are the preliminary fast of
the candidates for initiation, the torchlight procession, the
all-night vigil, the sitting of the candidates, veiled and in
silence, on stools covered with sheepskins, the use of scurrilous
language, the breaking of ribald jests, and the solemn communion with the divinity by participation in a draught of
barley-water from a holy chalice.[1]

Revelation of a reaped ear of corn the crowning act of the mysteries.

But there is yet another and a deeper secret of the
mysteries which the author of the poem appears to have
divulged under cover of his narrative.   He tells us how, as
soon as she had transformed the barren brown expanse of the
Eleusinian plain into a field of golden grain, she gladdened
the eyes of Triptolemus and the other Eleusinian princes by
shewing them the growing or standing corn.   When we
compare this part of the story with the statement of a
Christian writer of the second century, Hippolytus, that the
very heart of the mysteries consisted in shewing to the
initiated a reaped ear of corn,[2] we can hardly doubt that

---

[1] *Hymn to Demeter*, 47-50, 191-
211, 292-295, with the notes of
Messrs. Allen and Sikes in their edition of the Homeric Hymns (London,
1904).   As to representations of the
candidates for initiation seated on stools
draped with sheepskins, see L. R.
Farnell, *The Cults of the Greek States*,
iii. (Oxford, 1907) pp. 237 *sqq.*, with
plate xva. On a well-known marble
vase there figured the stool is covered
with a lion's skin and one of the candi-
date's feet rests on a ram's skull or horns;
but in two other examples of the same
scene the ram's fleece is placed on the
seat (Farnell, *op. cit.* p. 240 note a),
just as it is said to have been placed
on Demeter's stool in the Homeric
hymn.   As to the form of communion
in the Eleusinian mysteries, see
Clement of Alexandria, *Protrept.* 21,
p. 18 ed. Potter ; Arnobius, *Adversus
nationes*, v. 26 ; L. R. Farnell, *op. cit.*
iii. 185 *sq.*, 195 *sq.* For discussions
of the ancient evidence bearing on the
Eleusinian mysteries it may suffice to
refer to Chr. A. Lobeck, *Aglaophamus*
(Königsberg, 1829), pp. 3 *sqq.* ; G. F.
Schoemann, *Griechische Alterthümer*,[4]

ii. 387 *sqq.* ; Aug. Mommsen, *Heortologie* (Leipsic, 1864), pp. 222 *sqq.* ;
id., *Feste der Stadt Athen im Altertum*
(Leipsic, 1898), pp. 204 *sqq.* ; P.
Foucart, *Recherches sur l'Origine et
la Nature des Mystères d'Eleusis*
(Paris, 1895) (*Mémoires de l'Académie
des Inscriptions*, xxxv.) ; *id.*, *Les
grands Mystères d'Eleusis* (Paris,
1900) (*Mémoires de l'Académie des
Inscriptions*, xxxvii.) ; F. Lenormant
and E. Pottier, *s.v.* "Eleusinia," in
Daremberg et Saglio, *Dictionnaire
des Antiquités Grecques et Romaines*,
ii. 544 *sqq.* ; L. R. Farnell, *The Cults
of the Greek States*, iii. 126 *sqq.*
[2] Hippolytus, *Refutatio Omnium
Haeresium*, v. 8, p. 162, ed. L.
Duncker et F. G. Schneidewin (Göttingen, 1859).   The word which the
poet uses to express the revelation
(δεῖξε, *Hymn to Demeter*, verse 474) is
a technical one in the mysteries ; the
full phrase was δεικνύναι τὰ ἱερά. See
Plutarch, *Alcibiades*, 22 ; Xenophon,
Hellenica, vi. 3. 6 ; Isocrates, *Panegyricus*, 6 ; Lysias, *Contra Andocidem*,
51 ; Chr. A. Lobeck, *Aglaophamus*,
p. 51.

the poet of the hymn was well acquainted with this solemn rite, and that he deliberately intended to explain its origin in precisely the same way as he explained other rites of the mysteries, namely by representing Demeter as having set the example of performing the ceremony in her own person. Thus myth and ritual mutually explain and confirm each other. The poet of the seventh century before our era gives us the myth—he could not without sacrilege have revealed the ritual : the Christian father reveals the ritual, and his revelation accords perfectly with the veiled hint of the old poet. On the whole, then, we may, with many modern scholars, confidently accept the statement of the learned Christian father Clement of Alexandria, that the myth of Demeter and Persephone was acted as a sacred drama in the mysteries of Eleusis.[1]

But if the myth was acted as a part, perhaps as the principal part, of the most famous and solemn religious rites of ancient Greece, we have still to enquire, What was, after all, stripped of later accretions, the original kernel of the myth which appears to later ages surrounded and transfigured by an aureole of awe and mystery, lit up by some of the most brilliant rays of Grecian literature and art ? If we follow the indications given by our oldest literary authority on the subject, the author of the Homeric hymn to Demeter, the riddle is not hard to read ; the figures of the two goddesses, the mother and the daughter, resolve themselves into personifications of the corn.[2] At least this appears to be fairly certain for the daughter Persephone.

Demeter and Persephone personifications of the corn.

---

[1] Clement of Alexandria, *Protrept.* ii. 12, p. 12 ed. Potter : Δηὼ δὲ καὶ Κόρη δρᾶμα ἤδη ἐγενέσθην μυστικόν· καὶ τὴν πλάνην καὶ τὴν ἁρπαγὴν καὶ τὸ πένθος αὐταῖν Ἐλευσὶς δᾳδουχεῖ. Compare F. Lenormant, *s.v.* "Eleusinia," in Daremberg et Saglio, *Dictionnaire des Antiquités Grecques et Romaines,* iii. 578 : "*Que le drame mystique des aventures de Déméter et de Coré constituât le spectacle essentiel de l'initiation, c'est ce dont il nous semble impossible de douter.*" A similar view is expressed by G. F. Schoemann (*Griechische Alterthümer,*⁴ ii. 402) ; Preller - Robert (*Griechische Mytho-*

logie, i. 793) ; P. Foucart (*Recherches sur l'Origine et la Nature des Mystères d'Eleusis,* Paris, 1895, pp. 43 *sqq.* ; *id., Les Grands Mystères d'Eleusis,* Paris, 1900, p. 137) ; E. Rohde (*Psyche,*³ i. 289) ; and L. R. Farnell (*The Cults of the Greek States,* iii. 134, 173 *sqq.*).

[2] On Demeter and Proserpine as goddesses of the corn, see L. Preller, *Demeter und Persephone* (Hamburg, 1837), pp. 315 *sqq.* ; and especially W. Mannhardt, *Mythologische Forschungen* (Strasburg, 1884), pp. 202 *sqq.*

Per-
sephone
the seed
sown in
autumn
and
sprouting
in spring.

Demeter
the old
corn of
last year.

The view
that
Demeter
was the
Earth
goddess is
implicitly
rejected by
the author
of the
Homeric
*Hymn to
Demeter.*

The goddess who spends three or, according to another
version of the myth, six months of every year with the
dead under ground and the remainder of the year with the
living above ground ;[1] in whose absence the barley seed is
hidden in the earth and the fields lie bare and fallow ; on
whose return in spring to the upper world the corn shoots
up from the clods and the earth is heavy with leaves and
blossoms—this goddess can surely be nothing else than a
mythical embodiment of the vegetation, and particularly of
the corn, which is buried under the soil for some months of
every winter and comes to life again, as from the grave, in
the sprouting cornstalks and the opening flowers and foliage
of every spring.   No other reasonable and probable explanation of Persephone seems possible.[2]   And if the
daughter goddess was a personification of the young corn
of the present year, may not the mother goddess be a
personification of the old corn of last year, which has given
birth to the new crops ?   The only alternative to this view
of Demeter would seem to be to suppose that she is a
personification of the earth, from whose broad bosom the
corn and all other plants spring up, and of which accordingly
they may appropriately enough be regarded as the daughters.
This view of the original nature of Demeter has indeed been
taken by some writers, both ancient and modern,[3] and it is

[1] According to the author of the
Homeric Hymn to Demeter (verses
398 *sqq.*, 445 *sqq.*) and Apollodorus
(*Bibliotheca*, i. 5. 3) the time which
Persephone had to spend under ground
was one third of the year ; according
to Ovid (*Fasti*, iv. 613 *sq.* ; *Metamorphoses*, v. 564 *sqq.*) and Hyginus
(*Fabulae*, 146) it was one half.

[2] This view of the myth of Persephone is, for example, accepted and
clearly stated by L. Preller (*Demeter
und Persephone*, pp. 128 *sq.*).

[3] See, for example, Firmicus Maternus, *De errore profanarum religionum*,
17. 3 : "*Frugum substantiam volunt
Proserpinam dicere, quia fruges
hominibus cum seri coeperint prosunt.
Terram ipsam Cererem nominant,
nomen hoc a gerendis fructibus mutuati*";
L. Preller, *Demeter und Persephone*,
p. 128, "*Der Erdboden wird Demeter,*

die Vegetation Persephone."   François
Lenormant, again, held that Demeter
was originally a personification of the
earth regarded as divine, but he
admitted that from the time of the
Homeric poems downwards she was
sharply distinguished from Ge, the
earth-goddess proper.   See Daremberg
et Saglio, *Dictionnaire des Antiquités
Grecques et Romaines*, *s.v.* "Ceres,"
ii. 1022 *sq.*   Some light might be
thrown on the question whether
Demeter was an Earth Goddess or a
Corn Goddess, if we could be sure of
the etymology of her name, which has
been variously explained as "Earth
Mother" (Δῆ μήτηρ equivalent to Γῆ
μήτηρ) and as "Barley Mother" (from
an alleged Cretan word δηαί "barley":
see *Etymologicum Magnum*, *s.v.* Δηώ,
pp. 263 *sq.*).   The former etymology
has been the most popular ; the latter

one which can be reasonably maintained.   But it appears
to have been rejected by the author of the Homeric hymn
to Demeter, for he not only distinguishes Demeter from the
personified Earth but places the two in the sharpest opposition to each other.   He tells us that it was Earth who, in
accordance with the will of Zeus and to please Pluto, lured
Persephone to her doom by causing the narcissuses to grow
which tempted the young goddess to stray far beyond the
reach of help in the lush meadow.[1]   Thus Demeter of the
hymn, far from being identical with the Earth-goddess, must
have regarded that divinity as her worst enemy, since it
was to her insidious wiles that she owed the loss of her
daughter.   But if the Demeter of the hymn cannot have
been a personification of the earth, the only alternative
apparently is to conclude that she was a personification of
the corn.

With this conclusion all the indications of the hymn-
writer seem to harmonise.   He certainly represents Demeter
as the goddess by whose power and at whose pleasure
the corn either grows or remains hidden in the ground ;
and to what deity can such powers be so fittingly ascribed
as to the goddess of the corn ?   He calls Demeter yellow
and tells how her yellow tresses flowed down on her
shoulders ;[2]   could any colour be more appropriate with
which to paint the divinity of the yellow grain ?   The same
identification of Demeter with the ripe, the yellow corn is
made even more clearly by a still older poet, Homer
himself, or at all events the author of the fifth book of the
Iliad.   There we read : " And even as the wind carries the
chaff about the sacred threshing-floors, when men are

The Yellow Demeter, the goddess who sifts the ripe grain from the chaff at the threshing-floor.

is maintained by W. Mannhardt.   See
L. Preller, *Demeter und Persephone*,
pp. 317, 366 *sqq.* ; F. G. Welcker,
Griechische Götterlehre, i. 385 *sqq.* ;
Preller-Robert, *Griechische Mythologie*,
i. 747 note [6] ; Kern, in Pauly-Wissowa's
*Real-Encyclopädie der classischen Alter-
tumswissenschaft*, iv. 2713 ; W. Mannhardt, *Mythologische Forschungen*, pp.
281 *sqq.*   But my learned friend the
Rev. Professor J. H. Moulton informs
me that both etymologies are open to
serious philological objections, and that

no satisfactory derivation of the first
syllable of Demeter's name has yet
been proposed.   Accordingly I prefer
to base no argument on an analysis of
the name, and to rest my interpretation
of the goddess entirely on her myth,
ritual, and representations in art.
Etymology is at the best a very slippery
ground on which to rear mythological
theories.

[1] *Hymn to Demeter*, 8 *sqq.*

[2] *Hymn to Demeter*, 279, 302.

winnowing, what time yellow Demeter sifts the corn from the chaff on the hurrying blast, so that the heaps of chaff grow white below, so were the Achaeans whitened above by the cloud of dust which the hoofs of the horses spurned to the brazen heaven."[1] Here the yellow Demeter who sifts the grain from the chaff at the threshing-floor can hardly be any other than the goddess of the yellow corn ; she cannot be the Earth-goddess, for what has the Earth-goddess to do with the grain and the chaff blown about a threshing-floor ? With this interpretation it agrees that elsewhere Homer speaks of men eating " Demeter's corn " ;[2] and still more definitely Hesiod speaks of " the annual store of food, which the earth bears, Demeter's corn,"[3] thus distinguishing the goddess of the corn from the earth which bears it. Still more clearly does a later Greek poet personify the corn as Demeter when, in allusion to the time of the corn-reaping, he says that then " the sturdy swains cleave Demeter limb from limb."[4] And just as the ripe or yellow corn was personified as the Yellow Demeter, so the unripe or green corn was personified as the Green Demeter. In that character the goddess had sanctuaries at Athens and other places ; sacrifices were appropriately offered to Green Demeter in spring when the earth was growing green with the fresh vegetation, and the victims included sows big with young,[5] which no doubt were intended not merely to symbolise but magically to promote the abundance of the crops.

The Green Demeter the goddess of the green corn.

In Greek the various kinds of corn were called by the general name of " Demeter's fruits,"[6] just as in Latin they were called the " fruits or gifts of Ceres,"[7] an expression

The cereals called "Demeter's fruits."

---

[1] Homer, *Iliad*, v. 499-504.
[2] *Iliad*, xiii. 322, xxi. 76.
[3] Hesiod, *Works and Days*, 31 *sq.*
[4] Quoted by Plutarch, *Isis et Osiris*, 66.
[5] Pausanias, i. 22. 3 with my note ; Dittenberger, *Sylloge Inscriptionum Graecarum*,[2] No. 615 ; J. de Prott et L. Ziehen, *Leges Graecorum Sacrae*, Fasciculus I. (Leipsic, 1896) p. 49 ; Cornutus, *Theologiae Graecae Compendium*, 28 ; Scholiast on Sophocles, *Oedipus Colon.* 1600 ; L. R. Farnell,

The Cults of the Greek States, iii. 312 *sq.*
[6] Herodotus, i. 193, iv. 198 ; Xenophon, *Hellenica*, vi. 3. 6 ; Aelian, *Historia Animalium*, xvii. 16 ; Cornutus, *Theologiae Graecae Compendium*, 28 ; *Geoponica*, i. 12. 36 ; *Paroemiographi Graeci*, ed. Leutsch et Schneidewin, Appendix iv. 20 (vol. i. p. 439).
[7] *Cerealia* in Pliny, *Nat. Hist.* xxiii. 1 ; *Cerealia munera* and *Cerealia dona* in Ovid, *Metamorphoses*, xi. 121 *sq.*

which survives in the English word cereals. Tradition ran that before Demeter's time men neither cultivated corn nor tilled the ground, but roamed the mountains and woods in search of the wild fruits which the earth produced spontaneously from her womb for their subsistence. The tradition clearly implies not only that Demeter was the goddess of the corn, but that she was different from and younger than the goddess of the Earth, since it is expressly affirmed that before Demeter's time the earth existed and supplied mankind with nourishment in the shape of wild herbs, grasses, flowers and fruits.[1]

In ancient art Demeter and Persephone are characterised as goddesses of the corn by the crowns of corn which they wear on their heads and by the stalks of corn which they hold in their hands.[2] Theocritus describes a smiling image of Demeter standing by a heap of yellow grain on a threshing-floor and grasping sheaves of barley and poppies in both her hands.[3] Indeed corn and poppies singly or together were a frequent symbol of the goddess, as we learn not only from the testimony of ancient writers[4] but from many existing monuments of classical art.[5] The naturalness of the symbol

Corn and poppies as symbols of Demeter.

---

[1] Libanius, ed. J. J. Reiske, vol. iv. p. 367, *Corinth. Oratio*: Οὐκ αὖθις ἡμῶν ἄκαρπος ἡ γῆ δοκεῖ γεγονέναι; οὐ πάλιν ὁ πρὸ Δήμητρος εἶναι βίος; καί τοι καὶ πρὸ Δήμητρος αἱ γεωργίαι μὲν οὐκ ἦσαν· οὐδὲ ἄροτοι, αὐτόφυτοι δὲ βοτάναι καὶ πόαι· καὶ πολλὰ εἶχεν εἰς σωτηρίαν ἀνθρώπων αὐτοσχέδια ἄνθη ἡ γῆ ὠδίνουσα καὶ κύουσα πρὸ τῶν ἡμέρων τὰ ἄγρια. Ἐπλανῶντο μὲν, ἀλλ' οὐκ ἐπ' ἀλλήλους· ἄλση καὶ ὄρη περιῄσαν, ζητοῦντες αὐτόματον τροφήν. In this passage, which no doubt represents the common Greek view on the subject, the earth is plainly personified (ὠδίνουσα καὶ κύουσα), which points the antithesis between her and the goddess of the corn. Diodorus Siculus also says (v. 68) that corn grew wild with the other plants before Demeter taught men to cultivate it and to sow the seed.

[2] Ovid, *Fasti*, iv. 616; Eusebius, *Praeparatio Evangelii*, iii. 11. 5; Cornutus, *Theologiae Graecae Compendium*, 28; *Anthologia Palatina*,

vi. 104. 8; W. Mannhardt, *Mythologische Forschungen*, p. 235; J. Overbeck, *Griechische Kunstmythologie*, iii. (Leipsic, 1873-1878) pp. 420, 421, 453, 479, 480, 502, 505, 507, 514, 522, 523, 524, 525 *sq.*; L. R. Farnell, *The Cults of the Greek States*, iii. 217 *sqq.*, 220 *sq.*, 222, 226, 232, 233, 237, 260, 265, 268, 269 *sq.*, 271.

[3] Theocritus, *Idyl.* vii. 155 *sqq.* That the sheaves which the goddess grasped were of barley is proved by verses 31-34 of the poem.

[4] Eusebius, *Praeparatio Evangelii*, iii. 11. 5; Cornutus, *Theologiae Graecae Compendium*, 28, p. 56, ed. C. Lang; Virgil, *Georg.* i. 212, with the comment of Servius.

[5] See the references to the works of Overbeck and Farnell above. For example, a fine statue at Copenhagen, in the style of the age of Phidias, represents Demeter holding poppies and ears of corn in her left hand. See Farnell, *op. cit.* iii. 268, with plate xxviii.

can be doubted by no one who has seen—and who has not seen ?—a field of yellow corn bespangled thick with scarlet poppies ; and we need not resort to the shifts of an ancient mythologist, who explained the symbolism of the poppy in Demeter's hand by comparing the globular shape of the poppy to the roundness of our globe, the unevenness of its edges to hills and valleys, and the hollow interior of the scarlet flower to the caves and dens of the earth.[1] If only students would study the little black and white books of men less and the great rainbow-tinted book of nature more ; if they would more frequently exchange the heavy air and the dim light of libraries for the freshness and the sunshine of the open sky ; if they would oftener unbend their minds by rural walks-between fields of waving corn, beside rivers rippling by under grey willows, or down green lanes, where the hedges are white with the hawthorn bloom or red with wild roses, they might sometimes learn more about primitive religion than can be gathered from many dusty volumes, in which wire-drawn theories are set forth with all the tedious parade of learning.

Persephone portrayed as the young corn sprouting from the ground.

Nowhere, perhaps, in the monuments of Greek art is the character of Persephone as a personification of the young corn sprouting in spring portrayed more gracefully and more truly than on a coin of Lampsacus of the fourth century before our era. On it we see the goddess in the very act of rising from the earth. "Her face is upraised ; in her hand are three ears of corn, and others together with grapes are springing behind her shoulder. Complete is here the identification of the goddess and her attribute : she is embowered amid the ears of growing corn, and like it half buried in the ground. She does not make the corn and vine grow, but she *is* the corn and vine growing, and returning again to the face of the earth after lying hidden in its depths. Certainly the artist who designed this beautiful figure thoroughly understood Hellenic religion." [2]

As the goddess who first bestowed corn on mankind and taught them to sow and cultivate it,[3] Demeter was

---

[1] Cornutus, *Theologiae Graecae Compendium*, 28, p. 56 ed. C. Lang.

[2] Percy Gardner, *Types of Greek*

Coins (Cambridge, 1883), p. 174, with plate x. No. 25.

[3] Diodorus Siculus, v. 68. 1.

naturally invoked and propitiated by farmers before they Demeter
undertook the various operations of the agricultural year. invoked
In autumn, when he heard the sonorous trumpeting of the and pro-pitiated by
cranes, as they winged their way southward in vast flocks Greek
high overhead, the Greek husbandman knew that the rains farmers before the
were near and that the time of ploughing was at hand ; but autumnal
before he put his hand to the plough he prayed to Under- sowing.
ground Zeus and to Holy Demeter for a heavy crop of
Demeter's sacred corn.   Then he guided the ox-drawn
plough down the field, turning up the brown earth with the
share, while a swain followed close behind with a hoe, who
covered up the seed as fast as it fell to protect it from the
voracious birds that fluttered and twittered at the plough-
tail.[1] But while the ordinary Greek farmer took the signal
for ploughing from the clangour of the cranes, Hesiod and
other writers who aimed at greater exactness laid it down
as a rule that the ploughing should begin with the autumnal
setting of the Pleiades in the morning, which in Hesiod's
time fell on the twenty-sixth of October.[2]   The month
in which the Pleiades set in the morning was generally
recognised by the Greeks as the month of sowing ; it
corresponded apparently in part to our October, in part to

---

[1] Hesiod, *Works and Days*, 448-
474 ; Epictetus, *Dissertationes*, iii.
21. 12.   For the autumnal migration
and clangour of the cranes as the
signal for sowing, see Aristophanes,
Birds, 711 ; compare Theognis, 1197
sqq. But the Greeks also ploughed in
spring (Hesiod, *op. cit.* 462 ; Xenophon,
Oeconom. 16) ; indeed they ploughed
thrice in the year (Theophrastus,
Historia Plantarum, vii. 13. 6).   At
the approach of autumn the cranes of
northern Europe collect about rivers
and lakes, and after much trumpeting
set out in enormous bands on their
southward journey to the tropical
regions of Africa and India.   In early
spring they return northward, and
their flocks may be descried passing at
a marvellous height overhead or halting
to rest in the meadows beside some
broad river.   The bird emits its
trumpet-like note both on the ground
and on the wing.   See Alfred Newton,
Dictionary of Birds (London, 1893-

1896), pp. 110 *sq.*

[2] Hesiod, *Works and Days*, 383 *sq.*,
615-617 ; Aratus, *Phaenomena*, 254-
267 ; L. Ideler, *Handbuch der mathematischen und technischen Chronologie*
(Berlin, 1825-1826), i. 241 *sq.*   According to Pliny (*Nat. Hist.* xviii. 49)
wheat, barley, and all other cereals
were sown in Greece and Asia from
the time of the autumn setting of the
Pleiades.   This date for ploughing
and sowing is confirmed by Hippo-
crates and other medical writers.   See
W. Smith's *Dictionary of Greek ana
Roman Antiquities*,[3] i. 234.   Latin
writers prescribe the same date for the
sowing of wheat. See Virgil, *Georg.*
i. 219-226 ; Columella, *De re rustica*,
ii. 8 ; Pliny, *Nat. Hist.* xviii. 223-226.
In Columella's time the Pleiades, he
tells us (*l.c.*), set in the morning of
October 24th of the Julian calendar,
which would correspond to the October
16th of our reckoning.

our November. The Athenians called it Pyanepsion ; the Boeotians named it significantly Damatrius, that is, Demeter's month, and they celebrated a feast of mourning because, says Plutarch, who as a Boeotian speaks with authority on such a matter, Demeter was then in mourning for the descent of Persephone.[1] Is it possible to express more clearly the true original nature of Persephone as the corn-seed which has just been buried in the earth? The obvious, the almost inevitable conclusion did not escape Plutarch. He tells us that the mournful rites which were held at the time of the autumn sowing nominally commemorated the actions of deities, but that the real sadness was for the fruits of the earth, some of which at that season dropped of themselves and vanished from the trees, while others in the shape of seed were committed with anxious thoughts to the ground by men, who scraped the earth and then huddled it up over the seed, just as if they were burying and mourning for the dead.[2] Surely this interpretation of the custom and of the myth of Persephone is not only beautiful but true.

And just as the Greek husbandman prayed to the Corn Goddess when he committed the seed, with anxious forebodings, to the furrows, so after he had reaped the harvest and brought back the yellow sheaves with rejoicing to the threshing-floor, he paid the bountiful goddess her dues in the form of a thank-offering of golden grain. Theocritus has painted for us in glowing colours a picture of a

[1] Plutarch, *Isis et Osiris*, 69.

[2] Plutarch, *Isis et Osiris*, 70. Similarly Cornutus says that "Hades is fabled to have carried off Demeter's daughter because the seed vanishes for a time under the earth," and he mentions that a festival of Demeter was celebrated at the time of sowing (*Theologiae Graecae Compendium*, 28, pp. 54, 55 ed. C. Lang). In a fragment of a Greek calendar which is preserved in the Louvre "the ascent (ἀναβάσις) of the goddess" is dated the seventh day of the month Dius, and "the descent or setting (δύσις) of the goddess" is dated the fourth day of the month Hephaestius, a month which seems to be other-

wise unknown. See W. Froehner, *Musée Nationale du Louvre, Les Inscriptions Grecques* (Paris, 1880), pp. 50 *sq.* Greek inscriptions found at Mantinea refer to a worship of Demeter and Persephone, who are known to have had a sanctuary there (Pausanias, viii. 9. 2). The people of Mantinea celebrated "mysteries of the goddess" and a festival called the *koragia*, which seems to have represented the return of Persephone from the lower world. See W. Immerwahr, *Die Kulte und Mythen Arkadiens* (Leipsic, 1891), pp. 100 *sq.* ; S. Reinach, *Traité d'Épigraphie Grecque* (Paris, 1885), pp. 141 *sqq.* ; Hesychius, *s.v.* κοράγειν.

rustic harvest-home, as it fell on a bright autumn day some two thousand years ago in the little Greek island of Cos.[1] The poet tells us how he went with two friends from the city to attend a festival given by farmers, who were offering first-fruits to Demeter from the store of barley with which she had filled their barns. The day was warm, indeed so hot that the very lizards, which love to bask and run about in the sun, were slumbering in the crevices of the stone-walls, and not a lark soared carolling into the blue vault of heaven. Yet despite the great heat there were everywhere signs of autumn. "All things," says the poet, "smelt of summer, but smelt of autumn too." Indeed the day was really autumnal; for a goat-herd who met the friends on their way to the rural merry-making, asked them whether they were bound for the treading of the grapes in the wine-presses. And when they had reached their destination and reclined at ease in the dappled shade of over-arching poplars and elms, with the babble of a neighbouring fountain, the buzz of the cicalas, the hum of bees, and the cooing of doves in their ears, the ripe apples and pears rolled in the grass at their feet and the branches of the wild-plum trees were bowed down to the earth with the weight of their purple fruit. So couched on soft beds of fragrant lentisk they passed the sultry hours singing ditties alternately, while a rustic image of Demeter, to whom the honours of the day were paid, stood smiling beside a heap of yellow grain on the threshing-floor, with corn-stalks and poppies in her hands.

In this description the time of year when the harvest-home was celebrated is clearly marked. Apart from the mention of the ripe apples, pears, and plums, the reference to the treading of the grapes is decisive. The Greeks gather and press the grapes in the first half of October,[2] and accordingly it is to this date that the harvest-festival described by Theocritus must be assigned. At the present

descrip- tion of a harvest- home in Cos.

The harvest- home de- scribed by Theocritus fell in autumn.

---

[1] Theocritus, *Idyl.* vii.

[2] In ancient Greece the vintage seems to have fallen somewhat earlier; for Hesiod bids the husbandman gather the ripe clusters at the time when

Arcturus is a morning star, which in the poet's age was on the 18th of September. See Hesiod, *Works and Days*, 609 *sqq.*; L. Ideler, *Handbuch der mathematischen und technischen Chronologie*, i. 247.

day in Greece the maize-harvest immediately precedes the vintage, the grain being reaped and garnered at the end of September.   Travelling in rural districts of Argolis and Arcadia at that time of the year you pass from time to time piles of the orange-coloured cobs laid up ready to be shelled, or again heaps of the yellow grain beside the pods.   But maize was unknown to the ancient Greeks, who, like their modern descendants, reaped their wheat and barley crops much earlier in the summer, usually from the end of April till June.[1]   However, we may conclude that the day immortalised by Theocritus was one of those autumn days of great heat and effulgent beauty which in Greece may occur at any time up to the very verge of winter.   I remember such a day at Panopeus on the borders of Phocis and Boeotia.   It was the first of November, yet the sun shone in cloudless splendour and the heat was so great, that when I had examined the magnificent remains of ancient Greek fortification-walls which crown the summit of the hill, it was delicious to repose on a grassy slope in the shade of some fine holly-oaks and to inhale the sweet scent of the wild thyme, which perfumed all the air.   But it was summer's farewell.   Next morning the weather had completely changed. A grey November sky lowered sadly overhead, and grey mists hung like winding-sheets on the lower slopes of the barren mountains which shut in the fatal plain of Chaeronea.

The Greeks seem to have deferred the offering of first-fruits till the autumn in order to propitiate the Corn Goddess at the moment of ploughing and sowing, when   Thus we may infer that in the rural districts of ancient Greece farmers offered their first-fruits of the barley harvest to Demeter in autumn about the time when the grapes were being trodden in the wine-presses and the ripe apples and pears littered the ground in the orchards.   At first sight the lateness of the festival in the year is surprising ; for in the lowlands of Greece at the present day barley is reaped at the end of April and wheat in May,[2] and in antiquity the time of harvest would seem not to have been very different, for Hesiod bids the husbandman put the sickle to the corn at the morning rising of the Pleiades,[3] which in his time

---

[1] See *Adonis, Attis, Osiris*, Second Edition, p. 190 note [2].

[2] See *Adonis, Attis, Osiris*, Second

Edition, p. 190 note [2].

[3] Hesiod, *Works and Days*, 383 *sq.*

took place on the eleventh of May.[1] But if the harvest was her help was urgently needed.
reaped in spring or early summer, why defer the offerings
of corn to the Corn Goddess until the middle of autumn?
The reason for the delay is not, so far as I am aware,
explained by any ancient author, and accordingly it must
remain for us a matter of conjecture.   I surmise that the
reason may have been a calculation on the part of the
practical farmer that the best time to propitiate the Corn
Goddess was not after harvest, when he had got all that was
to be got out of her, but immediately before ploughing and
sowing, when he had everything to hope from her good-will
and everything to fear from her displeasure.   When he had
reaped his corn, and the sheaves had been safely garnered
in his barns, he might, so to say, snap his fingers at the
Corn Goddess.   What could she do for him on the bare
stubble-field which lay scorched and baking under the fierce
rays of the sun all the long rainless summer through?   But
matters wore a very different aspect when, with the shorten-
ing and cooling of the days, he began to scan the sky for
clouds [2] and to listen for the cries of the cranes as they flew
southward, heralding by their trumpet-like notes the approach
of the autumnal rains.   Then he knew that the time had
come to break up the ground that it might receive the seed
and be fertilised by the refreshing water of heaven ; then he
bethought him of the Corn Goddess once more and brought
forth from the grange a share of the harvested corn with
which to woo her favour and induce her to quicken the grain
which he was about to commit to the earth.   On this theory
the Greek offering of first-fruits was prompted not so much
by gratitude for past favours as by a shrewd eye to favours to
come, and perhaps this interpretation of the custom does no
serious injustice to the cool phlegmatic temper of the bucolic
mind, which is more apt to be moved by considerations of profit
than by sentiment.   At all events the reasons suggested for
delaying the harvest-festival accord perfectly with the natural
conditions and seasons of farming in Greece.   For in that
country the summer is practically rainless, and during the

[1] L. Ideler, *Handbuch der mathe-matischen und technischen Chronologie,* i. 242.
[2] Compare Xenophon, *Oeconomicus,*

17, ἐπειδὰν γὰρ ὁ μετοπωρινὸς χρόνος ἔλθῃ, πάντες που οἱ ἄνθρωποι πρὸς τὸν θέον ἀποβλέπουσιν, ὁπότε βρέξας τὴν γῆν ἀφήσει αὐτοὺς σπείρειν.

long months of heat and drought the cultivation of the two
ancient cereals, barley and wheat, is at a standstill.   The
first rains of autumn fall about the middle of October,[1] and
that was the Greek farmer's great time for ploughing and
sowing.[2]   Hence we should expect him to make his offering
of first-fruits to the Corn Goddess shortly before he ploughed
and sowed, and this expectation is entirely confirmed by
the date which we have inferred for the offering from the
evidence of Theocritus.   Thus the sacrifice of barley to
Demeter in the autumn would seem to have been not so
much a thank-offering as a bribe judiciously administered
to her at the very moment of all the year when her services
were most urgently wanted.

The fes-
tival of the
Proerosia
("Before
the Plough-
ing") held
at Eleusis
in honour
of
Demeter.

When with the progress of civilisation a number of
petty agricultural communities have merged into a single
state dependent for its subsistence mainly on the cultivation of the ground, it commonly happens that, though
every farmer continues to perform for himself the simple old
rites designed to ensure the blessing of the gods on his
crops, the government undertakes to celebrate similar, though
more stately and elaborate, rites on behalf of the whole
people, lest the neglect of public worship should draw down
on the country the wrath of the offended deities.   Hence it
comes about that, for all their pomp and splendour, the
national festivals of such states are often merely magnified
and embellished copies of homely rites and uncouth observances carried out by rustics in the open fields, in barns,
and on threshing-floors.   In ancient Egypt the religion of
Isis and Osiris furnishes examples of solemnities which have
been thus raised from the humble rank of rural festivities
to the dignity of national celebrations;[3] and in ancient
Greece a like development may be traced in the religion of
Demeter.   If the Greek ploughman prayed to Demeter and
Underground Zeus for a good crop before he put his hand
to the plough in autumn, the authorities of the Athenian
state celebrated about the same time and for the same
purpose a public festival in honour of Demeter at Eleusis.

---

[1] August Mommsen, *Feste der Stadt Athen im Altertum*, p. 193.
[2] See above, pp. 44 *sqq.*

[3] See *Adonis, Attis, Osiris,* Second Edition, pp. 283 *sqq.*

It was called the Proerosia, which signifies "Before the Ploughing"; and as the festival was dedicated to her, Demeter herself bore the name of Proerosia. Tradition ran that once on a time the whole-world was desolated by a famine, and that to remedy the evil the Pythian oracle bade the Athenians offer the sacrifice of the Proerosia on behalf of all men. They did so, and the famine ceased accordingly. Hence to testify their gratitude for the deliverance people sent the first-fruits of their harvest from all quarters to Athens.[1]

But the exact date at which the Proerosia or Festival before Ploughing took place is somewhat uncertain, and enquirers are divided in opinion as to whether it fell before or after the Great Mysteries, which began on the fifteenth or sixteenth of Boedromion, a month corresponding roughly to our September. Another name for the festival was Proarcturia, that is, "Before Arcturus,"[2] which points to a date either before the middle of September, when Arcturus is a morning star, or before the end of October, when Arcturus is an evening star.[3] In favour of the earlier date it may be said, first, that the morning phase of Arcturus was well known and much observed, because it marked the middle of autumn, whereas little use was made of the evening phase of Arcturus for the purpose of dating;[4] and, second, that in an official Athenian inscription the Festival before Ploughing (*Proerosia*) is mentioned immediately before the Great Mys-

The *Proerosia* seems to have been held before the plough-ing in October but after the Great Mysteries in September.

---

[1] Scholiast on Aristophanes, *Knights*, 720; Suidas, *s.vv.* εἰρεσιώνη and προηροσίαι; *Etymologicum Magnum*, Hesychius, and Photius, *Lexicon, s.v.* προηρόσια; Plutarch, *Septem Sapientum Convivium*, 15; Dittenberger, *Sylloge Inscriptionum Graecarum*,[2] No. 521, line 29, and No. 628; Aug. Mommsen, *Feste der Stadt Athen im Altertum* (Leipsic, 1898), pp. 192 *sqq.* The inscriptions prove that the Proerosia was held at Eleusis and that it was distinct from the Great Mysteries, being mentioned separately from them. Some of the ancients accounted for the origin of the festival by a universal plague instead of a universal famine. But this version of the story no doubt arose from the common confusion be-

tween the similar Greek words for plague and famine (λοιμός and λιμός). That in the original version famine and not plague must have been alleged as the reason for instituting the Proerosia, appears plainly from the reference of the name to ploughing, from the dedication of the festival to Demeter, and from the offerings of first-fruits; for these circumstances, though quite appropriate to ceremonies designed to stay or avert dearth and famine, would be quite inappropriate in the case of a plague.

[2] Hesychius, *s.v.* προηρόσια.

[3] August Mommsen, *Feste der Stadt Athen im Altertum*, p. 194.

[4] August Mommsen, *l.c.*

teries.[1] On the other hand, in favour of the later date, it may be said that as the autumnal rains in Greece set in about the middle of October, the latter part of that month would be a more suitable time for a ceremony at the opening of ploughing than the middle of September, when the soil is still parched with the summer drought ; and, second, that this date is confirmed by a Greek inscription of the fourth or third century B.C., found at Eleusis, in which the Festival before Ploughing is apparently mentioned in the month of Pyanepsion immediately before the festival of the Pyanepsia, which was held on the seventh day of that month.[2] It is difficult to decide between these conflicting arguments, but on the whole I incline, not without hesitation, to agree with some eminent modern authorities in placing the Festival before Ploughing in Pyanepsion (October) after the Mysteries, rather than in Boedromion (September) before the Mysteries.[3] However, we must bear in mind that as the Attic months, like the Greek months generally, were lunar,[4] their position in the solar year necessarily varied from year to year, and though these variations were periodically corrected by intercalation, nevertheless the beginning of each Attic month sometimes diverged by several weeks from the beginning of the corresponding month to which we equate it.[5] From this it follows that the Great Mysteries, which were always dated by the calendar month, must have annually shifted their place somewhat in the solar year ; whereas the Festival before Ploughing, if it was indeed dated either by the morning or by the evening phase of Arcturus, must have occupied a fixed place in the solar year. Hence it appears to be not impossible that the Great Mysteries, oscillating to and fro with the inconstant moon,

However, the date of the Great Mysteries, being determined by the lunar calendar, must have fluctuated in the solar year ; whereas the date of the Proerosia, being determined by observation of Arcturus, must have been fixed.

[1] Dittenberger, *Sylloge Inscriptionum Graecarum*,[2] No. 521, lines 29 *sqq.*

[2] Dittenberger, *Sylloge Inscriptionum Graecarum*,[2] No. 628.

[3] The view that the Festival before Ploughing (*Proerosia*) fell in Pyanepsion is accepted by W. Mannhardt and W. Dittenberger. See W. Mannhardt, *Antike Wald- und Feldkulte* (Berlin, 1877), pp. 238 *sq.* ; *id.*, *Mythologische Forschungen*, p. 258 ; Dittenberger, *Sylloge Inscriptionum Graecarum*,[2] note [2] on Inscr. No. 628 (vol. ii. pp.

423 *sq.*). The view that the Festival before Ploughing fell in Boedromion is maintained by August Mommsen. See his *Heortologie* (Leipsic, 1864), pp. 218 *sqq.* ; *id.*, *Feste der Stadt Athen im Altertum* (Leipsic, 1898), pp. 192 *sqq.*

[4] See below, p. 82.

[5] L. Ideler, *Handbuch der mathematischen und technischen Chronologie* (Berlin, 1825-1826), i. 292 *sq.* ; compare August Mommsen, *Chronologie* (Leipsic, 1883), pp. 58 *sq.*

may sometimes have fallen before and sometimes after the Festival before Ploughing, which apparently always remained true to the constant star. At least this possibility, which seems to have been overlooked by previous enquirers, deserves to be taken into account. It is a corollary from the shifting dates of the lunar months that the official Greek calendar, in spite of its appearance of exactness, really furnished the ancient farmer with little trustworthy guidance as to the proper seasons for conducting the various operations of agriculture ; and he was well advised in trusting to various natural timekeepers, such as the rising and setting of the constellations, the arrival and departure of the migratory birds, the flowering of certain plants,[1] the ripening of fruits, and the setting in of the rains, rather than to the fallacious indications of the public calendar. It is by natural timekeepers, and not by calendar months, that Hesiod determines the seasons of the farmer's year in the poem which is the oldest existing treatise on husbandry.[2]

Just as the ploughman's prayer to Demeter, before he drove the share through the clods of the field, was taken up and reverberated, so to say, with a great volume of sound in the public prayers which the Athenian state annually offered to the goddess before the ploughing on behalf of the whole world, so the simple first-fruits of barley, presented to the rustic Demeter under the dappled shade of rustling poplars and elms on the threshing-floor in Cos, were repeated year by year on a grander scale in the first-fruits of the barley and wheat harvest, which were presented to the Corn Mother and the Corn Maiden at Eleusis, not merely by every husbandman in Attica, but by all the allies and subjects of Athens far and near, and even by many free Greek communities beyond the sea. The reason why year by year these offerings of grain poured from far countries into the public granaries at Eleusis, was

Offerings of the first-fruits of the barley and wheat to Demeter and Persephone at Eleusis.

---

[1] For example, Theophrastus notes that squills flowered thrice a year, and that each flowering marked the time for one of the three ploughings. See Theophrastus, *Historia Plantarum*, vii. 13. 6.

[2] Hesiod, *Works and Days*, 383 *sqq.*

The poet indeed refers (*vv.* 765 *sqq.*) to days of the month as proper times for engaging in certain tasks ; but such references are always simply to days of the lunar month and apply equally to every month ; they are never to days as dates in the solar year.

the widespread belief that the gift of corn had been first
bestowed by Demeter on the Athenians and afterwards
disseminated by them among all mankind through the
agency of Triptolemus, who travelled over the world in
his dragon-drawn car teaching all peoples to plough the
earth and to sow the seed.[1] In the fifth century before our
era the legend was celebrated by Sophocles in a play called
Triptolemus, in which he represented Demeter instructing
the hero to carry the seed of the fruits which she had
bestowed on men to all the coasts of Southern Italy,[2] from
which we may infer that the cities of Magna Graecia were
among the number of those that sent the thank-offering of
barley and wheat every year to Athens. Again, in the
fourth century before our era Xenophon represents Callias,
the braggart Eleusinian Torchbearer, addressing the
Lacedaemonians in a set speech, in which he declared
that " Our ancestor Triptolemus is said to have bestowed the
seed of Demeter's corn on the Peloponese before any other
land. How then," he asked with pathetic earnestness, "can
it be right that you should come to ravage the corn of the
men from whom you received the seed ? "[3] Again, writing

Isocrates
on the
offerings of
first-fruits
at Eleusis. in the fourth century before our era Isocrates relates with
a swell of patriotic pride how, in her search for her lost
daughter Persephone, the goddess Demeter came to Attica
and gave to the ancestors of the Athenians the two greatest
of all gifts, the gift of the corn and the gift of the mysteries,
of which the one reclaimed men from the life of beasts and
the other held out hopes to them of a blissful eternity beyond
the grave. The antiquity of the tradition, the orator proceeds to say, was no reason for rejecting it, but quite the
contrary it furnished a strong argument in its favour, for
what many affirmed and all had heard might be accepted as
trustworthy. " And moreover," he adds, " we are not driven
to rest our case merely on the venerable age of the tradition
we can appeal to stronger evidence in its support. For
most of the cities send us every year the first-fruits of the
corn as a memorial of that ancient benefit, and when any of

---

[1] See below, p. 72.
[2] Dionysius Halicarnasensis, *Anti-quit. Rom.* i. 12. 2.

[3] Xenophon, *Historia Graeca*, vi. 3. 6.

them have failed to do so the Pythian priestess has commanded them to send the due portions of the fruits and to
act towards our city according to ancestral custom. Can
anything be supported by stronger evidence than by the
oracle of god, the assent of many Greeks, and the harmony
of ancient legend with the deeds of to-day ? " [1]

This testimony of Isocrates to the antiquity both of
the legend and of the custom might perhaps have been set
aside, or at least disparaged, as the empty bombast of a
wordy rhetorician, if it had not happened by good chance
to be amply confirmed by an official decree of the Athenian
people passed in the century before Isocrates wrote. The
decree was found inscribed on a stone at Eleusis and is
dated by scholars in the latter half of the fifth century before
our era, sometime between 446 and 420 B.C.[2] It deals
with the first-fruits of barley and wheat which were offered
to the Two Goddesses, that is, to Demeter and Persephone,
not only by the Athenians and their allies but by the
Greeks in general. It prescribes the exact amount of barley
and wheat which was to be offered by the Athenians and
their allies, and it directs the highest officials at Eleusis,
namely the Hierophant and the Torchbearer, to exhort the
other Greeks at the mysteries to offer likewise of the first-fruits
of the corn. The authority alleged in the decree for requiring or inviting offerings of first-fruits alike from Athenians
and from foreigners is ancestral custom and the bidding of
the Delphic oracle. The Senate is further enjoined to
send commissioners, so far as it could be done, to all
Greek cities whatsoever, exhorting, though not commanding,
them to send the first-fruits in compliance with ancestral
custom and the bidding of the Delphic oracle, and the state
officials are directed to receive the offerings from such states in
the same manner as the offerings of the Athenians and their
allies. Instructions are also given for the building of three
subterranean granaries at Eleusis, where the contributions
of grain from Attica were to be stored. The best of the corn

<small>Athenian decree concerning the offerings of first-fruits at Eleusis.</small>

---

[1] Isocrates, *Panegyric*, 6 *sq.*

[2] Dittenberger, *Sylloge Inscriptionum Graecarum*,[2] No. 20 (vol. i.

pp. 33 *sqq.*) ; E. S. Roberts and E. A. Gardner, *An Introduction to Greek Epigraphy*, Part ii. (Cambridge, 1905) No. 9, pp. 22 *sqq.*

was to be offered in sacrifice as the Eumolpids might direct :
oxen were to be bought and sacrificed, with gilt horns, not
only to the two Goddesses but also to the God (Pluto),
Triptolemus, Eubulus, and Athena ; and the remainder of
the grain was to be sold and with the produce votive offerings
were to be dedicated with inscriptions setting forth that they
had been dedicated from the offerings of first-fruits, and
recording the names of all the Greeks who sent the offerings
to Eleusis. The decree ends with a prayer that all who
comply with these injunctions or exhortations and render
their dues to the city of Athens and to the Two Goddesses,
may enjoy prosperity together with good and abundant crops.
Writing in the second century of our era, under the Roman
empire, the rhetorician Aristides records the custom which
the Greeks observed of sending year by year the first-fruits
of the harvest to Athens in gratitude for the corn, but he
speaks of the practice as a thing of the past.[1]

Even after foreign states ceased to send first-fruits of the corn to Eleusis, they continued to acknowledge the benefit which the Athenians had conferred on mankind by diffusing among them Demeter's gift of the corn.

We may suspect that the tribute of corn ceased to flow
from far countries to Athens, when, with her falling fortunes
and decaying empire, her proud galleys had ceased to carry
the terror of the Athenian arms into distant seas. But if
the homage was no longer paid in the substantial shape of
cargoes of grain, it continued down to the latest days of
paganism to be paid in the cheaper form of gratitude for
that inestimable benefit, which the Athenians claimed to have
received from the Corn Goddess and to have liberally communicated to the rest of mankind. Even the Sicilians, who,
inhabiting a fertile corn-growing island, worshipped Demeter
and Persephone above all the gods and claimed to have been
the first to receive the gift of the corn from the Corn Goddess,[2] nevertheless freely acknowledged that the Athenians
had spread, though they had not originated, the useful
discovery among the nations. Thus the patriotic Sicilian
historian Diodorus, while giving the precedence to his fellow-

[1] Aristides, *Panathen.* and *Eleusin.*,
vol. i. pp. 167 *sq.*, 417 ed. G. Dindorf
(Leipsic, 1829).

[2] Diodorus Siculus, v. 2 and 4;
Cicero, *In C. Verrem*, act. ii. bk. iv.
chapters 48 *sq.* Both writers mention
that the whole of Sicily was deemed

sacred to Demeter and Persephone,
and that corn was said to have grown
in the island before it appeared anywhere else. In support of the latter
claim Diodorus Siculus (v. 2. 4) asserts
that wheat grew wild in many parts of
Sicily.

countrymen, strives to be just to the Athenian pretensions in the following passage.[1] " Mythologists," says he, " relate that Demeter, unable to find her daughter, lit torches at the craters of Etna [2] and roamed over many parts of the world. Those people who received her best she rewarded by giving them in return the fruit of the wheat ; and because the Athenians welcomed her most kindly of all, she bestowed the fruit of the wheat on them next after the Sicilians. Wherefore that people honoured the goddess more than any other folk by magnificent sacrifices and the mysteries at Eleusis, which for their extreme antiquity and sanctity have become famous among all men. From the Athenians many others received the boon of the corn and shared the seed with their neighbours, till they filled the whole inhabited earth with it. But as the people of Sicily, on account of the intimate relation in which they stood to Demeter and the Maiden, were the first to participate in the newly discovered corn, they appointed sacrifices and popular festivities in honour of each of the two goddesses, naming the celebrations after them and signifying the nature of the boons they had received by the dates of the festivals. For they celebrated the bringing home of the Maiden at the time when the corn was ripe, performing the sacrifice and holding the festivity with all the solemnity and zeal that might be reasonably expected of men who desired to testify their gratitude for so signal a gift bestowed on them before all the rest of mankind. But the sacrifice to Demeter they assigned to the time when the sowing of the corn begins ; and for ten days they hold a popular festivity which bears the name of the goddess, and is remarkable as well for the

[1] Diodorus Siculus, v. 4.

[2] This legend, which is mentioned also by Cicero (*In C. Verrem*, act. ii. bk. iv. ch. 48), was no doubt told to explain the use of torches in the mysteries of Demeter and Persephone. The author of the Homeric *Hymn to Demeter* tells us (verses 47 *sq.*) that Demeter searched for her lost daughter for nine days with burning torches in her hands, but he does not say that the torches were kindled at the flames of Etna. In art Demeter and Persephone and their attendants were often represented with torches in their hands. See L. R. Farnell, *The Cults of the Greek States*, iii. (Oxford, 1907) plates xiii., xv.*a*, xvi., xvii., xviii., xix., xx., xxi.*a*, xxv., xxvii.*b*. Perhaps the legend of the torchlight search for Persephone and the use of the torches in the mysteries may have originated in a custom of carrying fire about the fields as a charm to secure sunshine for the corn. See *The Golden Bough*,[2] iii. 313.

magnificence of its pomp as for the costumes then worn in imitation of the olden time. During these days it is customary for people to rail at each other in foul language, because when Demeter was mourning for the rape of the Maiden she laughed at a ribald jest."[1] Thus despite his natural prepossession in favour of his native land, Diodorus bears testimony both to the special blessing bestowed on the Athenians by the Corn Goddess, and to the generosity with which they had imparted the blessing to others, until it gradually spread to the ends of the earth. Again, Cicero, addressing a Roman audience, enumerates among the benefits which Athens was believed to have conferred on the world, the gift of the corn and its origin in Attic soil; and the cursory manner in which he alludes to it seems to prove that the tradition was familiar to his hearers.[2] Four centuries later the rhetorician Himerius speaks of Demeter's gift of the corn and the mysteries to the Athenians as the source of the first and greatest service rendered by their city to mankind;[3] so ancient, widespread, and persistent was the legend which ascribed the origin of the corn to the goddess Demeter and associated it with the institution of the Eleusinian mysteries. No wonder that the Delphic oracle called Athens "the Metropolis of the Corn."[4]

From the passage of Diodorus which I have quoted we learn that the Sicilians celebrated the festival of Demeter at the beginning of sowing, and the festival of Persephone at harvest. This proves that they associated, if they did not identify, the Mother Goddess with the seed-corn and the Daughter Goddess with the ripe ears. Could any association or identification be more easy and obvious to people who personified the processes of nature under the form of

Margin notes:

Testimony of Cicero and Himerius.

The Sicilians seem to have associated Demeter with the seed-corn and Persephone with the ripe ears.

---

[1] The words which I have translated "the bringing home of the Maiden" (τῆς Κόρης τὴν καταγωγήν) are explained with great probability by Professor M.P. Nilsson as referring to the bringing of the ripe corn to the barn or the threshing-floor (*Griechische Feste*, Leipsic, 1906, pp. 356 *sq.*). This interpretation accords perfectly with a well-attested sense of καταγωγή and its cognate verb κατάγειν, and is preferable to the other possible interpretation "the bringing down," which would refer to the descent of Persephone into the nether world; for such a descent is hardly appropriate to a harvest festival.

[2] Cicero, *Pro L. Flacco*, 26.

[3] Himerius, *Orat.* ii. 5.

[4] Μητρόπολις τῶν καρπῶν, Aristides, *Panathen.* vol. i. p. 168 ed. G. Dindorf (Leipzig, 1829).

anthropomorphic deities?   As the seed brings forth the ripe
ear, so the Corn Mother Demeter gave birth to the Corn
Daughter Persephone.   It is true that difficulties arise when   Difficulty
we attempt to analyse this seemingly simple conception.   of distinguishing
How, for example, are we to divide exactly the two persons   between
of the divinity?   At what precise moment does the seed   Demeter
and Per-
cease to be the Corn Mother and begins to burgeon out   sephone as
into the Corn Daughter?   And how far can we identify the   personifications of
material substance of the barley and wheat with the divine   different
aspects of
bodies of the Two Goddesses?   Questions of this sort prob-   the corn.
ably gave little concern to the sturdy swains who ploughed,
sowed, and reaped the fat fields of Sicily.   We cannot imagine
that their night's rest was disturbed by uneasy meditations
on these knotty problems.   It would hardly be strange if the
muzzy mind of the Sicilian bumpkin, who looked with blind
devotion to the Two Goddesses for his daily bread, totally
failed to distinguish Demeter from the seed and Persephone from the ripe sheaves, and if he accepted implicitly
the doctrine of the real presence of the divinities in the corn
without discriminating too curiously between the material
and the spiritual properties of the barley or the wheat.
And if he had been closely questioned by a rigid logician as
to the exact distinction to be drawn between the two persons
of the godhead who together represented for him the annual
vicissitudes of the cereals, Hodge might have scratched his
head and confessed that it puzzled him to say where
precisely the one goddess ended and the other began, or
why the seed buried in the ground should figure at one time
as the dead daughter Persephone descending into the nether
world, and at another as the living Mother Demeter about
to give birth to next year's crop.   Theological subtleties
like these have posed longer heads than are commonly to be
found on bucolic shoulders.

The time of year at which the first-fruits were offered   The time of
to Demeter and Persephone at Eleusis is not explicitly   the year
when the
mentioned by ancient authorities, and accordingly no   first-fruits
inference can be drawn from the date of the offering as   of the corn
were
to its religious significance.   It is true that at the Eleusinian   offered to
mysteries the Hierophant and Torchbearer publicly exhorted   Demeter
and Per-
the Greeks in general, as distinguished from the Athenians   sephone at

Eleusis is
not known. and their allies, to offer the first-fruits in accordance with
ancestral custom and the bidding of the Delphic oracle.[1]
But there is nothing to shew that the offerings were made
immediately after the exhortation. Nor does any ancient
authority support the view of a modern scholar that the
offering of the first-fruits, or a portion of them, took place at
the Festival before Ploughing (*Proerosia*),[2] though that festival
would no doubt be an eminently appropriate occasion for
propitiating with such offerings the goddess on whose bounty
the next year's crop was believed to depend.

The
Festival
of the
Threshing-
floor
(*Haloa*)
at Eleusis. On the other hand, we are positively told that the first-
fruits were carried to Eleusis to be used at the Festival of
the Threshing-floor (*Haloa*).[3] But the statement, cursorily
reported by writers of no very high authority, cannot be
implicitly relied upon ; and even if it could, we should
hardly be justified in inferring from it that all the first-fruits
of the corn were offered to Demeter and Persephone at this

---

[1] Dittenberger, *Sylloge Inscriptionum
Graecarum*,[2] No. 20, lines 25 *sqq.* ;
E. S. Roberts and E. A. Gardner,
Introduction to Greek Epigraphy, ii.
(Cambridge, 1905) No. 9, lines 25
sqq., κελευέτω δὲ καὶ ὁ ἱεροφάντης καὶ ὁ
δᾳδοῦχος μυστηρίοις ἀπάρχεσθαι τοὺς
Ἕλληνας τοῦ καρποῦ κατὰ τὰ πάτρια καὶ
τὴν μαντείαν τὴν ἐγ Δελφῶν. By coup-
ling μυστηρίοις with ἀπάρχεσθαι instead
of with κελεύετω, Miss J. E. Harrison
understands the offering instead of the
exhortation to have been made at the
mysteries (*Prolegomena to the Study of
Greek Religion*, Second Edition, p. 155,
"Let the Hierophant and the Torchbearer command that at the mysteries
the Hellenes should offer first-fruits of
their crops," etc.). This interpretation
is no doubt grammatically permissible,
but the context seems to plead strongly,
if not to be absolutely decisive, in favour
of the other. It is to be observed
that the exhortation was addressed not
to the Athenians and their allies (who
were compelled to make the offering)
but only to the other Greeks, who
might make it or not as they pleased ;
and the amount of such voluntary contributions was probably small compared
to that of the compulsory contributions,
as to the date of which nothing is said.
That the proclamation to the Greeks in
general was an exhortation (κελευέτω),
not a command, is clearly shewn by
the words of the decree a few lines
lower down, where commissioners are
directed to go to all Greek states
exhorting but not commanding them
to offer the first-fruits (ἐκείνοις δὲ μὴ
ἐπιτάττοντας, κελεύοντας δὲ ἀπάρχεσθαι
ἐὰν βούλωνται κατὰ τὰ πάτρια καὶ τὴν
μαντείαν ἐγ Δελφῶν). The Athenians
could not command free and independent states to make such offerings, still
less could they prescribe the exact date
when the offerings were to be made.
All that they could and did do was,
taking advantage of the great assembly
of Greeks from all quarters at the
mysteries, to invite or exhort, by the
mouth of the great priestly function-
aries, the foreigners to contribute.

[2] August Mommsen, *Feste der Stadt
Athen im Altertum* (Leipsic, 1898),
pp. 192 *sqq.*

[3] Eustathius on Homer, *Iliad*, ix.
534, p. 772 ; Im. Bekker, *Anecdota
Graeca*, i. 384 *sq.*, *s.v.* Ἁλῶα. Compare O. Rubensohn, *Die Mysterienheiligtümer in Eleusis und Samothrake*
(Berlin, 1892), p. 116.

festival. Be that as it may, the Festival of the Threshing-floor was intimately connected with the worship both of Demeter and of Dionysus, and accordingly it deserves our attention. It is said to have been sacred to both these deities ;[1] and while the name seems to connect it rather with the Corn Goddess than with the Wine God, we are yet informed that it was held by the Athenians on the occasion of the pruning of the vines and the tasting of the stored-up wine.[2] The festival is frequently mentioned in Eleusinian inscriptions, from some of which we gather that it included sacrifices to the two goddesses and a so-called Ancestral Contest, as to the nature of which we have no information.[3] We may suppose that the festival or some part of it was celebrated on the Sacred Threshing-floor of Triptolemus at Eleusis ;[4] for as Triptolemus was the hero who is said to have diffused the knowledge of the corn all over the world, nothing could be more natural than that the Festival of the Threshing-floor should be held on the sacred threshing-floor which bore his name. As for Demeter, we have already seen how intimate was her association with the threshing-floor and the operation of threshing ; according to Homer, she is the yellow goddess who parts the yellow grain from the white chaff at the threshing, and in Cos her image with the corn-stalks and the poppies

[1] Eustathius on Homer, *Iliad*, ix. 534, p. 772 ; Im. Bekker, *Anecdota Graeca*, i. 384 *sq.*, *s.v.* Ἀλῷα.

[2] *Scholia in Lucianum*, ed. H. Rabe (Leipsic, 1906), pp. 279 *sq.* (scholium on *Dialog. Meretr.* vii. 4).

[3] Dittenberger, *Sylloge Inscriptionum Graecarum*,[2] Nos. 192, 246, 587, 640 ; Ἐφημερὶς Ἀρχαιολογική, 1884, coll. 135 *sq.* The passages of inscriptions and of ancient authors which refer to the festival are collected by Dr. L. R. Farnell, *The Cults of the Greek States*, iii. (Oxford, 1907) pp. 315 *sq.* For a discussion of the evidence see August Mommsen, *Feste der Stadt Athen im Altertum* (Leipsic, 1898), pp. 359 *sqq.* ; Miss J. E. Harrison, *Prolegomena to the Study of Greek Religion*, Second Edition (Cambridge, 1908), pp. 145 *sqq.*

[4] The threshing-floor of Triptolemus at Eleusis (Pausanias, i. 38. 6) is no doubt identical with the Sacred Threshing-floor mentioned in the great Eleusinian inscription of 329 B.C. (Dittenberger, *Sylloge Inscriptionum Graecarum*,[2] No. 587, line 234). We read of a hierophant who, contrary to ancestral custom, sacrificed a victim on the hearth in the Hall at Eleusis during the Festival of the Threshing-floor, "it being unlawful to sacrifice victims on that day" (Demosthenes, *Contra Neaeram*, 116, pp. 1384 *sq.*), but from such an unlawful act no inference can be drawn as to the place where the festival was held. That the festival probably had special reference to the threshing-floor of Triptolemus has already been pointed out by O. Rubensohn (*Die Mysterienheiligtümer in Eleusis und Samothrake*, Berlin, 1892, p. 118).

Date of the Festival of the Threshing-floor (*Haloa*) at Eleusis.

in her hands stood on the threshing-floor.[1]   The festival lasted one day, and no victims might be sacrificed at it ;[2] but special use was made, as we have seen, of the first-fruits of the corn.   With regard to the dating of the festival we are informed that it fell in the month Poseideon, which corresponds roughly to our December, and as the date rests on the high authority of the ancient Athenian antiquary Philochorus,[3] and is, moreover, indirectly confirmed by inscriptional evidence,[4] we are bound to accept it.   But it is certainly surprising to find a Festival of the Threshing-floor held so late in the year, long after the threshing, which in Greece usually takes place not later than midsummer, though on high ground in Crete it is sometimes prolonged till near the end of August.[5]   We seem bound to conclude that the Festival of the Threshing-floor was quite distinct from the actual threshing of the corn.[6]   It is said to have included certain mystic rites performed by women alone, who feasted and quaffed wine, while they broke filthy jests on each other and exhibited cakes baked in the form of the male and female organs of generation.[7]   If the latter particulars are correctly reported we may suppose that these indecencies, like certain obscenities which seem to have formed part of the Great Mysteries at Eleusis,[8] were no mere wanton outbursts of licentious passion, but were deliberately practised as rites calculated to promote the fertility of the ground by means of homoeopathic or imitative magic.   A like association of

[1] See above, pp. 41 *sq.*, 43. Maximus Tyrius observes (*Dissertat.* xxx. 5) that husbandmen were the first to celebrate sacred rites in honour of Demeter at the threshing-floor.

[2] See above, p. 61, note [4].

[3] Harpocration, *s.v.* Ἁλῶα (vol. i. p. 24, ed. G. Dindorf).

[4] Dittenberger, *Sylloge Inscriptionum Graecarum*,[2] No. 587, lines 124, 144, with the editor's notes ; August Mommsen, *Feste der Stadt Athen im Altertum*, p. 360.

[5] So I am informed by my friend Professor J. L. Myres, who speaks from personal observation.

[6] This is recognised by Professor M. P. Nilsson. See his *Studia de Dionysiis Atticis* (Lund, 1900), pp.

95 *sqq.*, and his *Griechische Feste*, p. 329. To explain the lateness of the festival, Miss J. E. Harrison suggests that "the shift of date is due to Dionysos.   The rival festivals of Dionysos were in mid - winter.   He possessed himself of the festivals of Demeter, took over her threshing-floor and compelled the anomaly of a winter threshing festival" (*Prolegomena to the Study of Greek Religion*, Second Edition, p. 147).

[7] Scholiast on Lucian, *Dial. Meretr.* vii. 4 (*Scholia in Lucianum*, ed. H. Rabe, Leipsic, 1906, pp. 279-281).

[8] Clement of Alexandria, *Protrept.* ii. 15 and 20, pp. 13 and 17 ed. Potter ; Arnobius, *Adversus Nationes*, v. 25-27, 35, 39.

what we might call indecency with rites intended to promote the growth of the crops meets us in the Thesmophoria, a festival of Demeter celebrated by women alone, at which the character of the goddess as a source of fertility comes out clearly in the custom of mixing the remains of the sacrificial pigs with the seed-corn in order to obtain a plentiful crop. We shall return to this festival later on.[1]

Other festivals held at Eleusis in honour of Demeter and Persephone were known as the Green Festival and the Festival of the Cornstalks.[2]   Of the manner of their celebration we know nothing except that they comprised sacrifices, which were offered to Demeter and Persephone. But their names suffice to connect the two festivals with the green and the standing corn. We have seen that Demeter herself bore the title of Green, and that sacrifices were offered to her under that title which plainly aimed at promoting fertility.[3]   Among the many epithets applied to Demeter which mark her relation to the corn may further be mentioned " Wheat-lover,"[4] " She of the Corn,"[5] " Sheaf-bearer,"[6] " She of the Threshing-floor,"[7] " She of the Win-nowing-fan,"[8] " Nurse of the Corn-ears,"[9] " Crowned with Ears of Corn,"[10] " She of the Seed,"[11] " She of the Green Fruits,"[12] " Heavy with Summer Fruits,"[13] " Fruit-bearer,"[14]

The Green Festival and the Festival of the Cornstalks at Eleusis.

Epithets of Demeter referring to the corn.

---

[1] See below, p. 116; vol. ii. pp. 17 *sqq.*

[2] Dittenberger, *Sylloge Inscriptionum Graecarum,*[2] No. 640; Ch. Michel, *Recueil d'Inscriptions Grecques* (Brussels, 1900), No. 135, p. 145. To be exact, while the inscription definitely mentions the sacrifices to Demeter and Persephone at the Green Festival, it does not record the deities to whom the sacrifice at the Festival of the Cornstalks (τὴν τῶν Καλαμαίων θυσίαν) was offered. But mentioned as it is in immediate connexion with the sacrifices to Demeter and Persephone at the Green Festival, we may fairly suppose that the sacrifice at the Festival of the Cornstalks was also offered to these goddesses.

[3] See above, p. 42.

[4] *Anthologia Palatina,* vi. 36. 1 *sq.*

[5] Polemo, cited by Athenaeus, iii. 9, p. 416 B.

[6] Nonnus, *Dionys.* xvii. 153. The Athenians sacrificed to her under this title (Eustathius, on Homer, *Iliad,* xviii. 553, p. 1162).

[7] Theocritus, *Idyl.* vii. 155; *Orphica,* xl. 5.

[8] *Anthologia Palatina,* vi. 98. 1.

[9] *Orphica,* xl. 3.

[10] *Anthologia Palatina,* vi. 104. 8.

[11] *Orphica,* xl. 5.

[12] *Ibid.*

[13] *Orphica,* xl. 18.

[14] This title she shared with Persephone at Tegea (Pausanias, viii. 53. 7), and under it she received annual sacrifices at Ephesus (Dittenberger, *Sylloge Inscriptionum Graecarum,*[2] No. 655). It was applied to her also at Epidaurus ('Εφημ. 'Αρχ., 1883, col. 153) and at Athens (Aristophanes, *Frogs,* 382), and appears to have been a common title of the goddess. See L. R. Farnell, *The Cults of the Greek States,* iii. 318 note[30].

"She of the Great Loaf," and "She of the Great Barley Loaf."[1] Of these epithets it may be remarked that though all of them are quite appropriate to a Corn Goddess, some of them would scarcely be applicable to an Earth Goddess and therefore they add weight to the other arguments which turn the scale in favour of the corn as the fundamental attribute of Demeter.

Belief in ancient and modern times that the corn-crops depend on possession of an image of Demeter.

How deeply implanted in the mind of the ancient Greeks was this faith in Demeter as goddess of the corn may be judged by the circumstance that the faith actually persisted among their Christian descendants at her old sanctuary of Eleusis down to the beginning of the nineteenth century. For when the English traveller Dodwell revisited Eleusis, the inhabitants lamented to him the loss of a colossal image of Demeter, which was carried off by Clarke in 1802 and presented to the University of Cambridge, where it still remains. "In my first journey to Greece," says Dodwell, "this protecting deity was in its full glory, situated in the centre of a threshing-floor, amongst the ruins of her temple. The villagers were impressed with a persuasion that their rich harvests were the effect of her bounty, and since her removal, their abundance, as they assured me, has disappeared."[2] Thus we see the Corn Goddess Demeter

---

[1] Polemo, cited by Athenaeus, iii. 73, p. 109 A B, x. 9. p. 416 C.

[2] E. Dodwell, *A Classical and Topographical Tour through Greece* (London, 1819), i. 583. E. D. Clarke found the image "on the side of the road, immediately before entering the village, and in the midst of a heap of dung, buried as high as the neck, a little beyond the farther extremity of the pavement of the temple. Yet even this degrading situation had not been assigned to it wholly independent of its antient history. The inhabitants of the small village which is now situated among the ruins of Eleusis still regarded this statue with a very high degree of superstitious veneration. They attributed to its presence the fertility of their land; and it was for this reason that they heaped around it the manure intended for their fields. They believed that the loss of it would be followed by no less a calamity than the failure of their annual harvests; and they pointed to the ears of bearded wheat, upon the sculptured ornaments upon the head of the figure, as a never-failing indication of the produce of the soil." When the statue was about to be removed, a general murmur ran among the people, the women joining in the clamour. "They had been always," they said, "famous for their corn; and the fertility of the land would cease when the statue was removed." See E. D. Clarke, *Travels in various Countries of Europe, Asia, and Africa*, iii. (London, 1814) pp. 772-774, 787 *sq.* Compare J. C. Lawson, *Modern Greek Folklore and Ancient Greek Religion* (Cambridge, 1910), p. 80, who tells us that "the statue was regularly crowned with flowers in the avowed hope of obtaining good harvests."

standing on the threshing-floor of Eleusis and dispensing corn to her worshippers in the nineteenth century of the Christian era, precisely as her image stood and dispensed corn to her worshippers on the threshing-floor of Cos in the days of Theocritus. And just as the people of Eleusis last century attributed the diminution of their harvests to the loss of the image of Demeter, so in antiquity the Sicilians, a corn-growing people devoted to the worship of the two Corn Goddesses, lamented that the crops of many towns had perished because the unscrupulous Roman governor Verres had impiously carried off the image of Demeter from her famous temple at Henna.[1]   Could we ask for a clearer proof that Demeter was indeed the goddess of the corn than this belief, held by the Greeks down to modern times, that the corn-crops depended on her presence and bounty and perished when her image was removed?

In a former part of this work I followed an eminent French scholar in concluding, from various indications, that part of the religious drama performed in the mysteries of Eleusis may have been a marriage between the sky-god Zeus and the corn-goddess Demeter, represented by the hierophant and the priestess of the goddess respectively.[2] The conclusion is arrived at by combining a number of passages, all more or less vague and indefinite, of late Christian writers ; hence it must remain to some extent uncertain and cannot at the best lay claim to more than a fair degree of probability.   It may be, as Professor W. Ridgeway holds, that this dramatic marriage of the god and goddess was an innovation foisted into the Eleusinian Mysteries in that great welter of religions which followed the meeting of the East and the West in the later ages of antiquity.[3]   If a marriage of Zeus and Demeter did indeed form an important feature of the Mysteries in the fifth century before our era, it is certainly remarkable, as Professor Ridgeway has justly pointed out, that no mention of Zeus

Sacred marriage of Zeus and Demeter at Eleusis.

---

[1] Cicero, *In C. Verrem*, act. ii. lib. iv. 51.

[2] *The Magic Art and the Evolution of Kings*, ii. 138 *sq.*

[3] This view was expressed by my friend Professor Ridgeway in a paper which I had the advantage of hearing him read at Cambridge in the early part of 1911.   Compare *The Athenaeum*, No. 4360, May 20th, 1911, p. 576.

occurs in the public decree of that century which regulates the offerings of first-fruits and the sacrifices to be made to the gods and goddesses of Eleusis.[1] At the same time we must bear in mind that, if the evidence for the ritual marriage of Zeus and Demeter is late and doubtful, the evidence for

Homer on the love of Zeus for Demeter. the myth is ancient and indubitable. The story was known to Homer, for in the list of beauties to whom he makes Zeus, in a burst of candour, confess that he had lost his too susceptible heart, there occurs the name of "the fair-haired Queen Demeter";[2] and in another passage the poet represents the jealous god smiting with a thunderbolt the favoured lover with whom the goddess had forgotten her dignity among the furrows of a fallow field.[3] Moreover, according to one tradition, Dionysus himself was the offspring of the intrigue between Zeus and Demeter.[4] Thus there is no intrinsic improbability in the view that one or other of these unedifying incidents in the backstairs chronicle of Olympus should have formed part of the sacred peep-show in the Eleusinian Mysteries. But it seems just possible that the

Zeus the Sky God may have been confused with Subterranean Zeus, that is, Pluto. marriage to which the Christian writers allude with malicious joy may after all have been of a more regular and orthodox pattern. We are positively told that the rape of Persephone was acted at the Mysteries;[5] may that scene not have been followed by another representing the solemnisation of her nuptials with her ravisher and husband Pluto? It is to be remembered that Pluto was sometimes known as a god of fertility under the title of Subterranean Zeus. It was to him under that title as well as to Demeter, that the Greek ploughman prayed at the beginning of the ploughing;[6] and the people of Myconus used to sacrifice to Subterranean Zeus and Subterranean Earth for the prosperity of the crops on the twelfth day of the month Lenaeon.[7] Thus it may be that the Zeus whose marriage was dramatically represented at the Mysteries was not the sky-god Zeus, but his

[1] Dittenberger, *Sylloge Inscriptionum Graecarum*,[2] No. 20; E. S. Roberts and E. A. Gardner, *Introduction to Greek Epigraphy*, ii. (Cambridge, 1905) No. 9, pp. 22 *sq.* See above, pp. 55 *sq.*
[2] Homer, *Iliad*, xiv. 326.
[3] Homer, *Odyssey*, v. 125 *sqq.*
[4] Diodorus Siculus, iii. 62. 6.

[5] Clement of Alexandria, *Protrept.* 12, p. 12, ed. Potter.
[6] Hesiod, *Works and Days*, 465 *sqq.*
[7] Dittenberger, *Sylloge Inscriptionum Graecarum*,[2] No. 615, lines 25 *sq.*; Ch. Michel, *Recueil d'Inscriptions Grecques*, No. 714; J. de Prott et L. Ziehen, *Leges Graecorum Sacrae*, No. 4.

brother Zeus of the Underworld, and that the writers who refer to the ceremony have confused the two brothers. This view, if it could be established, would dispose of the difficulty raised by the absence of the name of Zeus in the decree which prescribes the offerings to be made to the gods of Eleusis ; for although in that decree Pluto is not mentioned under the name of Subterranean Zeus, he is clearly referred to, as the editors of the inscription have seen, under the vague title of "the God," while his consort Persephone is similarly referred to under the title of "the Goddess," and it is ordained that perfect victims shall be sacrificed to both of them.   However, if we thus dispose of one difficulty, it must be confessed that in doing so we raise another.   For if the bridegroom in the Sacred Marriage at Eleusis was not the sky-god Zeus, but the earth-god Pluto, we seem driven to suppose that, contrary to the opinion of the reverend Christian scandal-mongers, the bride was his lawful wife Persephone and not his sister and mother-in-law Demeter. In short, on the hypothesis which I have suggested we are compelled to conclude that the ancient busybodies who lifted the veil from the mystic marriage were mistaken as to the person both of the divine bridegroom and of the divine bride.   In regard to the bridegroom I have conjectured that they may have confused the two brothers, Zeus of the Upper World and Zeus of the Lower World.   In regard to the bride, can any reason be suggested for confounding the persons of the mother and daughter?   On the view here taken of the nature of Demeter and Persephone nothing could be easier than to confuse them with each other, for both of them were mythical embodiments of the corn, the mother Demeter standing for the old corn of last year and the daughter Persephone standing for the new corn of this year.   In point of fact Greek artists, both of the archaic and of later periods, frequently represent the Mother and Daughter side by side in forms which resemble each other so closely that eminent modern experts have sometimes differed from each other on the question, which is Demeter and which is Persephone ; indeed in some cases it might be quite impossible to distinguish the two if it were not for the inscriptions attached to the

Demeter may have been confused with Persephone ; in art the types of the two goddesses are often very similar.

figures.[1] The ancient sculptors, vase-painters, and engravers must have had some good reason for portraying the two goddesses in types which are almost indistinguishable from each other ; and what better reason could they have had than the knowledge that the two persons of the godhead were one in substance, that they stood merely for two different aspects of the same simple natural phenomenon, the growth of the corn ? Thus it is easy to understand why Demeter and Persephone may have been confused in ritual as well as in art, why in particular the part of the divine bride in a Sacred Marriage may sometimes have been assigned to the Mother and sometimes to the Daughter. But all this, I fully admit, is a mere speculation, and I only put it forward as such. We possess far too little information as to a Sacred Marriage in the Eleusinian Mysteries to be justified in speaking with confidence on so obscure a subject.

---

[1] See L. R. Farnell, *The Cults of the Greek States*, iii. (Oxford, 1907), p. 259, " It was long before the mother could be distinguished from the daughter by any organic difference of form or by any expressive trait of countenance. On the more ancient vases and terracottas they appear rather as twin-sisters, almost as if the inarticulate artist were aware of their original identity of substance. And even among the monuments of the transitional period it is difficult to find any representation of the goddesses in characters at once clear and impressive. We miss this even in the beautiful vase of Hieron in the British Museum, where the divine pair are seen with Triptolemos : the style is delicate and stately, and there is a certain impression of inner tranquil life in the group, but without the aid of the inscriptions the mother would not be known from the daughter " ; *id.*, vol. iii. 274, " But it would be wrong to give the impression that the numismatic artists of this period were always careful to distinguish—in such a manner as the above works indicate —between mother and daughter. The old idea of their unity of substance still seemed to linger as an art-tradition : the very type we have just been examining appears on a fourth-century coin of Hermione, and must have been used here to designate Demeter Chthonia who was there the only form that the corn-goddess assumed. And even at Metapontum, where coin-engraving was long a great art, a youthful head crowned with corn, which in its own right and on account of its resemblance to the masterpiece of Euainetos could claim the name of Kore [Persephone], is actually inscribed ' Damater.' " Compare J. Overbeck, *Griechische Kunstmythologie*, iii. (Leipsic, 1873-1878), p. 453. In regard, for example, to the famous Eleusinian bas-relief, one of the most beautiful monuments of ancient religious art, which seems to represent Demeter giving the corn-stalks to Triptolemus, while Persephone crowns his head, there has been much divergence of opinion among the learned as to which of the goddesses is Demeter and which Persephone. See J. Overbeck, *op. cit.* iii. 427 *sqq.* ; L. R. Farnell, *op. cit.* iii. 263 *sq.* On the close resemblance of the artistic types of Demeter and Persephone see further E. Gerhard, *Gesammelte akademische Abhandlungen* (Berlin, 1866-1868), ii. 357 *sqq.* ; F. Lenormant, in Daremberg et Saglio, *Dictionnaire des Antiquités Grecques et Romaines*, i. 2, *s.v.* " Ceres," p. 1049.

One thing, however, which we may say with a fair The date degree of probability is that, if such a marriage did take of the Eleusinian place at Eleusis, no date in the agricultural year could well Mysteries have been more appropriate for it than the date at which in September would the Mysteries actually fell, namely about the middle of have been September. The long Greek summer is practically rainless a very appropriate and in the fervent heat and unbroken drought all nature time for a languishes. The river-beds are dry, the fields parched. The Sacred Marriage farmer awaits impatiently the setting-in of the autumnal rains, of the Sky which begin in October and mark the great season for plough- God with the Corn ing and sowing. What time could be fitter for celebrating Goddess the union of the Corn Goddess with her husband the Earth or the Earth God or perhaps rather with her paramour the Sky God, who Goddess. will soon descend in fertilising showers to quicken the seed in the furrows? Such embraces of the divine powers or their human representatives might well be deemed, on the principles of homoeopathic or imitative magic, indispensable to the growth of the crops. At least similar ideas have been entertained and similar customs have been practised by many peoples;[1] and in the legend of Demeter's love-adventure among the furrows of the thrice-ploughed fallow[2] we seem to catch a glimpse of rude rites of the same sort performed in the fields at sowing-time by Greek ploughmen for the sake of ensuring the growth of the seed which they were about to commit to the bosom of the naked earth. In this connexion a statement of ancient writers as to the rites of Eleusis receives fresh significance. We are told that at these rites the worshippers looked up to the sky and cried "Rain!" and then looked down at the earth and cried "Conceive!"[3] Nothing could be more appropriate at a marriage of the Sky God and the Earth or Corn Goddess than such invocations to the heaven to pour down rain and to the earth or the corn to conceive seed under the fertilising shower; in Greece no time could well be more suitable for

---

[1] *The Magic Art and the Evolution of Kings*, ii. 97 *sqq.*

[2] Homer, *Odyssey*, v. 125 *sqq.*

[3] Proclus, on Plato, *Timaeus*, p. 293 C, quoted by L. F. Farnell, *The Cults of the Greek States*, iii. 357, where Lobeck's emendation of ὕε, κύε for ὕε, τοκύε (*Aglaophamus*, p. 782) may be accepted as certain, confirmed as it is by Hippolytus, *Refutatio Omnium Haeresium*, v. 7, p. 146, ed. Duncker and Schneidewin (Göttingen, 1859), τὸ μέγα καὶ ἄρρητον Ἐλευσινίων μυστήριον ὕε κύε.

the utterance of such prayers than just at the date when the Great Mysteries of Eleusis were celebrated, at the end of the long drought of summer and before the first rains of autumn.

The Eleusinian games distinct from the Eleusinian Mysteries.

Different both from the Great Mysteries and the offerings of first-fruits at Eleusis were the games which were celebrated there on a great scale once in every four years and on a less scale once in every two years.[1] That the games were distinct from the Mysteries is proved by their periods, which were quadriennial and biennial respectively, whereas the Mysteries were celebrated annually. Moreover, in Greek epigraphy, our most authentic evidence in such matters, the games and the Mysteries are clearly distinguished from each other by being mentioned separately in the same inscription.[2] But like the Mysteries the games seem to have been very ancient; for the Parian Chronicler, who wrote in the year 264 B.C., assigns the foundation of the Eleusinian games to the reign of Pandion,

The Eleusinian games of later origin than the Eleusinian Mysteries.

the son of Cecrops. However, he represents them as of later origin than the Eleusinian Mysteries, which according to him were instituted by Eumolpus in the reign of Erechtheus, after Demeter had planted corn in Attica and Triptolemus had sown seed in the Rarian plain at Eleusis.[8] This testimony to the superior antiquity of the Mysteries is in harmony with our most ancient authority on the rites of Eleusis, the author of the *Hymn to Demeter*, who describes the origin of the Eleusinian Mysteries, but makes no reference or allusion to the Eleusinian Games. However, the great age of the games is again vouched for at a much

---

[1] As to the Eleusinian games see August Mommsen, *Feste der Stadt Athen im Altertum*, pp. 179-204; P. Foucart, *Les Grands Mystères d'Éleusis* (Paris, 1900), pp. 143-147; P. Stengel, in Pauly-Wissowa's *Real-Encyclopädie der classischen Altertumswissenschaft*, v. coll. 2330 *sqq.* The quadriennial celebration of the Eleusinian Games is mentioned by Aristotle (*Constitution of Athens*, 54), and in the great Eleusinian inscription of 329 B.C., which is also our only authority for the biennial celebration of the games. See Dittenberger, *Sylloge Inscriptionum Grae-*

carum,[2] No. 587, lines 258 *sqq.* The regular and official name of the games was simply *Eleusinia* (τὰ Ἐλευσίνια), a name which late writers applied incorrectly to the Mysteries. See August Mommsen, *op. cit.* pp. 179 *sqq.*; Dittenberger, *op. cit.* No. 587, note [171].

[2] Dittenberger, *Sylloge Inscriptionum Graecarum*,[2] No. 246, lines 25 *sqq.*; *id.* No. 587, lines 244 *sq.*, 258 *sqq.*

[8] *Marmor Parium*, in *Fragmenta Historicorum Graecorum*, ed. C. Müller, i. 544 *sq.*

later date by the rhetorician Aristides, who even declares
that they were the oldest of all Greek games.[1] With
regard to the nature and meaning of the games our information is extremely scanty, but an old scholiast on Pindar
tells us that they were celebrated in honour of Demeter and
Persephone as a thank-offering at the conclusion of the corn-
harvest.[2]   His testimony is confirmed by that of the
rhetorician Aristides, who mentions the institution of the
Eleusinian games in immediate connexion with the offerings
of the first-fruits of the corn, which many Greek states sent
to Athens ;[3] and from an inscription dated about the close
of the third century before our era we learn that at the
Great Eleusinian Games sacrifices were offered to Demeter
and Persephone.[4]   Further, we gather from an official
Athenian inscription of 329 B.C. that both the Great and
the Lesser Games included athletic and musical contests, a horse-race, and a competition which bore the
name of the Ancestral or Hereditary Contest, and which
accordingly may well have formed the original kernel of
the games.[5] Unfortunately nothing is known about this
Ancestral Contest. We might be tempted to identify it
with the Ancestral Contest included in the Eleusinian
Festival of the Threshing-floor,[6] which was probably held

The
Eleusinian
games
sacred to
Demeter
and Per-
sephone.

[1] Aristides, *Panathen.* and *Eleusin.*
vol. i. pp. 168, 417, ed. G. Dindorf.
[2] Schol. on Pindar, *Olymp.* ix.
150, p. 228, ed. Aug. Boeckh.
[3] Aristides, *ll.cc.*
[4] Dittenberger, *Sylloge Inscriptionum Graecarum,*[2] No. 246, lines 25
sqq. The editor rightly points out
that the Great Eleusinian Games are
identical with the games celebrated
every fourth year, which are mentioned in the decree of 329 B.C.
(Dittenberger, *Sylloge Inscriptionum
Graecarum,*[2] No. 587, lines 260 *sq.*).
[5] Dittenberger, *Sylloge Inscriptionum
Graecarum,*[2] No. 587, lines 259 *sqq.*
From other Attic inscriptions we learn
that the Eleusinian games comprised a
long foot-race, a race in armour, and
a pancratium. See Dittenberger, *op.
cit.* No. 587 note [171] (vol. ii. p. 313).
The Great Eleusinian Games also included the pentathlum (Dittenberger,

op. cit. No. 678, line 2). The pancratium included wrestling and boxing ;
the pentathlum included a foot-race,
leaping, throwing the quoit, throwing
the spear, and wrestling. See W.
Smith, *Dictionary of Greek and Roman
Antiquities,* Third Edition, *s.vv.* "Pancratium " and " Pentathlon."
[6] Dittenberger, *Sylloge Inscriptionum Graecarum,*[2] No. 246, lines 46
sqq. ; Ch. Michel, *Recueil d'Inscriptions Grecques,* No. 609. See above,
p. 61. The identification lies all the
nearer to hand because the inscription
records a decree in honour of a man
who had sacrificed to Demeter and
Persephone at the Great Eleusinian
Games, and a provision is contained in
the decree that the honour should be proclaimed "at the Ancestral Contest of the
Festival of the Threshing-floor." The
same Ancestral Contest at the Festival
of the Threshing-floor is mentioned in

on the Sacred Threshing-floor of Triptolemus at Eleusis.[1]

If the identification could be proved, we should have another confirmation of the tradition which connects the games with Demeter and the corn ; for according to the prevalent tradition it was to Triptolemus that Demeter first revealed the secret of the corn, and it was he whom she sent out as an itinerant missionary to impart the beneficent discovery of the cereals to all mankind and to teach them to sow the seed.[2] On monuments of art, especially in vase-paintings, he is constantly represented along with Demeter in this capacity, holding corn-stalks in his hand and sitting in his car, which is sometimes winged and sometimes drawn by dragons, and from which he is said to have sowed the seed down on the whole world as he sped through the air.[3] At Eleusis victims bought with the first-fruits of the wheat and barley were sacrificed to him as well as to Demeter and Persephone.[4] In short, if we may judge from the combined testimony of Greek literature and art, Triptolemus was the corn-hero first and foremost. Even beyond the limits of the Greek world, all men, we are told, founded sanctuaries and erected altars in his honour because he had bestowed on them the gift of the corn.[5] His very name has been plausibly explained both in ancient and modern times as " Thrice-ploughed " with reference to the Greek custom of

another Eleusinian inscription, which records honours decreed to a man who had sacrificed to Demeter and Persephone at the Festival of the Threshing-floor. See 'Εφημερὶς 'Αρχαιολογική, 1884, coll. 135 *sq.*

[1] See above, p. 61.

[2] Diodorus Siculus, v. 68 ; Arrian, *Indic.* 7 ; Lucian, *Somnium,* 15 ; *id., Philopseudes,* 3 ; Plato, *Laws,* vi. 22, p. 782 ; Apollodorus, *Bibliotheca,* i. 5, 2 ; Cornutus, *Theologiae Graecae Compendium,* 28, p. 53, ed. C. Lang ; Pausanias, i. 14. 2, vii. 18. 2, viii. 4. 1 ; Aristides, *Eleusin.* vol. i. pp. 416 *sq.,* ed. G. Dindorf ; Hyginus, *Fabulae,* 147, 259, 277 ; Ovid, *Fasti,* iv. 549 *sqq.* ; *id., Metamorph.* v. 645 *sqq.* ; Servius, on Virgil, *Georg.* i. 19. See also above, p. 54. As to Triptolemus, see L. Preller, *Demeter und Persephone* (Hamburg, 1837), pp. 282 *sqq.* ; *id.,*

Griechische Mythologie,[4] i. 769 *sqq.*

[3] C. Strube, *Studien über den Bilderkreis von Eleusis* (Leipsic, 1870), pp. 4 *sqq.* ; J. Overbeck, *Griechische Kunstmythologie,* iii. (Leipsic, 1873-1880), pp. 530 *sqq.* ; A. Baumeister, *Denkmäler des classischen Altertums,* iii. 1855 *sqq.* That Triptolemus sowed the earth with corn from his car is mentioned by Apollodorus, *Bibliotheca,* i..5. 2 ; Cornutus, *Theologiae Graecae Compendium,* 28, pp. 53 *sq.,* ed. C. Lang ; Hyginus, *Fabulae,* 147 ; and Servius, on Virgil, *Georg.* i. 19.

[4] Dittenberger, *Sylloge Inscriptionum Graecarum,*[2] No. 20, lines 37 *sqq.*; E. S. Roberts and E. A. Gardner, *Introduction to Greek Epigraphy,* ii. (Cambridge, 1905), No. 9, p. 24.

[5] Arrian, *Epicteti Dissertationes,* i. 4. 30.

ploughing the land thrice a year,[1] and the derivation is said to be on philological principles free from objection.[2]   In fact it would seem as if Triptolemus, like Demeter and Persephone themselves, were a purely mythical being, an embodiment of the conception of the first sower.   At all events in the local Eleusinian legend, according to an eminent scholar, who has paid special attention to Attic genealogy, " Triptolemus does not, like his comrade Eumolpus or other founders of Eleusinian priestly families, continue his kind, but without leaving offspring who might perpetuate his priestly office, he is removed from the scene of his beneficent activity.   As he appeared, so he vanishes again from the legend, after he has fulfilled his divine mission."[3]

However, there is no sufficient ground for identifying the Ancestral Contest of the Eleusinian games with the Ancestral Contest of the Threshing-festival at Eleusis, and accordingly the connexion of the games with the corn-harvest and with the corn-hero Triptolemus must so far remain uncertain.   But a clear trace of such a connexion may be seen in the custom of rewarding the victors in the Eleusinian games with measures of barley ; in the official Athenian inscription of 329 B.C., which contains the accounts of the superintendents of Eleusis and the Treasurers of the Two Goddesses, the amounts of corn handed over by these officers to the priests and priestesses for the purposes of the games is exactly specified.[4]   This of itself is sufficient to prove that the

Prizes of barley given to victors in the Eleusinian games.

---

[1] Scholiast on Homer, *Iliad*, xviii. 483 ; L. Preller, *Demeter und Persephone*, p. 286 ; F. A. Paley on Hesiod, *Works and Days*, 460. The custom of ploughing the land thrice is alluded to by Homer (*Iliad*, xviii. 542, *Odyssey*, v. 127) and Hesiod (*Theogony*, 971), and is expressly mentioned by Theophrastus (*Historia Plantarum*, vii. 13. 6).

[2] So I am informed by my learned friend the Rev. Professor J. H. Moulton.

[3] J. Toepffer, *Attische Genealogie* (Berlin, 1889), pp. 138 *sq.* However, the Eleusinian Torchbearer Callias apparently claimed to be descended from Triptolemus, for in a speech addressed to the Lacedaemonians he is

said by Xenophon (*Hellenica*, vi. 3. 6) to have spoken of Triptolemus as " our ancestor " (ὁ ἡμέτερος πρόγονος). See above, p. 54.   But it is possible that Callias was here speaking, not as a direct descendant of Triptolemus, but merely as an Athenian, who naturally ranked Triptolemus among the most illustrious of the ancestral heroes of his people.   Even if he intended to claim actual descent from the hero, this would prove nothing as to the historical character of Triptolemus, for many Greek families boasted of being descended from gods.

[4] The prize of barley is mentioned by the Scholiast on Pindar, *Olymp.* ix. 150.   The Scholiast on Aristides (vol. iii. pp. 55, 56, ed. G. Dindorf) men-

Eleusinian games were closely connected with the worship of Demeter and Persephone. The grain thus distributed in prizes was probably reaped on the Rarian plain near Eleusis, where according to the legend Triptolemus sowed the first corn.[1]   Certainly we know that the barley grow'n on that plain was used in sacrifices and for the baking of the sacrificial cakes,[2] from which we may reasonably infer that the prizes of barley, to which no doubt a certain sanctity attached in the popular mind, were brought from the same holy fields.   So sacred was the Rarian plain that no dead body was allowed to defile it.   When such a pollution accidentally took place, it was expiated by the sacrifice of a pig,[3] the usual victim employed in Greek purificatory rites.

The Eleusinian games primarily concerned with Demeter and Persephone. The Ancestral Contest in the games may have been originally a contest between the reapers to finish reaping.

Thus, so far as the scanty eviden_e at our disposal permits us to judge, the Eleusinian games, like the Eleusinian Mysteries, would seem to have been primarily concerned with Demeter and Persephone as goddesses of the corn.   At least that is expressly affirmed by the old scholiast on Pindar and it is borne out by the practice of rewarding the victors with measures of barley.   Perhaps the Ancestral Contest, which may well have formed the original nucleus of the games, was a contest between the reapers on the sacred Rarian plain to see who should finish his allotted task before his fellows.   For success in such a contest no prize could be more appropriate than a measure of the sacred barley which the victorious reaper had just cut on the barley-field.   In the sequel we shall see that similar contests between reapers have been common on the harvest fields of modern Europe, and it will appear that such competitions are not purely

tions ears of corn as the prize without specifying the kind of corn. In the official Athenian inscription of 329 B.C., though the amount of corn distributed in prizes both at the quadriennial and at the biennial games is stated, we are not told whether the corn was barley or wheat. See Dittenberger, *Sylloge Inscriptionum Graecarum,*[2] No. 587, lines 259 *sqq.* According to Aristides (*Eleusin.* vol. i. p. 417, ed. G. Dindorf, compare p. 168) the prize consisted of the corn which had first appeared at Eleusis.

[1] *Marmor Parium,* in *Fragmenta Historicorum Graecorum,* ed. C. Müller, i. 544.   That the Rarian plain was the first to be sown and the first to bear crops is affirmed by Pausanias (i. 38. 6).

[2] Pausanias, i. 38. 6.

[3] Dittenberger, *Sylloge Inscriptionum Graecarum,*[2] No. 587, lines 119 *sq.* In the same inscription, a few lines lower down, mention is made of two pigs which were used in purifying the sanctuary at Eleusis. On the pig in Greek purificatory rites, see my notes on Pausanias, ii. 31. 8 and v. 16. 8.

athletic ; their aim is not simply to demonstrate the superior
strength, activity, and skill of the victors ; it is to secure for
the particular farm the possession of the blooming young
Corn-maiden of the present year, conceived as the embodiment
of the vigorous grain, and to pass on to laggard neighbours
the aged Corn-mother of the past year, conceived as an
embodiment of the effete and outworn energies of the corn.[1]
May it not have been so at Eleusis ? may not the reapers
have vied with each other for possession of the young corn-
spirit Persephone and for avoidance of the old corn-spirit
Demeter ? may not the prize of barley, which rewarded the
victor in the Ancestral Contest, have been supposed to house
in the ripe ears no less a personage than the Corn-maiden
Persephone herself?   And if there is any truth in these conjectures (for conjectures they are and nothing more), we may
hazard a guess as to the other Ancestral Contest which took
place at the Eleusinian Festival of the Threshing-floor.
Perhaps it in like manner was originally a competition between
threshers on the sacred threshing-floor of Triptolemus to determine who should finish threshing his allotted quantity of
corn before the rest.   Such competitions have also been
common, as we shall see presently, on the threshing-floors of
modern Europe, and their motive again has not been simple
emulation between sturdy swains for the reward of strength
and dexterity ; it has been a dread of being burdened with
the aged and outworn spirit of the corn conceived as present
in the bundle of corn-stalks which receives the last stroke at
threshing.[2]   We know that effigies of Demeter with corn and
poppies in her hands stood on Greek threshing-floors.[3]
Perhaps at the conclusion of the threshing these effigies, as
representatives of the old Corn-spirit, were passed on to
neighbours who had not yet finished threshing the corn.   At
least the supposition is in harmony with modern customs
observed on the threshing-floor.

It is possible that the Eleusinian games were no more
than a popular merrymaking celebrated at the close of the
harvest.   This view of their character might be supported by
modern analogies ; for in some parts of Germany it has been

The Ancestral Contest in the Festival of the Threshing-floor may have been originally a contest between the threshers to finish threshing.

Games at harvest festivals in modern Europe.

[1] See below, pp. 140 *sqq.*, 155 *sqq.*, 164 *sqq.*, compare 218 *sqq.*   [2] See below, pp. 147 *sqq.*, 221 *sq.*, 223 *sq.*   [3] See above, p. 43.

customary for the harvesters, when their work is done, to engage in athletic competitions of various kinds, which have at first sight no very obvious connexion with the business of harvesting. For example, at Besbau near Luckau great cakes were baked at the harvest-festival, and the labourers, both men and women, ran races for them. He or she who reached them first received not only a cake, but a handkerchief or the like as a prize. Again, at Bergkirchen, when the harvest was over, a garland was hung up and the harvesters rode at it on horseback and tried to bring it down with a stab or a blow as they galloped past. He who succeeded in bringing it down was proclaimed King. Again, in the villages near Fürstenwald at harvest the young men used to fetch a fir-tree from the wood, peel the trunk, and set it up like a mast in the middle of the village. A handkerchief and other prizes were fastened to the top of the pole and the men clambered up for them.[1] Among the peasantry of Silesia, we are told, the harvest-home broadened out into a popular festival, in which athletic sports figured prominently. Thus, for example, at Järischau, in the Strehlitz district, a scythe, a rake, a flail, and a hay-fork or pitchfork were fastened to the top of a smooth pole and awarded as prizes, in order of merit, to the men who displayed most agility in climbing the pole. Younger men amused themselves with running in sacks, high jumps, and so forth. At Prauss, near Nimptsch, the girls ran a race in a field for aprons as prizes. In the central parts of Silesia a favourite amusement at harvest was a race between girls for a garland of leaves or flowers.[2] Yet it seems probable that all such sports at harvest were in origin not mere pastimes, but that they were serious attempts to secure in one way or another the help and blessing of the corn-spirit. Thus in some parts of Prussia, at the close of the rye-harvest, a few sheaves used to be left standing in the field after all the rest of the rye had been carted home. These sheaves were then made up into the shape of a man and dressed out in masculine costume, and all the young women were obliged to run a race, of which the corn-man

---

[1] A. Kuhn und W. Schwartz, *Norddeutsche Sagen, Märchen und Gebräuche* (Leipsic, 1848), pp. 398, 399, 400.

[2] P. Drechsler, *Sitte, Brauch und Volksglaube in Schlesien* (Leipsic, 1903-1906), ii. 70 *sq.*

was the goal. She who won the race led off the dancing in the evening.[1] Here the aim of the foot-race among the young women is clearly to secure the corn-spirit embodied in the last sheaf left standing on the field ; for, as we shall see later on, the last sheaf is commonly supposed to harbour the corn-spirit and is treated accordingly like a man or a woman.[2]

If the Ancestral Contest at the Eleusinian games was, as I have conjectured, a contest between the reapers on the sacred barley-field, we should have to suppose that the games were celebrated at barley-harvest, which in the lowlands of Greece falls in May or even at the end of April. This theory is in harmony with the evidence of the scholiast on Pindar, who tells us that the Eleusinian games were celebrated after the corn-harvest.[3] No other ancient authority, so far as I am aware, mentions at what time of the year these games were held. Modern authorities, arguing from certain slight and to some extent conjectural data, have variously assigned them to Metageitnion (August) and to Boedromion (September), and those who assign them to Boedromion (September) are divided in opinion as to whether they preceded or followed the Mysteries.[4] However, the evidence is far too slender and uncertain to allow of any conclusions being based on it.

But there is a serious difficulty in the way of connecting the Eleusinian games with the goddesses of the corn. How is the quadriennial or the biennial period of the games to be reconciled with the annual growth of the crops ? Year by year the barley and the wheat are sown and reaped ; how

Date of the Eleusinian games uncertain.

Why should games intended to promote the annual growth of the crops be held only every second or fourth year?

---

[1] A. Kuhn, *Märkische Sagen und Märchen* (Berlin, 1843), pp. 341 *sq.*

[2] See below, pp. 133 *sqq.*

[3] Scholiast on Pindar, *Olymp.* ix. 150, p. 228, ed, Aug. Boeckh.

[4] The games are assigned to Metageitnion by P. Stengel (Pauly-Wissowa, *Real-Encyclopädie der classischen Altertumswissenschaft,* v. 2. coll. 2331 *sq.*) and to Boedromion by August Mommsen and W. Dittenberger. The last-mentioned scholar supposes that the games immediately followed the Mysteries, and August Mommsen formerly thought so too, but he afterwards changed his

view and preferred to suppose that the games preceded the Mysteries. See Aug. Mommsen, *Heortologie* (Leipsic, 1864), p. 263 ; *id., Feste der Stadt Athen im Altertum* (Leipsic, 1898), pp. 182 *sqq.* ; Dittenberger, *Sylloge Inscriptionum Graecarum,*[2] No. 587, note [171] (vol. ii. pp. 313 *sq.*). The dating of the games in Metageitnion or in the early part of Boedromion depends on little more than a series of conjectures, particularly the conjectural restoration of an inscription and the conjectural dating of a certain sacrifice to Democracy.

then could the games, held only every fourth or every second year, have been regarded as thank-offerings for the annual harvest? On this view of their nature, which is the one taken by the old scholiast on Pindar, though the harvest was received at the hands of the Corn Goddess punctually every year, men thanked her for her bounty only every second year or even only every fourth year. What were her feelings likely to be in the blank years when she got no thanks and no games? She might naturally resent such negligence and ingratitude and punish them by forbidding the seed to sprout, just as she did at Eleusis when she mourned the loss of her daughter. In short, men could hardly expect to reap crops in years in which they offered nothing to the Corn Goddess. That would indeed appear to be the view generally taken by the ancient Greeks; for we have seen that year by year they presented the first-fruits of the barley and the wheat to Demeter, not merely in the solemn state ritual of Eleusis, but also in rustic festivals held by farmers on their threshing-floors. The pious Greek husbandman would no doubt have been shocked and horrified at a proposal to pay the Corn Goddess her dues only every second or fourth year. "No offerings, no crops," he would say to himself, and would anticipate nothing but dearth and famine in any year when he failed to satisfy the just and lawful demands of the divinity on whose good pleasure he believed the growth of the corn to be directly dependent. Accordingly we may regard it as highly probable that from the very beginning of settled and regular agriculture in Greece men annually propitiated the deities of the corn with a ritual of some sort, and rendered them their dues in the shape of offerings of the ripe barley and wheat. Now we know that the Mysteries of Eleusis were celebrated every year, and accordingly, if I am right in interpreting them as essentially a dramatic representation of the annual vicissitudes of the corn performed for the purpose of quickening the seed, it becomes probable that in some form or another they were annually held at Eleusis long before the practice arose of celebrating games there every fourth or every second year. In short, the Eleusinian mysteries were in all prob-

The Eleusinian Mysteries probably much older than the Eleusinian games.

ability far older than the Eleusinian games.   How old they
were we cannot even guess.   But when we consider that the
cultivation of barley and wheat, the two cereals specially
associated with Demeter, appears to have been practised in
prehistoric Europe from the Stone Age onwards,[1] we shall
be disposed to admit that the annual performance of religious or magical rites at Eleusis for the purpose of ensuring
good crops, whether by propitiating the Corn Goddess with
offerings of first-fruits or by dramatically representing the
sowing and the growth of the corn in mythical form, probably dates from an extremely remote antiquity.

But in order to clear our ideas on this subject it is
desirable to ascertain, if possible, the reason for holding the
Eleusinian games at intervals of two or four years.   The
reason for holding a harvest festival and thanksgiving every
year is obvious enough ; but why hold games only every
second or every fourth year?   The reason for such limita-
tions is by no means obvious on the face of them, especially
if the growth of the crops is deemed dependent on the
celebration.   In order to find an answer to this question it
may be well at the outset to confine our attention to the
Great Eleusinian Games, which were celebrated only every
fourth year.   That these were the principal games appears
not only from their name, but from the testimony of Aristotle, or at least of the author of *The Constitution of Athens*,
who notices only the quadriennial or, as in accordance with
Greek idiom he calls it, the penteteric celebration of the
games.[2]   Now the custom of holding games at intervals of

*Quad-
riennial
period of
many of
the great
games of
Greece.*

---

[1] A. de Candolle, *Origin of Cultivated Plants* (London, 1884), pp. 354
sq., 367 *sqq.* ; R. Munro, *The Lake-
dwellings of Europe* (London, Paris,
and Melbourne, 1890), pp. 497 *sqq.* ;
O. Schrader, *Reallexikon der indogermanischen Altertumskunde* (Strasburg,
1901), pp. 8 *sqq.* ; *id.*, *Sprachvergleichung und Urgeschichte* (Jena, 1906-
1907), ii. 185 *sqq.* ; H. Hirt, *Die
Indogermanen* (Strasburg, 1905-1907),
i. 254 *sqq.*, 273 *sq.*, 276 *sqq.*, ii. 640
sqq. ; M. Much, *Die Heimat der
Indogermanen* (Jena and Berlin, 1904),
pp. 221 *sqq.* ; T. E. Peet, *The Stone
and Bronze Ages in Italy and Sicily*

(Oxford, 1909), p. 362.
[2] Aristotle, *Constitution of Athens*,
54, where the quadriennial (penteteric)
festival of the Eleusinian Games is
mentioned along with the quadriennial
festivals of the Panathenaica, the Delia,
the Brauronia, and the Heraclea.   The
biennial (trieteric) festival of the Eleusinian Games is mentioned only in the
inscription of 329 B.C. (Dittenberger,
Sylloge Inscriptionum Graecarum,[2] No.
587, lines 259 *sq.*).   As to the identity of the Great Eleusinian Games
with the quadriennial games see Dittenberger, *Sylloge Inscriptionum Graecarum*, No. 246 note [9], No. 587 note [171].

four years was very common in Greece ; to take only a few
conspicuous examples the Olympic games at Olympia, the
Pythian games at Delphi, the Panathenaic games at Athens,
and the Eleutherian games at Plataea [1] were all celebrated
at quadriennial or, as the Greeks called them, penteteric
periods ; and at a later time when Augustus instituted, or
rather renewed on a more splendid scale, the games at
Actium to commemorate his great victory, he followed a well-
established Greek precedent by ordaining that they should
be quadriennial.[2]   Still later the emperor Hadrian instituted
quadriennial games at Mantinea in honour of his dead
favourite Antinous.[3]   But in regard to the two greatest of
all the Greek games, the Olympian and the Pythian, I have
shewn reasons for thinking that they were originally celebrated at intervals of eight instead of four years ; certainly
this is attested for the Pythian games,[4] and the mode of
calculating the Olympiads by alternate periods of fifty and
forty-nine lunar months,[5] which added together make up
eight solar years, seems to prove that the Olympic cycle of
four years was really based on a cycle of eight years, from
which it is natural to infer that in the beginning the
Olympic, like the Pythian, games may have been octennial
instead of quadriennial.[6]   Now we know from the testimony
of the ancients themselves that the Greeks instituted the
eight-years' cycle for the purpose of harmonising solar and
lunar time.[7]   They regulated their calendar primarily by observation of the moon rather than of the sun ; their months
were lunar, and their ordinary year consisted of twelve lunar

Old octen-nial period of the Pythian and prob-ably of the Olympian games.

The octen-nial cycle was in-stituted by the Greeks at a very early era for the purpose of harmonis-ing solar and lunar time.

[1] As to the Plataean games see Plutarch, *Aristides*, 21 ; Pausanias, ix. 2. 6.
[2] Strabo, vii. 7. 6, p. 325 ; Sue-tonius, *Augustus*, 18 ; Dio Cassius, li. 1 ; Daremberg et Saglio, *Dictionnaire des Antiquités Grecques et Romaines*, *s.v.* " Actia."
[3] Pausanias, viii. 9. 8.
[4] Scholiast on Pindar, *Pyth.*, Argu-ment, p. 298, ed. Aug. Boeckh ; Censorinus, *De die natali*, xviii. 6. According to the scholiast on Pindar (*l.c.*) the change from the octennial to the quadriennial period was occasioned by the nymphs of Parnassus bringing

ripe fruits in their hands to Apollo, after he had slain the dragon at Delphi.
[5] Scholiast on Pindar, *Olymp.* iii. 35 (20), p. 98, ed. Aug. Boeckh. Compare Boeckh's commentary on Pindar (vol. iii. p. 138 of his edition) ; L. Ideler, *Handbuch der mathematischen und technischen Chronologie*, i. 366 *sq.*, ii. 605 *sqq.*
[6] See *The Dying God*, chapter ii. § 4, " Octennial Tenure of the King-ship," especially pp. 68 *sq.*, 80, 89 *sq.*
[7] Geminus, *Elementa Astronomiae*, viii. 25 *sqq.*, pp. 110 *sqq.*, ed. C. Manitius (Leipsic, 1898) ; Censorinus, *De die natali*, xviii. 2-6.

months. But the solar year of three hundred and sixty-five and a quarter days exceeds the lunar year of twelve lunar months or three hundred and fifty-four days by eleven and a quarter days, so that in eight solar years the excess amounts to ninety days or roughly three lunar months. Accordingly the Greeks equated eight solar years to eight lunar years of twelve months each by intercalating three lunar months of thirty days each in the octennial cycle; they intercalated one lunar month in the third year of the cycle, a second lunar month in the fifth year, and a third lunar month in the eighth year.[1] In this way they, so to say, made the sun and moon keep time together by reckoning ninety-nine lunar months as equivalent to eight solar years; so that if, for example, the full moon coincided with the summer solstice in one year, it coincided with it again after the revolution of the eight years' cycle, but not before. The equation was indeed not quite exact, and in order to render it so the Greeks afterwards found themselves obliged, first, to intercalate three days every sixteen years, and, next, to omit one intercalary month in every period of one hundred and sixty years.[2] But these corrections were doubless refinements of a later age; they may have been due to the astronomer Eudoxus of Cnidus, or to Cleostratus of Tenedos, who were variously, but incorrectly, supposed to have instituted the octennial cycle.[3] There are strong grounds for holding that in its simplest form the octennial cycle of ninety-nine lunar months dates from an extremely remote antiquity in Greece; that it was in fact, as a well-informed Greek writer tell us,[4] the first systematic attempt to bring solar and the lunar time into harmony. Indeed, if the

---

[1] Geminus, *l.c.*

[2] Geminus, *Elementa Astronomiae*, viii. 36-41.

[3] Censorinus, *De die natali*, xviii. 5. As Eudoxus flourished in the fourth century B.C., some sixty or seventy years after Meton, who introduced the nineteen years' cycle to remedy the defects of the octennial cycle, the claim of Eudoxus to have instituted the latter cycle may at once be put out of court. The claim of Cleostratus, who seems to have lived in the sixth

or fifth century B.C., cannot be dismissed so summarily; but for the reasons given in the text he can hardly have done more than suggest corrections or improvements of the ancient octennial cycle.

[4] Geminus, *Elementa Astronomiae*, viii. 27. With far less probability Censorinus (*De die natali*, xviii. 2-4) supposes that the octennial cycle was produced by the successive duplication of biennial and quadriennial cycles. See below, pp. 86 *sq.*

Olympiads were calculated, as they appear to have been, on the eight years' cycle, this of itself suffices to place the origin of the cycle not later than 776 B.C., the year with which the reckoning by Olympiads begins. And when we bear in mind the very remote period from which, judged by the wonderful remains of Mycenae, Tiryns, Cnossus and other cities, civilisation in Greek lands appears to date, it seems reasonable to suppose that the octennial cycle, based as it was on very simple observations, for which nothing but good eyes and almost no astronomical knowledge was necessary,[1] may have been handed down among the inhabitants of these countries from ages that preceded by many centuries, possibly by thousands of years, the great period of Greek literature and art. The supposition is confirmed by the traces which the octennial cycle has left of itself in certain ancient Greek customs and superstitions, particularly by the evidence which points to the conclusion that at two of the oldest seats of monarchy in Greece, namely Cnossus and Sparta, the king's tenure of office was formerly limited to eight years.[2]

The motive for instituting the eight years' cycle was religious, not practical or scientific.

We are informed, and may readily believe, that the motive which led the Greeks to adopt the eight years' cycle was religious rather than practical or scientific : their aim was not so much to ensure the punctual despatch of business or to solve an abstract problem in astronomy, as to ascertain the exact days on which they ought to sacrifice to the gods. For the Greeks regularly employed lunar months in their reckonings,[3] and accordingly if they had dated their religious festivals simply by the number of the month and the day of

---

[1] L. Ideler, *Handbuch der mathematischen und technischen Chronologie*, ii. 605.

[2] *The Dying God*, pp. 58 *sqq.* Speaking of the octennial cycle Censorinus observes that " *Ob hoc in Graecia multae religiones hoc intervallo temporis summa caerimonia coluntur* " (*De die natali*, xviii. 6). Compare L. Ideler, *op. cit.* ii. 605 *sq.* ; G. F. Unger, " Zeitrechnung der Griechen und Römer," in Iwan Müller's *Handbuch der classischen Altertumswissenschaft*, i.[2] 732 *sq.* The great age and

the wide diffusion of the octennial cycle in Greece are rightly maintained by A. Schmidt (*Handbuch der griechischen Chronologie*, Jena, 1888, pp. 61 *sqq.*), who suggests that the cycle may have owed something to the astronomy of the Egyptians, with whom the inhabitants of Greece are known to have had relations from a very early time.

[3] Aratus, *Phaenomena*, 733 *sqq.* ; L. Ideler, *Handbuch der mathematischen und technischen Chronologie*, i. 255 *sq.*

the month, the excess of eleven and a quarter days of the
solar over the lunar year would have had the effect of causing the festivals gradually to revolve throughout the whole
circle of the seasons, so that in time ceremonies which
properly belonged to winter would come to be held in
summer, and on the contrary ceremonies which were only
appropriate to summer would come to be held in winter.
To avoid this anomaly, and to ensure that festivals dated by
lunar months should fall at fixed or nearly fixed points in
the solar year, the Greeks adopted the octennial cycle by
the simple expedient of intercalating three lunar months in
every period of eight years.   In doing so they acted, as one
of their writers justly pointed out, on a principle precisely
the reverse of that followed by the ancient Egyptians, who
deliberately regulated their religious festivals by a purely
lunar calendar for the purpose of allowing them gradually to
revolve throughout the whole circle of the seasons.[1]

Thus at an early stage of culture the regulation of the
calendar is largely an affair of religion : it is a means of
maintaining the established relations between gods and men
on a satisfactory footing ; and in public opinion the great
evil of a disordered calendar is not so much that it disturbs
and disarranges the ordinary course of business and the
various transactions of civil life, as that it endangers the
welfare or even the existence both of individuals and of
the community by interrupting their normal intercourse with
those divine powers on whose favour men believe themselves
to be absolutely dependent.   Hence in states which take
this view of the deep religious import of the calendar its
superintendence is naturally entrusted to priests rather than
to astronomers, because the science of astronomy is regarded
merely as ancillary to the deeper mysteries of theology.
For example, at Rome the method of determining the
months and regulating the festivals was a secret which the
pontiffs for ages jealously guarded from the profane vulgar ;
and in consequence of their ignorance and incapacity the
calendar fell into confusion and the festivals were celebrated
out of their natural seasons, until the greatest of all the
Roman pontiffs, Julius Caesar, remedied the confusion and

*In early
times the
regulation
of the
calendar is
largely an
affair of
religion.*

[1] Geminus, *Elementa Astronomiae*, viii. 15-45.

placed the calendar of the civilised world on the firm foundation on which, with little change, it stands to this day.[1]

The quad-
riennial
period of
games and
festivals in
Greece was
probably
arrived at
by bisect-
ing an
older
octennial
period.

On the whole, then, it appears probable that the octennial
cycle, based on considerations of religion and on elementary
observations of the two great luminaries, dated from a very
remote period among the ancient Greeks ; if they did not
bring it with them when they migrated southwards from the
oakwoods and beechwoods of Central Europe, they may
well have taken it over from their civilised predecessors of
different blood and different language whom they found
leading a settled agricultural life on the lands about the
Aegean Sea. Now we have seen reasons to hold that the
two most famous of the great Greek games, the Pythian and
the Olympian, were both based on the ancient cycle of
eight years, and that the quadriennial period at which they
were regularly celebrated in historical times was arrived at
by a subdivision of the older octennial cycle. It is hardly
rash, therefore, to conjecture that the quadriennial period in
general, regarded as the normal period for the celebration of
great games and festivals, was originally founded on elementary religious and astronomical considerations of the same
kind, that is, on a somewhat crude attempt to harmonise
the discrepancies of solar and lunar time and thereby to
ensure the continued favour of the gods. It is, indeed,
certain or probable that some of these quadriennial festivals
were celebrated in honour of the dead ;[2] but there seems to
be nothing in the beliefs or customs of the ancient Greeks
concerning the dead which would suggest a quadriennial
period as an appropriate one for propitiating the ghosts of
the departed. At first sight it is different with the octennial
period ; for according to Pindar, the souls of the dead who
had been purged of their guilt by an abode of eight years
in the nether world were born again on earth in the ninth
year as glorious kings, athletes, and sages.[3] Now if this
belief in the reincarnation of the dead after eight years were

[1] Macrobius, *Saturnalia*, i. 15. 9
sqq. ; Livy, ix. 46. 5 ; Valerius Maximus, ii. 5. 2 ; Cicero, *Pro Muraena*,
xi. 25 ; *id.*, *De legibus*, ii. 12. 29 ;
Suetonius, *Divus Iulius*, 40 ; Plutarch,
Caesar, 59.

[2] See *The Dying God*, pp. 92
sqq.

[3] Plato, *Meno*, p. 81 A-C ; Pindar,
ed. Aug. Boeckh, vol. iii. pp. 623 *sq.*,
Frag. 98. See further *The Dying God*,
pp. 69 *sq.*

primitive, it might certainly furnish an excellent reason for honouring the ghosts of great men at their graves every eight years in order to facilitate their rebirth into the world. Yet the period of eight years thus rigidly applied to the life of disembodied spirits appears too arbitrary and conventional to be really primitive, and we may suspect that in this application it was nothing but an inference drawn from the old octennial cycle, which had been instituted for the purpose of reconciling solar and lunar time. If that was so, it will follow that the quadriennial period of funeral games was, like the similar period of other religious festivals, obtained through the bisection of the octennial cycle, and hence that it was ultimately derived from astronomical considerations rather than from any beliefs touching a quadriennial revolution in the state of the dead. Yet in historical times it may well have happened that these considerations were forgotten, and that games and festivals were instituted at quadriennial intervals, for example at Plataea[1] in honour of the slain, at Actium to commemorate the great victory, and at Mantinea in honour of Antinous,[2] without any conscious reference to the sun and moon, and merely because that period had from time immemorial been regarded as the proper and normal one for the celebration of certain solemn religious rites.

If we enquire why the Greeks so often bisected the old octennial period into two quadriennial periods for purposes of religion, the answer can only be conjectural, for no positive information appears to be given us on the subject by ancient writers. Perhaps they thought that eight years was too long a time to elapse between the solemn services, and that it was desirable to propitiate the deities at shorter intervals. But it is possible that political as well as religious motives may have operated to produce the change. We have seen reason to think that at two of the oldest seats of monarchy in Greece, namely Cnossus and Sparta, kings formerly held office for periods of eight years only, after which their sovereignty either terminated or had to be formally renewed. Now with the gradual growth of that democratic

The reasons for bisecting the old octennial period into two quadriennial periods may have been partly religious, partly political.

---

[1] Plutarch, *Aristides*, 21 ; Pausanias, ix. 2. 6.
[2] See above, p. 80.

sentiment, which ultimately dominated Greek political life, men would become more and more jealous of the kingly power and would seek to restrict it within narrower limits, and one of the most obvious means of doing so was to shorten the king's tenure of office. We know that this was done at Athens, where the dynasty of the Medontids was reduced from the rank of monarchs for life to that of magistrates holding office for ten years only.[1] It is possible that else-where the king's reign was cut down from eight years to four years; and if I am right in my explanation of the origin of the Olympic games this political revolution actu-ally took place at Olympia, where the victors in the chariot-race would seem at first to have personated the Sun-god and perhaps held office in the capacity of divine kings during the intervals between successive celebrations of the games.[2] If at Olympia and elsewhere the games were of old primarily contests in which the king had personally to take part for the purpose of attesting his bodily vigour and therefore his capacity for office, the repetition of the test at intervals of four instead of eight years might be regarded as furnishing a better guarantee of the maintenance of the king's efficiency and thereby of the general welfare, which in primitive society is often supposed to be sympathetically bound up with the health and strength of the king.

The bien-nial period of some Greek games may have been obtained by bisect-ing the quadrien-nial period. But while many of the great Greek games were celebrated at intervals of four years, others, such as the Nemean and the Isthmian, were celebrated at intervals of two years only ; and just as the quadriennial period seems to have been arrived at through a bisection of the octennial period, so we may surmise that the biennial period was produced by a bisection of the quadriennial period. This was the view which the admirable modern chronologer L. Ideler took of the origin of the quad-riennial and biennial festivals respectively,[3] and it appears far more probable than the contrary opinion of the ancient chrono-loger Censorinus, that the quadriennial period was reached by doubling the biennial, and the octennial period by doubling

[1] Pausanias, iv. 5. 10 ; compare Aristotle, *Constitution of Athens*, iii. 1 ; G. Gilbert, *Handbuch der griechischen Staatsalterthumer*, i.[2] (Leipsic, 1893) pp. 122 *sq.*

[2] See *The Dying God*, pp. 89-92.

[3] L. Ideler, *Handbuch der mathe-matischen und technischen Chronologie*, ii. 606 *sq.*

the quadriennial.[1] The theory of Censorinus was that the Greeks started with a biennial cycle of twelve and thirteen lunar months alternately in successive years for the purpose of harmonising solar and lunar time.[2] But as the cycle so produced exceeds the true solar time by seven and a half days,[3] the discrepancy which it leaves between the two great celestial clocks, the sun and moon, was too glaring to escape the observation even of simple farmers, who would soon have been painfully sensible that the times were out of joint, if they had attempted to regulate the various operations of the agricultural year by reference to so very inaccurate an almanac. It is unlikely, therefore, that the Greeks ever made much use of a biennial cycle of this sort.

Now to apply these conclusions to the Eleusinian games, which furnished the starting-point for the preceding discussion. Whatever the origin and meaning of these games may have been, we may surmise that the quadriennial and biennial periods at which they were held were originally derived from astronomical considerations, and that they had nothing to do directly either with the agricultural cycle, which is annual, nor with the worship of the dead, which can scarcely be said to have any cycle at all, unless indeed it be an annual one. In other words, neither the needs of husbandry nor the superstitions relating to ghosts furnish any natural explanation of the quadriennial and biennial periods of the Eleusinian games, and to discover such an explanation we are obliged to fall back on astronomy or, to be more exact, on that blend of astronomy with religion which appears to be mainly responsible for such Greek festivals as exceed a year in their period. To admit this is not to decide the question whether the Eleusinian games were agricultural or funereal in character; but it is implicitly to acknowledge that the games were of later origin than the annual ceremonies, including the Great Mysteries, which were designed to propitiate the deities of the corn for the very simple and practical purpose of ensuring good crops within the year. For it cannot but be that men

Application of the foregoing conclusion to the Eleusinian games.

---

[1] Censorinus, *De die natali*, xviii. 2-4.

[2] Censorinus, *De die natali*, xviii. 2.

[3] L. Ideler, *Handbuch der mathematischen und technischen Chronologie*, i. 270.

observed and laid their account with the annual changes of
the seasons, especially as manifested by the growth and
maturity of the crops, long before they attempted to recon-
cile the discrepancies of solar and lunar time by a series of
observations extending over several years.

Varro on
the rites of
Eleusis.

On the whole, then, if, ignoring theories, we adhere to
the evidence of the ancients themselves in regard to the
rites of Eleusis, including under that general term the
Great Mysteries, the games, the Festival before Ploughing
(*proerosia*), the Festival of the Threshing-floor, the Green
Festival, the Festival of the Cornstalks, and the offerings
of first-fruits, we shall probably incline to agree with the
most learned of ancient antiquaries, the Roman Varro,
who, to quote Augustine's report of his opinion, "interpreted the whole of the Eleusinian mysteries as relating
to the corn which Ceres (Demeter) had discovered, and
to Proserpine (Persephone), whom Pluto had carried off
from her. And Proserpine herself, he said, signifies the
fecundity of the seeds, the failure of which at a certain time
had caused the earth to mourn for barrenness, and therefore
had given rise to the opinion that the daughter of Ceres, that
is, fecundity itself, had been ravished by Pluto and detained
in the nether world; and when the dearth had been
publicly mourned and fecundity had returned once more,
there was gladness at the return of Proserpine and solemn
rites were instituted accordingly. After that he says,"
continues Augustine, reporting Varro, "that many things
were taught in her mysteries which had no reference but to
the discovery of the corn." [1]

The close
resem-
blance
between
the artistic
types of
Demeter
and Per-
sephone

Thus far I have for the most part assumed an identity
of nature between Demeter and Persephone, the divine
mother and daughter personifying the corn in its double
aspect of the seed-corn of last year and the ripe ears of
this, and I pointed out that this view of the substantial
unity of mother and daughter is borne out by their portraits

---

[1] Augustine, *De civitate Dei*, vii. 20.
"*In Cereris autem sacris praedi-
cantur illa Eleusinia, quae apud
Athenienses nobilissima fuerunt. De
quibus iste [Varro] nihil interpretatur,
nisi quod attinet ad frumentum, quod*
*Ceres invenit, et ad Proserpinam,
quam rapiente Orco perdidit. Et hanc
ipsam dicit significare foecunditatem
seminum. . . . Dicit deinde multa in
mysteriis ejus tradi, quae nisi ad
frugum inventionem non pertineant.*"

in Greek art, which are often so alike as to be indistinguish- militates against the theory that the two goddesses personified two things so different as the earth and the corn.
able. Such a close resemblance between the artistic types
of Demeter and Persephone militates decidedly against the
view that the two goddesses are mythical embodiments of
two things so different and so easily distinguishable from
each other as the earth and the vegetation which springs
from it. Had Greek artists accepted that view of Demeter
and Persephone, they could surely have devised types of
them which would have brought out the deep distinction
between the goddesses. That they were capable of doing
so is proved by the simple fact that they regularly represented the Earth Goddess by a type which differed widely
both from that of Demeter and from that of Persephone.[1]
Not only so, but they sometimes set the two types of the
Earth Goddess and the Corn Goddess (Demeter) side by
side as if on purpose to demonstrate their difference. Thus
at Patrae there was a sanctuary of Demeter, in which she
and Persephone were portrayed standing, while Earth was
represented by a seated image;[2] and on a vase-painting
the Earth Goddess is seen appropriately emerging from
the ground with a horn of plenty and an infant in her
uplifted arms, while Demeter and Persephone, scarcely distinguishable from each other, stand at full height behind her,
looking down at her half-buried figure, and Triptolemus in
his wheeled car sits directly above her.[3] In this instructive
picture, accordingly, we see grouped together the principal
personages in the myth of the corn : the Earth Goddess, the
two Goddesses of the old and the new corn, and the hero
who is said to have been sent forth by the Corn Goddess
to sow the seed broadcast over the earth. Such representations seem to prove that the artists clearly distinguished
Demeter from the Earth Goddess.[4] And if Demeter did

[1] A. Baumeister, *Denkmäler des classischen Altertums*, i. 577 *sq.* ; Drexler, *s.v.* "Gaia," in W. H. Roscher's *Lexikon der griech. und röm. Mythologie*, i. 1574 *sqq.* ; L. R. Far-nell, *The Cults of the Greek States*, iii. (Oxford, 1907) p. 27.
[2] Pausanias, vii. 21. 11. At Athens there was a sanctuary of Earth the Nursing - Mother and of Green Demeter (Pausanias, i. 22. 3), but we

do not know how the goddesses were represented.
[3] L. R. Farnell, *The Cults of the Greek States*, iii. 256 with plate xxi. b.
[4] The distinction between Demeter (Ceres) and the Earth Goddess is clearly marked by Ovid, *Fasti*, iv. 673 *sq.* :
" *Officium commune Ceres et Terra tuentur;*
Haec praebet causam frugibus,
illa locum."

not personify the earth, can there be any reasonable doubt that, like her daughter, she personified the corn which was so commonly called by her name from the time of Homer downwards? The essential identity of mother and daughter is suggested, not only by the close resemblance of their artistic types, but also by the official title of "the Two Goddesses" which was regularly applied to them in the great sanctuary at Eleusis without any specification of their individual attributes and titles,[1] as if their separate individualities had almost merged in a single divine substance.[2]

As goddesses of the corn Demeter and Persephone came to be associated with the ideas of death and resurrection.

Surveying the evidence as a whole, we may say that from the myth of Demeter and Persephone, from their ritual, from their representations in art, from the titles which they bore, from the offerings of first-fruits which were presented to them, and from the names applied to the cereals, we are fairly entitled to conclude that in the mind of the ordinary Greek the two goddesses were essentially personifications of the corn, and that in this germ the whole efflorescence of their religion finds implicitly its explanation. But to maintain this is not to deny that in the long course of religious evolution high moral and spiritual conceptions were grafted on this simple original stock and blossomed out into fairer flowers than the bloom of the barley and the wheat. Above all, the thought of the seed buried in the earth in order to spring up to new and higher life readily suggested a comparison with human destiny, and strengthened the hope that for man too the grave may be but the beginning of a better and happier existence in some brighter world unknown. This simple and natural reflection seems perfectly sufficient to explain the association of the Corn Goddess at Eleusis with the mystery of death and the hope of a blissful immortality. For that the ancients regarded initiation in

[1] Dittenberger, *Sylloge Inscriptionum Graecarum*,[2] Nos. 20, 408, 411, 587, 646, 647, 652, 720, 789. Compare the expression διώνυμοι θέαι applied to them by Euripides, *Phoenissae*, 683, with the Scholiast's note.

[2] The substantial identity of Demeter and Persephone has been recognised by some modern scholars, though their interpretations of the

myth do not altogether agree with the one adopted in the text. See F. G. Welcker, *Griechische Götterlehre* (Göttingen, 1857-1862), ii. 532; L. Preller, in Pauly's *Realencyclopädie der classischen Altertumswissenschaft*, vi. 106 *sq.*; F. Lenormant, in Daremberg et Saglio, *Dictionnaire des Antiquités Grecques et Romaines*, i. 2. pp. 1047 *sqq.*

the Eleusinian mysteries as a key to unlock the gates of Paradise appears to be proved by the allusions which well-informed writers among them drop to the happiness in store for the initiated hereafter.[1] No doubt it is easy for us to discern the flimsiness of the logical foundation on which such high hopes were built.[2] But drowning men clutch at straws, and we need not wonder that the Greeks, like ourselves, with death before them and a great love of life in their hearts, should not have stopped to weigh with too nice a hand the arguments that told for and against the prospect of human immortality. The reasoning that satisfied Saint Paul[3] and has brought comfort to untold thousands of sorrowing Christians, standing by the deathbed or the open grave of their loved ones, was good enough to pass muster with ancient pagans, when they too bowed their heads under the burden of grief, and, with the taper of life burning low in the socket, looked forward into the darkness of the unknown. Therefore we do no indignity to the myth of Demeter and Persephone—one of the few myths in which the sunshine and clarity of the Greek genius are crossed by the shadow and mystery of death—when we trace its origin to some of the most familiar, yet eternally affecting aspects of nature, to the melancholy gloom and decay of autumn and to the freshness, the brightness, and the verdure of spring.

[1] *Homeric Hymn to Demeter*, 480 *sqq.*; Pindar, quoted by Clement of Alexandria, *Strom.* iii. 3.17, p. 518, ed. Potter; Sophocles, quoted by Plutarch, *De audiendis poetis*, 4; Isocrates, *Panegyricus*, 6; Cicero, *De legibus*, ii. 14. 36; Aristides, *Eleusin.* vol. i. p. 421, ed. G. Dindorf.

[2] A learned German professor has thought it worth while to break the poor butterfly argument on the wheel of his inflexible logic. The cruel act, while it proves the hardness of the professor's head, says little for his knowledge of human nature, which does not always act in strict accordance with the impulse of the syllogistic machinery. See Erwin Rohde, *Psyche*[3] (Tübingen and Leipsic, 1903), i. 290 *sqq.*

[3] 1 Corinthians xv. 35 *sqq.*

CHAPTER III

MAGICAL SIGNIFICANCE OF GAMES IN PRIMITIVE
AGRICULTURE

Games
played as
magical
ceremonies
to promote
the growth
of the
crops.

IN the preceding chapter we saw that among the rites of Eleusis were comprised certain athletic sports, such as foot-races, horse-races, leaping, wrestling, and boxing, the victors in which were rewarded with measures of barley distributed among them by the priests.[1]   These sports the ancients themselves associated with the worship of Demeter and Persephone, the goddesses of the corn, and strange as such an association may seem to us, it is not without its analogy among the harvest customs of modern European peasantry.[2]   But to discover clear cases of games practised for the express purpose of promoting the growth of the crops, we must turn to more primitive agricultural communities than the Athenians of classical antiquity or the peoples of modern Europe.   Such communities may be found at the present day among the savage tribes of Borneo and New Guinea, who subsist mainly by tilling the ground.   Among them we take the Kayans or Bahaus of central Borneo as typical. They are essentially an agricultural people, and devote themselves mainly to the cultivation of rice, which furnishes their staple food ; all other products of the ground are of subordinate importance.   Hence agriculture, we are told, dominates the whole life of these tribes : their year is the year of the cultivation of the rice, and they divide it into various periods which are determined by the conditions necessary for the tilling of the fields and the manipulation

The
Kayans
of central
Borneo, a
primitive
agricultural
people.

---

[1] See above, p. 71, with the footnote [5].
[2] See above, pp. 74 *sqq.*

of the rice. "In tribes whose thoughts are so much engrossed by agriculture it is no wonder that they associate with it their ideas of the powers which rule them for good or evil. The spirit-world stands in close connexion with the agriculture of the Bahaus; without the consent of the spirits no work in the fields may be undertaken. Moreover, all the great popular festivals coincide with the different periods of the cultivation of the rice. As the people are in an unusual state of affluence after harvest, all family festivals which require a large outlay are for practical reasons deferred till the New Year festival at the end of harvest. The two mighty spirits Amei Awi and his wife Buring Une, who, according to the belief of the Kayans, live in a world under ground, dominate the whole of the tillage and determine the issue of the harvest in great measure by the behaviour of the owner of the land, not so much by his moral conduct, as by the offerings he has made to the spirits and the attention he has paid to their warnings. An important part in agriculture falls to the chief : at the festivals he has, in the name of the whole tribe, to see to it that the prescribed conjurations are carried out by the priestesses. All religious ceremonies required for the cultivation of the ground take place in a small rice-field specially set apart for that purpose, called *luma lali* : here the chief's family ushers in every fresh operation in the cultivation of the rice, such as sowing, hoeing, and reaping : the solemn actions there performed have a symbolical significance."[1]

The sacred rice-fields (luma lali) on which all religious ceremonies requisite for agriculture are performed.

Not only the chief's family among the Kayans has such a consecrated field ; every family possesses one of its own. These little fields are never cultivated for the sake of their produce : they serve only as the scene of religious ceremonies and of those symbolical operations of agriculture which are afterwards performed in earnest on the real rice-fields.[2] For example, at the festival before sowing a priestess sows some rice on the consecrated field of the chief's family and then calls on a number of young men and girls to complete the work ; the young men then dig holes in the ground with digging-sticks, and the girls come behind them and

Ceremonies observed at the sowing festival.

[1] A. W. Nieuwenhuis, *Quer durch Borneo* (Leyden, 1904-1907), i. 156 *sq.*
[2] A. W. Nieuwenhuis, *op. cit.* i. 164.

plant the rice-seed in the holes.   Afterwards the priestesses
lay offerings of food, wrapt in banana-leaves, here and there
on the holy field, while they croon prayers to the spirits in
soft tones, which are half drowned in the clashing music of
the gongs.   On another day women gather all kinds of edible
leaves in their gardens and fields, boil them in water, and
then sprinkle the water on the consecrated rice-field.   But
on that and other days of the festival the people attend also
to their own wants, banqueting on a favourite species of rice

Taboos observed at the sowing festival. and other dainties.   The ceremonies connected with sowing
last several weeks, and during this time certain taboos have
to be observed by the people.   Thus on the first day of the
festival the whole population, except the very old and the
very young, must refrain from bathing; after that there
follows a period of rest for eight nights, during which the
people may neither work nor hold intercourse with their
neighbours.   On the tenth day the prohibition to bathe is
again enforced; and during the eight following days the
great rice-field of the village, where the real crops are raised,
is sowed.[1]   The reason for excluding strangers from the
village at these times is a religious one.   It is a fear lest
the presence of strangers might frighten the spirits or put
them in a bad humour, and so defeat the object of the
ceremony; for, while the religious ceremonies which accompany the cultivation of the rice differ somewhat from each
other in different tribes, the ideas at the bottom of them,
we are told, are everywhere the same : the aim always is to
appease and propitiate the souls of the rice and the other
spirits by sacrifices of all sorts.[2]

Games played at the sowing festival. However, during this obligatory period of seclusion and
rest the Kayans employ themselves in various pursuits,
which, though at first sight they might seem to serve no
other purpose than that of recreation, have really in the
minds of the people a much deeper significance.   For

[1] A. W. Nieuwenhuis, *Quer durch
Borneo*, i. 164-167.
[2] A. W. Nieuwenhuis, *op. cit.* i.
163.   The motive assigned for the ex-
clusion of strangers at the sowing festival applies equally to all religious rites.
"In all religious observances," says
Dr. Nieuwenhuis, "the Kayans fear

the presence of strangers, because these
latter might frighten and annoy the
spirits which are invoked."   On the
periods of seclusion and quiet observed
in connexion with agriculture by the
Kayans of Sarawak, see W. H. Fur-
ness, *Home-life of Borneo Head-hunters*
(Philadelphia, 1902), pp. 160 *sqq.*

example, at this time the men often play at spinning tops. The tops are smooth, flat pieces of wood weighing several pounds. Each man tries to spin his own top so that it knocks down those of his neighbours and continues itself to revolve triumphantly. New tops are commonly carved for the festival. The older men sometimes use heavy tops of iron-wood. Again, every evening the young men assemble in the open space before the chief's house and engage in contests of strength and agility, while the women watch them from the long gallery or verandah of the house. Another popular pastime during the festival of sowing is a masquerade. It takes place on the evening of the tenth day, the day on which, for the second time, the people are forbidden to bathe. The scene of the performance is again the open space in front of the chief's house. As the day draws towards evening, the villagers begin to assemble in the gallery or verandah of the house in order to secure good places for viewing the masquerade. All the maskers at these ceremonies represent evil spirits. The men wear ugly wooden masks on their faces, and their bodies are swathed in masses of slit banana leaves so as to imitate the hideous faces and hairy bodies of the demons. The young women wear on their heads cylindrical baskets, which conceal their real features, while they exhibit to the spectators grotesque human faces formed by stitches on pieces of white cotton, which are fastened to the baskets. On the occasion when Dr. Nieuwenhuis witnessed the ceremony, the first to appear on the scene were some men wearing wooden masks and helmets and so thickly wrapt in banana leaves that they looked like moving masses of green foliage. They danced silently, keeping time to the beat of the gongs. They were followed by other figures, some of whom executed war-dances ; but the weight of their leafy envelope was such that they soon grew tired, and though they leaped high, they uttered none of the wild war-whoops which usually accompany these martial exercises. When darkness fell, the dances ceased and were replaced by a little drama representing a boar brought to bay by a pack of hounds. The part of the boar was played by an actor wearing a wooden boar's head mask, who ran about on all fours and

Masquer-
ade at the
sowing
festival.

grunted in a life-like manner, while the hounds, acted by young men, snarled, yelped, and made dashes at him. The play was watched with lively interest and peals of laughter by the spectators. Later in the evening eight disguised girls danced, one behind the other, with slow steps and waving arms, to the glimmering light of torches and the strains of a sort of jew's harp.[1]

Rites at hoeing.

The rites which accompany the sowing of the fields are no sooner over than those which usher in the hoeing begin. Like the sowing ceremonies, they are inaugurated by a priestess, who hoes the sacred field round about a sacrificial stage and then calls upon other people to complete the work. After that the holy field is again sprinkled with a decoction of herbs.[2]

The Kayan New Year festival.

But the crowning point of the Kayan year is the New Year festival. The harvest has then been fully housed : abundance reigns in every family, and for eight days the people, dressed out in all their finery, give themselves up to mirth and jollity. The festival was witnessed by the Dutch explorer Dr. Nieuwenhuis.

Offerings and addresses to the spirits.

To lure the good spirits from the spirit land baskets filled with precious objects were set out before the windows, and the priestesses made long speeches, in which they invited these beneficent beings to come to the chief's house and to stay there during the whole of the ceremonies. Two days afterwards one of the priestesses harangued the spirits for three-quarters of an hour, telling them who the Kayans were, from whom the chief's family was descended, what the tribe was doing, and what were its wishes, not forgetting to implore the vengeance of the spirits on the Batang-Lupars, the hereditary foes of the Kayans. The harangue was couched in rhyming verse and delivered in sing-song tones. Five days later eight priestesses ascended a sacrificial stage, on which food was daily set forth for the spirits. There they joined hands and crooned another long address to the spirits, marking the time with their hands. Then a basket containing offerings of food was handed up to them, and one of the priestesses opened it and invited the spirits to enter the basket. When they were supposed to have done so, the lid

---

[1] A. W. Nieuwenhuis, *op. cit.* i. 167-169.   [2] A. W. Nieuwenhuis, *op. cit.* i. 169.

was shut down on them, and the basket with the spirits in it was conveyed into the chief's house. As the priestesses in the performance of the sacred ceremonies might not touch the ground, planks were cut from a fruit-tree and laid on the ground for them to step on. But the great feature of the New Year festival is the sacrifice of pigs, of which the spiritual essence is appropriately offered to the spirits, while their material substance is consumed by the worshippers. In carrying out this highly satisfactory arrangement, while the live pigs lay tethered in a row on the ground, the priestesses danced solemnly round a sacrificial stage, each of them arrayed in a war-mantle of panther-skin and wearing a war-cap on her head, and on either side two priests armed with swords executed war dances for the purpose of scaring away evil spirits. By their gesticulations the priestesses indicated to the powers above that the pigs were intended for their benefit. One of them, a fat but dignified lady, dancing composedly, seemed by her courteous gestures to invite the souls of the pigs to ascend up to heaven ; but others, not content with this too ideal offering, rushed at the pigs, seized the smallest of them by the hind legs, and exerting all their strength danced with the squealing porker to and from the sacrificial stage. In the evening, before darkness fell, the animals were slaughtered and their livers examined for omens : if the under side of the liver was pale, the omen was good ; but if it was dark, the omen was evil. On the last day of the festival one of the chief priestesses, in martial array, danced round the sacrificial stage, making passes with her old sword as if she would heave the whole structure heavenward ; while others stabbed with spears at the foul fiends that might be hovering in the air, intent on disturbing the sacred ministers at their holy work.[1]

" Thus," says Dr. Nieuwenhuis, reviewing the agricultural rites which he witnessed among the Kayans on the Mendalam river, " every fresh operation on the rice-field was ushered in by religious and culinary ceremonies, during which the community had always to observe taboos for several nights and to play certain definite games. As we saw, spinning-top games

Sacrifice of pigs.

Dr. Nieuwenhuis on the games played by the Kayans in connexion with agriculture.

[1] A. W. Nieuwenhuis, *Quer durch Borneo*, i. 171-182.

and masquerades were played during the sowing festival: at the first bringing in of the rice the people pelted each other with clay pellets discharged from small pea-shooters, but in former times sham fights took place with wooden swords; while during the New Year festival the men contend with each other in wrestling, high leaps, long leaps, and running. The women also fight each other with great glee, using bamboo vessels full of water for their principal weapons."[1]

Serious religious or magical significance of the games.

What is the meaning of the sports and pastimes which custom prescribes to the Kayans on these occasions? Are they mere diversions meant to while away the tedium of the holidays? or have they a serious, perhaps a religious or magical significance? To this question it will be well to let Dr. Nieuwenhuis give his answer. "The Kayans on the Mendalam river," he says, "enjoy tolerably regular harvests, and their agricultural festivals accordingly take place every year; whereas the Kayans on the Mahakam river, on account of the frequent failure of the harvests, can celebrate a New Year's festival only once in every two or three years. Yet although these festivities are celebrated more regularly on the Mendalam river, they are followed on the Mahakam river with livelier interest, and the meaning of all ceremonies and games can also be traced much better there. On the Mendalam river I came to the false conclusion that the popular games which take place at the festivals are undertaken quite arbitrarily at the seasons of sowing and harvest; but on the Mahakam river, on the contrary, I observed that even the masquerade at the sowing festival is invested with as deep a significance as any of the ceremonies performed by the priestesses."[2]

"The influence of religious worship, which dominates the whole life of the Dyak tribes, manifests itself also in their games. This holds good chiefly of pastimes in which all adults take part together, mostly on definite occasions; it is less applicable to more individual pastimes which are not restricted to any special season. Pastimes of the former sort are very rarely indulged in at ordinary times, and properly speaking they attain their full significance only on

[1] A. W. Nieuwenhuis, *op. cit.* i. 169 *sq.*

[2] A. W. Nieuwenhuis, *op. cit.* i. 163 *sq.*

the occasion of the agricultural festivals which bear a strictly religious stamp. Even then the recreations are not left to choice, but definite games belong to definite festivals ; thus at the sowing festivals other amusements are in vogue than at the little harvest festival or the great harvest festival at the beginning of the reaping, and at the New Year festival. . . . Is this connexion between festivals and games merely an accidental one, or is it based on a real affinity ? The latter seems to me the more probable view, for in the case of one of the most important games played by men I was able to prove directly a religious significance ; and although I failed to do so in the case of the others, I conjecture, nevertheless, that a religious idea lies at the bottom of all other games which are connected with definite festivals." [1]

If the reader should entertain any doubt on the subject, and should suspect that in arriving at this conclusion the Dutch traveller gave the reins to his fancy rather than followed the real opinion of the people, these doubts and suspicions will probably be dispelled by comparing the similar games which another primitive agricultural people avowedly play for the purpose of ensuring good crops. The people in question are the Kai of German New Guinea, who inhabit the rugged, densely wooded mountains inland from Finsch Harbour. They subsist mainly on the produce of the taro and yams which they cultivate in their fields, though the more inland people also make much use of sweet potatoes. All their crops are root crops. No patch of ground is cultivated for more than a year at a time. As soon as it has yielded a crop, it is deserted for another and is quickly overgrown with rank weeds, bamboos, and bushes. In six or eight years, when the undergrowth has died out under the shadow of the taller trees which have shot up, the land may again be cleared and brought under cultivation. Thus the area of cultivation shifts from year to year ; and the villages are not much more permanent ; for in the damp tropical climate the wooden houses soon rot and fall into

The Kai, an agricultural people of German New Guinea.

[1] A. W. Nieuwenhuis, *Quer durch Borneo*, ii. 130 *sq.* The game as to the religious significance of which Dr. Nieuwenhuis has no doubt is the masquerade performed by the Kayans of the Mahakam river, where disguised men personate spirits and pretend to draw home the souls of the rice from the far countries to which they may have wandered. See below, pp 186 *sq.*

Super-
stitious
practices
observed
by the Kai
for the
good of
the crops.

ruins, and when this happens the site of the village is changed.[1] To procure good crops of the taro and yams, on which they depend for their subsistence, the Kai resort to many superstitious practices. For example, in order to make the yams strike deep roots, they touch the shoots with the bone of a wild animal that has been killed in the recesses of a cave, imagining that just as the creature penetrated deep into the earth, so the shoots that have been touched with its bone will descend deep into the ground. And in order that the taro may bear large and heavy fruit, they place the shoots, before planting them, on a large and heavy block of stone, believing that the stone will communicate its valuable properties of size and weight to the future fruit. Moreover, great use is made of spells and incantations to promote the growth of the crops, and all persons who utter such magical formulas for this purpose have to abstain from eating certain foods until the plants have sprouted and give promise of a good crop. For example, they may not eat young bamboo shoots, which are a favourite article of diet with the people. The reason is that the young shoots are covered with fine prickles, which cause itching and irritation of the skin ; from which the Kai infer that if an enchanter of field fruits were to eat bamboo shoots, the contagion of their prickles would be conveyed through him to the fruits and would manifest itself in a pungent disagreeable flavour. For a similar reason no charmer of the crops who knows his business would dream of eating crabs, because he is well aware that if he were to do so the leaves and stalks of the plants would be dashed in pieces by a pelting rain, just like the long thin brittle legs of a dead crab. Again, were such an enchanter to eat any of the edible kinds of locusts, it seems obvious to the Kai that locusts would devour the crops over which the imprudent wizard had recited his spells. Above all, people who are concerned in planting fields must on no account eat pork ; because pigs, whether wild or tame, are the most deadly enemies of the crops, which they grub up and destroy ; from which it follows, as surely as the night does the day, that if you eat pork while

[1] Ch. Keysser, "Aus dem Leben der Kaileute," in R. Neuhauss, *Deutsch* *Neu-Guinea*, iii. (Berlin, 1911) pp. 3, 9 *sq.*, 12 *sq.*

you are at work on the farm, your fields will be devastated by inroads of pigs.[1]

However, these precautions are not the only measures which the Kai people adopt for the benefit of the yams and the taro. "In the opinion of the natives various games are important for a proper growth of the field-fruits; hence these games may only be played in the time after the work on the fields has been done. Thus to swing on a long Spanish reed fastened to a branch of a tree is thought to have a good effect on the newly planted yams. Therefore swinging is practised by old and young, by men and women. No one who has an interest in the growth of his crop in the field leaves the swing idle. As they swing to and fro they sing swing-songs. These songs often contain only the names of the kinds of yams that have been planted, together with the joyous harvest-cry repeated with variations, 'I have found a fine fruit!' In leaping from the swing, they cry '*Kakulili!*' By calling out the name of the yams they think to draw their shoots upwards out of the ground. A small bow with a string, on which a wooden flag adorned with a feather is made to slide down (the Kai call the instrument *tawatawa*), may only be used when the yams are beginning to wind up about their props. The tender shoots are then touched with the bow, while a song is sung which is afterwards often repeated in the village. It runs thus : ' *Mama gelo, gelowaineja, gelowaineja ; kiki tambai, kiki tambai.*' The meaning of the words is unknown. The intention is to cause a strong upward growth of the plants. In order that the foliage of the yams may sprout luxuriantly and grow green and spread, the Kai people play cat's cradle. Each of the intricate figures has a definite meaning and a name to match : for example 'the flock of pigeons' (*Hulua*), 'the Star,' 'the Flying Fox,' 'the Sago-palm Fan,' 'the Araucaria,' 'the Lizard and the Dog,' ' the Pig,' 'the Sentinel-box in the Fields,' 'the Rat's Nest,' ' the Wasp's Nest in the Bamboo-thicket,' 'the Kangaroo,' 'the Spider's Web,' 'the Little Children,' 'the Canoe,' 'Rain and Sunshine,' 'the Pig's Pitfall,' 'the Fish-spawn,' 'the Two Cousins, Kewâ and Imbiâwâ, carrying their dead Mother to the

Games played by the Kai people to promote the growth of the yams and taro.

---

[1] Ch. Keysser, *op. cit.* pp. 123-125.

Grave,' etc.   By spinning large native acorns or a sort
of wild fig they think that they foster the growth of the
newly-planted taro ; the plants will ' turn about and broaden.'
The game must therefore only be played at the time when
the taro is planted.   The same holds good of spearing at
the stalks of taro leaves with the ribs of sago leaves used as
miniature spears.   This is done when the taro leaves have
unfolded themselves, but when the plants have not yet set
any tubers.   A single leaf is cut from a number of stems, and
these leaves are brought into the village.   The game is played
by two partners, who sit down opposite to each other at a distance of three or four paces.   A number of taro stalks lie beside
each.   He who has speared all his adversary's stalks first is
victor ; then they change stalks and the game begins again.
By piercing the leaves they think that they incite the plants

*Tales and
legends
told by the
Kai to
cause the
fruits of
the earth
to thrive.*
to set tubers.   Almost more remarkable than the limita-
tion of these games to the time when work on the fields
is going forward is the custom of the Kai people which
only permits the tales of the olden time or popular
legends to be told at the time when the newly planted
fruits are budding and sprouting." [1]   At the end of every
such tale the Kai story-teller mentions the names of
the various kinds of yams and adds, " Shoots (for the new
planting) and fruits (to eat) in abundance ! "   " From their
concluding words we see that the Kai legends are only
told for a quite definite purpose, namely, to promote the
welfare of the yams planted in the field.   By reviving the
memory of the ancient beings, to whom the origin of
the field-fruits is referred, they imagine that they influence
the growth of the fruits for good.   When the planting is
over, and especially when the young plants begin to sprout,
the telling of legends comes to an end.   In the villages it is
always only a few old men who as good story-tellers can
hold the attention of their hearers." [2]

*Thus
among
these New
Guinea
people
games are
played and*
Thus with these New Guinea people the playing of
certain games and the recital of certain legends are alike
magical in their intention ; they are charms practised to
ensure good crops.   Both sets of charms appear to be based
on the principles of sympathetic magic.   In playing the

[1] Ch. Keysser, *op. cit.* iii. 125 *sq.*   [2] Ch. Keysser, *op. cit.* iii. 161.

games the players perform acts which are supposed to mimic stories told as charms to ensure good crops. or at all events to stimulate the corresponding processes in the plants : by swinging high in the air they make the plants grow high ; by playing cat's cradle they cause the leaves of the yams to spread and the stalks to intertwine, even as the players spread their hands and twine the string about their fingers ; by spinning fruits they make the taro plants to turn and broaden ; and by spearing the taro leaves they induce the plants to set tubers.[1] In telling the legends the story-tellers mention the names of the powerful beings who first created the fruits of the earth, and the mere mention of their names avails, on the principle of the magical equivalence of names and persons or things, to reproduce the effect.[2] The recitation of tales as a charm to promote the growth of the crops is not peculiar to the Kai. It is practised also by the Bakaua, another tribe of German New Guinea, who inhabit the coast of Huon Gulf, not far from the Kai. These people tell stories in the evening at the time when the yams and taro are ripe, and the stories always end with a prayer to the ancestral spirits, invoked under various more or less figurative designations, such as "a man" or "a cricket," that they would be pleased to cause countless shoots to sprout, the great tubers to swell, the sugar-cane to

[1] On the principles of homoeopathic or imitative magic, see *The Magic Art and the Evolution of Kings,* i. 52 *sqq.* The Esquimaux play cat's cradle as a charm to catch the sun in the meshes of the string and so prevent him from sinking below the horizon in winter. See *The Magic Art and the Evolution of Kings,* i. 316 *sq.* Cat's cradle is played as a game by savages in many parts of the world, including the Torres Straits Islands, the Andaman Islands, Africa, and America. See A. C. Haddon, *The Study of Man* (London and New York, 1898), pp. 224-232 ; Miss Kathleen Haddon, *Cat's Cradles from Many Lands* (London, 1911). For example, the Indians of North-western Brazil play many games of cat's cradle, each of which has its special name, such as the Bow, the Moon, the Pleiades, the Armadillo, the Spider, the Caterpillar, and the Guts of the Tapir. See Th.

Koch-Grünberg, *Zwei Jahre unter den Indianern* (Berlin, 1909-1910), i. 120, 123, 252, 253, ii. 127, 131. Finding the game played as a magical rite to stay the sun or promote the growth of the crops among peoples so distant from each other as the Esquimaux and the natives of New Guinea, we may reasonably surmise that it has been put to similar uses by many other peoples, though civilised observers have commonly seen in it nothing more than a pastime. Probably many games have thus originated in magical rites. When their old serious meaning was forgotten, they continued to be practised simply for the amusement they afforded the players. Another such game seems to be the "Tug of War." See *The Golden Bough,*[2] iii. 95.

[2] See *Taboo and the Perils of the Soul,* pp. 318 *sqq.*

thrive, and the bananas to hang in long clusters. " From this we see," says the missionary who reports the custom, " that the object of telling the stories is to prove to the ancestors, whose spirits are believed to be present at the recitation of the tales which they either invented or inherited, that people always remember them ; for which reason they ought to be favourable to their descendants, and above all to bestow their blessings on the shoots which are ready to be planted or on the plants already in the ground." As the story-teller utters the prayer, he looks towards the house in which the young shoots ready for planting or the ripe fruits are deposited.[1]

The Yabim of German New Guinea also tell tales on purpose to obtain abundant crops.

Similarly, the Yabim, a neighbouring tribe of German New Guinea, at the entrance to Huon Gulf, tell tales for the purpose of obtaining a plentiful harvest of yams, taro, sugar-cane, and bananas.[2] They subsist chiefly by the fruits of the earth which they cultivate, and among which taro, yams, and sugar-cane supply them with their staple food.[3] In their agricultural labours they believe themselves to be largely dependent on the spirits of their dead, the *balum*, as they call them. Before they plant the first taro in a newly cleared field they invoke the souls of the dead to make the plants grow and prosper ; and to propitiate these powerful spirits they bring valuable objects, such as boar's tusks and dog's teeth, into the field, in order that the ghosts may deck themselves with the souls of these ornaments, while at the same time they minister to the grosser appetites of the disembodied spirits by offering them a savoury mess of taro porridge. Later in the season they whirl bull-roarers in the fields and call out the names of the dead, believing that this makes the crops to thrive.[4]

Specimens of Yabim tales told as charms to procure a good harvest.

But besides the prayers which they address to the spirits of the dead for the sake of procuring an abundant harvest, the Yabim utter spells for the same purpose, and these spells sometimes take the form, not of a command, but of a narrative. Here, for instance, is one of their spells : " Once upon a time a man laboured in his field and complained that he had no

[1] Stefan Lehner, " Bukaua," in R. Neuhauss, *Deutsch Neu-Guinea*, iii. (Berlin, 1911) pp. 478 *sq.*

[2] See *Taboo and the Perils of the Soul*, p. 386.

[3] H. Zahn, " Die Jabim," in R. Neuhauss, *Deutsch Neu-Guinea*, iii. (Berlin, 1911) p. 290.

[4] H. Zahn, *op. cit.* pp. 332 *sq.*

taro shoots. Then came two doves flying from Poum. They had devoured much taro, and they perched on a tree in the field, and during the night they vomited all the taro up. Thus the man got so many taro shoots that he was even able to sell some of them to other people." Or, again, if the taro will not bud, the Yabim will have recourse to the following spell : " A muraena lay at ebb-tide on the shore. It seemed to be at its last gasp. Then the tide flowed on, and the muraena came to life again and plunged into the deep water." This spell is pronounced over twigs of a certain tree (*kalelong*), while the enchanter smites the ground with them. After that the taro is sure to bud.[1] Apparently the mere recitation of such simple tales is thought to produce the same effect as a direct appeal, whether in the shape of a prayer or a command, addressed to the spirits. Such incantations may be called narrative spells to distinguish them from the more familiar imperative spells, in which the enchanter expresses his wishes in the form of direct commands. Much use seems to be made of such narrative spells among the natives of this part of German New Guinea. For example, among the Bukaua, who attribute practically boundless powers to sorcerers in every department of life and nature, the spells by which these wizards attempt to work their will assume one of two forms : either they are requests made to the ancestors, or they are short narratives, addressed to nobody in particular, which the sorcerer mutters while he is performing his magical rites.[2] It is true, that here the distinction is drawn between narratives and requests rather than between narratives and commands ; but the difference of a request from a command, though great in theory, may be very slight in practice ; so that prayer and spell, in the ordinary sense of the words, may melt into each other almost imperceptibly. Even the priest or the enchanter who utters the one may be hardly conscious of the hairbreadth that divides it from the other. In regard to narrative spells, it seems probable that they have been used much more extensively among mankind than the evidence at our disposal per-

Such tales may be called narrative spells.

[1] H. Zahn, *op. cit.* p. 333.
[2] Stefan Lehner, "Bukaua," in R.   Neuhauss, *Deutsch Neu-Guinea*, iii. (Berlin, 1911) p. 448.

mits us positively to affirm ; in particular we may conjecture that many ancient narratives, which we have been accustomed to treat as mere myths, used to be regularly recited in magical rites as spells for the purpose of actually producing events like those which they describe.

Use of the bull-roarer to quicken the fruits of the earth.

The use of the bull-roarer to quicken the fruits of the earth is not peculiar to the Yabim. On the other side of New Guinea the instrument is employed for the same purpose by the natives of Kiwai, an island at the mouth of the Fly River. They think that by whirling bull-roarers they produce good crops of yams, sweet potatoes, and bananas ; and in accordance with this belief they call the implement "the mother of yams."[1] Similarly in Mabuiag, an island in Torres Straits, the bull-roarer is looked upon as an instrument that can be used to promote the growth of garden produce, such as yams and sweet potatoes ; certain spirits were supposed to march round the gardens at night swinging bull-roarers for this purpose.[2] Indeed a fertilising or prolific virtue appears to be attributed to the instrument by savages who are totally ignorant of agriculture. Thus among the Dieri of central Australia, when a young man had undergone the painful initiatory ceremony of having a number of gashes cut in his back, he used to be given a bull-roarer, whereupon it was believed that he became inspired by the spirits of the men of old, and that by whirling it, when he went in search of game before his wounds were healed, he had power to cause a good harvest of lizards, snakes, and other reptiles. On the other hand, the Dieri thought that if a woman were to see a bull-roarer that had been used at the initiatory ceremonies and to learn its secret, the tribe would ever afterwards be destitute of snakes, lizards, and other such food.[3] It may

[1] A. C. Haddon, in *Reports of the Cambridge Anthropological Expedition to Torres Straits*, v. (Cambridge, 1904) pp. 218, 219. Compare *id., Head - hunters, Black, White, and Brown* (London, 1901) p. 104.

[2] A. C. Haddon, in *Reports of the Cambridge Anthropological Expedition to Torres Straits*, v. (Cambridge, 1904) pp. 346 *sq.*

[3] A. W. Howitt, "The Dieri and other kindred Tribes of Central Australia," *Journal of the Anthropological Institute*, xx. (1891) p. 83 ; *id., Native Tribes of South-East Australia* (London, 1904), p. 660. The first, I believe, to point out the fertilising power ascribed to the bull-roarer by some savages was Dr. A. C. Haddon. See his essay,

very well be that a similar power to fertilise or multiply edible plants and animals has been ascribed to the bull-roarer by many other peoples who employ the implement in their mysteries.

Further, it is to be observed that just as the Kai of New Guinea swing to and fro on reeds suspended from the branches of trees in order to promote the growth of the crops, in like manner Lettish peasants in Russia devote their leisure to swinging in spring and early summer for the express purpose of making the flax grow as high as they swing in the air.[1]   And we may suspect that wherever swinging is practised as a ceremony at certain times of the year, particularly in spring and at harvest, the pastime is not so much a mere popular recreation as a magical rite designed to promote the growth of the crops.[2]

Swinging as an agricultural charm.

With these examples before us we need not hesitate to believe that Dr. Nieuwenhuis is right when he attributes a deep religious or magical significance to the games which the Kayans or Bahaus of central Borneo play at their various agricultural festivals.

It remains to point out how far the religious or magical practices of these primitive agricultural peoples of Borneo and New Guinea appear to illustrate by analogy the original nature of the rites of Eleusis.   So far as we can recompose, from the broken fragments of tradition, a picture of the religious and political condition of the Eleusinian people in the olden time, it appears to tally fairly well with the picture which Dr. Nieuwenhuis has drawn for us of the Kayans or Bahaus at the present day in the forests of central Borneo.   Here as there we see a petty agricultural community ruled by hereditary chiefs who, while they unite religious to civil authority, being bound to preside over the numerous ceremonies performed for the good of

Analogy of the Kayans of Borneo to the Greeks of Eleusis in the early time.

"The Bull-roarer," in *The Study of Man* (London and New York, 1898), pp. 277-327.   In this work Dr. Haddon recognises the general principle of the possible derivation of many games from magical rites.   As to the bull-roarer compare my paper "On some Ceremonies of the Central Australian Tribes," in the *Report of the Austral-* asian Association for the Advancement of Science for the year 1900 (Melbourne, 1901), pp. 313-322.

[1] J. G. Kohl, *Die deutsch-russischen Ostseeprovinzen* (Dresden and Leipsic, 1841), ii. 25.

[2] For the evidence see *The Dying God*, pp. 277-285.

the crops,[1] nevertheless lead simple patriarchal lives and are so little raised in outward dignity above their fellows that their daughters do not deem it beneath them to fetch water for the household from the village well.[2] Here as there we see a people whose whole religion is dominated and coloured by the main occupation of their lives ; who believe that the growth of the crops, on which they depend for their subsistence, is at the mercy of two powerful spirits, a divine husband and his wife, dwelling in a subterranean world ; and who accordingly offer sacrifices and perform ceremonies in order to ensure the favour of these mighty beings and so to obtain abundant harvests. If we knew more about the Rarian plain at Eleusis,[3] we might discover that it was the scene of many religious ceremonies like those which are performed on the little consecrated rice-fields (the *luma lali*) of the Kayans, where the various operations of the agricultural year are performed in miniature by members of the chief's family before the corresponding operations may be performed on a larger

The Sacred Ploughing at Eleusis.

scale by common folk on their fields. Certainly we know that the Rarian plain witnessed one such ceremony in the year. It was a solemn ceremony of ploughing, one of the three Sacred Ploughings which took place annually in various parts of Attica.[4] Probably the rite formed part of the *Proerosia* or Festival before Ploughing, which was intended to ensure a plentiful crop.[5] Further, it appears that the priests who guided the sacred slow-paced oxen as they dragged the plough down the furrows of the Rarian Plain, were drawn from the old priestly family of Bouzygai or "Ox-yokers," whose eponymous ancestor is said to have been the first man to yoke oxen and to plough the fields. As they performed this time-honoured ceremony, the priests uttered many quaint curses against all churls who should refuse to lend fire or water to neighbours, or to shew the way to wanderers, or who should

---

[1] On the Kayan chiefs and their religious duties, see A. W. Nieuwenhuis, *Quer durch Borneo*, i. 58-60.

[2] See above, p. 36.

[3] See above, p. 74.

[4] Plutarch, *Praecepta Conjugalia*, 42. Another of these Sacred Plough-

ings was performed at Scirum, and the third at the foot of the Acropolis at Athens ; for in this passage of Plutarch we must, with the latest editor, read ὑπὸ πόλιν for the ὑπὸ πέλιν of the manuscripts.

[5] See above, pp. 50 *sqq.*

leave a corpse unburied.[1]   If we had a complete list of the execrations fulminated by the holy ploughmen on these occasions, we might find that some of them were levelled at the impious wretches who failed to keep all the rules of the Sabbath, as we may call those periods of enforced rest and seclusion which the Kayans of Borneo and other primitive agricultural peoples observe for the good of the crops.[2]

[1] *Etymologicum Magnum*, *s.v.* Βουζύγια, p. 206, lines 47 *sqq.* ; Im. Bekker, *Anecdota Graeca* (Berlin, 1814-1821), i. 221 ; Pliny, *Nat. Hist.* vii. 199 ; Hesychius, *s.v.* Βουζύγης · καθίστατο δὲ παρ' αὐτοῖς καὶ ὁ τοὺς ἱεροὺς ἀρότους ἐπιτελῶν Βουζύγης; *Paroemiographi Graeci*, ed. E. L. Leutsch und F. G. Schneidewin (Göttingen, 1839-1851), i. 388, Βουζύγης · ἐπὶ τῶν πολλὰ ἀρωμένων. Ὁ γὰρ Βουζύγης Ἀθήνησιν ὁ τὸν ἱερὸν ἄροτον ἐπιτελῶν * * ἄλλα τε πολλὰ ἀρᾶται καὶ τοῖς μὴ κοινωνοῦσι κατὰ τὸν βίον ὕδατος ἢ πυρὸς ἢ μὴ ὑποφαίνουσιν ὁδὸν πλανωμένοις; Scholiast on Sophocles, *Antigone*, 255, λόγος δὲ ὅτι Βουζύγης Ἀθήνησι κατηράσατο τοῖς περιορῶσιν ἄταφον σῶμα. The Sacred Ploughing at the foot of the Acropolis was specially called *bouzygios* (Plutarch, *Praecepta Conjugalia*, 42). Compare J. Toepffer, *Attische Genealogie* (Berlin, 1889) pp. 136 *sqq.*

[2] Such Sabbaths are very commonly and very strictly observed in connexion with the crops by the agricultural hill tribes of Assam. The native name for such a Sabbath is *genna*. See T. C. Hodson, " The *Genna* amongst the Tribes of Assam," *Journal of the Anthropological Institute*, xxxvi. (1906) pp. 94 *sq.* : " Communal tabus are observed by the whole village. . . . Those which are of regular occurrence are for the most part connected with the crops. Even where irrigated terraces are made, the rice plant is much affected by deficiencies of rain and excess of sun. Before the crop is sown, the village is tabu or *genna*. The gates are closed and the friend without has to stay outside, while the stranger that is within the gates remains till all is ended. The festival is marked among some tribes by an outburst of licentiousness, for, so long

as the crops remain ungarnered, the slightest incontinence might ruin all. An omen of the prosperity of the crops is taken by a mock contest, the girls pulling against the men. In some villages the *gennas* last for ten days, but the tenth day is the crowning day of all. The men cook, and eat apart from the women during this time, and the food tabus are strictly enforced. From the conclusion of the initial crop *genna* to the commencement of the *genna* which ushers· in the harvest-time, all trade, all fishing, all hunting, all cutting grass and felling trees is forbidden. Those tribes which specialise in cloth - weaving, salt - making or pottery-making are forbidden the exercise of these minor but valuable industries. Drums and bugles are silent all the while. . . . Between the initial crop *genna* and the harvest-home, some tribes interpose a *genna* day which depends on the appearance of the first blade of rice. All celebrate the commencement of the gathering of the crops by a *genna*, which lasts at least two days. It is mainly a repetition of the initial *genna* and, just as the first seed was sown by the *gennabura*, the religious head of the village, so he is obliged to cut the first ear of rice before any one else may begin." On such occasions among the Kabuis, in spite of the licence accorded to the people generally, the strictest chastity is required of the religious head of the village who initiates the sowing and the reaping, and his diet is extremely limited ; for example, he may not eat dogs or tomatoes. See T. C. Hodson, "The Native Tribes of Manipur," *Journal of the Anthropological Institute*, xxxi. (1901) pp. 306 *sq.* ; and for more details, *id.*, *The Naga Tribes of Mani-*

The con-
nexion
of the
Eleusinian
games with
agriculture,
attested
by the
ancients,
is con-
firmed by
modern
savage
analogies.

Further, when we see that many primitive peoples practise what we call games but what they regard in all seriousness as solemn rites for the good of the crops, we may be the more inclined to accept the view of the ancients, who associated the Eleusinian games directly with the worship of Demeter and Persephone, the Corn Goddesses.[1] One of the contests at the Eleusinian games was in leaping,[2] and we know that even in modern Europe to this day leaping or dancing high is practised as a charm to make the crops grow tall.[3]   Again, the bull-roarer was swung so as to produce a humming sound at the Greek mysteries;[4] and when we find the same simple instrument whirled by savages in New Guinea for the sake of ensuring good crops, we may reasonably conjecture that it was whirled with a like intention by the rude forefathers of the Greeks among the cornfields of Eleusis.   If that were so— though the conjecture is hardly susceptible of demonstration —it would go some way to confirm the theory that the

pur (London, 1911), pp. 168 *sqq.* The resemblance of some of these customs to those of the Kayans of Borneo is obvious. We may conjecture that the "tug of war" which takes place between the sexes on several of these Sabbaths was originally a magical ceremony to ensure good crops rather than merely a mode of divination to forecast the coming harvest.   Magic regularly dwindles into divination before it degenerates into a simple game.   At one of these taboo periods the men set up an effigy of a man and throw pointed bamboos at it.   He who hits the figure in the head will kill an enemy; he who hits it in the belly will have plenty of food. See T. C. Hodson, in *Journal of the Anthropological Institute*, xxxvi. (1906) p. 95; *id.*, *The Naga Tribes of Manipur*, p. 171.   Here also we probably have an old magical ceremony passing through a phase of divination before it reaches the last stage of decay.   On Sabbaths observed in connexion with agriculture in Borneo and Assam, see further Hutton Webster, *Rest Days, a Sociological Study*, pp. 11 *sqq.* (*University Studies*, Lincoln, Nebraska,

vol. xi. Nos. 1-2, January-April, 1911).
[1] See above, p. 71.
[2] See above, p. 71 note 5.
[3] See *The Magic Art and the Evolution of Kings*, i. 137-139.
[4] See the old Greek scholiast on Clement of Alexandria, quoted by Chr. Aug. Lobeck, *Aglaophamus* (Königsberg, 1829), p. 700; Andrew Lang, *Custom and Myth* (London, 1884), p. 39.   It is true that the bull-roarer seems to have been associated with the rites of Dionysus rather than of Demeter; perhaps the sound of it was thought to mimick the bellowing of the god in his character of a bull.   But the worship of Dionysus was from an early time associated with that of Demeter in the Eleusinian mysteries; and the god himself, as we have seen, had agricultural affinities.   See above, p. 5.   An annual festival of swinging (which, as we have seen, is still practised both in New Guinea and Russia for the good of the crops) was held by the Athenians in antiquity and was believed to have originated in the worship of Dionysus.   See *The Dying God*, pp. 281 *sq.*

Eleusinian mysteries were in their origin nothing more than simple rustic ceremonies designed to make the farmer's fields to wave with yellow corn. And in the practice of the Kayans, whose worship of the rice offers many analogies to the Eleusinian worship of the corn, may we not detect a hint of the origin of that rule of secrecy which always characterised the Eleusinian mysteries? May it not have been that, just as the Kayans exclude strangers from their villages while they are engaged in the celebration of religious rites, lest the presence of these intruders should frighten or annoy the shy and touchy spirits who are invoked at these times, so the old Eleusinians may have debarred foreigners from participation in their most solemn ceremonies, lest the coy goddesses of the corn should take fright or offence at the sight of strange faces and so refuse to bestow on men their annual blessing? The admission of foreigners to the privilege of initiation in the mysteries was probably a late innovation introduced at a time when the fame of their sanctity had spread far and wide, and when the old magical meaning of the ritual had long been obscured, if not forgotten.

Lastly, it may be suggested that in the masked dances and dramatic performances, which form a conspicuous and popular feature of the Sowing Festival among the Kayans,[1] we have the savage counterpart of that drama of divine death and resurrection which appears to have figured so prominently in the mysteries of Eleusis.[2] If my interpretation of that solemn drama is correct, it represented in mythical guise the various stages in the growth of the corn for the purpose of magically fostering the natural processes which it simulated. In like manner among the Kaua and Kobeua Indians of North-western Brazil, who subsist chiefly by the cultivation of manioc, dances or rather pantomimes are performed by masked men, who represent spirits or demons of fertility, and by imitating the act of procreation are believed to stimulate the growth of plants as well as to quicken the wombs of women and to promote the multiplication of animals. Coarse and grotesque as these dramatic performances may seem to us, they convey no suggestion of

The sacred drama of the Eleusinian mysteries compared to the masked dances of agricultural savages.

---

[1] See above, pp. 95 *sq.*, and below, pp. 186 *sq.*   [2] See above, p. 39.

indecency to the minds either of the actors or of the spectators, who regard them in all seriousness as rites destined to confer the blessing of fruitfulness on the inhabitants of the village, on their plantations, and on the whole realm of nature.[1]   However, we possess so little exact information as to the rites of Eleusis that all attempts to elucidate them by the ritual of savages must necessarily be conjectural. Yet the candid reader may be willing to grant that conjectures supported by analogies like the foregoing do not exceed the limits of a reasonable hypothesis.

[1] Th. Koch-Grünberg, *Zwei Jahre unter den Indianern* (Berlin, 1909-1910), i. 137-140, ii. 193-196.   As to the cultivation of manioc among these Indians see *id.* ii. 202 *sqq.*

CHAPTER IV

WOMAN'S PART IN PRIMITIVE AGRICULTURE

IF Demeter was indeed a personification of the corn, it is natural to ask, why did the Greeks personify the corn as a goddess rather than a god? why did they ascribe the origin of agriculture to a female rather than to a male power? They conceived the spirit of the vine as masculine; why did they conceive the spirit of the barley and wheat as feminine? To this it has been answered that the personification of the corn as feminine, or at all events the ascription of the discovery of agriculture to a goddess, was suggested by the prominent part which women take in primitive agriculture.[1] The theory illustrates a recent tendency of mythologists to explain many myths as reflections of primitive society rather than as personifications of nature. For that reason, apart from its intrinsic interest, the theory deserves to be briefly considered.

Theory that the personification of corn as feminine was suggested by the part played by women in primitive agriculture.

Before the invention of the plough, which can hardly be worked without resort to the labour of men, it was and still is customary in many parts of the world to break up the soil for cultivation with hoes, and among not a few savage peoples to this day the task of hoeing the ground and sowing the seed devolves mainly or entirely upon the women, while the men take little or no part in cultivation beyond clearing the land by felling the forest trees and burning the fallen timber and brushwood which encumber the soil. Thus, for example, among the Zulus, " when a piece of land has been selected for cultivation, the task of clearing it

Among many savage tribes the labour of hoeing the ground and sowing the seed devolves on women.

---

[1] F. B. Jevons, *Introduction to the History of Religion* (London, 1896), p. 240; H. Hirt, *Die Indogermanen* (Strasburg, 1905-1907), i. 251 *sqq.*

belongs to the men. If the ground be much encumbered, this becomes a laborious undertaking, for their axe is very small, and when a large tree has to be encountered, they can only lop the branches; fire is employed when it is needful to remove the trunk. The reader will therefore not be surprised that the people usually avoid bush-land, though they seem to be aware of its superior fertility. As a general rule the men take no further share in the labour of cultivation; and, as the site chosen is seldom much encumbered and frequently bears nothing but grass, their part of the work is very slight. The women are the real labourers; for (except in some particular cases) the entire business of digging, planting, and weeding devolves on them; and, if we regard the assagai and shield as symbolical of the man, the hoe may be looked upon as emblematic of the woman. . . . With this rude and heavy instrument the woman digs, plants, and weeds her garden. Digging and sowing are generally one operation, which is thus performed; the seed is first scattered on the ground, when the soil is dug or picked up with the hoe, to the depth of three or four inches, the larger roots and tufts of grass being gathered out, but all the rest left in or on the ground."[1] A special term of contempt is applied to any Zulu man, who, deprived of the services of his wife and family, is compelled by hard necessity to handle the hoe himself.[2] Similarly among the Baronga of Delagoa Bay, "when the rains begin to fall, sometimes as early as September but generally later, they hasten to sow. With her hoe in her hands, the mistress of the field walks with little steps; every time she lifts a clod of earth well broken up, and in the hole thus made she plants three or four grains of maize and covers them up. If she has not finished clearing all the patch of the bush which she contemplated, she proceeds to turn up again the fields she tilled last year. The crop will be less abundant than in virgin soil, but they plant three or four years successively in the

---

[1] Rev. J. Shooter, *The Kafirs of Natal and the Zulu Country* (London, 1857), pp. 17 *sq.* Speaking of the Zulus another writer observes: "In gardening, the men clear the land, if need be, and sometimes fence it in;

the women plant, weed, and harvest" (Rev. L. Grout, *Zulu-land*, Philadelphia, N.D., p. 110).

[2] A. Delegorgue, *Voyage dans l'Afrique Australe* (Paris, 1847), ii. 225.

same field before it is exhausted.   As for enriching the soil with manure, they never think of it."[1]   Among the Barotsé, who cultivate millet, maize, and peas to a small extent and in a rudimentary fashion, women alone are occupied with the field-work, and their only implement is a spade or hoe.[2]   Of the Matabelé we are told that "most of the hard work is performed by the women ; the whole of the cultivation is done by them.   They plough with short spades of native manufacture ; they sow the fields, and they clear them of weeds."[3]   Among the Awemba, to the west of Lake Tanganyika, the bulk of the work in the plantations falls on the women ; in particular the men refuse to hoe the ground. They have a saying, "Is not each male child born for the axe and each female child for the hoe?"[4]

The natives of the Tanganyika plateau "cultivate the banana, and have a curious custom connected with it.   No man is permitted to sow ; but when the hole is prepared a little girl is carried to the spot on a man's shoulders.   She first throws into the hole a sherd of broken pottery, and then scatters the seed over it."[5]   The reason of the latter practice has been explained by more recent observers of these natives.   "Young children, it may here be noted, are often employed to administer drugs, remedies, even the Poison Ordeal, and to sow the first seeds.   Such acts, the natives say, must be performed by chaste and innocent hands, lest a contaminated touch should destroy the potency of the medicine or of the seedlings planted.   It used to be a very common sight upon the islands of Lake Bangweolo to watch how a Bisa woman would solve the problem of her own moral unfitness by carrying her baby-girl to the banana-plot, and inserting seedlings in the tiny hands for dropping into the holes already prepared."[6]   Similarly among the people of the Lower Congo "women must remain chaste while planting pumpkin and calabash seeds, they are not allowed to touch any pig-meat, and they must wash their

Chastity required in the sowers of seed.

[1] H. A. Junod, *Les Ba-Ronga* (Neuchatel, 1908), pp. 195 *sq.*

[2] L. Decle, *Three Years in Savage Africa* (London, 1898), p. 85.

[3] L. Decle, *op. cit.* p. 160.

[4] C. Gouldsbury and H. Sheane, *The Great Plateau of Northern Rhodesia* (London, 1911), p. 302.

[5] L. Decle, *op. cit.* p. 295.

[6] C. Gouldsbury and H. Sheane, *The Great Plateau of Northern Nigeria* (London, 1911), p. 179.

hands before touching the seeds. If a woman does not observe all these rules, she must not plant the seeds, or the crop will be bad ; she may make the holes, and her baby girl, or another who has obeyed the restrictions, can drop in the seeds and cover them over."[1] We can now perhaps understand why Attic matrons had to observe strict chastity when they celebrated the festival of the Thesmophoria.[2] In Attica that festival was held in honour of Demeter in the month of Pyanepsion, corresponding to October,[3] the season of the autumn sowing ; and the rites included certain ceremonies which bore directly on the quickening of the seed.[4] We may conjecture that the rule of chastity imposed on matrons at this festival was a relic of a time when they too, like many savage women down to the present time, discharged the important duty of sowing the seed and were bound for that reason to observe strict continence, lest any impurity on their part should defile the seed and prevent it from bearing fruit.

Woman's part in agriculture among the Caffres of South Africa in general. Of the Caffres of South Africa in general we read that "agriculture is mainly the work of the women, for in olden days the men were occupied in hunting and fighting. The women do but scratch the land with hoes, sometimes using long-handled instruments, as in Zululand, and sometimes short-handled ones, as above the Zambesi. When the ground is thus prepared, the women scatter the seed, throwing it over the soil quite at random. They know the time to sow by the position of the constellations, chiefly by that of the Pleiades. They date their new year from the time they can see this constellation just before sunrise."[5] In Basutoland, where

[1] Rev. J. H. Weeks, "Notes on some Customs of the Lower Congo People," *Folk-lore*, xx. (1909) p. 311.

[2] In order to guard against any breach of the rule they strewed *Agnus castus* and other plants, which were esteemed anaphrodisiacs, under their beds. See Dioscorides, *De Materia Medica*, i. 134 (135), vol. i. p. 130, ed. C. Sprengel (Leipsic, 1829-1830); Pliny, *Nat. Hist.* xxiv. 59 ; Aelian, *De Natura Animalium*, ix. 26 ; Hesychius, *s.v.* κνέωρον ; Scholiast on Theocritus, iv. 25 ; Scholiast on Nicander, *Ther.* 70 *sq.*

[3] Scholiast on Aristophanes, *Thes-*

mophor. 80 ; Plutarch, *Demosthenes*, 30; Aug. Mommsen, *Feste der Stadt Athen im Altertum* (Leipsic, 1898), pp. 310 *sq.* That Pyanepsion was the month of sowing is mentioned by Plutarch (*Isis et Osiris*, 69). See above, pp. 45 *sq.*

[4] See below, vol. ii. p. 17 *sq.*

[5] Dudley Kidd, *The Essential Kaffir* (London, 1904), p. 323. Compare B. Ankermann, "L'Ethnographie actuelle de l'Afrique méridionale," *Anthropos*, i. (1906) pp. 575 *sq.* As to the use of the Pleiades to determine the time of sowing, see note at the end of the volume, "The Pleiades in Primitive Calendars."

the women also till the fields, though the lands of chiefs are dug and sowed by men, an attempt is made to determine the time of sowing by observation of the moon, but the people generally find themselves out in their reckoning, and after much dispute are forced to fall back upon the state of the weather and of vegetation as better evidence of the season of sowing. Intelligent chiefs rectify the calendar at the summer solstice, which they call the summer-house of the sun.[1]

Among the Nandi of British East Africa "the rough work of clearing the bush for plantations is performed by the men, after which nearly all work in connexion with them is done by the women. The men, however, assist in sowing the seed, and in harvesting some of the crops. As a rule trees are not felled, but the bark is stripped off for about four feet from the ground and the trees are then left to die. The planting is mostly, if not entirely, done during the first half of the *Kiptamo* moon (February), which is the first month of the year, and when the *Iwat-kut* moon rises (March) all seed should be in the ground. The chief medicine man is consulted before the planting operations begin, but the Nandi know by the arrival in the fields of the guinea-fowl, whose song is supposed to be, *O-kol, o-kol*; *mi-i tokoch* (Plant, plant; there is luck in it), that the planting season is at hand. When the first seed is sown, salt is mixed with it, and the sower sings mournfully : *Ak o-siek-u o-chok-chi* (And grow quickly), as he sows. After fresh ground has been cleared, eleusine grain is planted. This crop is generally repeated the second year, after which millet is sown, and finally sweet potatoes or some other product. Most fields are allowed to lie fallow every fourth or fifth year. The Nandi manure their plantations with turf ashes. . . . The eleusine crops are harvested by both men and women. All other crops are reaped by the women only, who are at times assisted by the children. The corn is pounded and winnowed by the women and girls." [2]   Among

Agricul-
tural work
done by
women
among the
Nandi and
other tribes
of Central
and
Western
Africa.

[1] Rev. E. Casalis, *The Basutos* (London, 1861), pp. 143 (with plate), pp. 162-165.
[2] A. C. Hollis, *The Nandi* (Oxford, 1909), p. 19. However, among the Bantu Kavirondo, an essentially agricultural people of British East Africa, both men and women work in the fields with large iron hoes. See Sir Harry Johnston, *The Uganda Protectorate* (London, 1904), ii. 738.

the Suk and En-jemusi of British East Africa it is the women who cultivate the fields and milk the cows.[1] Among the Wadowe of German East Africa the men clear the forest and break up he hard ground, but the women sow and reap the crops.[2] So among the Wanyamwezi, who are an essentially agricultural people, to the south of Lake Victoria Nyanza, the men cut down the bush and hoe the hard ground, but leave the rest of the labour of weeding, sowing, and reaping to the women.[3] The Baganda of Central Africa subsist chiefly on bananas, and among them "the garden and its cultivation have always been the woman's department. Princesses and peasant women alike looked upon cultivation as their special work ; the garden with its produce was essentially the wife's domain, and she would under no circumstances allow her husband to do any digging or sowing in it. No woman would remain with a man who did not give her a garden and a hoe to dig it with ; if these were denied her, she would seek an early opportunity to escape from her husband and return to her relations to complain of her treatment, and to obtain justice or a divorce. When a man married he sought a plot of land for his wife in order that she might settle to work and provide food for the household. . . . In initial clearing of the land it was customary for the husband to take part ; he cut down the tall grass and shrubs, and so left the ground ready for his wife to begin her digging. The grass and the trees she heaped up and burned, reserving only so much as she needed for firewood. A hoe was the only implement used in cultivation ; the blade was heart-shaped with a prong at the base, by which it was fastened to the handle. The hoe-handle was never more than two feet long, so that a woman had to stoop when using it."[4] In Kiziba, a district immediately to the south of Uganda, the tilling of the soil is exclusively the work of the women. They turn up the soil with hoes, make holes in the ground with digging-sticks or their fingers, and drop a few seeds into

Agricultural work of women among the Baganda.

[1] M. W. H. Beech, *The Suk* (Oxford, 1911), p. 33.
[2] F. Stuhlmann, *Mit Emin Pascha ins Herz von Afrika* (Berlin, 1894), p. 36.

[3] F. Stuhlmann, *op. cit.* p. 75.
[4] Rev. J. Roscoe, *The Baganda* (London, 1911), pp. 426, 427 ; compare pp. 5, 38, 91 *sq.*, 93, 94, 95, 268.

each hole.[1]   Among the Niam-Niam of Central Africa "the men most studiously devote themselves to their hunting, and leave the culture of the soil to be carried on exclusively by the women";[2] and among the Monbuttoo of the same region in like manner, "whilst the women attend to the tillage of the soil and the gathering of the harvest, the men, unless they are absent either for war or hunting, spend the entire day in idleness."[3]   As to the Bangala of the Upper Congo we read that "large farms were made around the towns.   The men did the clearing of the bush, felling the trees, and cutting down the undergrowth; the women worked with them, heaping up the grass and brushwood ready for burning, and helping generally.   As a rule the women did the hoeing, planting, and weeding, but the men did not so despise this work as never to do it."   In this tribe "the food belonged to the woman who cultivated the farm, and while she supplied her husband with the vegetable food, he had to supply the fish and meat and share them with his wife or wives."[4]   Amongst the Tofoke, a tribe of the Congo State on the equator, all the field labour, except the clearing away of the forest, is performed by the women.   They dig the soil with a hoe and plant maize and manioc.   A field is used only once.[5]   So with the Ba-Mbala, a Bantu tribe between the rivers Inzia and Kwilu, the men clear the ground for cultivation, but all the rest of the work of tillage falls to the women, whose only tool is an iron hoe.   Fresh ground is cleared for cultivation every year.[6] The Mpongwe of the Gaboon, in West Africa, cultivate manioc (cassava), maize, yams, plantains, sweet potatoes, and ground nuts.   When new clearings have to be made in the forest, the men cut down and burn the trees, and the women put in the crop.   The only tool they use is a dibble, with which they turn up a sod, put in a seed, and cover it

Agricultural work of women on the Congo.

[1] H. Rehse, *Kiziba, Land und Leute* (Stuttgart, 1910), p. 53.

[2] G. Schweinfurth, *The Heart of Africa*[3] (London, 1878), i. 281.

[3] G. Schweinfurth, *op. cit.* ii. 40.

[4] Rev. J. H. Weeks, "Anthropological Notes on the Bangala of the Upper Congo River," *Journal of the* *Royal Anthropological Institute*, xxxix. (1909) pp. 117, 128.

[5] E. Torday, "Der Tofoke," *Mitteilungen der Anthropologischen Gesellschaft in Wien*, xli. (1911) p. 198.

[6] E. Torday and T. A. Joyce, "Notes on the Ethnography of the Ba-Mbala," *Journal of the Anthropological Institute*, xxxv. (1905) p. 405.

over.[1]   Among the Ashira of the same region the cultivation of the soil is in the hands of the women.[2]

Agricul-
tural work
done by
women
among the
Indian
tribes of
South
America.

A similar division of labour between men and women
prevails among many primitive agricultural tribes of Indians
in South America.   " In the interior of the villages," says an
eminent authority on aboriginal South America, " the man
often absents himself to hunt or to go into the heart of the
forest in search of the honey of the wild bees, and he always
goes alone.   He fells the trees in the places where he
wishes to make a field for cultivation, he fashions his
weapons, he digs out his canoe, while the woman rears the
children, makes the garments, busies herself with the
interior, cultivates the field, gathers the fruits, collects the
roots, and prepares the food.   Such is, generally at least,
the respective condition of the two sexes among almost
all the Americans.   The Peruvians alone had already, in
their semi-civilised state, partially modified these customs ;
for among them the man shared the toils of the other sex or
took on himself the most laborious tasks." [3]   Thus, to take
examples, among the Caribs of the West Indies the men
used to fell the trees and leave the fallen trunks to cumber
the ground, burning off only the smaller boughs.   Then the
women came and planted manioc, potatoes, yams, and
bananas wherever they found room among the tree-trunks.
In digging the ground to receive the seed or the shoots
they did not use hoes but simply pointed sticks.   The men,
we are told, would rather have died of hunger than undertake
such agricultural labours.[4]   Again, the staple vegetable food
of the Indians of British Guiana is cassava bread, made
from the roots of the manioc or cassava plant, which the
Indians cultivate in clearings of the forest.   The men fell
the trees, cut down the undergrowth, and in dry weather set
fire to the fallen lumber, thus creating open patches in the
forest which are covered with white ashes.   When the rains

[1] P. B. du Chaillu, *Explorations
and Adventures in Equatorial Africa*
(London, 1861), p. 22.

[2] P. B. du Chaillu, *op. cit.* p. 417.

[3] A. D'Orbigny, *L'Homme Améri-
cain (de l'Amérique Méridionale)* (Paris,
1839), i. 198 *sq.*

[4] Le Sieur de la Borde, "Relation
de l'Origine, Mœurs, Coustumes,
Religion, Guerres et Voyages des
Caraibes Sauvages des Isles Antilles
de l'Amerique," pp. 21-23, in *Recueil
de divers Voyages faits en Afrique et
en l'Amerique* (Paris, 1684).

set in, the women repair to these clearings, heavily laden with baskets full of cassava sticks to be used as cuttings. These they insert at irregular intervals in the soil, and so the field is formed. While the cassava is growing, the women do just as much weeding as is necessary to prevent the cultivated plants from being choked by the rank growth of the tropical vegetation, and in doing so they plant bananas, pumpkin seeds, yams, sweet potatoes, sugar-cane, red and yellow peppers, and so forth, wherever there is room for them. At last in the ninth or tenth month, when the seeds appearing on the straggling branches of the cassava plants announce that the roots are ripe, the women cut down the plants and dig up the roots, not all at once, but as they are required. These roots they afterwards peel, scrape, and bake into cassava bread.[1]

In like manner the cassava or manioc plant is cultivated generally among all the Indian tribes of tropical South America, wherever the plant will grow ; and the cultivation of it is altogether in the hands of the women, who insert the sticks in the ground after the fashion already described.[2] For example, among the tribes of the Uaupes River, in the upper valley of the Amazon, who are an agricultural people with settled abodes, "the men cut down the trees and brushwood, which, after they have lain some months to dry, are burnt ; and the mandiocca is then planted by the women, together with little patches of cane, sweet potatoes, and various fruits. The women also dig up the mandiocca, and prepare from it the bread which is their main sub-sistence. . . . The bread is made fresh every day, as when it gets cold and dry it is far less palatable. The women thus have plenty to do, for every other day at least they have to go to the field, often a mile or two distant, to fetch the root, and every day to grate, prepare, and bake the bread ; as it forms by far the greater part of their food, and they often pass days without eating anything else, especially

Cultivation of manioc by women among the Indian tribes of tropical South America.

---

[1] E. F. im Thurn, *Among the Indians of Guiana* (London, 1883), pp. 250 *sqq.*, 260 *sqq.*

[2] C. F. Phil. v. Martius, *Zur Ethnographie Amerika's, zumal Brasiliens* (Leipsic, 1867), pp. 486-489. On the economic importance of the manioc or cassava plant in the life of the South American Indians, see further E. J. Payne, *History of the New World called America*, i. (Oxford, 1892) pp. 310 *sqq.*, 312 *sq.*

when the men are engaged in clearing the forest."[1] Among the Tupinambas, a tribe of Brazilian Indians, the wives "had something more than their due share of labour, but they were not treated with brutality, and their condition was on the whole happy. They set and dug the mandioc ; they sowed and gathered the maize. An odd superstition prevailed, that if a sort of earth-almond, which the Portugueze call *amendoens*, was planted by the men, it would not grow."[2] Similar accounts appear to apply to the Brazilian Indians in general : the men occupy themselves with hunting, war, and the manufacture of their weapons, while the women plant and reap the crops, and search for fruits in the forest ;[3] above all they cultivate the manioc, scraping the soil clear of weeds with pointed sticks and inserting the shoots in the earth.[4] Similarly among the Indians of Peru, who cultivate maize in clearings of the forest, the cultivation of the fields is left to the women, while the men hunt with bows and arrows and blowguns in the woods, often remaining away from home for weeks or even months together.[5]

Agricultural work done by women among savage tribes in India, New Guinea, and New Britain.

A similar distribution of labour between the sexes prevails among some savage tribes in other parts of the world. Thus among the Lhoosai of south-eastern India the men employ themselves chiefly in hunting or in making forays on their weaker neighbours, but they clear the ground and help to carry home the harvest. However, the main burden of the bodily labour by which life is supported falls on the women ; they fetch water, hew wood, cultivate the ground,

[1] A. R. Wallace, *Narrative of Travels on the Amazon and Rio Negro* (London, 1889), pp. 336, 337 (*The Minerva Library*). Mr. Wallace's account of the agriculture of these tribes is entirely confirmed by the observations of a recent explorer in north-western Brazil. See Th. Koch-Grünberg, *Zwei Jahre unter den Indianern* (Berlin, 1909-1910), ii. 202-209 ; id., "Frauenarbeit bei den Indianern Nordwest-Brasiliens," *Mitteilungen der Anthropologischen Gesellschaft in Wien*, xxxviii. (1908) pp. 172-174. This writer tells us (*Zwei Jahre unter den Indianern*, ii. 203) that these Indians determine the time

for planting by observing certain constellations, especially the Pleiades. The rainy season begins when the Pleiades have disappeared below the horizon. See Note at end of the volume.

[2] R. Southey, *History of Brazil*, vol. i. Second Edition (London, 1822), p. 253.

[3] J. B. von Spix und C. F. Ph. von Martius, *Reise in Brasilien* (Munich, 1823-1831), i. 381.

[4] K. von den Steinen, *Unter den Naturvölkern Zentral-Brasiliens* (Berlin, 1894), p. 214.

[5] J. J. von Tschudi, *Peru* (St. Gallen, 1846), ii. 214.

and help to reap the crops.[1]   Among the Miris of Assam almost the whole of the field work is done by the women. They cultivate a patch of ground for two successive years, then suffer it to lie fallow for four or five. But they are deterred by superstitious fear from breaking new ground so long as the fallow suffices for their needs; they dread to offend the spirits of the woods by needlessly felling the trees. They raise crops of rice, maize, millet, yams, and sweet potatoes. But they seldom possess any implement adapted solely for tillage; they have never taken to the plough nor even to a hoe. They use their long straight swords to clear, cut, and dig with.[2]   Among the Korwas, a savage hill tribe of Bengal, the men hunt with bows and arrows, while the women till the fields, dig for wild roots, or cull wild vegetables. Their principal crop is pulse (*Cajanus Indicus*).[3]   Among the Papuans of Ayambori, near Doreh in Dutch New Guinea, it is the men who lay out the fields by felling and burning the trees and brushwood in the forest, and it is they who enclose the fields with fences, but it is the women who sow and reap them and carry home the produce in sacks on their backs. They cultivate rice, millet, and bananas.[4]   So among the natives of Kaimani Bay in Dutch New Guinea the men occupy themselves only with fishing and hunting, while all the field work falls on the women.[5]   In the Gazelle Peninsula of New Britain, when the natives have decided to convert a piece of grassland into a plantation, the men cut down the long grass, burn it, dig up the soil with sharp-pointed sticks, and enclose the land with a fence of saplings. Then the women plant the banana shoots, weed the ground, and in the intervals between the bananas insert slips of yams, sweet potatoes, sugar-cane, or ginger. When the produce is ripe, they carry it to the village. Thus the bulk of the labour of cultivation devolves on the women.[6]

[1] Captain T. H. Lewin, *Wild Races of South-Eastern India* (London, 1870), p. 255.

[2] E. T. Dalton, *Descriptive Ethnology of Bengal* (Calcutta, 1872), p. 33.

[3] E. T. Dalton, *op. cit.* pp. 226, 227.

[4] *Nieuw Guinea, ethnographisch en natuurkundig onderzocht en beschreven* (Amsterdam, 1862), p. 159.

[5] *Op. cit.* p. 119; H. von Rosenberg, *Der Malayische Archipel* (Leipsic, 1878), p. 433.

[6] P. A. Kleintitschen, *Die Küstenbewohner der Gazellehalbinsel* (Hiltrup

Division of agricultural work between men and women in the Indian Archipelago.

Among some peoples of the Indian Archipelago, after the land has been cleared for cultivation by the men, the work of planting and sowing is divided between men and women, the men digging holes in the ground with pointed sticks, and the women following them, putting the seeds or shoots into the holes, and then huddling the earth over them ; for savages seldom sow broadcast, they laboriously dig holes and insert the seed in them. This division of agricultural labour between the sexes is adopted by various tribes of Celebes, Ceram, Borneo, Nias, and New Guinea.[1] Sometimes the custom of entrusting the sowing of the seed to women appears to be influenced by superstitious as well as economic considerations. Thus among the Indians of the Orinoco, who with an infinitude of pains cleared the jungle for cultivation by cutting down the forest trees with their stone axes, burning the fallen lumber, and breaking up the ground with wooden instruments hardened in the fire, the task of sowing the maize and planting the roots was performed by the women alone ; and when the Spanish missionaries expostulated with the men for not helping their wives in this toilsome duty, they received for answer that as women knew how to conceive seed and bear children, so the seeds and roots planted by them bore fruit far more abundantly than if they had been planted by male hands.[2]

Among savages who have not learned to till the ground the task of collecting the vege-

Even among savages who have not yet learned to cultivate any plants the task of collecting the edible seeds and digging up the edible roots of wild plants appears to devolve mainly on women, while the men contribute their share to the common food supply by hunting and fishing, for which their superior strength, agility, and courage especi-

bei Münster, preface dated Christmas, 1906), pp. 60 sq.; G. Brown, D.D., Melanesians and Polynesians (London, 1910), pp. 324 sq.

[1] A. C. Kruijt, "Een en ander aangaande het geestelijk en maatschappelijk leven van den Poso-Alfoer," Mededeelingen van wege het Nederlandsche Zendelinggenootschap, xxxix. (1895) pp. 132, 134; J. Boot, "Korte schets der noordkust van Ceram," Tijdschrift van het Nederlandsch Aardrijkskundig Genootschap, Tweede Serie, x. (1893) p. 672 ; E. H. Gomes,

Seventeen Years among the Sea Dyaks of Borneo (London, 1911), p. 46 ; E. Modigliani, Un Viaggio a Nías (Milan, 1890), pp. 590 sq.; K. Vetter, Komm herüber und hilf uns! Heft 2 (Barmen, 1898), pp. 6 sq.; Ch. Keysser, "Aus dem Leben der Kaileute," in R. Neuhauss, Deutsch Neu-Guinea, iii. (Berlin, 1911) pp. 14, 85.

[2] J. Gumilla, Histoire Naturelle, Civile et Géographique de l'Orénoque (Avignon, 1758), ii. 166 sqq., 183 sqq. Compare The Magic Art and the Evolution of Kings, i. 139 sqq.

ally qualify them.   For example, among the Indians of table food California, who were entirely ignorant of agriculture, the in the form of wild general division of labour between the sexes in the search seeds and for food was that the men killed the game and caught the roots generally salmon, while the women dug the roots and brought in devolves on most of the vegetable food, though the men helped them to women. Examples gather acorns, nuts, and berries.[1]   Among the Indians of furnished by the San Juan Capistrano in California, while the men passed Californian their time in fowling, fishing, dancing, and lounging, " the Indians. women were obliged to gather seeds in the fields, prepare them for cooking, and to perform all the meanest offices, as well as the most laborious.   It was painful in the extreme, to behold them, with their infants hanging upon their shoulders, groping about in search of herbs or seeds, and exposed as they frequently were to the inclemency of the weather." [2]   Yet these rude savages possessed a calendar containing directions as to the seasons for collecting the different seeds and produce of the earth.   The calendar consisted of lunar months corrected by observation of the solstices, " for at the conclusion of the moon in December, that is, at the conjunction, they calculated the return of the sun from the tropic of Capricorn ; and another year commenced, the Indian saying ' the sun has arrived at his home.' . . . They observed with greater attention and celebrated with more pomp, the sun's arrival at the tropic of Capricorn than they did his reaching the tropic of Cancer, for the reason, that, as they were situated ten degrees from the latter, they were pleased at the sun's approach towards them ; for it returned to ripen their fruits and seeds, to give warmth to the atmosphere, and enliven again the fields with beauty and increase."   However, the knowledge of the calendar was limited to the *puplem* or general council of the tribe, who sent criers to make proclamation when the time had come to go forth and gather the seeds and other produce of the earth.   In their calculations they were assisted by a *pul* or

[1] S. Powers, *Tribes of California* (Washington, 1877), p. 23.
[2] Father Geronimo Boscana, "Chinigchinich," in [A. Robinson's] *Life in California* (New York, 1846), p. 287. Elsewhere the same well - informed writer observes of these Indians that " they neither cultivated the ground, nor planted any kind of grain ; but lived upon the wild seeds of the field, the fruits of the forest, and upon the abundance of game " (*op. cit.* p. 285).

astrologer, who observed the aspect of the moon.[1] When we consider that these rude Californian savages, destitute alike of agriculture and of the other arts of civilised life, yet succeeded in forming for themselves a calendar based on observation both of the moon and of the sun, we need not hesitate to ascribe to the immeasurably more advanced Greeks at the dawn of history the knowledge of a somewhat more elaborate calendar founded on a cycle of eight solar years.[2]

Among the aborigines of Australia the women provided the vegetable food, while the men hunted.

Among the equally rude aborigines of Australia, to whom agriculture in every form was totally unknown, the division of labour between the sexes in regard to the collection of food appears to have been similar. While the men hunted game, the labour of gathering and preparing the vegetable food fell chiefly to the women. Thus with regard to the Encounter Bay tribe of South Australia we are told that while the men busied themselves, according to the season, either with fishing or with hunting emus, opossums, kangaroos, and so forth, the women and children searched for roots and plants.[3] Again, among the natives of Western Australia " it is generally considered the province of women to dig roots, and for this purpose they carry a long, pointed stick, which is held in the right hand, and driven firmly into the ground, where it is shaken, so as to loosen the earth, which is scooped up and thrown out with the fingers of the left hand, and in this manner they dig with great rapidity. But the labour, in proportion to the amount obtained, is great. To get a yam about half an inch in circumference and a foot in length, they have to dig a hole above a foot square and two feet in depth ; a considerable portion of the time of the women and children is, therefore, passed in this employment. If the men are absent upon any expedition, the females are left in charge of one who is

[1] Father Geronimo Boscana, *op. cit.* pp. 302-305. As to the *puplem*, see *id.* p. 264. The writer says that criers informed the people " when to cultivate their fields " (p. 302). But taken along with his express statement that they " neither cultivated the ground, nor planted any kind of grain " (p. 285, see above, p. 125 note [2]), this expression " to cultivate their fields " must be understood loosely to denote merely the gathering of the wild seeds and fruits.

[2] See above, pp. 81 *sq.*

[3] H. E. A. Meyer, " Manners and Customs of the Encounter Bay Tribe," in *Native Tribes of South Australia* (Adelaide, 1879), pp. 191 *sq.*

old or sick ; and in traversing the bush you often stumble on a large party of them, scattered about in the forest, digging roots and collecting the different species of fungus." [1] In fertile districts, where the yams which the aborigines use as food grow abundantly, the ground may sometimes be seen riddled with holes made by the women in their search for these edible roots. Thus to quote Sir George Grey : " We now crossed the dry bed of a stream, and from that emerged upon a tract of light fertile soil, quite overrun with *warran* [yam] plants, the root of which is a favourite article of food with the natives. This was the first time we had yet seen this plant on our journey, and now for three and a half consecutive miles we traversed a fertile piece of land, literally perforated with the holes the natives had made to dig this root ; indeed we could with difficulty walk across it on that account, whilst this tract extended east and west as far as we could see." [2] Again, in the valley of the Lower Murray River a kind of yam (*Microseris Forsteri*) grew plentifully and was easily found in the spring and early summer, when the roots were dug up out of the earth by the women and children. The root is small and of a sweetish taste and grows throughout the greater part of Australia outside the tropics ; on the alpine pastures of the high Australian mountains it attains to a much larger size and furnishes a not unpalatable food.[3] But the women gather edible herbs and seeds as well as roots ; and at evening they may be seen trooping in to the camp, each with a great bundle of sow-thistles, dandelions, or trefoil on her head,[4] or carrying wooden vessels filled with seeds, which they afterwards grind up between stones and knead into a paste with water or bake into cakes.[5] Among the aborigines of central Victoria, while the men hunted, the women dug up edible

[1] (Sir) George Grey, *Journals of Two Expeditions of Discovery in North-West and Western Australia* (London, 1841), ii. 292 *sq.* The women also collect the nuts from the palms in the month of March (*id.* ii. 296).

[2] (Sir) George Grey, *op. cit.* ii. 12. The yam referred to is a species of *Diascorea*, like the sweet potato.

[3] R. Brough Smyth, *The Aborigines*

of *Victoria* (Melbourne, 1878), i. 209.

[4] P. Beveridge, " Of the Aborigines inhabiting the Great Lacustrine and Riverine Depression of the Lower Murray, Lower Murrumbidgee, Lower Lachlan, and Lower Darling," *Journal and Proceedings of the Royal Society of New South Wales for 1883*, vol. xvii. (Sydney, 1884) p. 36.

[5] R. Brough Smyth, *The Aborigines of Victoria*, i. 214.

roots and gathered succulent vegetables, such as the young tops of the *munya*, the sow-thistle, and several kinds of fig-marigold. The implement which they used to dig up roots with was a pole seven or eight feet long, hardened in the fire and pointed at the end, which also served them as a weapon both of defence and of offence.[1] Among the tribes of Central Australia the principal vegetable food is the seed of a species of Claytonia, called by white men *munyeru*, which the women gather in large quantities and winnow by pouring the little black seeds from one vessel to another so as to let the wind blow the loose husks away.[2]

The digging of the earth for wild fruits may have led to the origin of agriculture.

In these customs observed by savages who are totally ignorant of agriculture we may perhaps detect some of the steps by which mankind have advanced from the enjoyment of the wild fruits of the earth to the systematic cultivation of plants. For an effect of digging up the earth in the search for roots has probably been in many cases to enrich and fertilise the soil and so to increase the crop of roots or herbs ; and such an increase would naturally attract the natives in larger numbers and enable them to subsist for longer periods on the spot without being compelled by the speedy exhaustion of the crop to shift their quarters and wander away in search of fresh supplies. Moreover, the winnowing of the seeds on ground which had thus been turned up by the digging-sticks of the women would naturally contribute to the same result. For though savages at the level of the Californian Indians and the aborigines of Australia have no idea of using seeds for any purpose but that of immediate consumption, and it has never occurred to them to incur a temporary loss for the sake of a future gain by sowing them in the ground, yet it is almost certain that in the process of winnowing the seeds as a preparation for eating them many of the grains must have escaped and, being wafted by the wind, have fallen on the upturned soil and borne fruit. Thus by the operations of turning up the ground and winnowing the seed, though neither operation

[1] W. Stanbridge, " Some Particulars of the General Characteristics, Astronomy, and Mythology of the Tribes in the Central Part of Victoria, South Australia," *Transactions of the Ethno-* *logical Society of London*, N.S., i. (1861) p. 291.

[2] Baldwin Spencer and F. J. Gillen, *Native Tribes of Central Australia* (London, 1899), p. 22.

aimed at anything beyond satisfying the immediate pangs of hunger, savage man or rather savage woman was unconsciously preparing for the whole community a future and more abundant store of food, which would enable them to multiply and to abandon the old migratory and wasteful manner of life for a more settled and economic mode of existence.   So curiously sometimes does man, aiming his shafts at a near but petty mark, hit a greater and more distant target.

On the whole, then, it appears highly probable that as a consequence of a certain natural division of labour between the sexes women have contributed more than men towards the greatest advance in economic history, namely, the transition from a nomadic to a settled life, from a natural to an artificial basis of subsistence. *The discovery of agriculture due mainly to women.*

Among the Aryan peoples of Europe the old practice of hoeing the ground as a preparation for sowing appears to have been generally replaced at a very remote period by the far more effective process of ploughing;[1] and as the labour of ploughing practically necessitates the employment of masculine strength, it is hardly to be expected that in Europe many traces should remain of the important part formerly played by women in primitive agriculture.   However, we are told that among the Iberians of Spain and the Athamanes of Epirus the women tilled the ground,[2] and that among the ancient Germans the care of the fields was left to the women and old men.[3]   But these indications of an age when the cultivation of the ground was committed mainly to feminine hands are few and slight; and if the Greek conception of Demeter as a goddess of corn and agriculture really dates from such an age and was directly suggested by such a division of labour between the sexes, it *Women as agricultural labourers among the Aryans of Europe.* *The Greek conception of the Corn Goddess probably originated in a simple personification of the corn.*

<hr>

[1] O. Schrader, *Reallexikon der indogermanischen Altertumskunde* (Strasburg, 1901), pp. 6 *sqq.*, 630 *sqq.* ; *id.*, *Sprachvergleichung und Urgeschichte*[3] (Jena, 1905-1907), ii. 201 *sqq.* ; H. Hirt, *Die Indogermanen*, i. 251 *sqq.*, 263, 274.   The use of oxen to draw the plough is very ancient in Europe. On the rocks at Bohuslän in Sweden there is carved a rude representation

of a plough drawn by oxen and guided by a ploughman : it is believed to date from the Bronze Age.   See H. Hirt, *op. cit.* i. 286.

[2] Strabo, iii. 4. 17, p. 165 ; Heraclides Ponticus, "De rebus publicis," 33, in *Fragmenta Historicorum Graecorum*, ed. C. Müller, ii. 219.

[3] Tacitus, *Germania*, 15.

seems clear that its origin must be sought at a period far back in the history of the Aryan race, perhaps long before the segregation of the Greeks from the common stock and their formation into a separate people. It may be so, but to me I confess that this derivation of the conception appears somewhat far-fetched and improbable ; and I prefer to suppose that the idea of the corn as feminine was suggested to the Greek mind, not by the position of women in remote prehistoric ages, but by a direct observation of nature, the teeming head of corn appearing to the primitive fancy to resemble the teeming womb of a woman, and the ripe ear on the stalk being likened to a child borne in the arms or on the back of its mother. At least we know that similar sights suggest similar ideas to some of the agricultural negroes of West Africa. Thus the Hos of Togoland, who plant maize in February and reap it in July, say that the maize is an image of a mother ; when the cobs are forming, the mother is binding the infant on her back, but in July she sinks her head and dies and the child is taken away from her, to be afterwards multiplied at the next sowing.[1] When the rude aborigines of Western Australia observe that a seed-bearing plant has flowered, they call it the Mother of So-and-so, naming the particular kind of plant, and they will not allow it to be dug up.[2] Apparently they think that respect and regard are due to the plant as to a mother and her child. Such simple and natural comparisons, which may occur to men in any age and country, suffice to explain the Greek personification of the corn as mother and daughter, and we need not cast about for more recondite theories. Be that as it may, the conception of the corn as a woman and a mother was certainly not peculiar to the ancient Greeks, but has been shared by them with many other races, as will appear abundantly from the instances which I shall cite in the following chapter.

[1] J. Spieth, *Die Ewe-Stämme* (Berlin, 1906), p. 313.
[2] (Sir) G. Grey, *Journals of Two Expeditions of Discovery in North-west and Western Australia* (London, 1841), ii. 292.

CHAPTER V

THE CORN-MOTHER AND THE CORN-MAIDEN IN NORTHERN EUROPE

IT has been argued by W. Mannhardt that the first part Suggested of Demeter's name is derived from an alleged Cretan word derivation of the name *deai*, "barley," and that accordingly Demeter means neither Demeter. more nor less than " Barley-mother " or " Corn-mother " ;[1] for the root of the word seems to have been applied to different kinds of grain by different branches of the Aryans.[2] As Crete appears to have been one of the most ancient seats of the worship of Demeter,[3] it would not be surprising if her name were of Cretan origin. But the etymology is open to serious objections,[4] and it is safer therefore to lay no stress on it. Be that as it may, we have found independent reasons for identifying Demeter as the Corn-mother, and of the two species of corn associated with her in Greek

---

[1] W. Mannhardt, *Mythologische Forschungen* (Strasburg, 1884), pp. 292 *sqq.* See above, p. 40, note[3].

[2] O. Schrader, *Reallexikon der indogermanischen Altertumskunde* (Strasburg, 1901), pp. 11, 289 ; *id., Sprachvergleichung und Urgeschichte*[2] (Jena, 1890), pp. 409, 422 ; *id., Sprachvergleichung und Urgeschichte*[3] (Jena, 1905-1907), ii. 188 *sq.* Compare V. Hehn, *Kulturpflanzen und Hausthiere in ihrem Uebergang aus Asien*[7] (Berlin, 1902), pp. 58 *sq.*

[3] Hesiod, *Theog.* 969 *sqq.* ; F. Lenormant, in Daremberg et Saglio, *Dictionnaire des Antiquités Grecques et Romaines*, i. 2, p. 1029 ; Kern, in Pauly - Wissowa's *Real - Encyclopädie*

der classischen Altertumswissenschaft, iv. 2, coll. 2720 *sq.*

[4] My friend Professor J. H. Moulton tells me that there is great doubt as to the existence of a word δηαί, "barley" (*Etymologicum Magnum*, p. 264, lines 12 *sq.*), and that the common form of Demeter's name, *Dāmāter* (except in Ionic and Attic) is inconsistent with η in the supposed Cretan form. "Finally if δηαί = ζειαί, you are bound to regard her as a Cretan goddess, or as arising in some other area where the dialect changed Indogermanic *y* into δ and not ζ: since Ionic and Attic have ζ, the two crucial letters of the name tell different tales" (Professor J. H. Moulton, in a letter to me, dated 19 December 1903).

religion, namely barley and wheat, the barley has perhaps the better claim to be her original element; for not only would it seem to have been the staple food of the Greeks in the Homeric age, but there are grounds for believing that it is one of the oldest, if not the very oldest, cereal cultivated by the Aryan race. Certainly the use of barley in the religious ritual of the ancient Hindoos as well as of the ancient Greeks furnishes a strong argument in favour of the great antiquity of its cultivation, which is known to have been practised by the lake-dwellers of the Stone Age in Europe.[1]

Analogies to the Corn-mother or Barley-mother of ancient Greece have been collected in great abundance by W. Mannhardt from the folk-lore of modern Europe. The following may serve as specimens.

The Corn-mother among the Germans and the Slavs.

In Germany the corn is very commonly personified under the name of the Corn-mother. Thus in spring, when the corn waves in the wind, the peasants say, " There comes the Corn-mother," or " The Corn-mother is running over the field," or " The Corn-mother is going through the corn."[2] When children wish to go into the fields to pull the blue corn-flowers or the red poppies, they are told not to do so, because the Corn-mother is sitting in the corn and will catch them.[3] Or again she is called, according to the crop, the Rye-mother or the Pea-mother, and children are warned against straying in the rye or among the peas by threats of the Rye-mother or the Pea-mother. In Norway also the Pea-mother is said to sit among the peas.[4] Similar expressions are current among the Slavs. The Poles and

---

[1] A. Kuhn, *Die Herabkunft des Feuers und des Göttertranks*[2] (Gütersloh, 1886), pp. 68 *sq.*; O. Schrader, *Reallexikon der indogermanischen Altertumskunde*, pp. 11, 12, 289; *id.*, *Sprachvergleichung und Urgeschichte*,[3] ii. 189, 191, 197 *sq.*; H. Hirt, *Die Indogermanen* (Strasburg, 1905-1907), i. 276 *sqq.* In the oldest Vedic ritual barley and not rice is the cereal chiefly employed. See H. Oldenberg, *Die Religion des Veda* (Berlin, 1894), p. 353. For evidence that barley was cultivated in Europe by the lake-dwellers of the Stone Age, see A. de Candolle, *Origin*

of Cultivated Plants (London, 1884), pp. 368, 369; R. Munro, *The Lake-dwellings of Europe* (London, Paris, and Melbourne, 1890), pp. 497 *sq.* According to Pliny (*Nat. Hist.* xviii. 72) barley was the oldest of all foods.

[2] W. Mannhardt, *Mythologische Forschungen* (Strasburg, 1884), p. 296. Compare O. Hartung, "Zur Volkskunde aus Anhalt," *Zeitschrift des Vereins für Volkskunde*, vii. (1897) p. 150.

[3] W. Mannhardt, *Mythologische Forschungen* (Strasburg, 1884), p. 297.

[4] *Ibid.* pp. 297 *sq.*

Czechs warn children against the Corn-mother who sits in the corn. Or they call her the old Corn-woman, and say that she sits in the corn and strangles the children who tread it down.[1] The Lithuanians say, "The Old Rye-woman sits in the corn."[2] Again the Corn-mother is believed to make the crop grow. Thus in the neighbour-hood of Magdeburg it is sometimes said, "It will be a good year for flax ; the Flax-mother has been seen." At Dinkelsbühl, in Bavaria, down to the latter part of the nine-teenth century, people believed that when the crops on a particular farm compared unfavourably with those of the neighbourhood, the reason was that the Corn-mother had punished the farmer for his sins.[3] In a village of Styria it is said that the Corn-mother, in the shape of a female puppet made out of the last sheaf of corn and dressed in white, may be seen at midnight in the corn-fields, which she fertilises by passing through them ; but if she is angry with a farmer, she withers up all his corn.[4]

Further, the Corn-mother plays an important part in harvest customs. She is believed to be present in the handful of corn which is left standing last on the field ; and with the cutting of this last handful she is caught, or driven away, or killed. In the first of these cases, the last sheaf is carried joyfully home and honoured as a divine being. It is placed in the barn, and at threshing the corn-spirit appears again.[5] In the Hanoverian district of Hadeln the reapers stand round the last sheaf and beat it with sticks in order to drive the Corn-mother out of it. They call to each other, "There she is! hit her! Take care she doesn't catch you!" The beating goes on till the grain is com-pletely threshed out ; then the Corn-mother is believed to be driven away.[6] In the neighbourhood of Danzig the person who cuts the last ears of corn makes them into a doll, which is called the Corn-mother or the Old Woman and is brought home on the last waggon.[7] In some parts

The Corn-mother in the last sheaf.

[1] *Ibid.* p. 299. Compare R. Andree, *Braunschweiger Volkskunde* (Bruns-wick, 1896), p. 281.
[2] W. Mannhardt, *Mythologische Forschungen*, p. 300.
[3] W. Mannhardt, *Mythologische Forschungen*, p. 310.
[4] *Ibid.* pp. 310 *sq.* Compare O. Hartung, *l.c.*
[5] W. Mannhardt, *op. cit.* p. 316.
[6] *Ibid.* p. 316.
[7] *Ibid.* pp. 316 *sq.*

of Holstein the last sheaf is dressed in woman's clothes and called the Corn-mother. It is carried home on the last waggon, and then thoroughly drenched with water. The drenching with water is doubtless a rain-charm.[1] In the district of Bruck in Styria the last sheaf, called the Corn-mother, is made up into the shape of a woman by the oldest married woman in the village, of an age from fifty to fifty-five years. The finest ears are plucked out of it and made into a wreath, which, twined with flowers, is carried on her head by the prettiest girl of the village to the farmer or squire, while the Corn-mother is laid down in the barn to keep off the mice.[2] In other villages of the same district the Corn-mother, at the close of harvest, is carried by two lads at the top of a pole. They march behind the girl who wears the wreath to the squire's house, and while he receives the wreath and hangs it up in the hall, the Corn-mother is placed on the top of a pile of wood, where she is the centre of the harvest supper and dance. Afterwards she is hung up in the barn and remains there till the threshing is over. The man who gives the last stroke at threshing is called the son of the Corn-mother; he is tied up in the Corn-mother, beaten, and carried through the village. The wreath is dedicated in church on the following Sunday; and on Easter Eve the grain is rubbed out of it by a seven-years-old girl and scattered amongst the young corn. At Christmas the straw of the wreath is placed in the manger to make the cattle thrive.[3] Here the fertilising power of the Corn-mother is plainly brought out by scattering the seed taken from her body (for the wreath is made out of the Corn-mother) among the new corn; and her influence over animal life is indicated by placing the straw in the manger. At Westerhüsen, in Saxony, the last corn cut is made in the shape of a woman decked with ribbons and cloth. It is fastened to a pole and brought home on the last waggon. One of the people in the waggon keeps waving the pole, so that the figure moves as if alive. It is placed on the threshing-floor, and stays there till the threshing is done.[4]

Fertilising power of the Corn-mother.

---

[1] *Ibid.* p. 317. As to such rain-charms see *Adonis, Attis, Osiris,* Second Edition, pp. 195-197.

[2] W. Mannhardt, *Mythologische Forschungen,* p. 317.

[3] *Ibid.* pp. 317 *sq.*

[4] *Ibid.* p. 318.

Amongst the Slavs also the last sheaf is known as the Rye - mother, the Wheat - mother, the Oats - mother, the Barley-mother, and so on, according to the crop. In the district of Tarnow, Galicia, the wreath made out of the last stalks is called the Wheat-mother, Rye-mother, or Pea-mother. It is placed on a girl's head and kept till spring, when some of the grain is mixed with the seed-corn.[1] Here again the fertilising power of the Corn-mother is indicated. In France, also, in the neighbourhood of Auxerre, the last sheaf goes by the name of the Mother of the Wheat, Mother of the Barley, Mother of the Rye, or Mother of the Oats. They leave it standing in the field till the last waggon is about to wend homewards. Then they make a puppet out of it, dress it with clothes belonging to the farmer, and adorn it with a crown and a blue or white scarf. A branch of a tree is stuck in the breast of the puppet, which is now called the Ceres. At the dance in the evening the Ceres is set in the middle of the floor, and the reaper who reaped fastest dances round it with the prettiest girl for his partner. After the dance a pyre is made. All the girls, each wearing a wreath, strip the puppet, pull it to pieces, and place it on the pyre, along with the flowers with which it was adorned. Then the girl who was the first to finish reaping sets fire to the pile, and all pray that Ceres may give a fruitful year. Here, as Mannhardt observes, the old custom has remained intact, though the name Ceres is a bit of schoolmaster's learning.[2] In Upper Brittany the last sheaf is always made into human shape ; but if the farmer is a married man, it is made double and consists of a little corn-puppet placed inside of a large one. This is called the Mother-sheaf. It is delivered to the farmer's wife, who unties it and gives drink-money in return.[3]

Sometimes the last sheaf is called, not the Corn-mother, but the Harvest - mother or the Great Mother. In the province of Osnabrück, Hanover, it is called the Harvest-mother ; it is made up in female form, and then the reapers dance about with it. In some parts of Westphalia the last sheaf at the rye-harvest is made especially heavy by fastening

---

[1] *Ibid.*

[2] W. Mannhardt, *op. cit.* pp. 318 *sq.*

[3] P. Sébillot, *Coutumes populaires de la Haute-Bretagne* (Paris, 1886), p. 306.

stones in it. They bring it home on the last waggon and call it the Great Mother, though they do not fashion it into any special shape. In the district of Erfurt a very heavy sheaf, not necessarily the last, is called the Great Mother, and is carried on the last waggon to the barn, where all hands lift it down amid a fire of jokes.[1]

The Grand-mother in the last sheaf. Sometimes again the last sheaf is called the Grand-mother, and is adorned with flowers, ribbons, and a woman's apron. In East Prussia, at the rye or wheat harvest, the reapers call out to the woman who binds the last sheaf, "You are getting the Old Grandmother." In the neighbourhood of Magdeburg the men and women servants strive who shall get the last sheaf, called the Grandmother. Who-ever gets it will be married in the next year, but his or her spouse will be old; if a girl gets it, she will marry a widower; if a man gets it, he will marry an old crone. In Silesia the Grandmother—a huge bundle made up of three or four sheaves by the person who tied the last sheaf—was formerly fashioned into a rude likeness of the human form.[2] In the neighbourhood of Belfast the last sheaf sometimes goes by the name of the Granny. It is not cut in the usual way, but all the reapers throw their sickles at it and try to bring it down. It is plaited and kept till the (next?) autumn. Whoever gets it will marry in the course of the year.[3]

The Old Woman or the Old Man in the last sheaf. Oftener the last sheaf is called the Old Woman or the Old Man. In Germany it is frequently shaped and dressed as a woman, and the person who cuts it or binds it is said to "get the Old Woman."[4] At Altisheim, in Swabia, when all the corn of a farm has been cut except a single strip, all the reapers stand in a row before the strip; each cuts his share rapidly, and he who gives the last cut "has the Old Woman."[5] When the sheaves are being set up in heaps, the person who gets hold of the Old Woman, which is the largest and thickest of all the sheaves, is jeered at by the rest, who call out to him, "He has the Old Woman and must keep her."[6] The woman who binds the last sheaf is

[1] W. Mannhardt, *Mythologische Forschungen*, p. 319.

[2] W. Mannhardt, *Mythologische Forschungen*, p. 320.

[3] *Ibid.* p. 321.

[4] *Ibid.* pp. 321, 323, 325 *sq.*

[5] *Ibid.* p. 323; F. Panzer, *Beitrag zur deutschen Mythologie* (Munich, 1848-1855), ii. p. 219, § 403.

[6] W. Mannhardt, *op. cit.* p. 325.

sometimes herself called the Old Woman, and it is said that she will be married in the next year.[1] In Neusaass, West Prussia, both the last sheaf—which is dressed up in jacket, hat, and ribbons—and the woman who binds it are called the Old Woman. Together they are brought home on the last waggon and are drenched with water.[2] In various parts of North Germany the last sheaf at harvest is made up into a human effigy and called "the Old Man"; and the woman who bound it is said "to have the Old Man."[3] At Hornkampe, near Tiegenhof (West Prussia), when a man or woman lags behind the rest in binding the corn, the other reapers dress up the last sheaf in the form of a man or woman, and this figure goes by the laggard's name, as "the old Michael," "the idle Trine." It is brought home on the last waggon, and, as it nears the house, the bystanders call out to the laggard, "You have got the Old Woman and must keep her."[4] In Brandenburg the young folks on the harvest-field race towards a sheaf and jump over it. The last to jump over it has to carry a straw puppet, adorned with ribbons, to the farmer and deliver it to him while he recites some verses. Of the person who thus carries the puppet it is said that "he has the Old Man." Probably the puppet is or used to be made out of the last corn cut.[5] In many districts of Saxony the last sheaf used to be adorned with ribbons and set upright so as to look like a man. It was then known as "the Old Man," and the young women brought it back in procession to the farm, singing as they went, "Now we are bringing the Old Man."[6]

In West Prussia, when the last rye is being raked together, the women and girls hurry with the work, for none of them likes to be the last and to get "the Old Man," that is, a puppet made out of the last sheaf, which must be carried before the other reapers by the person who was the last

The Old Man or the Old Woman in the last sheaf.

---

[1] *Ibid.* p. 323.

[2] *Ibid.*

[3] A. Kuhn and W. Schwartz, *Norddeutsche Sagen, Märchen und Gebräuche* (Leipsic, 1848), pp. 396 *sq.*, 399 ; K. Bartsch, *Sagen, Märchen und Gebräuche aus Meklenburg* (Vienna, 1879-1880), ii. 309, § 1494.

[4] W. Mannhardt, *op. cit.* pp. 323 *sq.*

[5] H. Prahn, "Glaube und Brauch in der Mark Brandenburg," *Zeitschrift des Vereins für Volkskunde*, i. (1891) pp. 186 *sq.*

[6] K. Haupt, *Sagenbuch der Lausitz* (Leipsic, 1862-1863), i. p. 233, No. 277 note.

to finish.[1]   In Silesia the last sheaf is called the Old Woman
or the Old Man and is the theme of many jests ; it is made
unusually large and is sometimes weighted with a stone.
At Girlachsdorf, near Reichenbach, when this heavy sheaf is
lifted into the waggon, they say, " That is the Old Man
whom we sought for so long."[2]   Among the Germans of
West Bohemia the man who cuts the last corn is said to
" have the Old Man."   In former times it used to be
customary to put a wreath on his head and to play all kinds
of pranks with him, and at the harvest supper he was given
the largest portion.[3]   At Wolletz in Westphalia the last
sheaf at harvest is called the Old Man, and being made up
into the likeness of a man and decorated with flowers it is
presented to the farmer, who in return prepares a feast for the
reapers.   About Unna, in Westphalia, the last sheaf at
harvest is made unusually large, and stones are inserted to
increase its weight.   It is called *de greaute meaur* (the Grey
Mother?), and when it is brought home on the waggon
water is thrown on the harvesters who accompany it.[4]
Among the Wends the man or woman who binds the last
sheaf at wheat harvest is said to " have the Old Man."
A puppet is made out of the wheaten straw and ears in the
likeness of a man and decked with flowers.   The person
who bound the last sheaf must carry the Old Man home,
while the rest laugh and jeer at him.   The puppet is hung
up in the farmhouse and remains till a new Old Man is
made at the next harvest.[5]   At the close of the harvest the
Arabs of Moab bury the last sheaf in a grave in the corn-
field, saying as they do so, " We are burying the Old Man,"
or " The Old Man is dead."[6]

Identifica-
tion of the
harvester
with the
corn- spirit.

In some of these customs, as Mannhardt has remarked,
the person who is called by the same name as the last sheaf
and sits beside it on the last waggon is obviously identified

[1] R. Krause, *Sitten, Gebräuche und
Aberglauben in Westpreussen* (Berlin,
preface dated March 1904), p. 51.
   [2] P. Drechsler, *Sitte, Brauch und
Volksglaube in Schlesien* (Leipsic, 1903-
1906), ii. 65 *sqq.*
   [3] A. John, *Sitte, Brauch und
Volksglaube im deutschen Westböhmen*
(Prague, 1905), p. 189.

[4] A. Kuhn, *Sagen, Gebräuche und
Märchen aus Westfalen* (Leipsic, 1859),
ii. 184, §§ 512 b, 514.
   [5] W. von Schulenburg, *Wendisches
Volksthum* (Berlin, 1882), p. 147.
   [6] A. Jaussen, *Coutumes des Arabes
au pays de Moab* (Paris, 1908), pp.
252 *sq.*

with it ; he or she represents the corn-spirit which has been
caught in the last sheaf ; in other words, the corn-spirit is
represented in duplicate, by a human being and by a sheaf.[1]
The identification of the person with the sheaf is made still
clearer by the custom of wrapping up in the last sheaf the
person who cuts or binds it. Thus at Hermsdorf in Silesia
it used to be the regular practice to tie up in the last sheaf
the woman who had bound it.[2] At Weiden, in Bavaria, it
is the cutter, not the binder, of the last sheaf who is tied
up in it.[3] Here the person wrapt up in the corn represents the corn-spirit, exactly as a person wrapt in branches
or leaves represents the tree-spirit.[4]

The last sheaf, designated as the Old Woman, is often   The last
distinguished from the other sheaves by its size and weight.   sheaf made
Thus in some villages of West Prussia the Old Woman is   large and
made twice as long and thick as a common sheaf, and a   heavy.
stone is fastened in the middle of it. Sometimes it is made
so heavy that a man can barely lift it.[5] At Alt-Pillau,
in Samland, eight or nine sheaves are often tied together
to make the Old Woman, and the man who sets it up
grumbles at its weight.[6] At Itzgrund, in Saxe-Coburg,
the last sheaf, called the Old Woman, is made large with
the express intention of thereby securing a good crop next
year.[7] Thus the custom of making the last sheaf unusually
large or heavy is a charm, working by sympathetic magic,
to ensure a large and heavy crop at the following harvest.
In Denmark also the last sheaf is made larger than the
others, and is called the Old Rye-woman or the Old Barley-
woman. No one likes to bind it, because whoever does so
will be sure, they think, to marry an old man or an old
woman. Sometimes the last wheat-sheaf, called the Old
Wheat-woman, is made up in human shape, with head,

[1] W. Mannhardt, *Mythologische
Forschungen*, p. 324.

[2] *Ibid.* p. 320.

[3] W. Mannhardt, *op. cit.* p. 325.

[4] See *The Magic Art and the
Evolution of Kings*, ii. 74 *sqq.*

[5] W. Mannhardt, *op. cit.* p. 324.

[6] *Ibid.* pp. 324 *sq.*

[7] *Ibid.* p. 325. The author of *Die*

gestriegelte Rockenphilosophie (Chem-
nitz, 1759) mentions (p. 891) the
German superstition that the last sheaf
should be made large in order that
all the sheaves next year may be of
the same size ; but he says nothing as
to the shape or name of the sheaf.
Compare A. John, *Sitte, Brauch und
Volksglaube im deutschen Westböhmen*
(Prague, 1905), p. 188.

arms, and legs, and being dressed in clothes is carried home on the last waggon, while the harvesters sit beside it drinking and huzzaing.[1]   Of the person who binds the last sheaf it is said, " She or he is the Old Rye-woman." [2]

The Carlin and the Maiden in Scotland.

In Scotland, when the last corn was cut after Hallowmas, the female figure made out of it was sometimes called the Carlin or Carline, that is, the Old Woman.   But if cut before Hallowmas, it was called the Maiden ; if cut after sunset, it was called the Witch, being supposed to bring bad luck.[3]   Among the Highlanders of Scotland the last corn cut at harvest is known either as the Old Wife (*Cailleach*) or as the Maiden ; on the whole the former name seems to prevail in the western and the latter in the central and eastern districts.   Of the Maiden we shall speak presently ; here we are dealing with the Old Wife.   The following general account of the custom is given by a careful and well-informed enquirer, the Rev. J. G. Campbell, minister of the remote Hebridean island of Tiree : " The Harvest Old Wife (*a Chailleach*).—In harvest, there was a struggle to escape from being the last done with the shearing,[4] and when tillage in common existed, instances were known of a ridge being left unshorn (no person would claim it) because of it being behind the rest.   The fear entertained was that of having the ' famine of the farm ' (*gort a bhaile*), in the shape of an imaginary old woman (*cailleach*), to feed till next harvest.   Much emulation and amusement arose from the fear of this old woman. . . . The first done made a doll of some blades of corn, which was called the ' old wife,' and sent it to his nearest neighbour.   He in turn, when ready, passed it to another still less expeditious, and the person it last remained with had ' the old woman ' to keep for that year." [5]

The Old Wife (*Cail- leach*) at harvest in the High- lands of Scotland.

The Old Wife (*Cailleach*) in the last

To illustrate the custom by examples, in Bernera, on the west of Lewis, the harvest rejoicing goes by the name of the Old Wife (*Cailleach*) from the last sheaf

[1] W. Mannhardt, *op. cit.* p. 327.

[2] *Ibid.* p. 328.

[3] J. Jamieson, *Dictionary of the Scottish Language*, New Edition (Paisley, 1879-1882), iii. 206, *s.v.*

" Maiden," ; W. Mannhardt, *Mytholo- gische Forschungen*, p. 326.
[4] That is, with the reaping.
[5] Rev. J. G. Campbell, *Superstitions of the Highlands and Islands of Scotland* (Glasgow, 1900), pp. 243 *sq.*

cut, whether in a township, farm, or croft. Where there
are a number of crofts beside each other, there is always
great rivalry as to who shall first finish reaping, and so
have the Old Wife before his neighbours. Some people
even go out on a clear night to reap their fields after their
neighbours have retired to rest, in order that they may have
the Old Wife first. More neighbourly habits, however,
usually prevail, and as each finishes his own fields he goes
to the help of another, till the whole crop is cut. The reaping is still done with the sickle. When the corn has been
cut on all the crofts, the last sheaf is dressed up to look as
like an old woman as possible. She wears a white cap, a
dress, an apron, and a little shawl over the shoulders fastened
with a sprig of heather. The apron is tucked up to form a
pocket, which is stuffed with bread and cheese. A sickle,
stuck in the string of the apron at the back, completes her
equipment. This costume and outfit mean that the Old
Wife is ready to bear a hand in the work of harvesting.
At the feast which follows, the Old Wife is placed at the
head of the table, and as the whisky goes round each of the
company drinks to her, saying, " Here's to the one that has
helped us with the harvest." When the table has been
cleared away and dancing begins, one of the lads leads out
the Old Wife and dances with her ; and if the night is fine
the party will sometimes go out and march in a body to a
considerable distance, singing harvest-songs, while one of
them carries the Old Wife on his back. When the Harvest-
Home is over, the Old Wife is shorn of her gear and used
for ordinary purposes.[1] In the island of Islay the last corn
cut also goes by the name of the Old Wife (*Cailleach*), and
when she has done her duty at harvest she is hung up on the
wall and stays there till the time comes to plough the fields
for the next year's crop. Then she is taken down, and on the
first day when the men go to plough she is divided among
them by the mistress of the house. They take her in their
pockets and give her to the horses to eat when they reach
the field. This is supposed to secure good luck for the next
harvest, and is understood to be the proper end of the Old

[1] R. C. Maclagan, "Notes on folk-lore objects collected in Argyleshire,"
Folk-lore, vi. (1895) pp. 149 *sq.*

The Old Wife at harvest in Argyleshire.

Wife.[1] In Kintyre also the name of the Old Wife is given to the last corn cut.[2] On the shores of the beautiful Loch Awe, a long sheet of water, winding among soft green hills, above which the giant Ben Cruachan towers bold and rugged on the north, the harvest custom is somewhat different. The name of the Old Wife (*Cailleach*) is here bestowed, not on the last corn cut, but on the reaper who is the last to finish. He bears it as a term of reproach, and is not privileged to reap the last ears left standing. On the contrary, these are cut by the reaper who was the first to finish his *spagh* or strip (literally "claw"), and out of them is fashioned the Maiden, which is afterwards hung up, according to one statement, "for the purpose of preventing the death of horses in spring."[3] In the north-east of Scotland "the one who took the last of the grain from the field to the stackyard was called the 'winter.' Each one did what could be done to avoid being the last on the field, and when there were several on the field there was a race to get off. The unfortunate 'winter' was the subject of a good deal of teasing, and was dressed up in all the old clothes that could be gathered about the farm, and placed on the 'bink' to eat his supper."[4] So in Caithness the person who cuts the last sheaf is called Winter and retains the name till the next harvest.[5]

The reaper of the last sheaf called the Winter.

The Hag (*wrach*) at harvest in North Pembrokeshire.

Usages of the same sort are reported from Wales. Thus in North Pembrokeshire a tuft of the last corn cut, from six to twelve inches long, is plaited and goes by the name of the Hag (*wrach*) ; and quaint old customs used to be practised with it within the memory of many persons still alive. Great was the excitement among the reapers when the last patch of standing corn was reached. All in turn threw their sickles at it, and the one who succeeded in cutting it received a jug of home-brewed ale. The Hag (*wrach*) was then hurriedly made and taken to a neighbouring farm, where the reapers were still busy at their work. This was generally done by the ploughman ; but he had to be very

[1] R. C. Maclagan, *op. cit.* p. 151.
[2] R. C. Maclagan, *op. cit.* p. 149.
[3] *Ibid.* pp. 151 *sq.*
[4] Rev. Walter Gregor, *Notes on the*

Folk-lore of the North-East of Scotland (London, 1881), p. 182.
[5] Rev. J. Macdonald, *Religion and Myth* (London, 1893), p. 141.

careful not to be observed by his neighbours, for if they saw him coming and had the least suspicion of his errand they would soon make him retrace his steps. Creeping stealthily up behind a fence he waited till the foreman of his neighbour's reapers was just opposite him and within easy reach. Then he suddenly threw the Hag over the fence and, if possible, upon the foreman's sickle, crying out

> *" Boreu y codais i,*
> *Hwyr y dilynais i,*
> *Ar ei gwar hi."*

On that he took to his heels and made off as fast as he could run, and he was a lucky man if he escaped without being caught or cut by the flying sickles which the infuriated reapers hurled after him. In other cases the Hag was brought home to the farmhouse by one of the reapers. He did his best to bring it home dry and without being observed ; but he was apt to be roughly handled by the people of the house, if they suspected his errand. Sometimes they stripped him of most of his clothes, sometimes they would drench him with water which had been carefully stored in buckets and pans for the purpose. If, however, he succeeded in bringing the Hag in dry and unobserved, the master of the house had to pay him a small fine ; or sometimes a jug of beer " from the cask next to the wall," which seems to have commonly held the best beer, would be demanded by the bearer. The Hag was then carefully hung on a nail in the hall or elsewhere and kept there all the year. The custom of bringing in the Hag (*wrach*) into the house and hanging it up still exists in some farms of North Pembrokeshire, but the ancient ceremonies which have just been described are now discontinued.[1]

Similar customs at harvest were observed in South

---

[1] D. Jenkyn Evans, in an article entitled "The Harvest Customs of Pembrokeshire," *Pembroke County Guardian*, 7th December 1895. In a letter to me, dated 23 February 1901, Mr. E. S. Hartland was so good as to correct the Welsh words in the text. He tells me that they mean literally, "I rose early, I pursued late on her neck," and he adds : "The idea seems to be that the man has pursued the Hag or Corn-spirit to a later refuge, namely, his neighbour's field not yet completely reaped, and now he leaves her for the other reapers to catch. The proper form of the Welsh word for Hag is *Gwrach*. That is the radical from *gwr*, man ; *gwraig*, woman. *Wrach* is the 'middle mutation.' "

Pembrokeshire within living memory. In that part of the country there used to be a competition between neighbouring farms to see which would finish reaping first. The foreman of the reapers planned so as to finish the reaping in a corner of the field out of sight of the people on the next farm. There, with the last handful of corn cut, he would make two Old Women or Hags (*wrachs*). One of them he would send by a lad or other messenger to be laid secretly in the field where the neighbours were still at work cutting their corn. The messenger would disguise himself to look like a stranger, and jumping the fence and creeping through the corn he would lay the Hag (*wrach*) in a place where the reapers in reaping would be sure to find it. Having done so he fled for dear life, for were the reapers to catch him they would shut him up in a dark room and not let him out till he had cleaned all the muddy boots, shoes, and clogs in the house. The second Hag (*wrach*) was sent or taken by the foreman of the reapers to his master's farmhouse. Generally he tried to pop into the house unseen and lay the Hag on the kitchen table ; but if the people of the farm caught him before he laid it down, they used to drench him with water. If a foreman succeeded in getting both the Hags (*wrachs*) laid safe in their proper quarters, one at home, the other on a neighbour's farm, without interruption, it was deemed a great honour.[1]

In County Antrim, down to some years ago, when the sickle was finally expelled by the reaping machine, the few stalks of corn left standing last on the field were plaited together ; then the reapers, blindfolded, threw their sickles at the plaited corn, and whoever happened to cut it through took it home with him and put it over his door. This bunch of corn was called the Carley [2]—probably the same word as Carlin.

Similar customs are observed by Slavonic peoples. Thus in Poland the last sheaf is commonly called the Baba, that is, the Old Woman. "In the last sheaf," it is said, "sits the Baba." The sheaf itself is also called the Baba, and is

[1] M. S. Clark, "An old South Pembrokeshire Harvest Custom," *Folk-lore*, xv. (1904) pp. 194-196.

[2] Communicated by my friend Professor W. Ridgeway.

sometimes composed of twelve smaller sheaves lashed together.[1]   In some parts of Bohemia the Baba, made out of
the last sheaf, has the figure of a woman with a great straw
hat.   It is carried home on the last harvest-waggon and
delivered, along with a garland, to the farmer by two girls.
In binding the sheaves the women strive not to be last, for
she who binds the last sheaf will have a child next year.[2]
The last sheaf is tied up with others into a large bundle, and
a green branch is stuck on the top of it.[3]   Sometimes the
harvesters call out to the woman who binds the last sheaf,
"She has the Baba," or "She is the Baba."   She has then
to make a puppet, sometimes in female, sometimes in male
form, out of the corn; the puppet is occasionally dressed
with clothes, often with flowers and ribbons only.   The
cutter of the last stalks, as well as the binder of the last
sheaf, was also called Baba ; and a doll, called the Harvest-
woman, was made out of the last sheaf and adorned with
ribbons.   The oldest reaper had to dance, first with this doll,
and then with the farmer's wife.[4]   In the district of Cracow,
when a man binds the last sheaf, they say, "The Grandfather
is sitting in it " ; when a woman binds it, they say, "The Baba
is sitting in it," and the woman herself is wrapt up in the
sheaf, so that only her head projects out of it.   Thus encased in the sheaf, she is carried on the last harvest-waggon
to the house, where she is drenched with water by the whole
family.   She remains in the sheaf till the dance is over, and
for a year she retains the name of Baba.[5]

In Lithuania the name for the last sheaf is Boba (Old   The Old
Woman), answering to the Polish name Baba.   The Boba is   Woman
                                                           (the Baba)
said to sit in the corn which is left standing last.[6]   The   at harvest
person who binds the last sheaf or digs the last potato is the   in Lithu-
                                                                 ania.
subject of much banter, and receives and long retains the
name of the Old Rye-woman or the Old Potato-woman.[7]
The last sheaf—the Boba—is made into the form of a
woman, carried solemnly through the village on the last
harvest-waggon, and drenched with water at the farmer's
house ; then every one dances with it.[8]

[1] W. Mannhardt, *Mythologische*
Forschungen, p. 328.
[2] W. Mannhardt, *op. cit.* p. 238.
[3] *Ibid.* pp. 328 *sq.*

[4] *Ibid.* p. 329.
[5] *Ibid.* p. 330.   [6] *Ibid.*
[7] W. Mannhardt, *op. cit.* p. 331.
[8] *Ibid.*

The Corn-
queen and
the
Harvest-
queen.

In Russia also the last sheaf is often shaped and dressed as a woman, and carried with dance and song to the farm-house. Out of the last sheaf the Bulgarians make a doll which they call the Corn-queen or Corn-mother ; it is dressed in a woman's shirt, carried round the village, and then thrown into the river in order to secure plenty of rain and dew for the next year's crop. Or it is burned and the ashes strewn on the fields, doubtless to fertilise them.[1] The name Queen, as applied to the last sheaf, has its analogies in central and northern Europe. Thus, in the Salzburg district of Austria, at the end of the harvest a great procession takes place, in which a Queen of the Corn-ears (*Ährenkönigin*) is drawn along in a little carriage by young fellows.[2] The custom of the Harvest Queen appears to have been common in England. Brand quotes from Hutchinson's *History of Northumberland* the following : " I have seen, in some places, an image apparelled in great finery, crowned with flowers, a sheaf of corn placed under her arm, and a scycle in her hand, carried out of the village in the morning of the conclusive reaping day, with music and much clamour of the reapers, into the field, where it stands fixed on a pole all day, and when the reaping is done, is brought home in like manner. This they call the Harvest Queen, and it represents the Roman Ceres." [3] Again, the traveller Dr. E. D. Clarke tells us that " even in the town of Cambridge, and centre of our University, such curious remains of antient customs may be noticed, in different seasons of the year, which pass without observation. The custom of blowing horns upon the first of May (Old Style) is derived from a festival in honour of Diana. At the *Hawkie*, as it is called, or Harvest Home, I have seen a clown dressed in woman's clothes, having his face painted, his head decorated with ears of corn, and bearing about him other symbols of Ceres, carried in a waggon, with great pomp and loud shouts, through the streets, the horses being covered with white sheets : and when I inquired the meaning of the ceremony, was answered by the people that they were drawing the Morgay (ΜΗΤΗΡ ΓΗ)

[1] *Ibid.* p. 332.
[2] Th. Vernaleken, *Mythen und Bräuche des Volkes in Oesterreich* (Vienna, 1859), p. 310.
[3] Hutchinson, *History of Northumberland*, ii. *ad finem*, 17, quoted by J. Brand, *Popular Antiquities of Great Britain*, ii. 20, Bohn's edition.

or Harvest Queen." [1]   Milton must have been familiar with
the custom of the Harvest Queen, for in *Paradise Lost* [2]
he says :—

> "*Adam the while*
> *Waiting desirous her return, had wove*
> *Of choicest flow'rs a garland to adorn*
> *Her tresses, and her rural labours crown,*
> *As reapers oft are wont their harvest-queen.*"

Often customs of this sort are practised, not on the
harvest-field but on the threshing-floor.   The spirit of the
corn, fleeing before the reapers as they cut down the
ripe grain, quits the reaped corn and takes refuge in the
barn, where it appears in the last sheaf threshed, either to
perish under the blows of the flail or to flee thence to the
still unthreshed corn of a neighbouring farm. [3]   Thus the last
corn to be threshed is called the Mother-Corn or the Old
Woman.   Sometimes the person who gives the last stroke
with the flail is called the Old Woman, and is wrapt in the
straw of the last sheaf, or has a bundle of straw fastened on
his back.   Whether wrapt in the straw or carrying it on his
back, he is carted through the village amid general laughter.
In some districts of Bavaria, Thüringen, and elsewhere, the
man who threshes the last sheaf is said to have the Old
Woman or the Old Corn-woman ; he is tied up in straw,
carried or carted about the village, and set down at last

The corn-spirit as the Old Woman or Old Man at threshing.

---

[1] E. D. Clarke, *Travels in Various Countries of Europe, Asia, and Africa,* Part ii., Section First, Second Edition (London, 1813), p. 229.   Perhaps *Morgay* (which Clarke absurdly explains as μητὴρ γῆ) is a mistake for *Hawkie* or *Hockey.*   The waggon in which the last corn was brought from the harvest field was called the *hockey* cart or *hock* cart.   In a poem called "The Hock-cart or Harvest Home" Herrick has described the joyous return of the laden cart drawn by horses swathed in white sheets and attended by a merry crowd, some of whom kissed or stroked the sheaves, while others pranked them with oak leaves. See further J. Brand, *Popular Antiquities,* ii. 22 *sq.,* Bohn's edition. The name *Hockey* or *Hawkie* is no doubt the same with the German

hôkelmei, hörkelmei, or *harkelmei,* which in Westphalia is applied to a green bush or tree set up in the field at the end of harvest and brought home in the last waggon-load ; the man who carries it into the farmhouse is sometimes drenched with water.   See A. Kuhn, *Sagen, Gebräuche und Märchen aus Westfalen* (Leipsic, 1859), ii. 178-180, §§ 494-497.   The word is thought to be derived from the Low German *hokk* (plural *hokken*), "a heap of sheaves." See Joseph Wright, *English Dialect Dictionary,* iii. (London, 1902) p. 190, *s.v.* "Hockey," from which it appears that in England the word has been in use in Yorkshire, Cumberland, and Suffolk.

[2] Book ix. lines 838-842.

[3] W. Mannhardt, *Mythologische Forschungen,* pp. 333 *sq.*

on the dunghill, or taken to the threshing-floor of a neighbour-ing farmer who has not finished his threshing.[1]   In Poland the man who gives the last stroke at threshing is called Baba (Old Woman) ; he is wrapt in corn and wheeled through the village.[2]   Sometimes in Lithuania the last sheaf is not threshed, but is fashioned into female shape and carried to the barn of a neighbour who has not finished his threshing.[3]

The man who gives the last stroke at threshing is called the Corn-fool the Oats-fool, etc.

At Chorinchen, near Neustadt, the man who gives the last stroke at threshing is said to "get the Old Man."[4] In various parts of Austrian Silesia he is called the corn-fool, the oats-fool, and so forth according to the crop, and retains the name till the next kind of grain has been reaped. Sometimes he is called the *Klöppel* or mallet.   He is much ridiculed and in the Bennisch district he is dressed out in the threshing-implements and obliged to carry them about the farmyard to the amusement of his fellows.   In Dobischwald the man who gives the last stroke at threshing has to carry a log or puppet of wood wrapt in straw to a neighbour who has not yet finished his threshing.   There he throws his burden into the barn, crying, " There you have the Mallet (*Klöppel*)," and makes off as fast as he can. If they catch him, they tie the puppet on his back, and he is known as the Mallet (*Klöppel*) for the whole of the year ; he may be the Corn-mallet or the Wheat-mallet or so forth according to the particular crop.[5]

The man who gives the last stroke at threshing is said to get the Old Woman or the Old Man.

About Berneck, in Upper Franken, the man who gives the last stroke at threshing runs away.   If the others catch him, he gets " the Old Woman," that is, the largest dumpling, which elsewhere is baked in human shape.   The custom of setting a dumpling baked in the form of an old woman before the man who has given the last stroke at threshing is also observed in various parts of Middle Franken.   Some-times the excised genitals of a calf are served up to him at table.[6]   At Langenbielau in Silesia the last sheaf, which

[1] *Ibid.* p. 334.
[2] W. Mannhardt, *Mythologische For-schungen*, p. 334.   [3] *Ibid.* p. 336.
[4] A. Kuhn and W. Schwartz, *Norddeutsche Sagen, Märchen und Gebräuche* (Leipsic, 1848), p. 397.

[5] A. Peter, *Völksthümliches aus Öster-reichisch - Schlesien* (Troppau, 1865-1867), ii. 270.
[6] *Bavaria Landes- und Volkskunde des Königreichs Bayern*, iii. (Munich, 1865) pp. 344, 969.

is called "the Old Man," is threshed separately and the corn ground into meal and baked into a loaf. This loaf is believed to possess healing virtue and to bring a blessing ; hence none but members of the family may partake of it. At Wittichenau, in the district of Hoyerswerda (Silesia), when the threshing is ended, some of the straw of "the Old Man" is carried to a neighbour who has not yet finished his threshing, and the bearer is rewarded with a gratuity.[1] Among the Germans of the Falkenauer district in West Bohemia the man who gives the last stroke at threshing gets "the Old Man," a hideous scarecrow, tied on his back. If threshing is still proceeding at another farm, he may go thither and rid himself of his burden, but must take care not to be caught. In this way a farmer who is behind-hand with his threshing may receive several such scarecrows, and so become the target for many gibes. Among the Germans of the Planer district in West Bohemia, the man who gives the last stroke at threshing is himself called "the Old Man." Similarly at flax-dressing in Silberberg (West Bohemia), the woman who is the last to finish her task is said to get the Old Man, and a cake baked in human form is served up to her at supper.[2] The Wends of Saxony say of the man who gives the last stroke at threshing that "he has struck the Old Man" (wón je stareho bil), and he is obliged to carry a straw puppet to a neighbour, who has not yet finished his threshing, where he throws the puppet unobserved over the fence.[3] In some parts of Sweden, when a stranger woman appears on the threshing-floor, a flail is put round her body, stalks of corn are wound round her neck, a crown of ears is placed on her head, and the threshers call out, "Behold the Corn-woman." Here the stranger woman, thus suddenly appearing, is taken to be the corn-spirit who has just been expelled by the flails from the corn-stalks.[4] In other cases the farmer's wife represents the corn-spirit. Thus in the Commune of Saligné, Canton de Poiret (Vendée), the farmer's wife,

The Corn-woman at threshing.

[1] P. Drechsler, Sitte, Brauch und Volksglaube in Schlesien (Leipsic, 1903-1906), ii. 67.
[2] A. John, Sitte, Brauch und Volksglaube im deutschen Westböhmen (Prague, 1905), pp. 193, 194, 197.
[3] R. Wuttke, Sächsische Volkskunde? (Dresden, 1901), p. 360.
[4] W. Mannhardt, Mythologische Forschungen, p. 336.

along with the last sheaf, is tied up in a sheet, placed on a litter, and carried to the threshing machine, under which she is shoved. Then the woman is drawn out and the sheaf is threshed by itself, but the woman is tossed in the sheet, as if she were being winnowed.[1] It would be impossible to express more clearly the identification of the woman with the corn than by this graphic imitation of threshing and winnowing her. Mitigated forms of the custom are observed in various places. Thus among the Germans of Schüttarschen in West Bohemia it was customary at the close of the threshing to " throttle " the farmer's wife by squeezing her neck between the arms of a flail till she consented to bake a special kind of cake called a *drischala* (from *dreschen*, " to thresh ").[2] A similar custom of " throttling " the farmer's wife at the threshing is practised in some parts of Bavaria, only there the pressure is applied by means of a straw rope instead of a flail.[3]

The corn-spirit as a child at harvest.

In these customs the spirit of the ripe corn is regarded as old, or at least as of mature age. Hence the names of Mother, Grandmother, Old Woman, and so forth. But in other cases the corn-spirit is conceived as young. Thus at Saldern, near Wolfenbuttel, when the rye has been reaped, three sheaves are tied together with a rope so as to make a puppet with the corn ears for a head. This puppet is called the Maiden or the Corn-maiden (*Kornjunfer*).[4] Sometimes the corn-spirit is conceived as a child who is separated from its mother by the stroke of the sickle. This last view appears in the Polish custom of calling out to the man who cuts the last handful of corn, " You have cut the navel-string."[5] In some districts of West Prussia the figure made out of the last sheaf is called the Bastard, and a boy is wrapt up in it. The woman who binds the last sheaf and represents the Corn-mother is told that she is about to be brought to bed ; she cries like a woman in travail, and an old woman in the character of

[1] *Ibid.* p. 336 ; W. Mannhardt, *Baumkultus*, p. 612.

[2] A. John, *Sitte, Brauch und Volksglaube im deutschen Westböhmen* (Prague, 1905), p. 194.

[3] E. H. Meyer, *Badisches Volksleben*

(Strasburg, 1900), p. 437.

[4] A. Kuhn, *Sagen, Gebräuche und Märchen aus Westfalen* (Leipsic, 1859), ii. 184 *sq.*, § 515.

[5] W. Mannhardt, *Die Korndämonen* (Berlin, 1868), p. 28.

grandmother acts as midwife. At last a cry is raised that
the child is born; whereupon the boy who is tied up in the
sheaf whimpers and squalls like an infant. The grandmother wraps a sack, in imitation of swaddling bands, round
the pretended baby, who is carried joyfully to the barn, lest
he should catch cold in the open air.[1] In other parts of North
Germany the last sheaf, or the puppet made out of it, is
called the Child, the Harvest-Child, and so on, and they
call out to the woman who binds the last sheaf, "you are
getting the child."[2]

In the north of England, particularly in the counties of
Northumberland, Durham, and Yorkshire, the last corn cut
on the field at harvest is or used to be variously known
as the *mell* or the *kirn*, of which *kern* and *churn* are merely
local or dialectical variations. The corn so cut is either
plaited or made up into a doll-like figure, which goes by
the name of the mell-doll or the kirn-doll, or the kirn-baby,
and is brought home with rejoicings at the end of the
harvest.[3] In the North Riding of Yorkshire the last sheaf
gathered in is called the Mell-sheaf, and the expression
"We've gotten wer mell" is as much as to say "The
Harvest is finished." Formerly a Mell-doll was made out of
a sheaf of corn decked with flowers and wrapped in such of
the reapers' garments as could be spared. It was carried with
music and dancing to the scene of the harvest-supper, which
was called the mell-supper.[4] In the north of Yorkshire

The last
corn cut
called the
mell, the
kirn, or
the *churn*
in various
parts of
England.

---

[1] W. Mannhardt, *l.c.*

[2] W. Mannhardt, *l.c.*

[3] Joseph Wright, *English Dialect
Dictionary*, vol. i. (London, 1898)
p. 605 *s.v.* "Churn"; *id.*, vol. iii.
(London, 1902) p. 453 *s.v.* "Kirn";
id. vol. iv. (London, 1903) pp. 82 *sq.*
Sir James Murray, editor of the *New
English Dictionary*, kindly informs me
that the popular etymology which
identifies *kern* or *kirn* in this sense with
corn is entirely mistaken; and that
"baby" or "babbie" in the same
phrase means only "doll," not
"infant." He writes, "*Kirn-babbie*
does not mean 'corn-baby,' but
merely *kirn-doll, harvest-home doll.*
Bab, babbie was even in my youth the
regular name for 'doll' in the district,

as it was formerly in England; the
only woman who sold dolls in Hawick
early in the [nineteenth] century, and
whose toy-shop all bairns knew, was
known as 'Betty o' the Babs,' Betty
of the dolls."

[4] W. Henderson, *Folk-lore of the
Northern Counties of England* (London,
1879), pp. 88 *sq.*; M. C. F. Morris,
Yorkshire Folk-talk, pp. 212-214.
Compare F. Grose, *Provincial Glossary*
(London, 1811), *s.v.* "Mell-supper";
J. Brand, *Popular Antiquities*, ii.
27 *sqq.*, Bohn's edition; *The Denham
Tracts*, edited by Dr. James Hardy
(London, 1892-1895), ii. 2 *sq.* The
sheaf out of which the Mell-doll was
made was no doubt the Mell-sheaf,
though this is not expressly said. Dr.

the mell-sheaf "was frequently made of such dimensions
as to be a heavy load for a man, and, within a few years
comparatively, was proposed as the prize to be won in a
race of old women. In other cases it was carefully preserved
and set up in some conspicuous place in the farmhouse."[1]
Where the last sheaf of corn cut was called the *kirn* or
kern instead of the *mell*, the customs concerned with it seem
to have been essentially similar. Thus we are told that
in the north it was common for the reapers, on the last day
of the reaping, "to have a contention for superiority in
quickness of dispatch, groups of three or four taking each a
ridge, and striving which should soonest get to its termina-
tion. In Scotland, this was called a *kemping*, which simply
means a striving. In the north of England, it was a *mell*.
. . . As the reapers went on during the last day, they took
care to leave a good handful of the grain uncut, but laid
down flat, and covered over ; and, when the field was done,
the 'bonniest lass' was allowed to cut this final handful,
which was presently dressed up with various sewings, tyings,
and trimmings, like a doll, and hailed as a *Corn Baby*. It
was brought home in triumph, with music of fiddles and
bagpipes, was set up conspicuously that night at supper,
and was usually preserved in the farmer's parlour for the
remainder of the year. The bonny lass who cut this handful of grain was deemed the *Har'st Queen*."[2] To cut the
last portion of standing corn in the harvest field was known
as "to get the kirn" or "to win the kirn"; and as soon as
this was done the reapers let the neighbours know that the
harvest was finished by giving three cheers, which was

Joseph Wright, editor of *The English
Dialect Dictionary*, kindly informs me
that the word *mell* is well known in
these senses in all the northern counties
of England down to Cheshire. He
tells me that the proposals to connect
mell with "meal" or with "maiden"
(through a form like the German
Mädel) are inadmissible.

[1] Joseph Wright, *The English
Dialect Dictionary*, vol. iv. (London,
1903) *s.v.* "Mell," p. 83.

[2] R. Chambers, *The Book of Days*
(Edinburgh, 1886), ii. 377 *sq.* The

expression "Corn Baby" used by the
writer is probably his interpretation of
the correct expression *kirn* or *kern*
baby. See above, p. 151, note [3]. It is
not clear whether the account refers to
England or Scotland. Compare F.
Grose, *Provincial Glossary* (London
1811), *s.v.* "Kern-baby," "an image
dressed up with corn, carried before the
reapers to their mell-supper, or harvest-
home" ; J. Brand, *Popular Antiquities*,
ii. 20 ; W. Henderson, *Folk-lore of
the Northern Counties of England*,
p. 87.

called "to cry or shout the kirn."[1]   Where the last handful **The** *churn* **cut by throwing sickles at it.** of standing corn was called the *churn*, the stalks were roughly plaited together, and the reapers threw their sickles at it till some one cut it through, which was called "cutting the churn." The severed churn (that is, the plaited corn) was then placed over the kitchen door or over the hob in the chimney for good luck, and as a charm against witchcraft.[2] In Kent the Ivy Girl is, or used to be, " a figure composed of some of the best corn the field produces, and made as well as they can into a human shape ; this is afterwards curiously dressed by the women, and adorned with paper trimmings, cut to resemble a cap, ruffles, handkerchief, etc., of the finest lace. It is brought home with the last load of corn from the field upon the waggon, and they suppose entitles them to a supper at the expense of the employer."[3]

In some parts of Scotland, as well as in the north of Eng- **The last corn cut called the** *kirn* **in some parts of Scotland.** land, the last handful of corn cut on the harvest-field was called the *kirn*, and the person who carried it off was said "to win the kirn." It was then dressed up like a child's doll and went by the name of the kirn-baby, the kirn-doll, or the Maiden.[4]   In Berwickshire down to about the middle of the nineteenth century there was an eager competition among the reapers to cut the last bunch of standing corn. They gathered round it at a little distance and threw their sickles in turn at it, and the man who succeeded in cutting it through gave it to the girl he preferred. She made the corn so cut into a kirn-dolly and dressed it, and the doll was then taken to the farmhouse and hung up there till the next harvest, when its place was taken by the new kirn-dolly.[5]   At Spottiswoode **The** *kirn* **cut by reapers blindfold.** (Westruther Parish) in Berwickshire the reaping of the last corn at harvest was called "cutting the Queen " almost as often as "cutting the kirn." The mode of cutting it was not by throwing sickles. One of the reapers consented to be blindfolded, and having been given a sickle in his hand

---

[1] Joseph Wright, *The English Dialect Dictionary*, iii. (London, 1902) s.v. " Kirn," p. 453.

[2] Joseph Wright, *The English Dialect Dictionary*, i. (London, 1898) p. 605.

[3] J. Brand, *Popular Antiquities*, ii.

21 *sq.*

[4] J. Jamieson, *Etymological Dictionary of the Scottish Language*, New Edition (Paisley, 1879-1882), iii. 42 *sq.*, *s.v.* " Kirn."

[5] Mrs. A. B. Gomme, " A Berwickshire Kirn-dolly," *Folk-lore*, xii. (1901) p. 215.

and turned twice or thrice about by his fellows, he was bidden to go and cut the kirn. His groping about and making wild strokes in the air with his sickle excited much hilarity. When he had tired himself out in vain and given up the task as hopeless, another reaper was blindfolded and pursued the quest, and so on, one after the other, till at last the kirn was cut. The successful reaper was tossed up in the air with three cheers by his brother harvesters. To decorate the room in which the kirn-supper was held at Spottiswoode as well as the granary, where the dancing took place, two women made kirn-dollies or Queens every year ; and many of these rustic effigies of the corn-spirit might be seen hanging up together.[1] At Lanfine in Ayrshire, down to near the end of the nineteenth century, the last bunch of standing corn at harvest was, occasionally at least, plaited together, and the reapers tried to cut it by throwing their sickles at it ; when they failed in the attempt, a woman has been known to run in and sever the stalks at a blow. In Dumfriesshire also, within living memory, it used to be customary to cut the last standing corn by throwing the sickles at it.[2]

The *churn* in Ireland cut by throwing the sickles at it.

In the north of Ireland the harvest customs were similar, but there, as in some parts of England, the last patch of standing corn bore the name of the *churn*, a dialectical variation of *kirn*. "The custom of 'Winning the Churn' was prevalent all through the counties of Down and Antrim fifty years ago. It was carried out at the end of the harvest, or reaping the grain, on each farm or holding, were it small or large. Oats are the main crop of the district, but the custom was the same for other kinds of grain. When the reapers had nearly finished the last field a handful of the best-grown stalks was selected, carefully plaited as it stood, and fastened at the top just under the ears to keep the plait in place. Then when all the corn was cut from about this, which was known as *The Churn*, and the sheaves about it had been removed to some distance, the reapers stood in a group about ten yards off it, and each

---

[1] Mrs. A. B. Gomme, "Harvest Customs," *Folk-lore*, xiii. (1902) p. 178.

[2] J. G. Frazer, "Notes on Harvest Customs," *Folk-lore*, vii. (1889) p. " 48.

whirled his sickle at the *Churn* till one lucky one succeeded in cutting it down, when he was cheered on his achievement. This person had then the right of presenting it to the master or mistress of the farm, who gave the reaper a shilling." A supper and a dance of the reapers in the farmhouse often concluded the day. The *Churn*, trimmed and adorned with ribbons, was hung up on a wall in the farmhouse and carefully preserved. It was no uncommon sight to see six or even twelve or more such *Churns* decorating the walls of a farmhouse in County Down or Antrim.[1]

In some parts of the Highlands of Scotland the last handful of corn that is cut by the reapers on any particular farm is called the Maiden, or in Gaelic *Maidhdeanbuain*, literally "the shorn Maiden." Superstitions attach to the winning of the Maiden. If it is got by a young person, they think it an omen that he or she will be married before another harvest. For that or other reasons there is a strife between the reapers as to who shall get the Maiden, and they resort to various stratagems for the purpose of securing it. One of them, for example, will often leave a handful of corn uncut and cover it up with earth to hide it from the other reapers, till all the rest of the corn on the field is cut down. Several may try to play the same trick, and the one who is coolest and holds out longest obtains the coveted distinction. When it has been cut, the Maiden is dressed with ribbons into a sort of doll and affixed to a wall of the farmhouse. In the north of Scotland the Maiden is carefully preserved till Yule morning, when it is divided among the cattle "to make them thrive all the year round."[2] In the island of Mull and some parts of the mainland of Argyleshire the last handful of corn cut is called the Maiden (*Maighdean-Bhuana*). Near Ardrishaig, in Argyleshire, the

The last corn cut called the Maiden in the Highlands of Scotland.

---

[1] (Rev.) H. W. Lett, "Winning the Churn (Ulster)," *Folk-lore*, xvi. (1905) p. 185. My friend Miss Welsh, formerly Principal of Girton College, Cambridge, told me (30th May 1901) that she remembers the custom of the *churn* being observed in the north of Ireland ; the reapers cut the last handful of standing corn (called the *churn*) by throwing their sickles at it, and the corn so cut was taken home and kept for some time.

[2] J. Jamieson, *Dictionary of the Scottish Language*, New Edition (Paisley, 1879-1882), iii. 206, *s.v.* "Maiden." An old Scottish name for the Maiden (*autumnalis nymphula*) was *Rapegyrne*. See Fordun, *Scotichron.* ii. 418, quoted by J. Jamieson, *op. cit.* iii. 624, *s.v.* "Rapegyrne."

Maiden is made up in a fanciful three-cornered shape, decorated with ribbons, and hung from a nail on the wall.[1]

The cutting of the Maiden at harvest in Argyleshire. The following account of the Maiden was obtained in the summer of 1897 from the manager of a farm near Kilmartin in Argyleshire : " The *Mhaighdean-Bhuana*, or *Reaping Maiden*, was the last sheaf of oats to be cut on a croft or farm. Before the reaping-machine and binder took the place of the sickle and the scythe, the young reapers of both sexes, when they neared the end of the last rig or field, used to manœuvre to gain possession of the *Mhaighdean-Bhuana*. The individual who was fortunate enough to obtain it was *ex officio* entitled to be the King or the Queen of the Harvest-Home festival. The sheaf so designated was carefully preserved and kept intact until the day they began leading home the corn. A tuft of it was then given to each of the horses, as they started from the corn-field with their first load. The rest of it was neatly made up, and hung in some conspicuous corner of the farmhouse, where it remained till it was replaced by a younger sister next season. On the first day of ploughing a tuft of it was given (as on the first day of leading home the corn) as a *Sainnseal* or handsel for luck to the horses. The *Mhaighdean-Bhuana* so preserved and used was a symbol that the harvest had been duly secured, and that the spring work had been properly inaugurated. It was also believed to be a protection against fairies and witchcraft." [2]

The cutting of the Maiden at harvest in Perthshire. In the parish of Longforgan, situated at the south-eastern corner of Perthshire, it used to be customary to give what was called the Maiden Feast at the end of the harvest. The last handful of corn reaped on the field was called the Maiden, and things were generally so arranged that it fell into the hands of a pretty girl. It was then decked out with ribbons and brought home in triumph to the music of bagpipes and fiddles. In the evening the reapers danced and made merry. Afterwards the Maiden was dressed out, generally in the

[1] R. C. Maclagan, in *Folk-lore*, vi. (1895) pp. 149, 151.
[2] Rev. M. MacPhail (Free Church Manse, Kilmartin, Lochgilphead), "Folk-lore from the Hebrides," *Folk-lore*, xi.(1900)p.441. That the Maiden, hung up in the house, is thought to keep out witches till the next harvest is mentioned also by the Rev. J. G. Campbell, *Superstitions of the Highlands and Islands of Scotland* (Glasgow, 1900), p. 20. So with the *churn* (above, p. 153)

form of a cross, and hung up, with the date attached to it, in a conspicuous part of the house.[1] In the neighbourhood of Balquhidder, Perthshire, the last handful of corn is cut by the youngest girl on the field, and is made into the rude form of a female doll, clad in a paper dress, and decked with ribbons. It is called the Maiden, and is kept in the farmhouse, generally above the chimney, for a good while, sometimes till the Maiden of the next year is brought in. The writer of this book witnessed the ceremony of cutting the Maiden at Balquhidder in September 1888.[2] A lady friend [3] informed me that as a young girl she cut the Maiden several times at the request of the reapers in the neighbourhood of Perth. The name of the Maiden was given to the last handful of standing corn ; a reaper held the top of the bunch while she cut it. Afterwards the bunch was plaited, decked with ribbons, and hung up in a conspicuous place on the wall of the kitchen till the next Maiden was brought in. The harvest-supper in this neighbourhood was also called the Maiden ; the reapers danced at it.

In the Highland district of Lochaber dancing and merry-making on the last night of harvest used to be universal and are still generally observed. Here, we are told, the festivity without the Maiden would be like a wedding without the bride. The Maiden is carried home with tumultuous rejoicing, and after being suitably decorated is hung up in the barn, where the dancing usually takes place. When supper is over, one of the company, generally the oldest man present, drinks a glass of whisky, after turning to the suspended sheaf and saying, " Here's to the Maiden." The company follow his example, each in turn drinking to the Maiden. Then the dancing begins.[4] On some farms on the Gareloch, in Dumbartonshire, about the year 1830, the last handful of standing corn was called the Maiden. It was divided in two, plaited, and then cut with the sickle by a girl, who, it was

The Maiden at harvest in Lochaber.

The cutting of the harvest on the Gareloch in Dumbartonshire.

[1] Sir John Sinclair, *Statistical Account of Scotland*, xix. (Edinburgh, 1797), pp. 550 *sq.* Compare Miss E. J. Guthrie, *Old Scottish Customs* (London and Glasgow, 1885), pp. 130 *sq.*

[2] *Folk-lore Journal*, vi. (1888) pp. 268 *sq.*

[3] The late Mrs. Macalister, wife of Professor Alexander Macalister, Cambridge. Her recollections referred especially to the neighbourhood of Glen Farg, some ten or twelve miles to the south of Perth.

[4] Rev. James Macdonald, *Religion and Myth* (London, 1893), pp. 141 *sq.*

thought, would be lucky and would soon be married. When it was cut the reapers gathered together and threw their sickles in the air. The Maiden was dressed with ribbons and hung in the kitchen near the roof, where it was kept for several years with the date attached. Sometimes five or six Maidens might be seen hanging at once on hooks. The harvest-supper was called the Kirn.[1] In other farms on the Gareloch the last handful of corn was called the Maidenhead or the Head ; it was neatly plaited, sometimes decked with ribbons, and hung in the kitchen for a year, when the grain was given to the poultry.[2]

The cutting of the *clyack* sheaf at harvest in Aberdeenshire.

In the north-east of Aberdeenshire the customs connected with the last corn cut at harvest have been carefully collected and recorded by the late Rev. Walter Gregor of Pitsligo. His account runs as follows : " The last sheaf cut is the object of much care : the manner of cutting it, binding it, and carrying it to the house varies a little in the different districts. The following customs have been reported to me by people who have seen them or who have practised them, and some of the customs have now disappeared. The information comes from the parishes of Pitsligo, Aberdour, and Tyrie, situated in the north-east corner of the county of Aberdeen, but the customs are not limited to these parishes.

" Some particulars relating to the sheaf may be noted as always the same ; thus (*a*) it is cut and gathered by the youngest person present in the field, the person who is supposed to be the purest ; (*b*) the sheaf is not allowed to touch the ground ; (*c*) it is made up and carried in triumph to the house ; (*d*) it occupies a conspicuous place in the festivals which follow the end of the reaping ; (*e*) it is kept till Christmas morning, and is then given to one or more of the horses or to the cattle of the farm.

The *clyack* sheaf cut by the youngest girl and not allowed to touch the ground.

" Before the introduction of the scythe, the corn was cut by the sickle or *heuck*, a kind of curved sickle. The last sheaf was shorn or cut by the youngest girl present. As the corn might not touch the ground, the master or ' gueed-

---

[1] From information supplied by Archie Leitch, late gardener to my father at Rowmore, Garelochhead. The Kirn was the name of the harvest festivity in the south of Scotland also.

See Lockhart's *Life of Scott*, ii. 184 (first edition); *Early Letters of Thomas Carlyle*, ed. Norton, ii. 325 *sq.*
[2] Communicated by the late Mr. Macfarlane of Faslane, Gareloch.

man' sat down, placed the band on his knees, and received thereupon each handful as it was cut. The sheaf was bound, dressed as a woman, and when it had been brought to the house, it was placed in some part of the kitchen, where everybody could see it during the meal which followed the end of the reaping. This sheaf was called the *clyack* sheaf.[1]

" The manner of receiving and binding the last sheaf is not always the same. Here is another : three persons hold the band in their hands, one of them at each end, while the third holds the knot in the middle. Each handful of corn is placed so that the cut end is turned to the breast of those who support the ears on the opposite side. When all is cut, the youngest boy ties the knot. Two other bands are fastened to the sheaf, one near the cut end, the other near the ears. The sheaf is carried to the house by those who have helped to cut or bind it (Aberdour).

" Since the introduction of the scythe, it is the youngest boy who cuts the last sheaf ; my informant (a woman) told me that when he was not strong enough to wield the scythe, his hand was guided by another. The youngest girl gathers it. When it is bound with three bands, it is cut straight, and it is not allowed to touch the ground. The youngest girls carry it to the house. My informant (a woman) told me that she had seen it decked and placed at the head of the bed. Formerly, and still sometimes, there was always a bed in the kitchen (Tyrie).

" The corn is not allowed to fall on the ground : the young girls who gather it take it by the ear and convey it handful by handful, till the whole sheaf is cut. A woman who 'has lost a feather of her wing,' as an old woman put it to me, may not touch it. Sometimes also they merely put the two hands round the sheaf (New Deer).

" Generally a feast and dance follow when all the wheat is cut. This feast and dance bear the name of *clyack* or

The *clyack* feast or "meal and ale."

---

[1] A slightly different mode of making up the *clyack* sheaf is described by the Rev. Walter Gregor elsewhere (*Notes on the Folk-lore of the North-east of Scotland*, London, 1881, pp. 181 *sq.*) : "The *clyack* sheaf was cut by the maidens on the harvest field. On no account was it allowed to touch the ground. One of the maidens seated herself on the ground, and over her knees was the band of the sheaf laid. Each of the maidens cut a handful, or more if necessary, and laid it on the band. The sheaf was then bound, still lying over the maiden's knees, and dressed up in woman's clothing."

'meal and ale.' However, some people do not give 'meal and ale' till all the cut corn has been got in: then the feast is called 'the Winter,' and they say that a farmer 'has the Winter' when all his sheaves have been carried home.

"At this feast two things are indispensable: a cheese called the *clyack-kebback* and 'meal and ale.'

"The cheese *clyack-kebback* must be cut by the master of the house. The first slice is larger than the rest; it is known by the name of 'the *kanave's faang*,'—the young man's big slice—and is generally the share of the herd boy (Tyrie).

"The dish called 'meal and ale' is made as follows. You take a suitable vessel, whether an earthenware pot or a milk-bowl, if the crockery is scanty; but if on the contrary the family is well off, they use other special utensils. In each dish ale is poured and treacle is added to sweeten it. Then oatmeal is mixed with the sweetened ale till the whole is of a sufficient consistency. The cook adds whisky to the mixture in such proportion as she thinks fit. In each plate is put a ring. To allow the meal time to be completely absorbed, the dish is prepared on the morning of the feast. At the moment of the feast the dish or dishes containing the strong and savoury mixture are set on the middle of the table. But it is not served up till the end. Six or seven persons generally have a plate to themselves. Each of them plunges his spoon into the plate as fast as possible in the hope of getting the ring; for he who is lucky enough to get it will be married within the year. Meantime some of the stuff is swallowed, but often in the struggle some of it is spilt on the table or the floor.

The *clyack* sheaf in the dance.

"In some districts there used to be and still is dancing in the evening of the feast. 'The sheaf' figured in the dances. It was dressed as a girl and carried on the back of the mistress of the house to the barn or granary which served as a ballroom. The mistress danced a reel with 'the sheaf' on her back.

The *clyack* sheaf given to a mare in foal or to a cow in calf.

"The woman who gave me this account had been a witness of what she described when she was a girl. The sheaf was afterwards carefully stored till the first day of Christmas, when it was given to eat to a mare in foal, if there was one on the farm, or, if there was not, to the oldest cow in calf. Elsewhere the sheaf was divided between all the cows and their calves or between all the horses and the cattle of the farm. (Related by an eye-witness.)" [1]

In these Aberdeenshire customs the sanctity attributed to the last corn cut at harvest is clearly manifested, not merely by the ceremony with which it is treated on the field, in the house, and in the barn, but also by the great care taken to prevent it from touching the ground or being handled by any unchaste person. The reason why the youngest person on the field, whether a girl or a boy, is chosen to cut the last standing corn and sometimes to carry it to the house is no doubt a calculation that the younger the person the more likely is he or she to be sexually pure. We have seen that for this reason some negroes entrust the sowing of the seed to very young girls,[2] and later on we shall meet with more evidence in Africa of the notion that the corn may be handled only by the pure.[3] And in the gruel of oat-meal and ale, which the harvesters sup with spoons as an indispensable part of the harvest supper, have we not the Scotch equivalent of the gruel of barley-meal and water, flavoured with pennyroyal, which the initiates at Eleusis drank as a solemn form of communion with the Barley Goddess Demeter?[4] May not that mystic sacrament have

Sanctity attributed to the clyack sheaf.

The sacrament of barley-meal and water at Eleusis.

---

[1] W. Gregor, "Quelques coutumes du Nord-est du Comté d'Aberdeen," *Revue des Traditions populaires,* iii. (October, 1888) pp. 484-487 (wrong pagination; should be 532-535). This account, translated into French by M.. Loys Brueyre from the author's English and translated by me back from French into English, is fuller than the account given by the same writer in his *Notes on the Folk-lore of the North-east of Scotland* (London, 1881), pp. 181-183. I have translated "*une jument ayant son poulain*" by "a mare in foal," and "*la plus ancienne vache ayant son veau*" by "the oldest cow in calf," because in the author's *Notes on the Folk-lore of the North-east of Scotland* (p. 182) we read that the last sheaf was "carefully preserved till Christmas or New Year morning. On that morning it was given to a mare in foal," etc. Otherwise the French words might

naturally be understood of a mare with its foal and a cow with its calf.

[2] See above, pp. 115 *sq.*

[3] See below, vol. ii. p. 110.

[4] The drinking of the draught (called the κυκεών) as a solemn rite in the Eleusinian mysteries is mentioned by Clement of Alexandria (*Protrept.* 21, p. 18, ed. Potter) and Arnobius (*Adversus Nationes,* v. 26). The composition of the draught is revealed by the author of the Homeric *Hymn to Demeter* (verses 206-211), where he represents Demeter herself partaking of the sacred cup. That the compound was a kind of thick gruel, half-solid, half-liquid, is mentioned by Eustathius (on Homer, *Iliad,* xi. 638, p. 870). Compare Miss J. E. Harrison, *Prolegomena to the Study of Greek Religion,* Second Edition (Cambridge, 1908), pp. 155 *sqq.*

originated in a simple harvest supper held by Eleusinian farmers at the end of the reaping? According to a briefer account of the Aberdeenshire custom, "the last sheaf cut, or 'maiden,' is carried home in merry procession by the harvesters. It is then presented to the mistress of the house, who dresses it up to be preserved till the first mare foals. The maiden is then taken down and presented to the mare as its first food. The neglect of this would have untoward effects upon the foal, and disastrous consequences upon farm operations generally for the season."[1] In Fifeshire the last handful of corn, known as the Maiden, is cut by a young girl and made into the rude figure of a doll, tied with ribbons, by which it is hung on the wall of the farm-kitchen till the next spring.[2] The custom of cutting the Maiden at harvest was also observed in Inverness-shire and Sutherlandshire.[3]

The corn-spirit as a bride.

A somewhat maturer but still youthful age is assigned to the corn-spirit by the appellations of Bride, Oats-bride, and Wheat-bride, which in Germany are sometimes bestowed both on the last sheaf and on the woman who binds it.[4] At wheat-harvest near Müglitz, in Moravia, a small portion of the wheat is left standing after all the rest has been reaped. This remnant is then cut, amid the rejoicing of the reapers, by a young girl who wears a wreath of wheaten ears on her head and goes by the name of the Wheat-bride. It is supposed that she will be a real bride that same year.[5]

[1] Rev. J. Macdonald, *Religion and Myth* (London, 1893), pp. 140 *sq.*, from MS. notes of Miss J. Ligertwood.

[2] *Folk-lore Journal*, vii. (1889) p. 51; *The Quarterly Review*, clxxii. (1891) p. 195.

[3] As to Inverness-shire my old friend Mr. Hugh E. Cameron, formerly of Glen Moriston, Inverness-shire, wrote to me many years ago: "As a boy, I remember the last bit of corn cut was taken home, and neatly tied up with a ribbon, and then stuck up on the wall above the kitchen fire-place, and there it often remained till the 'maiden' of the following year took its place. There was no ceremony about it, beyond often a struggle as to who would get, or cut, the last sheaf to

select the 'maiden' from" (*The Folk-lore Journal*, vii. 1889, pp. 50 *sq.*). As to Sutherlandshire my mother was told by a servant, Isabella Ross, that in that county "they hang up the 'maiden' generally over the mantel-piece (chimney-piece) till the next harvest. They have always a kirn, whipped cream, with often a ring in it, and sometimes meal sprinkled over it. The girls must all be dressed in lilac prints, they all dance, and at twelve o'clock they eat potatoes and herrings" (*op. cit.* pp. 53 *sq.*).

[4] W. Mannhardt, *Die Korndämonen* (Berlin, 1868), p. 30.

[5] W. Müller, *Beiträge zur Volkskunde der Deutschen in Mähren* (Vienna and Olmütz, 1893), p. 327.

In the upland valley of Alpach, in North Tyrol, the person who brings the last sheaf into the granary is said to have the Wheat-bride or the Rye-bride according to the crop, and is received with great demonstrations of respect and rejoicing. The people of the farm go out to meet him, bells are rung, and refreshments offered to him on a tray.[1]   In Austrian Silesia a girl is chosen to be the Wheat-bride, and much honour is paid to her at the harvest-festival.[2]   Near Roslin and Stonehaven, in Scotland, the last handful of corn cut "got the name of ' the bride,' and she was placed over the *bress* or chimney-piece ; she had a ribbon tied below her numerous *ears*, and another round her waist." [3]

Sometimes the idea implied by the name of Bride is worked out more fully by representing the productive powers of vegetation as bride and bridegroom. Thus in the Vorharz an Oats-man and an Oats-woman, swathed in straw, dance at the harvest feast.[4]   In South Saxony an Oats-bridegroom and an Oats-bride figure together at the harvest celebration. The Oats-bridegroom is a man completely wrapt in oats-straw ; the Oats-bride is a man dressed in woman's clothes, but not wrapt in straw. They are drawn in a waggon to the ale-house, where the dance takes place. At the beginning of the dance the dancers pluck the bunches of oats one by one from the Oats-bridegroom, while he struggles to keep them, till at last he is completely stript of them and stands bare, exposed to the laughter and jests of the company.[5]   In Austrian Silesia the ceremony of "the Wheat-bride" is celebrated by the young people at the end of the harvest. The woman who bound the last sheaf plays the part of the Wheat-bride, wearing the harvest-crown of wheat ears and flowers on her head. Thus adorned, standing beside her Bridegroom in a waggon and attended by bridesmaids, she is drawn by a pair of oxen, in full imitation of a marriage

The corn-spirit as Bride and Bridegroom.

---

[1] J. E. Waldfreund, "Volksge-bräuche und Aberglaube in Tirol und dem Salzburger Gebirg," *Zeitschrift für deutsche Mythologie und Sitten-kunde,* iii. (1855) p. 340.

[2] Th. Vernaleken, *Mythen und Bräuche des Volkes in Oesterreich* (Vienna, 1859), p. 310.

[3] Mr. R. Matheson, in *The Folk-lore Journal,* vii. (1889) pp. 49, 50.

[4] W. Mannhardt, *Die Korndämonen* (Berlin, 1868), p. 30.

[5] E. Sommer, *Sagen, Märchen una Gebräuche aus Sachsen und Thüringen* (Halle, 1846), pp. 160 *sq.* ; W. Mann-hardt, *l.c.*

procession, to the tavern, where the dancing is kept up till morning. Somewhat later in the season the wedding of the Oats-bride is celebrated with the like rustic pomp. About Neisse, in Silesia, an Oats-king and an Oats-queen, dressed up quaintly as a bridal pair, are seated on a harrow and drawn by oxen into the village.[1]

The corn-spirit in the double form of the Old Wife and the Maiden simultaneously at harvest in the Highlands of Scotland. In these last instances the corn-spirit is personified in double form as male and female. But sometimes the spirit appears in a double female form as both old and young, corresponding exactly to the Greek Demeter and Persephone, if my interpretation of these goddesses is right. We have seen that in Scotland, especially among the Gaelic-speaking population, the last corn cut is sometimes called the Old Wife and sometimes the Maiden. Now there are parts of Scotland in which both an Old Wife (*Cailleach*) and a Maiden are cut at harvest. As the accounts of this custom are not quite clear and consistent, it may be well to give them first in the words of the original authorities. Thus the late Sheriff Alexander Nicolson tells us that there is a Gaelic proverb, " A balk (*léum-iochd*) in autumn is better than a sheaf the more " ; and he explains it by saying that a *léum-iochd* or balk " is a strip of a corn-field left fallow. The fear of being left with the last sheaf of the harvest, called the *cailleach*, or *gobhar bhacach*, always led to an exciting competition among the reapers in the last field. The reaper who came on a *léum-iochd* would of course be glad to have so much the less to cut." [2]   In further explanation of the proverb the writer adds :

" The customs as to the *Cailleach* and *Maighdean-bhuana* seem to have varied somewhat. Two reapers were usually set to each rig, and according to one account, the man who was first done got the *Maighdean-bhuana* or ' Reaping-Maiden,' while the man who was last got the *Cailleach* or ' old woman.' The latter term is used in Argyleshire ; the term *Gobhar-bhacach*, the lame goat, is used in Skye.

" According to what appears to be the better version, the

[1] W. Mannhardt, *l.c.*; E. Peter, *Volksthümliches aus Österreichisch-Schlesien* (Troppau, 1865-1867), ii. 269.

[2] Alexander Nicolson, *A Collection of Gaelic Proverbs and Familiar Phrases, based on Macintosh's Collection* (Edinburgh and London, 1881), p. 248.

competition to avoid the *Cailleach* was not between reapers but
between neighbouring crofters, and the man who got his
harvest done first sent a handful of corn called the *Cailleach*
to his neighbour, who passed it on, till it landed with him
who was latest. That man's penalty was to provide for the
dearth of the township, *gort a' bhaile*, in the ensuing season.

"The *Maighdean-bhuana*, again, was the last cut handful of oats, on a croft or farm, and was an object of lively
competition among the reapers. It was tastefully tied
up with ribbons, generally dressed like a doll, and then
hung up on a nail till spring. On the first day of ploughing it was solemnly taken down, and given as a *Sainnseal*
(or handsel) to the horses for luck. It was meant as a symbol that the harvest had been secured, and to ward off the
fairies, representatives of the ethereal and unsubstantial, till
the time came to provide for a new crop."[1]   Again, the
Rev. Mr. Campbell of Kilchrenan, on Loch Awe, furnished Dr.
R. C. Maclagan with the following account of the Highland
customs at harvest. The recollections of Mrs. MacCorquodale,
then resident at Kilchrenan, refer to the customs practised
about the middle of the nineteenth century in the wild
and gloomy valley of Glencoe, infamous in history for
the treacherous massacre perpetrated there by the Government troops in 1692. "Mrs. MacCorquodale says that
the rivalry was for the Maiden, and for the privilege she
gave of sending the Cailleach to the next neighbour.
The Maiden was represented by the last stalks reaped ;
the Cailleach by a handful taken at random from the
field, perhaps the last rig of the reaper last to finish. The
Cailleach was not dressed but carried after binding to
the neighbour's field. The Maiden was cut in the following
manner. All the reapers gathered round her and kept a
short distance from her. They then threw their hooks
[sickles] at her. The person successful in cutting her down
in this manner was the man whose possession she became.
Mrs. MacCorquodale understood that the man of a township
who got the Cailleach finally was supposed to be doomed to
poverty for his want of energy. (Gaelic : *treubhantas*—
valour.)

[1] A. Nicolson, *op. cit.* pp. 415 *sq.*

" A sample of the toast to the Cailleach at the harvest entertainment was as follows : ' The Cailleach is with . . . and is now with (me) since I was the last.   I drink to her health.   Since she assisted me in harvest, it is likely that it is with me she will abide during the winter.'   In explaining the above toast Mr. Campbell says that it signifies that the Cailleach is always with agriculturists.   ' She has been with others before and is now with me (the proposer of the toast). Though I did my best to avoid her I welcome her as my assistant, and am prepared to entertain her during the winter.' Another form of the toast was as follows : ' To your health, good wife, who for harvest has come to help us, and if I live I'll try to support you when winter comes.'

" John MacCorquodale, Kilchrenan, says that at Crianlarich in Strath Fillan, they make a Cailleach of sticks and a turnip, old clothes and a pipe.   In this case the effigy passed in succession to seven farms, which he mentioned, and finally settled with an innkeeper.   The list suggested that the upper farms stood a bad chance, and perhaps that a prosperous innkeeper could more easily bear up against the reproach and loss (?) of supporting the Cailleach.

" Duncan MacIntyre, Kilchrenan, says that in one case where the last field to be reaped was the most fertile land on the farm, the corn first cut in it, which was taken near the edge, was reserved to make a Cailleach, should the owner be so happy as to be able to pass her on to his neighbour.   The last blades cut were generally in the middle or best part of the field.   These in any event became the Maiden."   Lastly, Dr. Maclagan observes that " having directed the attention of Miss Kerr, Port Charlotte, Islay, to the practice of having two different bunches on the mainland of Argyle, she informs me that in Islay and Kintyre the last handful is the Cailleach, and they have no Maiden.   The same is the custom in Bernara and other parts of the Western Isles, while in Mull the last handful is the Maiden, and they have no Cailleach.   In North Uist the habit still prevails of putting the Cailleach over-night among the standing corn of lazy crofters." [1]

The general rule to which these various accounts point

[1] R. C. Maclagan, " Corn-maiden in Argyleshire," *Folk-lore*, vii. (1896) pp. 78 *sq.*

seems to be that, where both a Maiden and an Old Wife (*Cailleach*) are fashioned out of the reaped corn at harvest, the Maiden is always made out of the last stalks left standing, and is kept by the farmer on whose land it was cut ; while the Old Wife is made out of other stalks, sometimes out of the first stalks cut, and is regularly passed on to a laggard farmer who happens to be still reaping after his brisker neighbour has cut all his corn.   Thus while each farmer keeps his own Maiden, as the embodiment of the young and fruitful spirit of the corn, he passes on the Old Wife as soon as he can to a neighbour, and so the old lady may make the round of all the farms in the district before she finds a place in which to lay her venerable head.   The farmer with whom she finally takes up her abode is of course the one who has been the last of all the countryside to finish reaping his crops, and thus the distinction of entertaining her is rather an invidious, one. Similarly we saw that in Pembrokeshire, where the last corn cut is called, not the Maiden, but the Hag, she is passed on hastily to a neighbour who is still at work in his fields and who receives his aged visitor with anything but a transport of joy.   If the Old Wife represents the corn-spirit of the past year, as she probably does wherever she is contrasted with and opposed to a Maiden, it is natural enough that her faded charms should have less attractions for the husbandman than the buxom form of her daughter, who may be expected to become in her turn the mother of the golden grain when the revolving year has brought round another autumn.   The same desire to get rid of the effete Mother of the Corn by palming her off on other people comes out clearly in some of the customs observed at the close of threshing, particularly in the practice of passing on a hideous straw puppet to a neighbour farmer who is still threshing his corn.[1]

The harvest customs just described are strikingly analogous to the spring customs which we reviewed in the first part of this work.   (1) As in the spring customs the tree-spirit is represented both by a tree and by a person,[2] so in

---

[1] See above, p. 149, where, however, the corn-spirit is conceived as an Old Man.

[2] See *The Magic Art and the Evolution of Kings*, ii. 73 *sqq.*

the harvest customs the corn-spirit is represented both by the last sheaf and by the person who cuts or binds or threshes it. The equivalence of the person to the sheaf is shewn by giving him or her the same name as the sheaf; by wrapping him or her in it; and by the rule observed in some places, that when the sheaf is called the Mother, it must be made up into human shape by the oldest married woman, but that when it is called the Maiden, it must be cut by the youngest girl.[1] Here the age of the personal representative of the corn-spirit corresponds with that of the supposed age of the corn-spirit, just as the human victims offered by the Mexicans to promote the growth of the maize varied with the age of the maize.[2] For in the Mexican, as in the European, custom the human beings were probably representatives of the corn-spirit rather than victims offered to it. (2) Again, the same fertilising influence which the tree-spirit is supposed to exert over vegetation, cattle, and even women[3] is ascribed to the corn-spirit. Thus, its supposed influence on vegetation is shewn by the practice of taking some of the grain of the last sheaf (in which the corn-spirit is regularly supposed to be present), and scattering it among the young corn in spring or mixing it with the seed-corn.[4] Its influence on animals is shewn by giving the last sheaf to a mare in foal, to a cow in calf, and to horses at the first ploughing.[5] Lastly, its influence on women is indicated by the custom of delivering the Mother-sheaf, made into the likeness of a pregnant woman, to the farmer's wife;[6] by the belief that the woman who binds the last sheaf will have a child next year;[7] perhaps, too, by the idea that the person who gets it will soon be married.[8]

The spring and harvest customs of Europe are parts of a primitive heathen ritual.

Plainly, therefore, these spring and harvest customs are based on the same ancient modes of thought, and form parts of the same primitive heathendom, which was doubtless practised by our forefathers long before the dawn of history.

---

[1] Above, pp. 134, 137, 138 sq., 142, 145, 147, 148, 149.

[2] See below, pp. 237 sq.

[3] The Magic Art and the Evolution of Kings, ii. 47 sqq.

[4] Above, pp. 134, 135.

[5] Above, pp. 141, 155, 156, 158, 160 sq., 162, 165.

[6] See above, p. 135.

[7] Above, p. 145. Compare A. Kuhn, Sagen, Gebräuche und Märchen aus Westfalen (Leipsic, 1859), ii. p. 185, § 516.

[8] Above, pp. 136, 139, 155, 157 sq., 162; compare p. 160.

Amongst the marks of a primitive ritual we may note the following :—

1. No special class of persons is set apart for the performance of the rites ; in other words, there are no priests. The rites may be performed by any one, as occasion demands.

2. No special places are set apart for the performance of the rites ; in other words, there are no temples. The rites may be performed anywhere, as occasion demands.

3. Spirits, not gods, are recognised. (*a*) As distinguished from gods, spirits are restricted in their operations to definite departments of nature. Their names are general, not proper. Their attributes are generic, rather than individual ; in other words, there is an indefinite number of spirits of each class, and the individuals of a class are all much alike ; they have no definitely marked individuality ; no accepted traditions are current as to their origin, life, adventures, and character. (*b*) On the other hand gods, as distinguished from spirits, are not restricted to definite departments of nature. It is true that there is generally some one department over which they preside as their special province ; but they are not rigorously confined to it ; they can exert their power for good or evil in many other spheres of nature and life. Again, they bear individual or proper names, such as Demeter, Persephone, Dionysus ; and their individual characters and histories are fixed by current myths and the representations of art.

4. The rites are magical rather than propitiatory. In other words, the desired objects are attained, not by propitiating the favour of divine beings through sacrifice, prayer, and praise, but by ceremonies which, as I have already explained,[1] are believed to influence the course of nature directly through a physical sympathy or resemblance between the rite and the effect which it is the intention of the rite to produce.

Judged by these tests, the spring and harvest customs of our European peasantry deserve to rank as primitive. For no special class of persons and no special places are set exclusively apart for their performance ; they may be performed by any one, master or man, mistress or maid, boy or

Marginal notes: Marks of a primitive ritual. Reasons for regarding the spring and harvest customs of modern

[1] *The Magic Art and the Evolution of Kings*, i. 220 *sqq.*

girl ; they are practised, not in temples or churches, but in
the woods and meadows, beside brooks, in barns, on harvest
fields and cottage floors.   The supernatural beings whose
existence is taken for granted in them are spirits rather than
deities : their functions are limited to certain well-defined
departments of nature : their names are general, like the
Barley-mother, the Old Woman, the Maiden, not proper
names like Demeter, Persephone, Dionysus.   Their generic
attributes are known, but their individual histories and
characters are not the subject of myths.   For they exist in
classes rather than as individuals, and the members of each
class are indistinguishable.   For example, every farm has its
Corn-mother, or its Old Woman, or its Maiden ; but every
Corn-mother is much like every other Corn-mother, and so
with the Old Women and Maidens.   Lastly, in these harvest,
as in the spring customs, the ritual is magical rather than
propitiatory.   This is shewn by throwing the Corn-mother
into the river in order to secure rain and dew for the
crops ;[1] by making the Old Woman heavy in order to get
a heavy crop next year ;[2] by strewing grain from the last
sheaf amongst the young crops in spring ;[3] and by giving
the last sheaf to the cattle to make them thrive.[4]

[1] Above, p. 146.   The common
custom of wetting the last sheaf and
its bearer is no doubt also a rain-
charm ; indeed the intention to procure rain or make the corn grow is
sometimes avowed.   See above, pp.
134, 137, 143, 144, 145 ; *Adonis,
Attis, Osiris*, Second Edition, pp.
195-197.
[2] Above, pp. 135 *sq.*, 138, 139, 152.
[3] Above, p. 134.
[4] Above, pp. 134, 155, 158, 161.

CHAPTER VI

THE CORN-MOTHER IN MANY LANDS

§ 1. *The Corn-mother in America*

EUROPEAN peoples, ancient and modern, have not been singular in personifying the corn as a mother goddess. The same simple idea has suggested itself to other agricultural races in distant parts of the world, and has been applied by them to other indigenous cereals than barley and wheat. If Europe has its Wheat-mother and its Barley-mother, America has its Maize-mother and the East Indies their Rice-mother. These personifications I will now illustrate, beginning with the American personification of the maize.

The Corn-mother in many lands.

We have seen that among European peoples it is a common custom to keep the plaited corn-stalks of the last sheaf, or the puppet which is formed out of them, in the farm-house from harvest to harvest.[1] The intention no doubt is, or rather originally was, by preserving the representative of the corn-spirit to maintain the spirit itself in life and activity throughout the year, in order that the corn may grow and the crops be good. This interpretation of the custom is at all events rendered highly probable by a similar custom observed by the ancient Peruvians, and thus described by the old Spanish historian Acosta:—" They take a certain portion of the most fruitful of the maize that grows in their farms, the which they put in a certain granary which they do call *Pirua*, with certain ceremonies, watching three nights; they put this maize in the richest garments they have, and being thus wrapped and dressed, they worship this *Pirua*, and hold

The Maize-mother among the Peruvian Indians.

[1] Above, pp. 136, 138, 140, 143, W. Mannhardt, *Die Korndämonen*, 152, 153, 154, 155, 156, 157, 158 : pp. 7, 26.

it in great veneration, saying it is the mother of the maize of their inheritances, and that by this means the maize augments and is preserved. In this month [the sixth month, answering to May] they make a particular sacrifice, and the witches demand of this *Pirua* if it hath strength sufficient to continue until the next year; and if it answers no, then they carry this maize to the farm to burn, whence they brought it, according to every man's power; then they make another *Pirua*, with the same ceremonies, saying that they renew it, to the end the seed of maize may not perish, and if it answers that it hath force sufficient to last longer, they leave it until the next year. This foolish vanity continueth to this day, and it is very common amongst the Indians to have these *Piruas.*" [1]

In this description of the custom there seems to be some error. Probably it was the dressed-up bunch of maize, not the granary (*Pirua*), which was worshipped by the Peruvians and regarded as the Mother of the Maize. This is confirmed by what we know of the Peruvian custom from another source. The Peruvians, we are told, believed all useful plants to be animated by a divine being who causes their growth. According to the particular plant, these divine beings were called the Maize-mother (*Zara-mama*), the Quinoa-mother (*Quinoa-mama*), the Coca-mother (*Coca-mama*), and the Potato-mother (*Axo-mama*). Figures of these divine mothers were made respectively of ears of maize and leaves of the quinoa and coca plants; they were dressed in women's clothes and worshipped. Thus the Maize-mother was represented by a puppet made of stalks of maize dressed in full female attire; and the Indians believed that "as mother, it had the power of producing and giving birth to much maize." [2] Probably, therefore, Acosta mis-

The Maize-mother, the Quinoa-mother, the Coca-mother, and the Potato-mother among the Peruvian Indians.

[1] J. de Acosta, *Natural and Moral History of the Indies*, bk. v. ch. 28, vol. ii. p. 374 (Hakluyt Society, London, 1880). In quoting the passage I have modernised the spelling. The original Spanish text of Acosta's work was reprinted in a convenient form at Madrid in 1894. See vol. ii. p. 117 of that edition.

[2] W. Mannhardt, *Mythologische*

Forschungen, pp. 342 *sq.* Mannhardt's authority is a Spanish tract (*Carta pastorale de exortacion e instruccion contra las idolatrias de los Indios del arçobispado de Lima*) by Pedro de Villagomez, Archbishop of Lima, published at Lima in 1649, and communicated to Mannhardt by J. J. v. Tschudi. The *Carta Pastorale* itself seems to be partly based on an earlier

understood his informant, and the Mother of the Maize which he describes was not the granary (*Pirua*), but the bunch of maize dressed in rich vestments. The Peruvian Mother of the Maize, like the harvest-Maiden at Balquhidder, was kept for a year in order that by her means the corn might grow and multiply. But lest her strength might not suffice to last

work, the *Extirpacion de la Idolatria del Piru. Dirigido al Rey N.S. en Su real conseio de Indias, por el Padre Pablo Joseph de Arriaga de la Compañia de Jesus* (Lima, 1621). A copy of this work is possessed by the British Museum, where I consulted it. The writer explains (p. 16) that the Maize-mothers (*Zaramamas*) are of three sorts, namely (1) those which are made of maize stalks, dressed up like women, (2) those which are carved of stone in the likeness of cobs of maize, and (3) those which consist simply of fruitful stalks of maize or of two maize-cobs naturally joined together. These last, the writer tells us, were the principal *Zaramamas*, and were revered by the natives as Mothers of the Maize. Similarly, when two potatoes were found growing together the Indians called them Potato-mothers (*Axomamas*) and kept them in order to get a good crop of potatoes. As Arriaga's work is rare, it may be well to give his account of the Maize-mothers, Coca-mothers, and Potato-mothers in his own words. He says (p. 16): "*Zaramamas, son de tres maneras, y son las que se quentan entre las cosas halladas en los pueblos. La primera es una como muñeca hecha de cañas de maiz, vestida como muger con su anaco, y llicilla, y sus topos de plata, y entienden, que como madre tiene virtud de engendrar, y parir mucho maiz. A este modo tienen tambien Cocamamas para augmento de la coca. Otras son de piedra labradas como choclos, o mazorcas de maiz, con sus granos relevados, y de estas suelen tener muchas en lugar de Conopas* [household gods]. *Otras son algunas cañas fertiles de maiz, que con la fertilidad de la tierra dieron muchas maçorcas, y grandes, o quando salen dos maçorcas juntas, y estas son las principales, Zaramamas, y assi las reverencian*

como a madres del maiz, a estas llaman tambien Huantayzara, o Ayrihuayzara. A este tercer genero no le dan la adoracion que a Huaca, ni Conopa, sino que le tienen supersticiosamente como una cosa sagrada, y colgando estas cañas con muchos choclos de unos ramos de sauce bailen con ellas el bayle, que llaman Ayrihua, y acabado el bayle, las queman, y sacrifican a Libiac para que les de buena cosecha. Con la misma supersticion guardan las mazorcas del maiz, que salen muy pintadas, que llaman Micsazara, o Mantayzara, o Caullazara, y otros que llaman Piruazara, que son otras maçorcas en que van subiendo los granos no derechos sino haziendo caracol. Estas Micsazara, o Piruazara, ponen supersticiosamente en los montones de maiz, y en las Piruas (que son donde guardan el maiz) paraque se las guarde, y el dia de las exhibiciones se junta tanto de estas maçorcas, que tienen bien que comer las mulas. La misma supersticion tienen con las que llaman Axomamas, que son quando salen algunas papas juntas, y las guardan para tener buena cosecha de papas." The *exhibiciones* here referred to are the occasions when the Indians brought forth their idols and other relics of superstition and delivered them to the ecclesiastical visitors. At Tarija in Bolivia, down to the present time, a cross is set up at harvest in the maize-fields, and on it all maize-spadices growing as twins are hung. They are called Pacha-mamas (Earth-mothers) and are thought to bring good harvests. See Baron E. Nordenskiöld, "Travels on the Boundaries of Bolivia and Argentina," *The Geographical Journal*, xxi. (1903) pp. 517, 518. Compare E. J. Payne, *History of the New World called America* (Oxford, 1892), i. 414 *sq.*

till the next harvest, she was asked in the course of the
year how she felt, and if she answered that she felt weak, she
was burned and a fresh Mother of the Maize made, "to the
end the seed of maize may not perish." Here, it may be
observed, we have a strong confirmation of the explanation
already given of the custom of killing the god, both periodically and occasionally. The Mother of the Maize was
allowed, as a rule, to live through a year, that being the
period during which her strength might reasonably be supposed to last unimpaired ; but on any symptom of her
strength failing she was put to death, and a fresh and vigorous
Mother of the Maize took her place, lest the maize which
depended on her for its existence should languish and decay.

Customs of
the ancient
Mexicans
at the
maize-
harvest.

Hardly less clearly does the same train of thought come
out in the harvest customs formerly observed by the Zapotecs
of Mexico. At harvest the priests, attended by the nobles
and people, went in procession to the maize fields, where they
picked out the largest and finest sheaf. This they took
with great ceremony to the town or village, and placed it in
the temple upon an altar adorned with wild flowers. After
sacrificing to the harvest god, the priests carefully wrapped
up the sheaf in fine linen and kept it till seed-time. Then
the priests· and nobles met again at the temple, one of them
bringing the skin of a wild beast, elaborately ornamented, in
which the linen cloth containing the sheaf was enveloped.
The sheaf was then carried once more in procession to the
field from which it had been taken. Here a small cavity or
subterranean chamber had been prepared, in which the
precious sheaf was deposited, wrapt in its various envelopes.
After sacrifice had been offered to the gods of the fields for
an abundant crop the chamber was closed and covered over
with earth. Immediately thereafter the sowing began.
Finally, when the time of harvest drew near, the buried sheaf
was solemnly disinterred by the priests, who distributed the
grain to all who asked for it. The packets of grain so distributed were carefully preserved as talismans till the harvest.[1]
In these ceremonies, which continued to be annually cele-

[1] Brasseur de Bourbourg, *Histoire
des Nations civilisées du Mexique et de
l'Amérique Centrale* (Paris, 1857-
1859), iii. 40 *sqq.* Compare *id.*, iii.
505 *sq.* ; E. J. Payne, *History of the
New World called America*, i. 419 *sq.*

brated long after the Spanish conquest, the intention of keeping the finest sheaf buried in the maize field from seed-time
to harvest was undoubtedly to quicken the growth of the
maize.

A fuller and to some extent different account of the
ancient Mexican worship of the maize has been given us
by the Franciscan monk Bernardino de Sahagun, who arrived
in Mexico in 1529, only eight years after its conquest by
the Spaniards, and devoted the remaining sixty-one years
of his long life to labouring among the Indians for their
moral and spiritual good. Uniting the curiosity of a
scientific enquirer to the zeal of a missionary, and adorning
both qualities with the humanity and benevolence of a
good man, he obtained from the oldest and most learned
of the Indians accounts of their ancient customs and beliefs,
and embodied them in a work which, for combined interest
of matter and fulness of detail, has perhaps never been
equalled in the records of aboriginal peoples brought into
contact with European civilisation. This great document,
after lying neglected in the dust of Spanish archives for centuries, was discovered and published almost simultaneously
in Mexico and England in the first half of the nineteenth
century. It exists in the double form of an Aztec text and
a Spanish translation, both due to Sahagun himself. Only
the Spanish version has hitherto been published in full, but
the original Aztec text, to judge by the few extracts of it
which have been edited and translated, appears to furnish
much more ample details on many points, and in the interest
of learning it is greatly to be desired that a complete edition
and translation of it should be given to the world.

Fortunately, among the sections of this great work which
have been edited and translated from the Aztec original into
German by Professor Eduard Seler of Berlin is a long one
describing the religious festivals of the ancient Mexican
calendar.[1] From it we learn some valuable particulars as to

Marginal notes: Sahagun's account of the ancient Mexican religion.

Marginal notes: Sahagun's description of the Mexican Maize-goddess and her festival.

---

[1] E. Seler, "Altmexikanische
Studien, ii.," *Veröffentlichungen aus
dem königlichen Museum für Völkerkunde*, vi. (Berlin, 1899) 2/4 Heft,
pp. 67 *sqq.* Another chapter of
Sahagun's work, describing the costumes
of the Mexican gods, has been edited
and translated into German by Professor E. Seler in the same series
of publications ("Altmexikanische
Studien," *Veröffentlichungen aus dem
königlichen Museum für Völkerkunde,*

the worship of the Maize-goddess and the ceremonies observed by the Mexicans for the purpose of ensuring a good crop of maize. The festival was the fourth of the Aztec year, and went by the name of the Great Vigil. It fell on a date which corresponds to the seventh of April. The name of the Maize-goddess was Chicome couatl, and the Mexicans conceived and represented her in the form of a woman, red in face and arms and legs, wearing a paper crown dyed vermilion, and clad in garments of the hue of ripe cherries. No doubt the red colour of the goddess and her garments referred to the deep orange hue of the ripe maize ; it was like the yellow hair of the Greek corn-goddess Demeter. She was supposed to make all kinds of maize, beans, and vegetables to grow. On the day of the festival the Mexicans sent out to the maize-fields and fetched from every field a plant of maize, which they brought to their houses and greeted as their maize - gods, setting them up in their dwellings, clothing them in garments, and placing food before them. And after sunset they carried the maize-plants to the temple of the Maize-goddess, where they snatched them from one another and fought and struck each other with them. Further, at this festival they brought to the temple of the Maize-goddess the maize-cobs which were to be used in the sowing. The cobs were carried by three maidens in bundles of seven wrapt in red paper. One of the girls was small with short hair, another was older with long hair hanging down, and the third was full-grown with her hair wound round her head. Red feathers were gummed to the arms and legs of the three maidens and their faces were painted, probably to resemble the red Maize-goddess, whom they may be supposed to have personated at various stages of the growth of the corn. The maize-cobs which they brought to the temple of the Maize-goddess were called by the name of the Maize-god Cinteotl, and they were afterwards deposited in the granary

i. 4 (Berlin, 1890) pp. 117 sqq.). Sahagun's work as a whole is known to me only in the excellent French translation of Messrs. D. Jourdanet and R. Simeon (*Histoire Générale des choses de la Nouvelle-Espagne par le*

R. P. Fray Bernardino de Sahagun, Paris, 1880). As to the life and character of Sahagun see M. R. Simeon's introduction to the translation, pp. vii. sqq.

and kept there as "the heart of the granary" till the sowing time came round, when they were used as seed.[1]

The eastern Indians of North America, who subsisted to a large extent by the cultivation of maize, generally conceived the spirit of the maize as a woman, and supposed that the plant itself had sprung originally from the blood drops or the dead body of the Corn Woman. In the sacred formulas of the Cherokee the corn is sometimes invoked as "the Old Woman," and one of their myths relates how a hunter saw a fair woman issue from a single green stalk of corn.[2] The Iroquois believe the Spirit of the Corn, the Spirit of Beans, and the Spirit of Squashes to be three sisters clad in the leaves of their respective plants, very fond of each other, and delighting to dwell together. This divine trinity is known by the name of *De-o-ha'-ko*, which means "Our Life" or "Our Supporters." The three persons of the trinity have no individual names, and are never mentioned separately except by means of description. The Indians have a legend that of old the corn was easily cultivated, yielded abundantly, and had a grain exceedingly rich in oil, till the Evil One, envious of this good gift of the Great Spirit to man, went forth into the fields and blighted them. And still, when the wind rustles in the corn, the pious Indian fancies he hears the Spirit of the Corn bemoaning her blighted fruitfulness.[3] The Huichol Indians of Mexico imagine maize to be a little girl, who may sometimes be heard weeping in the fields; so afraid is she of the wild beasts that eat the corn.[4]

The Corn-mother among the North American Indians.

---

[1] B. de Sahagun, Aztec text of book ii., translated by Professor E. Seler, "Altmexikanische Studien, ii.," *Veröffentlichungen aus dem königlichen Museum für Völkerkunde*, vi. 2/4 Heft (Berlin, 1899), pp. 188-194. The account of the ceremonies given in the Spanish version of Sahagun's work is a good deal more summary. See B. de Sahagun, *Histoire Générale des choses de la Nouvelle Espagne* (Paris, 1880), pp. 94-96.

[2] J. Mooney, "Myths of the Cherokee," *Nineteenth Annual Report*

of the *Bureau of American Ethnology*, Part I. (Washington, 1900) pp. 423, 432. See further *Adonis, Attis, Osiris*, Second Edition, pp. 296 *sq.*

[3] L. H. Morgan, *League of the Iroquois* (Rochester, 1851), pp. 161 *sq.*, 199. According to the Iroquois the corn plant sprang from the bosom of the mother of the Great Spirit after her burial (L. H. Morgan, *op. cit.* p. 199 note [1]).

[4] C. Lumholtz, *Unknown Mexico* (London, 1903), ii. 280.

§ 2. *The Mother-cotton in the Punjaub*

In the Punjaub, to the east of the Jumna, when the cotton boles begin to burst, it is usual to select the largest plant in the field, sprinkle it with butter-milk and rice-water, and then bind to it pieces of cotton taken from the other plants of the field. This selected plant is called Sirdar or *Bhogaldaí*, that is "mother-cotton," from *bhogla*, a name sometimes given to a large cotton-pod, and *daí* (for *daiya*), "a mother," and after it has been saluted, prayers are offered that the other plants may resemble it in the richness of their produce.[1]

§ 3. *The Barley Bride among the Berbers*

The conception of the corn-spirit as a bride seems to come out clearly in a ceremony still practised by the Berbers near Tangier, in Morocco. When the women assemble in the fields to weed the green barley or reap the crops, they take with them a straw figure dressed like a woman, and set it up among the corn. Suddenly a group of horsemen from a neighbouring village gallops up and carries off the straw puppet amid the screams and cries of the women. However, the ravished effigy is rescued by another band of mounted men, and after a struggle it remains, more or less dishevelled, in the hands of the women. That this pretended abduction is a mimic marriage appears from a Berber custom in accordance with which, at a real wedding, the bridegroom carries off his seemingly unwilling bride on horse-back, while she screams and pretends to summon her friends to her rescue. No fixed date is appointed for the simulated abduction of the straw woman from the barley-field, the time depends upon the state of the crops, but the day and hour are made public before the event. Each village used to practise this mimic contest for possession of the straw woman, who probably represents the Barley Bride, but nowadays the custom is growing obsolete.[2]

[1] H. M. Elliot, *Supplemental Glossary of Terms used in the North-Western Provinces*, edited by J. Beames (London, 1869), i. 254.

[2] W. B. Harris, "The Berbers of Morocco," *Journal of the Anthropological Institute*, xxvii. (1898) p. 68.

An earlier account of what seems to be the same practice runs as follows : " There is a curious custom which seems to be a relic of their pagan masters, who made this and the adjoining regions of North Africa the main granary of their Latin empire. When the young corn has sprung up, which it does about the middle of February, the women of the villages make up the figure of a female, the size of a very large doll, which they dress in the gaudiest fashion they can contrive, covering it with ornaments to which all in the village contribute something ; and they give it a tall, peaked head-dress. This image they carry in procession round their fields, screaming and singing a peculiar ditty. The doll is borne by the foremost woman, who must yield it to any one who is quick enough to take the lead of her, which is the cause of much racing and squabbling. The men also have a similar custom, which they perform on horseback. They call the image Mata. These ceremonies are said by the people to bring good luck. Their efficacy ought to be great, for you frequently see crowds of men engaged in their performances running and galloping recklessly over the young crops of wheat and barley. Such customs are directly opposed to the faith of Islam, and I never met with a Moor who could in any way enlighten me as to their origin. The Berber tribes, the most ancient race now remaining in these regions, to which they give the name, are the only ones which retain this antique usage, and it is viewed by the Arabs and dwellers in the town as a remnant of idolatry." [1] We may conjecture that this gaudily dressed effigy of a female, which the Berber women carry about their fields when the corn is sprouting, represents the Corn-mother, and that the procession is designed to promote the growth of the crops by imparting to them the quickening influence of the goddess. We can therefore understand why there should be a competition among the women for the possession of the effigy ; each woman probably hopes to secure for herself and her crops a larger measure of fertility by appropriating the image of the Corn - mother. The competition on horseback among the men is no doubt to be

---

[1] Sir John Drummond Hay, *Western Barbary, its Wild Tribes and Savage Animals* (1844), p. 9, quoted in *Folklore*, vii. (1896) pp. 306 *sq.*

explained similarly; they, too, race with each other in their eagerness to possess themselves of an effigy, perhaps of a male power of the corn, by whose help they expect to procure a heavy crop. Such contests for possession of the corn-spirit embodied in the corn-stalks are common, as we have seen, among the reapers on the harvest fields of Europe. Perhaps they help to explain some of the contests in the Eleusinian games, among which horse-races as well as foot-races were included.[1]

§ 4. *The Rice-mother in the East Indies*

Comparison of the European ritual of the corn with the Indonesian ritual of the rice.

If the reader still feels any doubts as to the meaning of the harvest customs which have been practised within living memory by European peasants, these doubts may perhaps be dispelled by comparing the customs observed at the rice-harvest by the Malays and Dyaks of the East Indies. For these Eastern peoples have not, like our peasantry, advanced beyond the intellectual stage at which the customs originated; their theory and their practice are still in unison; for them the quaint rites which in Europe have long dwindled into mere fossils, the pastime of clowns and the puzzle of the learned, are still living realities of which they can render an intelligible and truthful account. Hence a study of their beliefs and usages concerning the rice may throw some light on the true meaning of the ritual of the corn in ancient Greece and modern Europe.

The Indonesian ritual of the rice is based on the belief that the rice is animated by a soul.

Now the whole of the ritual which the Malays and Dyaks observe in connexion with the rice is founded on the simple conception of the rice as animated by a soul like that which these people attribute to mankind. They explain the phenomena of reproduction, growth, decay and death in the rice on the same principles on which they explain the corresponding phenomena in human beings. They imagine that in the fibres of the plant, as in the body of a man, there is a certain vital element, which is so far independent of the plant that it may for a time be completely separated from it without fatal effects, though if its absence be prolonged beyond certain limits the plant will wither and

[1] See above, pp. 70 *sqq.*

die. This vital yet separable element is what, for the want
of a better word, we must call the soul of a plant, just as a
similar vital and separable element is commonly supposed
to constitute the soul of man ; and on this theory or myth
of the plant-soul is built the whole worship of the cereals,
just as on the theory or myth of the human soul is built
the whole worship of the dead,—a towering superstructure
reared on a slender and precarious foundation.

The strict parallelism between the Indonesian ideas
about the soul of man and the soul of rice is well brought
out by Mr. R. J. Wilkinson in the following passage : " The
spirit of life,—which, according to the ancient Indonesian
belief, existed in all things, even in what we should now
consider inanimate objects—is known as the *sĕmangat*.   It
was not a ' soul ' in the modern English sense, since it was
not the exclusive possession of mankind, its separation from
the body did not necessarily mean death, and its nature may
possibly not have been considered immortal.   At the present
day, if a Malay feels faint, he will describe his condition by
saying that his ' spirit of life ' is weak or is ' flying ' from his
body ; he sometimes appeals to it to return : ' Hither, hither,
bird of my soul.'   Or again, if a Malay lover wishes to
influence the mind of a girl, he may seek to obtain control
of her *sĕmangat*, for he believes that this spirit of active and
vigorous life must quit the body when the body sleeps and
so be liable to capture by the use of magic arts.   It is,
however, in the ceremonies connected with the so-called
' spirit of the rice-crops ' that the peculiar characteristics of
the *sĕmangat* come out most clearly.   The Malay considers
it essential that the spirit of life should not depart from the
rice intended for next year's sowing as otherwise the dead
seed would fail to produce any crop whatever.   He, therefore, approaches the standing rice-crops at harvest-time in a
deprecatory manner ; he addresses them in endearing terms ;
he offers propitiatory sacrifices ; he fears that he may scare
away the timorous ' bird of life ' by the sight of a weapon or
the least sign of violence.   He must reap the seed-rice, but
he does it with a knife of peculiar shape, such that the cruel
blade is hidden away beneath the reaper's fingers and does
not alarm the ' soul of the rice.'   When once the seed-rice

Parallelism
between
the human
soul and
the rice-
soul.

has been harvested, more expeditious reaping-tools may be employed, since it is clearly unnecessary to retain the spirit of life in grain that is only intended for the cooking-pot. Similar rites attend all the processes of rice-cultivation—the sowing and the planting-out as well as the harvest,—for at each of these stages there is a risk that the vitality of the crop may be ruined if the bird of life is scared away. In the language used by the high-priests of these very ancient ceremonies we constantly find references to Sri (the Hindu Goddess of the Crops), to the fruit of the Tree of Knowledge, and to Adam who, according to Moslem tradition, was the first planter of cereals ;—many of these references only represent the attempts of the conservative Malays to make their old religions harmonize with later beliefs. Beneath successive layers of religious veneer, we see the animism of the old Indonesians, the theory of a bird-spirit of life, and the characteristic view that the best protection against evil lies in gentleness and courtesy to all animate and inanimate things." [1]

The soul-stuff of rice.

"It is a familiar fact," says another eminent authority on the East Indies, "that the Indonesian imagines rice to be animated, to be provided with ' soul-stuff.' Since rice is everywhere cultivated in the Indian Archipelago, and with some exceptions is the staple food, we need not wonder that the Indonesian conceives the rice to be not merely animated in the ordinary sense but to be possessed of a soul-stuff which in strength and dignity ranks with that of man. Thus the Bataks apply the same word *tondi* to the soul-stuff of rice and the soul-stuff of human beings. Whereas the Dyaks of Poelopetak give the name of *gana* to the soul-stuff of things, animals, and plants, they give the name of *hambaruan* to the soul-stuff of rice as well as of

[1] R. J. Wilkinson (of the Civil Service of the Federated Malay States), *Malay Beliefs* (London and Leyden, 1906), pp. 49-51. On the conception of the soul as a bird, see *Taboo and the Perils of the Soul*, pp. 33 *sqq*. The Toradjas of Central Celebes think that the soul of the rice is embodied in a pretty little blue bird, which builds its nest in the rice-field when the ears are forming and vanishes after harvest. Hence no one may drive away, much less kill, these birds ; to do so would not only injure the crop, the sacrilegious wretch himself would suffer from sickness, which might end in blindness. See A. C. Kruyt, "De Rijstmoeder in den Indischen Archipel," p. 374 (see the full reference in the next note).

man. So also the inhabitants of Halmahera call the soul-stuff of things and plants *giki* and *duhutu*, but in men and food they recognise a *gurumi*. Of the Javanese, Malays, Macassars, Buginese, and the inhabitants of the island of Buru we know that they ascribe a *sumangè*, *sumangat*, or *sĕmangat* to rice as well as to men. So it is with the Toradjas of Central Celebes ; while they manifestly conceive all things and plants as animated, they attribute a *tanoana* or soul-stuff only to men, animals, and rice. It need hardly be said that this custom originates in the very high value that is set on rice." [1]

Believing the rice to be animated by a soul like that of a man, the Indonesians naturally treat it with the deference and the consideration which they shew to their fellows. Thus they behave towards the rice in bloom as they behave towards a pregnant woman ; they abstain from firing guns or making loud noises in the field, lest they should so frighten the soul of the rice that it would mis-carry and bear no grain ; and for the same reason they will not talk of corpses or demons in the rice-fields. Moreover, they feed the blooming rice with foods of various kinds which are believed to be wholesome for women with child ; but when the rice-ears are just beginning to form, they are looked upon as infants, and women go through the fields feeding them with rice-pap as if they were human babes. [2] In such natural and obvious comparisons of the breeding plant to a breeding woman, and of the young grain to a young child, is to be sought the origin of the kindred Greek

Rice treated by the In-donesians as if it were a woman.

[1] A. C. Kruyt, " De Rijstmoeder in den Indischen Archipel," *Verslagen en Mededeelingen der koninklijke Akademie van Wetenschappen*, Afdeeling Letter-kunde, Vierde Reeks, v. part 4 (Am-sterdam, 1903), pp. 361 *sq*. This essay (pp. 361-411) contains a valuable collection of facts relating to what the writer calls the Rice-mother in the East Indies. But it is to be observed that while all the Indonesian peoples seem to treat a certain portion of the rice at harvest with superstitious respect and ceremony, only a part of them actually call it " the Rice-mother." Mr. Kruyt prefers to speak of " soul-stuff " rather than of " a soul," because, according to him, in living beings the animating principle is conceived, not as a tiny being confined to a single part of the body, but as a sort of fluid or ether diffused through every part of the body. See his work, *Het Ani-misme in den Indischen Archipel* (The Hague, 1906), pp. 1 *sqq*. In the latter work (pp. 145-150) the writer gives a more summary account of the Indonesian theory of the rice-soul.

[2] See *The Magic Art and the Evolu-tion of Kings*, ii. 28 *sq*. ; A. C. Kruyt, " De Rijstmoeder," *op. cit.* pp. 363 *sq*., 370 *sqq*.

conception of the Corn-mother and the Corn-daughter, Demeter and Persephone, and we need not go further afield to search for it in a primitive division of labour between the sexes.[1]   But if the timorous feminine soul of the rice can be frightened into a miscarriage even by loud noises, it is easy to imagine what her feelings must be at harvest, when people are under the sad necessity of cutting down the rice with the knife.   At so critical a season every precaution must be used to render the necessary surgical operation of reaping as inconspicuous and as painless as possible.   For that reason, as we have seen,[2] the reaping of the seed-rice is done with knives of a peculiar pattern, such that the blades are hidden in the reapers' hands and do not frighten the rice-spirit till the very last moment, when her head is swept off almost before she is aware ; and from a like delicate motive the reapers at work in the fields employ a special form of speech, which the rice-spirit cannot be expected to understand, so that she has no warning or inkling of what is going forward till the heads of rice are safely deposited in the basket.[3]

The Kayans of Borneo, their treatment of the soul of the rice.   Among the Indonesian peoples who thus personify the rice we may take the Kayans or Bahaus of Central Borneo as typical.   As we have already seen, they are essentially an agricultural people devoted to the cultivation of rice, which furnishes their staple food ; their religion is deeply coloured by this main occupation of their lives, and it presents many analogies to the Eleusinian worship of the corn-goddesses Demeter and Persephone.[4]   And just as the Greeks regarded corn as a gift of the goddess Demeter, so the Kayans believe that rice, maize, sweet potatoes, tobacco, and all the other products of the earth which they cultivate, were originally created for their benefit by the spirits.[5]

Instruments used by the Kayans for the purpose of   In order to secure and detain the volatile soul of the rice the Kayans resort to a number of devices.   Among the instruments employed for this purpose are a miniature ladder, a spatula, and a basket containing hooks, thorns, and

[1] See above, pp. 113 *sqq.*
[2] See above, p. 181.
[3] See *Taboo and the Perils of the Soul*, pp. 411 *sq.* ; A. C. Kruyt, "De

Rijstmoeder," *op. cit.* p. 372.
[4] See above, pp. 92 *sqq.*
[5] A. W. Nieuwenhuis, *Quer durch Borneo* (Leyden, 1904-1907), i. 157 *sq.*

cords.   With the spatula the priestess strokes the soul of
the rice down the little ladder into the basket, where it is
naturally held fast by the hooks, the thorn, and the cord;
and having thus captured and imprisoned the soul she
conveys it into the rice-granary.   Sometimes a bamboo box
and a net are used for the same purpose.   And in order to
ensure a good harvest for the following year it is necessary
not only to detain the soul of all the grains of rice which
are safely stored in the granary, but also to attract and
recover the soul of all the rice that has been lost through
falling to the earth or being eaten by deer, apes, and pigs.
For this purpose instruments of various sorts have been
invented by the priests.   One, for example, is a bamboo
vessel provided with four hooks made from the wood of a
fruit-tree, by means of which the absent rice-soul may be
hooked and drawn back into the vessel, which is then hung
up in the house.   Sometimes two hands carved out of the
wood of a fruit-tree are used for the same purpose.   And
every time that a Kayan housewife fetches rice from the
granary for the use of her household, she must propitiate
the souls of the rice in the granary, lest they should be
angry at being robbed of their substance.   To keep them
in good humour a bundle of shavings of a fruit-tree and
a little basket are always hung in the granary.   An egg
and a small vessel containing the juice of sugar-cane are
attached as offerings to the bundle of shavings, and the
basket contains a sacred mat, which is used at fetching the
rice.   When the housewife comes to fetch rice from the
granary, she pours juice of the sugar-cane on the egg, takes
the sacred mat from the basket, spreads it on the ground,
lays a stalk of rice on it, and explains to the souls of the
rice the object of her coming.   Then she kneels before the
mat, mutters some prayers or spells, eats a single grain from
the rice-stalk, and having restored the various objects to
their proper place, departs from the granary with the
requisite amount of rice, satisfied that she has discharged
her religious duty to the spirits of the rice.   At harvest the
spirits of the rice are propitiated with offerings of food and
water, which are carried by children to the rice-fields.   At
evening the first rice-stalks which have been cut are solemnly

brought home in a consecrated basket to the beating of a gong, and all cats and dogs are driven from the house before the basket with its precious contents is brought in.[1]

Masquerade performed by the Kayans before sowing for the purpose of attracting the soul of the rice.

Among the Kayans of the Mahakam river in Central Borneo the sowing of the rice is immediately preceded by a performance of masked men, which is intended to attract the soul or rather souls of the rice and so to make sure that the harvest will be a good one. The performers represent spirits ; for, believing that spirits are mightier than men, the Kayans imagine that they can acquire and exert superhuman power by imitating the form and actions of spirits.[2] To support their assumed character they wear grotesque masks with goggle eyes, great teeth, huge ears, and beards of white goat's hair, while their bodies are so thickly wrapt up in shredded banana-leaves that to the spectator they present the appearance of unwieldy masses of green foliage. The leader of the band carries a long wooden hook or rather crook, the shaft of which is partly whittled into loose fluttering shavings. These disguises they don at a little distance from the village, then dropping down the river in boats they land and march in procession to an open space among the houses, where the people, dressed out in all their finery, are waiting to witness the performance. Here the maskers range themselves in a circle and dance for some time under the burning rays of the midday sun, waving their arms, shaking and turning their heads, and executing a variety of steps to the sound of a gong, which is beaten according to a rigidly prescribed rhythm. After the dance they form a line, one behind the other, to fetch the vagrant soul of the rice from far countries. At the head of the procession marches the leader holding high his crook and behind him follow all the other masked men in their leafy costume, each holding his fellow by the hand. As he strides along, the leader makes a motion with his crook as if he were hooking something and drawing it to himself, and the gesture is imitated by all his followers. What

---

[1] A. W. Nieuwenhuis, *op. cit.* i. 118-121. Compare *id., In Centraal Borneo* (Leyden, 1900), i. 154 *sqq.*

[2] A similar belief probably explains the masked dances and pantomimes of many savage tribes. If that is so, it shews how deeply the principle of imitative magic has influenced savage religion.

he is thus catching are the souls of the rice, which sometimes wander far away, and by drawing them home to the village he is believed to ensure that the seed of the rice which is about to be sown will produce a plentiful harvest. As the spirits are thought not to possess the power of speech, the actors who personate them may not utter a word, else they would run the risk of falling down dead. The great field of the chief is sown by representatives of all the families, both free and slaves, on the day after the masquerade. On the same day the free families sacrifice on their fields and begin their sowing on one or other of the following days. Every family sets up in its field a sacrificial stage or altar, with which the sowers must remain in connexion during the time of sowing. Therefore no stranger may pass between them and the stage ; indeed the Kayans are not allowed to have anything to do with strangers in the fields ; above all they may not speak with them. If such a thing should accidentally happen, the sowing must cease for that day. At the sowing festival, but at no other time, Kayan men of the Mahakam river, like their brethren of the Mendalam river, amuse themselves with spinning tops. For nine days before the masquerade takes place the people are bound to observe certain taboos : no stranger may enter the village : no villager may pass the night out of his own house : they may not hunt, nor pluck fruits, nor fish with the casting-net or the drag-net.[1] In this tribe the proper day for sowing is officially determined by a priest from an observation of the sun setting behind the hills in a line with two stones which the priest has set up, one behind the other. However, the official day often does not coincide with the actual day of sowing.[2]

The masquerade thus performed by the Kayans of the Mahakum river before sowing the rice is an instructive example of a religious or rather magical drama acted for the express purpose of ensuring a good crop. As such it may be compared to the drama of Demeter and Persephone,

Comparison of the Kayan masquerade with the Eleusinian drama.

---

[1] A. W. Nieuwenhuis, *Quer durch Borneo*, i. 322-330. Compare *id.*, *In Centraal Borneo*, i. 185 *sq*. As to the masquerades performed and the taboos observed at the sowing season by the Kayans of the Mendalam river, see above, pp. 94 *sqq*.

[2] A. W. Nieuwenhuis, *op. cit.* i. 317.

the Corn-mother and the Corn-maiden, which was annually
played at the Eleusinian mysteries shortly before the
autumnal sowing of the corn.   If my interpretation of these
mysteries is correct, the intention of the Greek and of the
Kayan drama was one and the same.

Securing
the soul of
the rice
among the
Dyaks of
Northern
Borneo.

At harvest the Dyaks of Northern Borneo have a special
feast, the object of which is "to secure the soul of the rice,
which if not so detained, the produce of their farms would
speedily rot and decay.   At sowing time, a little of the
principle of life of the rice, which at every harvest is secured
by their priests, is planted with their other seeds, and is thus
propagated and communicated."   The mode of securing the
soul of the rice varies in different tribes.   In the Quop district
the ceremony is performed by the chief priest alone, first in the
long broad verandah of the common house and afterwards
in each separate family apartment.   As a preparation for
the ceremony a bamboo altar, decorated with green boughs
and red and white streamers, is erected in the verandah,
and presents a very gay appearance.   Here the people, old
and young, assemble, the priestesses dressed in gorgeous
array and the elder men wearing bright-coloured jackets and
trousers of purple, yellow, or scarlet hue, while the young
men and lads beat gongs and drums.   When the priest,
with a bundle of charms in either hand, is observed to be
gazing earnestly in the air at something invisible to common
eyes, the band strikes up with redoubled energy, and the
elderly men in the gay breeches begin to shriek and revolve
round the altar in the dance.   Suddenly the priest starts
up and makes a rush at the invisible object; men run to
him with white cloths, and as he shakes his charms over the
cloths a few grains of rice fall into them.   These grains are
the soul of the rice; they are carefully folded up in the
cloths and laid at the foot of the altar.   The same performance is afterwards repeated in every family apartment.   In
some tribes the soul of the rice is secured at midnight.   Outside the village a lofty altar is erected in an open space
surrounded by the stately forms of the tropical palms.
Huge bonfires cast a ruddy glow over the scene and light
up the dusky but picturesque forms of the Dyaks as they
move in slow and solemn dance round the altar, some

bearing lighted tapers in their hands, others brass salvers with offerings of rice, others covered baskets, of which the contents are hidden from all but the initiated.   The corner-posts of the altar are lofty bamboos, whose leafy tops are yet green and rustle in the wind ; and from one of them a long narrow streamer of white cloth hangs down.   Suddenly elders and priests rush at this streamer, seize the end of it, and amid the crashing music of drums and gongs and the yells of the spectators begin dancing and swaying themselves backwards and forwards, and to and fro.   A priest or elder mounts the altar amid the shouts of the bystanders and shakes the tall bamboos violently ; and in the midst of all this excitement and hubbub small stones, bunches of hair, and grains of rice fall at the feet of the dancers, and are carefully picked up by watchful attendants.   These grains are the soul of the rice.   The ceremony ends with several of the oldest priestesses falling, or pretending to fall, sense-less to the ground, where, till they come to themselves, their heads are supported and their faces fanned by their younger colleagues.   At the end of the harvest, when the year's crop has been garnered, another feast is held.   A pig and fowls are killed, and for four days gongs are beaten and dancing kept up.   For eight days the village is tabooed and no stranger may enter it.   At this festival the ceremony of catching the soul of the rice is repeated to prevent the crop from rotting ; and the soul so obtained is mixed with the seed-rice of the next year.[1]

The same need of securing the soul of the rice, if the crop is to thrive, is keenly felt by the Karens of Burma. When a rice-field does not flourish, they suppose that the soul (*kelah*) of the rice is in some way detained from the rice. If the soul cannot be called back, the crop will fail.   The following formula is used in recalling the *kelah* (soul) of the rice : " O come, rice-*kelah*, come !   Come to the field.   Come to the rice.   With seed of each gender, come.   Come from the river Kho, come from the river Kaw ; from the place where they meet, come.   Come from the West, come from

Recalling the soul of the rice among the Karens of Burma.

[1] Spenser St. John, *Life in the Forests of the Far East*[2] (London, 1863), i. 187, 192 *sqq.* ; W. Chalmers, quoted in H. Ling Roth's *Natives of Sarawak and British North Borneo* (London, 1896), i. 412-414.

the East.   From the throat of the bird, from the maw of the ape, from the throat of the elephant.   Come from the sources of rivers and their mouths.   Come from the country of the Shan and Burman.   From the distant kingdoms come. From all granaries come.   O rice-*kelah*, come to the rice." [1]

Securing the soul of the rice in various parts of Burma.

Among the Taungthu of Upper Burma it is customary, when all the rice-fields have been reaped, to make a trail of unhusked rice (paddy) and husks all the way from the fields to the farm-house in order to guide the spirit or butterfly, as they call it, of the rice home to the granary.   Care is taken that there should be no break in the trail, and the butterfly of the rice is invited with loud cries to come to the house.   Were the spirit of the rice not secured in this manner, next year's harvest would be bad.[2]   Similarly among the Cherokee Indians of North America " care was always taken to keep a clean trail from the field to the house, so that the corn might be encouraged to stay at home and not go wandering elsewhere," and " seven ears from the last year's crop were always put carefully aside, in order to *attract the corn*, until the new crop was ripened." [3]   In Hsa Möng Hkam, a native state of Upper Burma, when two men work rice-fields in partnership, they take particular care as to the division of the grain between them.   Each partner has a basket made, of which both top and bottom are carefully closed with wood to prevent the butterfly spirit of the rice from escaping ; for if it were to flutter away, the next year's crop would be but poor.[4]   Among the Talaings of Lower Burma "the last sheaf is larger than the rest ; it is brought home separately, usually if not invariably on the morning after the remainder of the harvest has been carted to the threshing-floor.   The cultivators drive out in their bullock-cart, taking with them a woman's comb, a looking-glass, and a woman's skirt.   The sheaf is dressed in the skirt, and apparently the form is gone through of presenting

[1] Rev. E. B. Cross, "On the Karens," *Journal of the American Oriental Society*, iv. (1854) p. 309.
[2] (Sir) J. G. Scott and J. P. Hardiman, *Gazetteer of Upper Burma and of the Shan States* (Rangoon, 1900-1901), Part i. vol. i. p. 559.
[3] J. Mooney, "Myths of the Cherokee," *Nineteenth Annual Report of the Bureau of American Ethnology*, Part i. (Washington, 1900) p. 423. Compare *Adonis, Attis, Osiris*, Second Edition, pp. 296 sq.
[4] (Sir) J. G. Scott and J. P. Hardiman, *op. cit.* Part ii. vol. i. p. 172.

it with the glass and comb. It is then brought home in triumph, the people decking the cart with their silk kerchiefs, and cheering and singing the whole way. On their arrival home they celebrate the occasion with a feast. Strictly speaking the sheaf should be kept apart from the rest of the harvest ; owing, however, to the high price of paddy it often finds its way to the threshing-floor. Even when this is not the case it is rarely tended so carefully as it is said to have been in former days, and if not threshed with the remaining crop is apt to be eaten by the cattle. So far as I could ascertain it had never been the custom to keep it throughout the year ; but on the first ploughing of the ensuing season there was some ceremony in connection with it. The name of the sheaf was *Bonmagyi* ; at first I was inclined to fancy that this was a contraction of *thelinbon ma gyi*, 'the old woman of the threshing-floor.' There are, however, various reasons for discarding this derivation, and I am unable to suggest any other."[1] In this custom the personification of the last sheaf of rice as a woman comes out clearly in the practice of dressing it up in female attire.

The Corn-mother of our European peasants has her match in the Rice-mother of the Minangkabauers of Sumatra. The Minangkabauers definitely attribute a soul to rice, and will sometimes assert that rice pounded in the usual way tastes better than rice ground in a mill, because in the mill the body of the rice was so bruised and battered that the soul has fled from it. Like the Javanese they think that the rice is under the special guardianship of a female spirit called Saning Sari, who is conceived as so closely knit up with the plant that the rice often goes by her name, as with the Romans the corn might be called Ceres. In particular Saning Sari is represented by certain stalks or grains called *indoea padi*, that is, literally, " Mother of Rice," a name that is often given to the guardian spirit herself. This so-called Mother of Rice is the occasion of a number of ceremonies observed at the planting and harvesting of the rice as well as during its preservation in the barn.

The Rice-mother among the Minangkabauers of Sumatra.

---

[1] From a letter written to me by Mr. J. S. Furnivall and dated Pegu Club, Rangoon, 6/6 (*sic*). Mr. Furnivall adds that in Upper Burma the custom of the *Bonmagyi* sheaf is unknown.

The Rice-
mother
among the
Minang-
kabauers of
Sumatra.
When the seed of the rice is about to be sown in the
nursery or bedding-out ground, where under the wet system
of cultivation it is regularly allowed to sprout before being
transplanted to the fields, the best grains are picked out to
form the Rice-mother. These are then sown in the middle
of the bed, and the common seed is planted round about
them. The state of the Rice-mother is supposed to exert
the greatest influence on the growth of the rice; if she
droops or pines away, the harvest will be bad in consequence.
The woman who sows the Rice-mother in the nursery lets
her hair hang loose and afterwards bathes, as a means of
ensuring an abundant harvest. When the time comes to
transplant the rice from the nursery to the field, the Rice-
mother receives a special place either in the middle or in a
corner of the field, and a prayer or charm is uttered as
follows : " Saning Sari, may a measure of rice come from a
stalk of rice and a basketful from a root ; may you be
frightened neither by lightning nor by passers-by ! Sunshine
make you glad ; with the storm may you be at peace ; and
may rain serve to wash your face ! " While the rice is
growing, the particular plant which was thus treated as the
Rice-mother is lost sight of ; but before harvest another
Rice-mother is found. When the crop is ripe for cutting,
the oldest woman of the family or a sorcerer goes out to
look for her. The first stalks seen to bend under a passing
breeze are the Rice-mother, and they are tied together but
not cut until the first-fruits of the field have been carried
home to serve as a festal meal for the family and their
friends, nay even for the domestic animals ; since it is Saning
Sari's pleasure that the beasts also should partake of her
good gifts. After the meal has been eaten, the Rice-mother
is fetched home by persons in gay attire, who carry her very
carefully under an umbrella in a neatly worked bag to the
barn, where a place in the middle is assigned to her. Every
one believes that she takes care of the rice in the barn and
even multiplies it not uncommonly.[1]

[1] J. L. van der Toorn, " Het
animisme bij den Minangkabauer der
Padangsche Bovenlanden," *Bijdragen
tot de Taal- Land- en Volkenkunde van
Nederlandsch Indië*, xxxix. (1890) pp.
63-65. In the charm recited at sowing
the Rice-mother in the bed, I have
translated the Dutch word *stoel* as
"root," but I am not sure of its precise
meaning in this connexion. It is

When the Tomori of Central Celebes are about to plant the rice, they bury in the field some betel as an offering to the spirits who cause the rice to grow. Over the spot where the offering is buried a small floor of wood is laid, and the family sits on it and consumes betel together as a sort of silent prayer or charm to ensure the growth of the crop. The rice that is planted round this spot is the last to be reaped at harvest. At the commencement of the reaping the stalks of this patch of rice are tied together into a sheaf, which is called "the Mother of the Rice" (*ineno pae*), and offerings in the shape of rice, fowl's liver, eggs, and other things are laid down before it. When all the rest of the rice in the field has been reaped, "the Mother of the Rice" is cut down and carried with due honour to the rice-barn, where it is laid on the floor, and all the other sheaves are piled upon it. The Tomori, we are told, regard the Mother of the Rice as a special offering made to the rice-spirit Omonga, who dwells in the moon. If that spirit is not treated with proper respect, for example if the people who fetch rice from the barn are not decently clad, he is angry and punishes the offenders by eating up twice as much rice in the barn as they have taken out of it; some people have heard him smacking his lips in the barn, as he devoured the rice. On the other hand the Toradjas of Central Celebes, who also practise the custom of the Rice-mother at harvest, regard her as the actual mother of the whole harvest, and therefore keep her carefully, lest in her absence the garnered store of rice should all melt away and disappear.[1] Among the Tomori, as among other Indonesian peoples, reapers at work in the field make use of special words which differ from the terms in ordinary use; the reason for adopting this peculiar form of speech at reaping appears to be, as I have already pointed out, a fear of alarming the timid soul of the rice by revealing the fate in store for it.[2] To the same

doubtless identical with the English agricultural term "to stool," which is said of a number of stalks sprouting from a single seed, as I learn from my friend Professor W. Somerville of Oxford.

[1] A. C. Kruijt, "Eenige ethno-grafische aanteekeningen omtrent de Toboengkoe en de Tomori," *Mede-deelingen van wege het Nederlandsche Zendelinggenootschap*, xliv. (1900) pp. 227, 230 sq.

[2] See *Taboo and the Perils of the Soul*, pp. 411 sq.

motive is perhaps to be ascribed the practice observed
by the Tomori of asking each other riddles at harvest.[1]

Riddles
and stories
in con-
nexion with
the rice.

Similarly among the Alfoors or Toradjas of Poso, in Central
Celebes, while the people are watching the crops in the fields
they amuse themselves with asking each other riddles and
telling stories, and when any one guesses a riddle aright, the
whole company cries out, " Let our rice come up, let fat ears
come up both in the lowlands and on the heights." But all
the time between harvest and the laying out of new fields
the asking of riddles and the telling of stories is strictly
forbidden.[2] Thus among these people it seems that the
asking of riddles is for some reason regarded as a charm
which may make or mar the crops.

The Rice-
mother
among the
Toradjas
of Celebes.

Among some of the Toradjas of Celebes the ceremony
of cutting and bringing home the Mother of the Rice
is observed as follows. When the crop is ripe in the
fields, the Mother of the Rice (*ânrong pâre*) must be
fetched before the rest of the harvest is reaped. The
ceremony is performed on a lucky day by a woman, who
knows the rites. For three days previously she observes
certain precautions to prevent the soul (*soemangâna âse*) of
the rice from escaping out of the field, as it might be apt to
do, if it got wind that the reapers with their cruel knives
were so soon to crop the ripe ears. With this view she ties
up a handful of standing stalks of the rice into a bunch in
each corner of the field, while she recites an invocation
to the spirits of the rice, bidding them gather in the field
from the four quarters of the heaven. As a further precaution she stops the sluices, lest with the outrush of the
water from the rice-field the sly soul of the rice should make
good its escape. And she ties knots in the leaves of the
rice-plants, all to hinder the soul of the rice from running
away. This she does in the afternoon of three successive
days. On the morning of the fourth day she comes again
to the field, sits down in a corner of it, and kisses the rice
three times, again inviting the souls of the rice to come
thither and assuring them of her affection and care. Then

[1] A. C. Kruijt, *op. cit.* p. 228.

[2] A. C. Kruijt, " Een en ander
aangaande het geestelijk en maatschap-

elijk leven van den Poso-Alfoer,"
*Mededeelingen van wege het Nederland-
sche Zendelinggenootschap,*xxxix.(1895)
pp. 142 *sq.*

she cuts the bunch of rice-stalks which she had tied together on one of the previous days. The stalks in the bunch must be nine in number, and their leaves must be cut with them, not thrown away. As she cuts, she may not look about her, nor cry out, nor speak to any one, nor be spoken to ; but she says to the rice, " The prophet reaps you. I take you, but you diminish not ; I hold you in my hand and you increase. You are the links of my soul, the support of my body, my blessing, my salvation. There is no God but God." Then she passes to another corner of the field to cut the bunch of standing rice in it with the same ceremony ; but before coming to it she stops half way to pluck another bunch of five stalks in like manner. Thus from the four sides of the field she collects in all fifty-six stalks of rice, which together make up the Mother of the Rice (*ânrong pâre*). Then in a corner of the field she makes a little stage and lays the Mother of the Rice on it, with the ears turned towards the standing rice and the cut stalks towards the dyke which encloses the field. After that she binds the fifty-six stalks of the Rice-mother into a sheaf with the bark of a particular kind of tree. As she does so, she says, " The prophet binds you into a sheaf ; the angel increases you ; the *awâlli* cares for you. We loved and cared for each other." Then, after anointing the sheaf and fumigating it with incense, she lays it on the little stage. On this stage she had previously placed several kinds of rice, betel, one or more eggs, sweetmeats, and young coco-nuts, all as offerings to the Mother of the Rice, who, if she did not receive these attentions, would be offended and visit people with sickness or even vanish away altogether. Some-times on large farms a fowl is killed and its blood deposited in the half of a coco-nut on the stage. The standing rice round about the stage is the last of the whole field to be reaped. When it has been cut, it is bound up with the Mother of the Rice into a single sheaf and carried home. Any body may carry the sheaf, but in doing so he or she must take care not to let it fall, or the Rice-mother would be angry and might disappear.[1]

[1] G. Maan, " Eenige mededeelingen omtrent de zeden en gewoonten der   Toerateya ten opzichte van den rijstbouw," *Tijdschrift voor Indische*

The rice
personified
as a young
woman
among the
Bataks of
Sumatra.

Among the Battas or Bataks of Sumatra the rice appears to be personified as a young unmarried woman rather than as a mother. On the first day of reaping the crop only a few ears of rice are plucked and made up into a little sheaf. After that the reaping may begin, and while it is going forward offerings of rice and betel are presented in the middle of the field to the spirit of the rice, who is personified under the name of Miss Dajang. The offering is accompanied by a common meal shared by the reapers. When all the rice has been reaped, threshed and garnered, the little sheaf which was first cut is brought in and laid on the top of the heap in the granary, together with an egg or a stone, which is supposed to watch over the rice.[1] Though we are not told, we may assume that the personified spirit of the rice is supposed to be present in the first sheaf cut and in that form to keep guard over the rice in the granary. Another writer, who has independently described the customs of the Karo-Bataks at the rice-harvest, tells us that the largest sheaf, which is usually the one first made up, is regarded as the seat of the rice-soul and is treated exactly like a person ; at the trampling of the paddy to separate the grain from the husks the sheaf in question is specially entrusted to a girl who has a lucky name, and whose parents are both alive.[2]

Taal- Land- en Volkenkunde, xlvi. (1903) pp. 330-337. The writer dates his article from Tanneteya (in Celebes?), but otherwise gives no indication of the geographical position of the people he describes. A similar omission is common with Dutch writers on the geography and ethnology of the East Indies, who too often appear to assume that the uncouth names of these barbarous tribes and obscure hamlets are as familiar to European readers as Amsterdam or the Hague. The Toerateyas whose customs Mr. Maan describes in this article are the inland inhabitants of Celebes. Their name Toerateyas or Toradjas signifies simply "inlanders" and is applied to them by their neighbours who live nearer the sea ; it is not a name used by the people themselves. The Toradjas include many tribes and the particular tribe whose

usages in regard to the Rice-mother are described in the text is probably not one of those whose customs and beliefs have been described by Mr. A. C. Kruijt in many valuable papers. See above, p. 183 note[1], and *The Magic Art and the Evolution of Kings*, i. 109 note[1].

[1] M. Joustra, "Het leven, de zeden en gewoonten der Bataks," *Mededeelingen van wege het Nederlandsche Zendelinggenootschap*, xlvi. (1902) pp. 425 *sq*.

[2] J. H. Neumann, "Iets over den landbouw bij de Karo-Bataks," *Mededeelingen van wege het Nederlandsche Zendelinggenootschap*, xlvi. (1902) pp. 380 *sq*. As to the employment in ritual of young people whose parents are both alive, see *Adonis, Attis, Osiris*, Second Edition, pp. 413 *sqq*.

In Mandeling, a district of Sumatra, contrary to what The King seems to be the usual practice, the spirit of the rice is personi- of the Rice in fied as a male instead of as a female and is called the Rajah Mandeling. or King of the Rice. He is supposed to be immanent in certain rice-plants, which are recognised by their peculiar formation, such as a concealment of the ears in the sheath, an unusual arrangement of the leaves, or a stunted growth, When one or more such plants have been discovered in the field, they are sprinkled with lime-juice, and the spirits are invoked by name and informed that they are expected at home and that all is ready for their reception. Then the King of the Rice is plucked with the hand and seven neighbouring rice-stalks cut with a knife. He and his seven companions are then carefully brought home ; the bearer may not speak a word, and the children in the house may make no noise till the King of the Rice has been safely lodged in the granary and tethered, for greater security, with a grass rope to one of the posts. As soon as that is done, the doors are shut to prevent the spirits of the rice from escaping. The person who fetches the King of the Rice from the field should prepare himself for the important duty by eating a hearty meal, for it would be an omen of a bad harvest if he presented himself before the King of the Rice with an empty stomach. For the same reason the sower of rice should sow the seed on a full stomach, in order that the ears which spring from the seed may be full also.[1]

Again, just as in Scotland the old and the young spirit The Rice- of the corn are represented as an Old Wife (*Cailleach*) and mother and the Rice- a Maiden respectively, so in the Malay Peninsula we find child at both the Rice-mother and her child represented by different harvest in the Malay sheaves or bundles of ears on the harvest-field. The follow- Peninsula. ing directions for obtaining both are translated from a native Malay work on the cultivation of rice : "When the rice is

[1] A. L. van Hasselt, "Nota, betref-fende de rijstcultuur in de Residentie Tapanoeli," *Tijdschrift voor Indische Taal- Land- en Volkenkunde*, xxxvi. (1893) pp. 526-529; Th. A. L. Heyting, "Beschrijving der Onderaf-deeling Groot- mandeling en Batang-natal," *Tijdschrift van het Nederlandsch*

Aardrijkskundig Genootschap, Tweede Serie, xiv. (1897) pp. 290 *sq*. As to the rule of sowing seed on a full stomach, which is a simple case of homoeopathic or imitative magic, see further *The Magic Art and the Evolution of Kings*, i. 136.

The Rice-
mother and
the Rice-
child at
harvest in
the Malay
Peninsula. ripe all over, one must first take the 'soul' out of all the plots of one's field. You choose the spot where the rice is best and where it is 'female' (that is to say, where the bunch of stalks is big) and where there are seven joints in the stalk. You begin with a bunch of this kind and clip seven stems to be the 'soul of the rice'; and then you clip yet another handful to be the 'mother-seed' for the following year. The 'soul' is wrapped in a white cloth tied with a cord of *těrap* bark, and made into the shape of a little child in swaddling clothes, and put into the small basket. The 'mother-seed' is put into another basket, and both are fumigated with benzoin, and then the two baskets are piled the one on the other and taken home, and put into the *kěpuk* (the receptacle in which rice is stored)."[1] The ceremony of cutting and bringing home the Soul of the Rice was witnessed by Mr. W. W. Skeat at Chodoi in Selangor on the twenty-eighth of January 1897. The particular bunch or sheaf which was to serve as the Mother of the Rice-soul had previously been sought and identified by means of the markings or shape of the ears. From this sheaf an aged sorceress, with much solemnity, cut a little bundle of seven ears, anointed them with oil, tied them round with parti-coloured thread, fumigated them with incense, and having wrapt them in a white cloth deposited them in a little oval-shaped basket. These seven ears were the infant Soul of the Rice and the little basket was its cradle. It was carried home to the farmer's house by another woman, who held up an umbrella to screen the tender infant from the hot rays of the sun. Arrived at the house the Rice-child was welcomed by the women of the family, and laid, cradle and all, on a new sleeping-mat with pillows at the head. After that the farmer's wife was instructed to observe certain rules of taboo for three days, the rules being in many respects identical with those which have to be observed for three days after the birth of a real child. For example, perfect quiet must be observed, as in a house where a baby has just been born; a light was placed near the head of the Rice-child's bed and might not go out at night, while the fire on the hearth had to be kept

[1] W. W. Skeat, *Malay Magic* (London, 1900), pp. 225 *sq.*

up both day and night till the three days were over ; hair might not be cut ; and money, rice, salt, oil, and so forth were forbidden to go out of the house, though of course these valuable articles were quite free to come in.   Something of the same tender care which is thus bestowed on the newly-born Rice-child is naturally extended also to its parent, the sheaf from whose body it was taken.   This sheaf, which remains standing in the field after the Rice-soul has been carried home and put to bed, is treated as a newly-made mother ; that is to say, young shoots of trees are pounded together and scattered broadcast every evening for three successive days, and when the three days are up you take the pulp of a coco-nut and what are called "goat-flowers," mix them up, eat them with a little sugar, and spit some of the mixture out among the rice.   So after a real birth the young shoots of the jack-fruit, the rose-apple, certain kinds of banana, and the thin pulp of young coco-nuts are mixed with dried fish, salt, acid, prawn-condiment, and the like dainties to form a sort of salad, which is administered to mother and child for three successive days.   The last sheaf is reaped by the farmer's wife, who carries it back to the house, where it is threshed and mixed with the Rice-soul.   The farmer then takes the Rice-soul and its basket and deposits it, together with the product of the last sheaf, in the big circular rice-bin used by the Malays.   Some grains from the Rice-soul are mixed with the seed which is to be sown in the following year.[1]   In this Rice-mother and Rice-child of the Malay Peninsula we may see the counterpart and in a sense the prototype of the Demeter and Persephone of ancient Greece.

Once more, the European custom of representing the corn-spirit in the double form of bride and bridegroom [2] has its parallel in a ceremony observed at the rice-harvest in Java.   Before the reapers begin to cut the rice, the priest or sorcerer picks out a number of ears of rice, which are tied together, smeared with ointment, and adorned with flowers.   Thus decked out, the ears are called the *padi-pĕngantèn*, that is, the Rice-bride and the Rice-bridegroom ; their wedding feast is celebrated, and the cutting of the rice begins im-

The Rice-bride and the Rice-bridegroom at harvest in Java.

[1] W. W. Skeat, *Malay Magic*, pp. 235-249.   [2] See above, pp. 163 *sq.*

mediately afterwards. Later on, when the rice is being got in, a bridal chamber is partitioned off in the barn, and furnished with a new mat, a lamp, and all kinds of toilet articles. Sheaves of rice, to represent the wedding guests, are placed beside the Rice-bride and the Rice-bridegroom. Not till this has been done may the whole harvest be housed in the barn. And for the first forty days after the rice has been housed, no one may enter the barn, for fear of disturbing the newly-wedded pair.[1]

Another account of the Javanese custom.

Another account of the Javanese custom runs as follows. When the rice at harvest is to be brought home, two handfuls of common unhusked rice (paddy) are tied together into a sheaf, and two handfuls of a special kind of rice (*kleefrijst*) are tied up into another sheaf; then the two sheaves are fastened together in a bundle which goes by the name of "the bridal pair" (*pĕn-gantenan*). The special rice is the bridegroom, the common rice is the bride. At the barn "the bridal pair" is received on a winnowing-fan by a wizard, who removes them from the fan and lays them on the floor with a couch of *kloewih* leaves under them "in order that the rice may increase," and beside them he places a *kĕmiri* nut, tamarind pips, and a top and string as playthings with which the young couple may divert themselves. The bride is called Emboq Sri and the bridegroom Sadana, and the wizard addresses them by name, saying : " Emboq Sri and Sadana, I have now brought you home and I have prepared a place for you. May you sleep agreeably in this agreeable place ! Emboq Sri and Sadana, you have been received by So-and-So (the owner), let So-

[1] P. J. Veth, *Java* (Haarlem, 1875-1884), i. 524-526. The ceremony has also been described by Miss Augusta de Wit (*Facts and Fancies about Java*, Singapore, 1898, pp. 229-241), who lays stress on the extreme importance of the rice-harvest for the Javanese. The whole island of Java, she tells us, "is one vast rice-field. Rice on the swampy plains, rice on the rising ground, rice on the slopes, rice on the very summits of the hills. From the sod under one's feet to the verge of the horizon, everything has one and the same colour, the bluish-green of the young, or the gold of the ripened rice. The natives are all, without exception, tillers of the soil, who reckon their lives by seasons of planting and reaping, whose happiness or misery is synonymous with the abundance or the dearth of the precious grain. And the great national feast is the harvest home, with its crowning ceremony of the Wedding of the Rice" (*op. cit.* pp. 229 *sq.*). I have to thank my friend Dr. A. C. Haddon for directing my attention to Miss de Wit's book.

and-So lead a life free from care.   May Emboq Sri's luck
continue in this very agreeable place!"[1]

The same idea of the rice-spirit as a husband and wife The rice-
meets us also in the harvest customs of Bali and Lombok, spirit as husband
two islands which lie immediately to the east of Java. "The and wife in Bali and
inhabitants of Lombok," we are told, "think of the rice-plant Lombok.
as animated by a soul.   They regard it as one with a
divinity and treat it with the distinction and honour that are
shewn to a very important person.   But as it is impossible
to treat all the rice-stalks in a field ceremoniously, the native,
feeling the need of a visible and tangible representative of
the rice-deity and taking a part for the whole, picks out
some stalks and conceives them as the visible abode of the
rice-soul, to which he can pay his homage and from which
he hopes to derive advantage.   These few stalks, the foremost among their many peers, form what is called the *ninin
pantun* by the people of Bali and the *inan paré* by the
Sassaks" of Lombok.[2]   The name *ina paré* is sometimes
translated Rice-mother, but the more correct translation is
said to be "the principal rice."   The stalks of which this
"principal rice" consists are the first nine shoots which the
husbandman himself takes with his own hands from the
nursery or bedding-out ground and plants at the upper end
of the rice-field beside the inlet of the irrigation water.   They
are planted with great care in a definite order, one of them
in the middle and the other eight in a circle about it.   When
the whole field has been planted, an offering, which usually
consists of rice in many forms, is made to "the principal
rice" (*inan paré*).   When the rice-stalks begin to swell the
rice is said to be pregnant, and the "principal rice" is
treated with the delicate attentions which are paid to a
woman with child.   Thus rice-pap and eggs are laid down
beside it, and sour fruits are often presented to it, because
pregnant women are believed to long for sour fruit.   More-

---

[1] A. C. Kruijt, "Gebruiken bij den
rijstoogst in enkele streken op Oost-
Java," *Mededeelingen van wege het
Nederlandsche   Zendelinggenootschap*,
xlvii. (1903) pp. 132-134.   Compare
id., "De rijst-moeder in den Indischen
Archipel," *Verslagen en Mededeelingen der koninklijke Akademie van*

Wetenschappen, Afdeeling Letterkunde,
Vierde Reeks, v. part 4 (Amsterdam,
1903), pp. 398 *sqq.*
[2] J. C. van Eerde, "Gebruiken bij
den rijstbouw en rijstoogst op Lombok,"
*Tijdschrift voor Indische Taal- Land-
en Volkenkunde*, xlv. (1902) pp. 563-
565 note.

The Rice-spirit as husband and wife in Bali and Lombok.

over the fertilisation of the rice by the irrigation water is compared to the union of the goddess Batari Sri with her husband Ida Batara (Vishnu), who is identified with the flowing water. Some people sprinkle the pregnant rice with water in which cooling drugs have been infused or with water which has stood on a holy grave, in order that the ears may fill out well. When the time of harvest has come, the owner of the field himself makes a beginning by cutting "the principal rice" (*inan paré* or *ninin pantun*) with his own hands and binding it into two sheaves, each composed of one hundred and eight stalks with their leaves attached to them. One of the sheaves represents a man and the other a woman, and they are called "husband and wife" (*istri kakung*). The male sheaf is wound about with thread so that none of the leaves are visible, whereas the female sheaf has its leaves bent over and tied so as to resemble the roll of a woman's hair. Sometimes, for further distinction, a necklace of rice-straw is tied round the female sheaf. The two sheaves are then fastened together and tied to a branch of a tree, which is stuck in the ground at the inlet of the irrigation water. There they remain while all the rest of the rice is being reaped. Sometimes, instead of being tied to a bough, they are laid on a little bamboo altar. The reapers at their work take great care to let no grains of rice fall on the ground, otherwise the Rice-goddess would grieve and weep at being parted from her sisters, who are carried to the barn. If any portion of the field remains unreaped at nightfall, the reapers make loops in the leaves of some of the standing stalks to prevent the evil spirits from proceeding with the harvest during the hours of darkness, or, according to another account, lest the Rice-goddess should go astray. When the rice is brought home from the field, the two sheaves representing the husband and wife are carried by a woman on her head, and are the last of all to be deposited in the barn. There they are laid to rest on a small erection or on a cushion of rice-straw along with three lumps of *nasi*, which are regarded as the attendants or watchers of the bridal pair. The whole arrangement, we are informed, has for its object to induce the rice to increase and multiply in the granary, so that the owner may get more out of it than he put in. Hence when the people of Bali bring the two sheaves, the husband and wife, into the barn, they say, " Increase ye and multiply without ceasing." When a woman fetches rice from the granary for the use of her household, she has to observe a number of rules, all of which are clearly dictated by respect for the spirit of the rice. She should not enter the barn in the dark or at noon, perhaps because the spirit may then be supposed to be sleeping. She must enter with her right foot first. She must be decently clad with her breasts covered. She must not chew betel, and she would do well to rinse her mouth before repairing to the barn, just as she would do if she waited on a person of distinction or on a divinity. No sick or menstruous woman may enter the barn, and there must be no talking in it, just as there must be no talking when shelled rice is being scooped up. When all the rice in the barn has been used up, the two sheaves representing the husband and wife remain in the empty building till they have gradually disappeared or been devoured by mice. The pinch of hunger sometimes drives individuals to eat up the rice of these two sheaves, but the wretches who do so are viewed with disgust by their fellows and branded as pigs and dogs. Nobody would ever sell these holy sheaves with the rest of their profane brethren.[1]

The same notion of the propagation of the rice by a male and female power finds expression amongst the Szis of Upper Burma. When the paddy, that is, the rice with the husks still on it, has been dried and piled in a heap for threshing, all the friends of the household are invited to the threshing-floor, and food and drink are brought out. The heap of paddy is divided and one half spread out for threshing, while the other half is left piled up. On the pile food and spirits are set, and one of the elders, addressing " the father and mother of the paddy-plant," prays for plenteous harvests in future, and begs that the seed may bear many fold. Then the whole party eat, drink, and make merry. This ceremony at the threshing-floor is the

The Father and Mother of the Rice among the Szis of Burma.

[1] J. C. van Eerde, " Gebruiken bij den rijstbouw en rijstoogst op Lombok," *Tijdschrift voor Indische Taal- Land- en Volkenkunde*, xlv.(1902)pp. 563-573.

only occasion when these people invoke "the father and mother of the paddy." [1]

§ 5. *The Spirit of the Corn embodied in Human Beings*

The spirit of the corn sometimes thought to be embodied in men or women.

Thus the theory which recognises in the European Corn-mother, Corn-maiden, and so forth, the embodiment in vegetable form of the animating spirit of the crops is amply confirmed by the evidence of peoples in other parts of the world, who, because they have lagged behind the European races in mental development, retain for that very reason a keener sense of the original motives for observing those rustic rites which among ourselves have sunk to the level of meaningless survivals. The reader may, however, remember that according to Mannhardt, whose theory I am expounding, the spirit of the corn manifests itself not merely in vegetable but also in human form ; the person who cuts the last sheaf or gives the last stroke at threshing passes for a temporary embodiment of the corn-spirit, just as much as the bunch of corn which he reaps or threshes. Now in the parallels which have been hitherto adduced from the customs of peoples outside Europe the spirit of the crops appears only in vegetable form. It remains, therefore, to prove that other races besides our European peasantry have conceived the spirit of the crops as incorporate in or represented by living men and women. Such a proof, I may remind the reader, is germane to the theme of this book ; for the more instances we discover of human beings representing in themselves the life or animating spirit of plants, the less difficulty will be felt at classing amongst them the King of the Wood at Nemi.

The Old Woman who Never Dies, the goddess of the crops among the Mandans and Minnitarees.

The Mandans and Minnitarees of North America used to hold a festival in spring which they called the corn-medicine festival of the women. They thought that a certain Old Woman who Never Dies made the crops to grow, and that, living somewhere in the south, she sent the migratory waterfowl in spring as her tokens and representatives. Each sort of bird represented a special kind of crop cultivated by

[1] (Sir) J. G. Scott and J. P. Hardiman, *Gazetteer of Upper Burma and the* Shan States, Part i. vol. i. (Rangoon, 1900) p. 426.

the Indians: the wild goose stood for the maize, the wild swan for the gourds, and the wild duck for the beans. So when the feathered messengers of the Old Woman began to arrive in spring the Indians celebrated the corn-medicine festival of the women. Scaffolds were set up, on which the people hung dried meat and other things by way of offerings to the Old Woman ; and on a certain day the old women of the tribe, as representatives of the Old Woman who Never Dies, assembled at the scaffolds each bearing in her hand an ear of maize fastened to a stick. They first planted these sticks in the ground, then danced round the scaffolds, and finally took up the sticks again in their arms. Meanwhile old men beat drums and shook rattles as a musical accompaniment to the performance of the old women. Further, young women came and put dried flesh into the mouths of the old women, for which they received in return a grain of the consecrated maize to eat. Three or four grains of the holy corn were also placed in the dishes of the young women, to be afterwards carefully mixed with the seed-corn, which they were supposed to fertilise. The dried flesh hung on the scaffold belonged to the old women, because they represented the Old Woman who Never Dies. A similar corn-medicine festival was held in autumn for the purpose of attracting the herds of buffaloes and securing a supply of meat. At that time every woman carried in her arms an uprooted plant of maize. They gave the name of the Old Woman who Never Dies both to the maize and to those birds which they regarded as symbols of the fruits of the earth, and they prayed to them in autumn saying, " Mother, have pity on us ! send us not the bitter cold too soon, lest we have not meat enough ! let not all the game depart, that we may have something for the winter ! " In autumn, when the birds were flying south, the Indians thought that they were going home to the Old Woman and taking to her the offerings that had been hung up on the scaffolds, especially the dried meat, which she ate.[1] Here then we have the spirit or divinity of the corn conceived as an Old Woman and represented in bodily form by old women, who in their

---

[1] Maximilian, Prinz zu Wied, *Reise in das innere Nord-America* (Coblenz, 1839-1841), ii. 182 *sq.*

Miami
myth of
the Corn-
spirit in
the form
of a
broken-
down
old man.

capacity of representatives receive some at least of the offerings which are intended for her.

The Miamis, another tribe of North American Indians, tell a tale in which the spirit of the corn figures as a broken-down old man. They say that corn, that is, maize, first grew in heaven, and that the Good Spirit commanded it to go down and dwell with men on earth. At first it was reluctant to do so, but the Good Spirit prevailed on it to go by promising that men would treat it well in return for the benefit they derived from it. "So corn came down from heaven to benefit the Indian, and this is the reason why they esteem it, and are bound to take good care of it, and to nurture it, and not raise more than they actually require, for their own consumption." But once a whole town of the Miamis was severely punished for failing in respect for the corn. They had raised a great crop and stored much of it under ground, and much of it they packed for immediate use in bags. But the corn was so plentiful that much of it still remained on the stalks, and the young men grew reckless and played with the shelled cobs, throwing them at each other, and at last they even broke the cobs from the growing stalks and pelted each other with them too. But a judgment soon followed on such wicked conduct. For when the hunters went out to hunt, though the deer seemed to abound, they could kill nothing. So the corn was gone and they could get no meat, and the people were hungry. Well, one of the hunters, roaming by himself in the woods to find something to eat for his aged father, came upon a small lodge in the wilderness where a decrepit old man was lying with his back to the fire. Now the old man was no other than the Spirit of the Corn. He said to the young hunter, "My grandson, the Indians have afflicted me much, and reduced me to the sad state in which you see me. In the side of the lodge you will find a small kettle. Take it and eat, and when you have satisfied your hunger, I will speak to you." But the kettle was full of such fine sweet corn as the hunter had never in his life seen before. When he had eaten his fill, the old man resumed the thread of his discourse, saying, "Your people have wantonly abused and reduced me to the state you now see me in : my back-bone is broken in many places; it was the foolish young men of your town who did me this evil, for I am Mondamin, or corn, that came down from heaven. In their play they threw corn-cobs and corn-ears at one another, treating me with contempt. I am the corn-spirit whom they have injured. That is why you experience bad luck and famine. I am the cause; you feel my just resentment, therefore your people are punished. Other Indians do not treat me so. They respect me, and so it is well with them. Had you no elders to check the youths at their wanton sport? You are an eye-witness of my sufferings. They are the effect of what you did to my body." With that he groaned and covered himself up. So the young hunter returned and reported what he had seen and heard; and since then the Indians have been very careful not to play with corn in the ear.[1]

In some parts of India the harvest-goddess Gauri is represented at once by an unmarried girl and by a bundle of wild balsam plants, which is made up into the figure of a woman and dressed as such with mask, garments, and ornaments. Both the human and the vegetable representative of the goddess are worshipped, and the intention of the whole ceremony appears to be to ensure a good crop of rice.[2]

The harvest-goddess Gauri represented by a girl and a bundle of plants.

§ 6. The Double Personification of the Corn as Mother and Daughter

Compared with the Corn-mother of Germany and the harvest-Maiden of Scotland, the Demeter and Persephone of Greece are late products of religious growth. Yet as members of the Aryan family the Greeks must at one time or another have observed harvest customs like those which are still practised by Celts, Teutons, and Slavs, and which, far beyond the limits of the Aryan world, have been practised by the Indians of Peru, the Dyaks of Borneo, and many other natives of the East Indies—a

Analogy of Demeter and Persephone to the Corn-mother, the Harvest-maiden, and similar figures in the harvest customs of modern European peasantry.

---

[1] H. R. Schoolcraft, *Indian Tribes of the United States*, v. (Philadelphia, 1856) pp. 193-195.
[2] B. A. Gupte, "Harvest Festivals in honour of Gauri and Ganesh," *Indian Antiquary*, xxxv. (1906) p. 61. For details see *The Magic Art and the Evolution of Kings*, ii. 77 *sq.*

sufficient proof that the ideas on which these customs rest are not confined to any one race, but naturally suggest themselves to all untutored peoples engaged in agriculture. It is probable, therefore, that Demeter and Persephone, those stately and beautiful figures of Greek mythology, grew out of the same simple beliefs and practices which still prevail among our modern peasantry, and that they were represented by rude dolls made out of the yellow sheaves on many a harvest-field long before their breathing images were wrought in bronze and marble by the master hands of Phidias and Praxiteles. A reminiscence of that olden time—a scent, so to say, of the harvest-field—lingered to the last in the title of the Maiden (*Kore*) by which Persephone was commonly known. Thus if the prototype of Demeter is the Corn-mother of Germany, the prototype of Persephone is the harvest-Maiden, which, autumn after autumn, is still made from the last sheaf on the Braes of Balquhidder. Indeed, if we knew more about the peasant-farmers of ancient Greece, we should probably find that even in classical times they continued annually to fashion their Corn-mothers (Demeters) and Maidens (Persephones) out of the ripe corn on the harvest-fields.[1] But unfortunately the Demeter and Persephone whom we know were the denizens of towns, the majestic inhabitants of lordly temples ; it was for such divinities alone that the refined writers of antiquity had eyes ; the uncouth rites performed by rustics amongst the corn were beneath their notice. Even if they noticed them, they probably never dreamed of any connexion between the puppet of corn-stalks on the sunny stubble-field and the marble divinity in the shady coolness of the temple. Still the writings even of these town-bred and cultured persons afford us an occasional glimpse of a Demeter as rude as the rudest that a remote German village can shew. Thus the story that Iasion begat a child Plutus ("wealth," "abundance") by Demeter on a thrice-ploughed field,[2] may

The rustic analogues of Demeter and Persephone.

[1] It is possible that the image of Demeter with corn and poppies in her hands, which Theocritus (vii. 155 *sqq.*) describes as standing on a rustic threshing-floor (see above, p. 47), may have been a Corn-mother or a Corn-maiden of the kind described in the text. The suggestion was made to me by my learned and esteemed friend Dr. W. H. D. Rouse.

[2] Homer, *Odyssey*, v. 125 *sqq.* ; Hesiod, *Theog.* 969 *sqq.*

be compared with the West Prussian custom of the mock birth of a child on the harvest-field.[1]   In this Prussian custom the pretended mother represents the Corn-mother (*Żytniamatka*); the pretended child represents the Corn-baby, and the whole ceremony is a charm to ensure a crop next year.[2] The custom and the legend alike point to an older practice of performing, among the sprouting crops in spring or the stubble in autumn, one of those real or mimic acts of procreation by which, as we have seen, primitive man often seeks to infuse his own vigorous life into the languid or decaying energies of nature.[3] Another glimpse of the savage under the civilised Demeter will be afforded farther on, when we come to deal with another aspect of these agricultural divinities.

The reader may have observed that in modern folk-customs the corn-spirit is generally represented either by a Corn-mother (Old Woman, etc.) or by a Maiden (Harvest-child, etc.), not both by a Corn-mother and by a Maiden. Why then did the Greeks represent the corn both as a mother and a daughter?   *Why did the Greeks personify the corn as a mother and a daughter?*

In the Breton custom the mother-sheaf—a large figure made out of the last sheaf with a small corn-doll inside of it—clearly represents both the Corn-mother and the Corn-daughter, the latter still unborn.[4] Again, in the Prussian custom just referred to, the woman who plays the part of Corn-mother represents the ripe grain; the child appears to represent next year's corn, which may be regarded, naturally enough, as the child of this year's corn, since it is from the seed of this year's harvest that next year's crop will spring. Further, we have seen that among the Malays of the Peninsula   *Demeter was perhaps the ripe crop and Persephone the seed-corn.*

[1] See above, pp. 150 *sq.*
[2] It is possible that a ceremony performed in a Cyprian worship of Ariadne may have been of this nature: at a certain annual sacrifice a young man lay down and mimicked a woman in child-bed. See Plutarch, *Theseus*, 20: ἐν δὴ τῇ θυσίᾳ τοῦ Γορπιαίου μηνὸς ἱσταμένου δευτέρᾳ κατακλινόμενόν τινα τῶν νεανίσκων φθέγγεσθαι καὶ ποιεῖν ἅπερ ὠδινοῦσαι γυναῖκες. We have already seen grounds for regarding Ariadne as a goddess or spirit of vegetation. See *The Magic Art and the Evolution of Kings*, ii. 138. Amongst the Minnitarees in North America, the Prince of Neuwied saw a tall strong woman pretend to bring up a stalk of maize out of her stomach; the object of the ceremony was to secure a good crop of maize in the following year. See Maximilian, Prinz zu Wied, *Reise in das innere Nord-America* (Coblenz, 1839-1841), ii. 269.

[3] See *The Magic Art and the Evolution of Kings*, ii. 97 *sqq.*

[4] See above, p. 135.

and sometimes among the Highlanders of Scotland the spirit of the grain is represented in double female form, both as old and young, by means of ears taken alike from the ripe crop: in Scotland the old spirit of the corn appears as the Carline or *Cailleach*, the young spirit as the Maiden ; while among the Malays of the Peninsula the two spirits of the rice are definitely related to each other as mother and child.[1] Judged by these analogies Demeter would be the ripe crop of this year ; Persephone would be the seed-corn taken from it and sown in autumn, to reappear in spring.[2] The descent of Persephone into the lower world would thus be a mythical expression for the sowing of the seed ; her reappearance in spring would signify the sprouting of the young corn. In this way the Persephone of one year becomes the Demeter of the next, and this may very well have been the original form of the myth. But when with the advance of religious thought the corn came to be personified, no longer as a being that went through the whole cycle of birth, growth, reproduction, and death within a year, but as an immortal goddess, consistency required that one of the two personifications, the mother or the daughter, should be sacrificed. However, the double conception of the corn as mother and daughter may have been too old and too deeply 'rooted in the popular mind to be eradicated by logic, and so room had to be found in the reformed myth both for mother and daughter. This was done by assigning to Persephone the character of the corn sown in autumn and sprouting in spring, while Demeter was left to play the somewhat vague part of the heavy mother of the corn, who laments its annual disappearance underground, and rejoices over its reappearance in spring. Thus instead of a regular succession of divine beings, each living a year and then giving birth to her successor, the reformed myth exhibits the conception of two divine and immortal beings, one of whom annually disappears into and reappears from the ground, while the other has little to do but to weep and rejoice at the appropriate seasons.[3]

---

[1] See above, pp. 140 *sqq.*, 155 *sqq.*, 164 *sqq.*, 197 *sqq.*

[2] However, the Sicilians seem on the contrary to have regarded Demeter as the seed-corn and Persephone as the ripe crop. See above, pp. 57, 58 *sq.*

[3] According to Augustine (*De civitate Dei*, iv. 8) the Romans imagined a whole series of distinct deities, mostly goddesses, who took charge of the corn

This theory of the double personification of the corn in Greek myth assumes that both personifications (Demeter and Persephone) are original.   But if we suppose that the Greek myth started with a single personification, the after-growth of a second personification may perhaps be explained as follows.   On looking over the harvest customs which have been passed under review, it may be noticed that they involve two distinct conceptions of the corn-spirit.   For whereas in some of the customs the corn-spirit is treated as immanent in the corn, in others it is regarded as external to it.   Thus when a particular sheaf is called by the name of the corn-spirit, and is dressed in clothes and handled with reverence,[1] the spirit is clearly regarded as immanent in the corn.   But when the spirit is said to make the crops grow by passing through them, or to blight the grain of those against whom she has a grudge,[2] she is apparently conceived as distinct from, though exercising power over, the corn.   Conceived in the latter way the corn-spirit is in a fair way to become a deity of the corn, if she has not become so already.   Of these two conceptions, that of the corn-spirit as immanent in the corn is doubtless the older, since the view of nature as animated by indwelling spirits appears to have generally preceded the view of it as controlled by external deities ; to put it shortly, animism precedes deism.   In the harvest customs of our European peasantry the corn-spirit seems to be conceived now as immanent in the corn and now as external to it.   In Greek mythology, on the other hand, Demeter is viewed rather as the deity of the corn than as the spirit immanent in it.[3]   The process of thought which leads

at all its various stages from the time when it was committed to the ground to the time when it was lodged in the granary.   Such a multiplication of mythical beings to account for the process of growth is probably late rather than early.

[1] In some places it was customary to kneel down before the last sheaf, in others to kiss it. See W. Mannhardt, *Korndämonen*, p. 26 ; *id.*, *Mythologische Forschungen*, p. 339.   The custom of kneeling and bowing before the last corn is said to have been observed, at least occasionally, in England.   See *Folk-lore Journal*, vii. (1888) p. 270 ; and Herrick's evidence, above, p. 147, note[1].   The Malay sorceress who cut the seven ears of rice to form the Rice-child kissed the ears after she had cut them (W. W. Skeat, *Malay Magic*, p. 241).

[2] Above, pp. 132 *sq.*

[3] Even in one of the oldest documents, the Homeric *Hymn to Demeter*, Demeter is represented as the goddess who controls the growth of the corn rather than as the spirit who is immanent in it. See above, pp. 36 *sq.*

Duplica-
tion of
deities as
a con-
sequence
of the
anthropo-
morphic
tendency. to the change from the one mode of conception to the other is anthropomorphism, or the gradual investment of the immanent spirits with more and more of the attributes of humanity.   As men emerge from savagery the tendency to humanise their divinities gains strength ; and the more human these become the wider is the breach which severs them from the natural objects of which they were at first merely the animating spirits or souls.   But in the progress upwards from savagery men of the same generation do not march abreast ; and though the new anthropomorphic gods may satisfy the religious wants of the more developed intelligences, the backward members of the community will cling by preference to the old animistic notions.   Now when the spirit of any natural object such as the corn has been invested with human qualities, detached from the object, and converted into a deity controlling it, the object itself is, by the withdrawal of its spirit, left inanimate ; it becomes, so to say, a spiritual vacuum.   But the popular fancy, intolerant of such a vacuum, in other words, unable to conceive anything as inanimate, immediately creates a fresh mythical being, with which it peoples the vacant object.   Thus the same natural object comes to be represented in mythology by two distinct beings : first by the old spirit now separated from it and raised to the rank of a deity ; second, by the new spirit, freshly created by the popular fancy to supply the place vacated by the old spirit on its elevation to a

Example
of such
duplication
in Japan,
where there
are two
distinct
deities of
the sun. higher sphere.   For example, in Japanese religion the solar character of Ama-terasu, the great goddess of the Sun, has become obscured, and accordingly the people have personified the sun afresh under the name of *Nichi-rin sama*, " sun-wheeling personage," and *O tentō sama*, " august-heaven-path-personage " ; to the lower class of Japanese at the present day, especially to women and children, *O tentō sama* is the actual sun, sexless, mythless, and unencumbered by any formal worship, yet looked up to as a moral being who rewards the good, punishes the wicked, and enforces oaths made in his name.[1]   In such cases the problem for mythology is, having got two distinct personifications of the same object, what to do with them ?   How are their relations to each other

---

[1] W. G. Aston, *Shinto* (London, 1905), p. 127.

to be adjusted, and room found for both in the mythological system ?   When the old spirit or new deity is conceived as creating or producing the object in question, the problem is easily solved.   Since the object is believed to be produced by the old spirit, and animated by the new one, the latter, as the soul of the object, must also owe its existence to the former ; thus the old spirit will stand to the new one as producer to produced, that is, in mythology, as parent to child, and if both spirits are conceived as female, their relation will be that of mother and daughter.   In this way, starting from a single personification of the corn as female, mythic fancy might in time reach a double personification of it as mother and daughter.   It would be very rash to affirm that this was the way in which the myth of Demeter and Persephone actually took shape ; but it seems a legitimate conjecture that the reduplication of deities, of which Demeter and Persephone furnish an example, may sometimes have arisen in the way indicated.   For example, among the pairs of deities dealt with in a former part of this work, it has been shewn that there are grounds for regarding both Isis and her companion god Osiris as personifications of the corn.[1]   On the hypothesis just suggested, Isis would be the old corn-spirit, and Osiris would be the newer one, whose relationship to the old spirit was variously explained as that of brother, husband, and son ;[2] for of course mythology would always be free to account for the coexistence of the two divinities in more ways than one.   It must not, however, be forgotten that this proposed explanation of such pairs of deities as Demeter and Persephone or Isis and Osiris is purely conjectural, and is only given for what it is worth.

Perhaps the Greek personification of the corn as a mother and a daughter (Demeter and Persephone) is a case of such a mythical duplication.

---

[1] See *Adonis, Attis, Osiris*, Second Edition, pp. 323 *sqq.*, 330 *sqq.*, 346 *sqq.*

[2] A. Pauly, *Real-Encyclopädie der classischen Alterthumswissenschaft*, v. (Stuttgart, 1849) p. 1011.

CHAPTER VII

LITYERSES

§ 1. *Songs of the Corn Reapers*

Death and resurrection a leading incident in the myth of Persephone, as in the myths of Adonis, Attis, Osiris, and Dionysus.

IN the preceding pages an attempt has been made to shew that in the Corn-mother and Harvest-maiden of Northern Europe we have the prototypes of Demeter and Persephone. But an essential feature is still wanting to complete the resemblance. A leading incident in the Greek myth is the death and resurrection of Persephone; it is this incident which, coupled with the nature of the goddess as a deity of vegetation, links the myth with the cults of Adonis, Attis, Osiris, and Dionysus; and it is in virtue of this incident that the myth finds a place in our discussion of the Dying God. It remains, therefore, to see whether the conception of the annual death and resurrection of a god, which figures so prominently in these great Greek and Oriental worships, has not also its origin or its analogy in the rustic rites observed by reapers and vine-dressers amongst the corn-shocks and the vines.

Popular harvest and vintage customs in ancient Egypt, Syria, and Phrygia.

Our general ignorance of the popular superstitions and customs of the ancients has already been confessed. But the obscurity which thus hangs over the first beginnings of ancient religion is fortunately dissipated to some extent in the present case. The worships of Osiris, Adonis, and Attis had their respective seats, as we have seen, in Egypt, Syria, and Phrygia; and in each of these countries certain harvest and vintage customs are known to have been observed, the resemblance of which to each other and to the national rites struck the ancients themselves, and, compared with the harvest customs of modern peasants and barbarians, seems to throw some light on the origin of the rites in question.

It has been already mentioned, on the authority of Diodorus, that in ancient Egypt the reapers were wont to lament over the first sheaf cut, invoking Isis as the goddess to whom they owed the discovery of corn.[1] To the plaintive song or cry sung or uttered by Egyptian reapers the Greeks gave the name of Maneros, and explained the name by a story that Maneros, the only son of the first Egyptian king, invented agriculture, and, dying an untimely death, was thus lamented by the people.[2] It appears, however, that the name Maneros is due to a misunderstanding of the formula *mââ-ne-hra*, " Come to the house," which has been discovered in various Egyptian writings, for example in the dirge of Isis in the Book of the Dead.[3] Hence we may suppose that the cry *mââ-ne-hra* was chanted by the reapers over the cut corn as a dirge for the death of the corn-spirit (Isis or Osiris) and a prayer for its return. As the cry was raised over the first ears reaped, it would seem that the corn-spirit was believed by the Egyptians to be present in the first corn cut and to die under the sickle. We have seen that in the Malay Peninsula and Java the first ears of rice are taken to represent either the Soul of the Rice or the Rice-bride and the Rice-bridegroom.[4] In parts of Russia the first sheaf is treated much in the same way that the last sheaf is treated elsewhere. It is reaped by the mistress herself, taken home and set in the place of honour near the holy pictures ; afterwards it is threshed separately, and some of its grain is mixed with the next year's seed-corn.[5] In Aberdeenshire, while the last corn cut was generally used to make the *clyack* sheaf,[6] it was sometimes, though rarely, the first corn

Maneros, a plaintive song of Egyptian reapers.

---

[1] Diodorus Siculus, i. 14, ἔτι γὰρ καὶ νῦν κατὰ τὸν θερισμὸν τοὺς πρώτους ἀμηθέντας στάχυς θέντας τοὺς ἀνθρώπους κόπτεσθαι πλησίον τοῦ δράγματος καὶ τὴν Ἶσιν ἀνακαλεῖσθαι κτλ. For θέντας we should perhaps read σύνθεντας, which is supported by the following δράγματος.

[2] Herodotus, ii. 79 ; Julius Pollux, iv. 54 ; Pausanias, ix. 29. 7 ; Athenaeus, xiv. 11, p. 620 A.

[3] H. Brugsch, *Die Adonisklage und das Linoslied* (Berlin, 1852), p. 24. According to another interpretation, however, Maneros is the Egyptian *manurosh*, " Let us be merry." See Lauth, " Über den ägyptischen Maneros," *Sitzungsberichte der königl. bayer. Akademie der Wissenschaften zu München*, 1869, ii. 163-194.

[4] Above, pp. 197 *sqq.*

[5] W. R. S. Ralston, *Songs of the Russian People* (London, 1872), pp. 249 *sq.*   [6] See above, pp. 158 *sq.*

cut that was dressed up as a woman and carried home with ceremony.[1]

Linus or Ailinus, a plaintive song sung at the vintage in Phoenicia.

In Phoenicia and Western Asia a plaintive song, like that chanted by the Egyptian corn-reapers, was sung at the vintage and probably (to judge by analogy) also at harvest. This Phoenician song was called by the Greeks Linus or Ailinus and explained, like Maneros, as a lament for the death of a youth named Linus.[2] According to one story Linus was brought up by a shepherd, but torn to pieces by his dogs.[3] But, like Maneros, the name Linus or Ailinus appears to have originated in a verbal misunderstanding, and to be nothing more than the cry *ai lanu,* that is " Woe to us," which the Phoenicians probably uttered in mourning for Adonis ;[4] at least Sappho seems to have regarded Adonis and Linus as equivalent.[5]

Bormus, a plaintive song sung by Mariandynian reapers in Bithynia.

In Bithynia a like mournful ditty, called Bormus or Borimus, was chanted by Mariandynian reapers. Bormus was said to have been a handsome youth, the son of King Upias or of a wealthy and distinguished man. One summer day, watching the reapers at work in his fields, he went to fetch them a drink of water and was never heard of more. So the reapers sought for him, calling him in plaintive strains, which they continued to chant at harvest ever afterwards.[6]

§ 2. *Killing the Corn-spirit*

Lityerses, a song sung at

In Phrygia the corresponding song, sung by harvesters both at reaping and at threshing, was called Lityerses.

---

[1] W. Gregor, "Quelques coutumes du Nord-est du comté d'Aberdeen," *Revue des Traditions populaires,* iii. (1888) p. 487 (should be 535).

[2] Homer, *Iliad,* xviii. 570 ; Herodotus, ii. 79 ; Pausanias, ix. 29. 6-9 ; Conon, *Narrat.* 19. For the form Ailinus see Suidas, *s.v.* ; Euripides, *Orestes,* 1395 ; Sophocles, *Ajax,* 627. Compare Moschus, *Idyl.* iii. 1 ; Callimachus, *Hymn to Apollo,* 20. See Greve, *s.v.* "Linos," in W. H. Roscher's *Ausführliches Lexikon der griech. und röm. Mythologie,* ii. 2053 *sqq.*

[3] Conon, *Narrat.* 19.

[4] F. C. Movers, *Die Phönizier,* i. (Bonn, 1841), p. 246 ; W. Mannhardt, *Antike Wald- und Feldkulte* (Berlin, 1877), p. 281. In Hebrew the expression would be *oï lanu* (‏אי לנו‎), which occurs in 1 Samuel, iv. 7 and 8 ; Jeremiah, iv. 13, vi. 4. However, the connexion of the Linus song with the lament for Adonis is regarded by Baudissin as very doubtful. See W. W. Graf Baudissin, *Adonis und Esmun* (Leipsic, 1911), p. 360, note [3].

[5] Pausanias, ix. 29. 8.

[6] Julius Pollux, iv. 54 ; Athenaeus, xiv. 11, pp. 619 F-620 A ; Hesychius, *svv.* Βῶρμον and Μαριανδυνὸς θρῆνος.

According to one story, Lityerses was a bastard son of reaping
Midas, King of Phrygia, and dwelt at Celaenae.   He threshing
used to reap the corn, and had an enormous appetite. in Phrygia.
When a stranger happened to enter the corn-field or to Lityerses.
pass by it, Lityerses gave him plenty to eat and drink,
then took him to the corn-fields on the banks of the
Maeander and compelled him to reap along with him.
Lastly, it was his custom to wrap the stranger in a sheaf,
cut off his head with a sickle, and carry away his
body, swathed in the corn stalks.   But at last Hercules
undertook to reap with him, cut off his head with the
sickle, and threw his body into the river.[1]   As Hercules
is reported to have slain Lityerses in the same way that
Lityerses slew others (as Theseus treated Sinis and Sciron),
we may infer that Lityerses used to throw the bodies of his
victims into the river.   According to another version of the
story, Lityerses, a son of Midas, was wont to challenge
people to a reaping match with him, and if he vanquished
them he used to thrash them ; but one day he met with a
stronger reaper, who slew him.[2]

There are some grounds for supposing that in these The
stories of Lityerses we have the description of a Phrygian story of
harvest custom in accordance with which certain persons, seems to
especially strangers passing the harvest field, were regularly reflect
regarded as embodiments of the corn-spirit, and as such were Phrygian
seized by the reapers, wrapt in sheaves, and beheaded, their harvest
bodies, bound up in the corn-stalks, being afterwards thrown killing
into water as a rain-charm.   The grounds for this sup- strangers
position are, first, the resemblance of the Lityerses story to ments of
the harvest customs of European peasantry, and, second, the spirit.
frequency of human sacrifices offered by savage races to

---

[1] The story was told by Sositheus in
his play of *Daphnis*. His verses have
been preserved in the tract of an
anonymous writer. See *Scriptores
rerum mirabilium Graeci*, ed. A.
Westermann (Brunswick, 1839), pp.
220 *sq.* ; also Athenaeus, x. 8, p.
415 B ; Scholiast on Theocritus, x.
41 ; Photius, *Lexicon*, Suidas, and
Hesychius, *s.v.* " Lityerses " ; Aposto-
lius, *Centur.* x. 74 ; Servius, on Virgil,
Bucol. viii. 68.   Photius mentions the
sickle with which Lityerses beheaded
his victims. Servius calls Lityerses a
king and says that Hercules cut off his
head with the sickle that had been given
him to reap with. Lityerses is the subject of a special study by W. Mannhardt
(*Mythologische Forschungen*, pp. 1 *sqq.*),
whom I follow. Compare O. Crusius,
s.v. " Lityerses," in W. H. Roscher's
*Ausführliches Lexikon der griech. und
röm. Mythologie*, ii. 2065 *sqq.*

[2] Julius Pollux, iv. 54.

promote the fertility of the fields. We will examine these grounds successively, beginning with the former.

In comparing the story with the harvest customs of Europe,[1] three points deserve special attention, namely : I. the reaping match and the binding of persons in the sheaves ; II. the killing of the corn-spirit or his representatives ; III. the treatment of visitors to the harvest field or of strangers passing it.

Contests among reapers, binders, and threshers in order not to be the last at their work.

I. In regard to the first head, we have seen that in modern Europe the person who cuts or binds or threshes the last sheaf is often exposed to rough treatment at the hands of his fellow-labourers. For example, he is bound up in the last sheaf, and, thus encased, is carried or carted about, beaten, drenched with water, thrown on a dunghill, and so forth. Or, if he is spared this horseplay, he is at least the subject of ridicule or is thought to be destined to suffer some misfortune in the course of the year. Hence the harvesters are naturally reluctant to give the last cut at reaping or the last stroke at threshing or to bind the last sheaf, and towards the close of the work this reluctance produces an emulation among the labourers, each striving to finish his task as fast as possible, in order that he may escape the invidious distinction of being last.[2] For example, in the neighbourhood of Danzig, when the winter corn is cut and mostly bound up in sheaves, the portion which still remains to be bound is divided amongst the women binders, each of whom receives a swath of equal length to bind. A crowd of reapers, children, and idlers gather round to witness the contest, and at the word, " Seize the Old Man," the women fall to work, all binding their allotted swaths as hard as they can. The spectators watch them narrowly, and the woman who cannot keep pace with the rest and consequently binds the last sheaf has to carry

---

[1] In this comparison I closely follow W. Mannhardt, *Mythologische Forschungen*, pp. 18 *sqq.*

[2] Compare above, pp. 134, 136, 137 *sq.*, 140, 142, 143, 144, 145, 147 *sq.*, 149, 164 *sq.* On the other hand, the last sheaf is sometimes an object of desire and emulation. See above, pp. 136, 141, 153, 154 *sq.*, 156, 162 note[3], 165. It is so at

Balquhidder also (*Folk-lore Journal*, vi. 269) ; and it was formerly so on the Gareloch, Dumbartonshire, where there was a competition for the honour of cutting it, and handfuls of standing corn used to be hidden under sheaves in order that the last to be uncovered should form the Maiden.—(From the information of Archie Leitch. See pp. 157 *sq.*)

the Old Man (that is, the last sheaf made up in the form of a man) to the farmhouse and deliver it to the farmer with the words, " Here I bring you the Old Man." At the supper which follows, the Old Man is placed at the table and receives an abundant portion of food, which, as he cannot eat it, falls to the share of the woman who carried him. Afterwards the Old Man is placed in the yard and all the people dance round him. Or the woman who bound the last sheaf dances for a good while with the Old Man, while the rest form a ring round them; afterwards they all, one after the other, dance a single round with him. Further, the woman who bound the last sheaf goes herself by the name of the Old Man till the next harvest, and is often mocked with the cry, " Here comes the Old Man." [1] In the Mittelmark district of Prussia, when the rye has been reaped, and the last sheaves are about to be tied up, the binders stand in two rows facing each other, every woman with her sheaf and her straw rope before her. At a given signal they all tie up their sheaves, and the one who is the last to finish is ridiculed by the rest. Not only so, but her sheaf is made up into human shape and called the Old Man, and she must carry it home to the farmyard, where the harvesters dance in a circle round her and it. Then they take the Old Man to the farmer and deliver it to him with the words, " We bring the Old Man to the Master. He may keep him till he gets a new one." After that the Old Man is set up against a tree, where he remains for a long time, the butt of many jests. [2] At Aschbach in Bavaria, when the reaping is nearly finished, the reapers say, " Now, we will drive out the Old Man." Each of them sets himself to reap a patch of corn as fast as he can ; he who cuts the last handful or the last stalk is greeted by the rest with an exulting cry, " You have the Old Man." Sometimes a black mask is fastened on the reaper's face and he is dressed in woman's clothes ; or if the reaper is a woman, she is dressed in man's clothes. A dance follows. At the supper the Old Man gets twice as large a portion of food as the others. The proceedings are similar at threshing ; the person who gives the last stroke is

---

[1] W. Mannhardt, *Mythologische Forschungen*, pp. 19 *sq*.

[2] A. Kuhn, *Märkische Sagen und Märchen* (Berlin, 1843), p. 342.

said to have the Old Man. At the supper given to the threshers he has to eat out of the cream-ladle and to drink a great deal. Moreover, he is quizzed and teased in all sorts of ways till he frees himself from further annoyance by treating the others to brandy or beer.[1]

Custom of wrapping up in corn-stalks the last reaper, binder, or thresher. These examples illustrate the contests in reaping, threshing, and binding which take place amongst the harvesters, from their unwillingness to suffer the ridicule and discomfort incurred by the one who happens to finish his work last. It will be remembered that the person who is last at reaping, binding, or threshing, is regarded as the representative of the corn-spirit,[2] and this idea is more fully expressed by binding him or her in corn-stalks. The latter custom has been already illustrated, but a few more instances may be added. At Kloxin, near Stettin, the harvesters call out to the woman who binds the last sheaf, "You have the Old Man, and must keep him." The Old Man is a great bundle of corn decked with flowers and ribbons, and fashioned into a rude semblance of the human form. It is fastened on a rake or strapped on a horse, and brought with music to the village. In delivering the Old Man to the farmer, the woman says :—

> "*Here, dear Sir, is the Old Man.*
> *He can stay no longer on the field,*
> *He can hide himself no longer,*
> *He must come into the village.*
> *Ladies and gentlemen, pray be so kind*
> *As to give the Old Man a present.*"

As late as the first half of the nineteenth century the custom was to tie up the woman herself in pease-straw, and bring her with music to the farmhouse, where the harvesters danced with her till the pease-straw fell off.[3] In other villages round Stettin, when the last harvest-waggon is being loaded, there is a regular race amongst the women, each striving not to be last. For she who places the last sheaf on the waggon is called the Old Man, and is completely

[1] W. Mannhardt, *Mythologische Forschungen*, p. 20; F. Panzer, *Beitrag zur deutschen Mythologie* (Munich, 1848-1855), ii. p. 217, § 397; A. Witzschel, *Sagen, Sitten und Gebräuche aus Thüringen* (Vienna, 1878), p. 222, § 69.

[2] Above, pp. 167 *sq.*

[3] W. Mannhardt, *Mythologische Forschungen*, p. 22.

swathed in corn-stalks ; she is also decked with flowers, and flowers and a helmet of straw are placed on her head.   In solemn procession she carries the harvest-crown to the squire, over whose head she holds it while she utters a string of good wishes.   At the dance which follows, the Old Man has the right to choose his, or rather her, partner ; it is an honour to dance with him.[1]   At Blankenfelde, in the district of Potsdam, the woman who binds the last sheaf at the rye-harvest is saluted with the cry, " You have the Old Man." A woman is then tied up in the last sheaf in such a way that only her head is left free ; her hair also is covered with a cap made of rye-stalks, adorned with ribbons and flowers. She is called the Harvest-man, and must keep dancing in front of the last harvest-waggon till it reaches the squire's house, where she receives a present and is released from her envelope of corn.[2]   At Gommern, near Magdeburg, the reaper who cuts the last ears of corn is often wrapt up in corn-stalks so completely that it is hard to see whether there is a man in the bundle or not.   Thus wrapt up he is taken by another stalwart reaper on his back, and carried round the field amidst the joyous cries of the harvesters.[3] At Neuhausen, near Merseburg, the person who binds the last sheaf is wrapt in ears of oats and saluted as the Oats-man, whereupon the others dance round him.[4]   At Brie, Isle de France, the farmer himself is tied up in the *first* sheaf.[5] At the harvest-home at Udvarhely, Transylvania, a person is encased in corn-stalks, and wears on his head a crown made out of the last ears cut.   On reaching the village he is soused with water over and over.[6]   At Dingelstedt, in the district of Erfurt, down to the first half of the nineteenth century it was the custom to tie up a man in the last sheaf. He was called the Old Man, and was brought home on the last waggon, amid huzzas and music.   On reaching the farm-yard he was rolled round the barn and drenched with water.[7] At Nördlingen in Bavaria the man who gives the last stroke at threshing is wrapt in straw and rolled on the threshing-

[1] W. Mannhardt, *Mythologische Forschungen*, p. 22.
[2] *Ibid.* pp. 22 *sq.*
[3] *Ibid.* p. 23.
[4] *Ibid.* pp. 23 *sq.*
[5] *Ibid.* p. 24.
[6] *Ibid.* p. 24.
[7] *Ibid.* p. 24.

floor.[1]   In some parts of Oberpfalz, Bavaria, he is said to
"get the Old Man," is wrapt in straw, and carried to a
neighbour who has not yet finished his threshing.[2]   In Silesia
the woman who binds the last sheaf has to submit to a good
deal of horse-play.   She is pushed, knocked down, and tied
up in the sheaf, after which she is called the corn-puppet
(*Kornpopel*).[3]   In Thüringen a sausage is stuck in the last
sheaf at threshing, and thrown, with the sheaf, on the
threshing-floor.   It is called the *Barrenwurst* or *Bazenwurst*,
and is eaten by all the threshers.   After they have eaten it a
man is encased in pease-straw, and thus attired is led through
the village.[4]

The corn-spirit, driven out of the last corn, lives in the barn during the winter.
"In all these cases the idea is that the spirit of the
corn—the Old Man of vegetation—is driven out of the corn
last cut or last threshed, and lives in the barn during the
winter.   At sowing-time he goes out again to the fields to
resume his activity as animating force among the sprouting
corn."[5]

Similar ideas as to the last corn in India.
Ideas of the same sort appear to attach to the last corn
in India.   At Hoshangábád, in Central India, when the reaping
is nearly done, a patch of corn, about a rood in extent, is left
standing in the cultivator's last field, and the reapers rest a little.
Then they rush at this remnant, tear it up, and cast it into the
air, shouting victory to one or other of the local gods, according
to their religious persuasion.   A sheaf is made out of this
corn, tied to a bamboo, set up in the last harvest cart, and
carried home in triumph.   Here it is fastened up in the
threshing-floor or attached to a tree or to the cattle-shed,
where its services are held to be essential for the purpose of
averting the evil-eye.[6]   A like custom prevails in the eastern
districts of the North-Western Provinces of India.   Sometimes
a little patch is left untilled as a refuge for the field-spirit;
sometimes it is sown, and when the corn of this patch has
been reaped with a rush and a shout, it is presented to the

[1] *Ibid.* pp. 24 *sq.*
[2] *Ibid.* p. 25.
[3] P. Drechsler, *Sitte, Brauch und Volksglaube in Schlesien* (Leipsic, 1903-1906), ii. 65.
[4] A. Witzschel, *Sagen, Sitten und Gebräuche aus Thüringen* (Vienna, 1878), p. 223, § 70.

[5] W.   Mannhardt,   *Mythologische Forschungen*, pp. 25 *sq.*
[6] C. A. Elliot, *Hoshangábád Settlement Report*, p. 178, quoted in *Panjab Notes and Queries*, iii. §§ 8, 168 (October and December, 1885); W. Crooke, *Popular Religion and Folklore of Northern India* (Westminster, 1896), ii. 306.

priest, who offers it to the local gods or bestows it on a beggar.[1]

II. Passing to the second point of comparison between the Lityerses story and European harvest customs, we have now to see that in the latter the corn-spirit is often believed to be killed at reaping or threshing. In the Romsdal and other parts of Norway, when the haymaking is over, the people say that "the Old Hay-man has been killed." In some parts of Bavaria the man who gives the last stroke at threshing is said to have killed the Corn-man, the Oats-man, or the Wheat-man, according to the crop.[2] In the Canton of Tillot, in Lothringen, at threshing the last corn the men keep time with their flails, calling out as they thresh, "We are killing the Old Woman! We are killing the Old Woman!" If there is an old woman in the house she is warned to save herself, or she will be struck dead.[3] Near Ragnit, in Lithuania, the last handful of corn is left standing by itself, with the words, "The Old Woman (*Boba*) is sitting in there." Then a young reaper whets his scythe, and, with a strong sweep, cuts down the handful. It is now said of him that "he has cut off the Boba's head"; and he receives a gratuity from the farmer and a jugful of water over his head from the farmer's wife.[4] According to another account, every Lithuanian reaper makes haste to finish his task; for the Old Rye-woman lives in the last stalks, and whoever cuts the last stalks kills the Old Rye-woman, and by killing her he brings trouble on himself.[5] In Wilkischken, in the district of Tilsit, the man who cuts the last corn goes by the name of "the killer of the Rye-woman."[6] In Lithuania, again, the corn-spirit is believed to be killed at threshing as well as at reaping. When only a single pile of corn remains to be threshed, all the threshers suddenly step back a few paces, as if at the word of command. Then they fall to work, plying their flails with the utmost rapidity and vehemence, till they come to the last bundle. Upon this they fling themselves with almost frantic fury, straining every nerve, and raining blows on it till the word "Halt!" rings out

The corn-spirit supposed to be killed at reaping or threshing.

---

[1] W. Crooke, *op. cit.* ii. 306 *sq.*

[2] W. Mannhardt, *Mythologische Forschungen*, p. 31.

[3] *Ibid.* p. 334.

[4] *Ibid.* p. 330.

[5] *Ibid.*

[6] *Ibid.* p. 331.

sharply from the leader. The man whose flail is the last to fall after the command to stop has been given is immediately surrounded by all the rest, crying out that "he has struck the Old Rÿe-woman dead." He has to expiate the deed by treating them to brandy; and, like the man who cuts the last corn, he is known as "the killer of the Old Rye-woman."[1] Sometimes in Lithuania the slain corn-spirit was represented by a puppet. Thus a female figure was made out of corn-stalks, dressed in clothes, and placed on the threshing-floor, under the heap of corn which was to be threshed last. Whoever thereafter gave the last stroke at threshing "struck the Old Woman dead."[2] We have already met with examples of burning the figure which represents the corn-spirit.[3] In the East Riding of Yorkshire a custom called "burning the Old Witch" is observed on the last day of harvest. A small sheaf of corn is burnt on the field in a fire of stubble; peas are parched at the fire and eaten with a liberal allowance of ale; and the lads and lasses romp about the flames and amuse themselves by blackening each other's faces.[4] Sometimes, again, the corn-spirit is represented by a man, who lies down under the last corn; it is threshed upon his body, and the people say that "the Old Man is being beaten to death."[5] We saw that sometimes the farmer's wife is thrust, together with the last sheaf, under the threshing-machine, as if to thresh her, and that afterwards a pretence is made of winnowing her.[6] At Volders, in the Tyrol, husks of corn are stuck behind the neck of the man who gives the last stroke at threshing, and he is throttled with a straw garland. If he is tall, it is believed that the corn will be tall next year. Then he is tied on a bundle and flung into the river.[7] In Carinthia, the thresher who gave the last stroke, and the person who

Corn-spirit represented by a man, who is threshed.

[1] W. Mannhardt, *Mythologische Forschungen*, p. 335.

[2] *Ibid.* p. 335.

[3] Above, pp. 135, 146.

[4] J. Nicholson, *Folk-lore of East Yorkshire* (London, Hull, and Driffield, 1890), p. 28, supplemented by a letter of the author's addressed to Mr. E. S. Hartland and dated 33 Leicester Street, Hull, 11th September, 1890. I have to thank Mr. E. S. Hartland for calling my attention to the custom and allowing me to see Mr. Nicholson's letter.

[5] W. Mannhardt, *Die Korndämonen*, p. 26.

[6] Above, pp. 149 *sq.*

[7] W. Mannhardt, *Mythologische Forschungen*, p. 50.

untied the last sheaf on the threshing-floor, are bound hand
and foot with straw bands, and crowns of straw are placed
on their heads. Then they are tied, face to face, on a
sledge, dragged through the village, and flung into a brook.[1]
The custom of throwing the representative of the corn-spirit
into a stream, like that of drenching him with water, is,
as usual, a rain-charm.[2]

III. Thus far the representatives of the corn-spirit have
generally been the man or woman who cuts, binds, or
threshes the last corn. We now come to the cases in which
the corn-spirit is represented either by a stranger passing
the harvest-field (as in the Lityerses tale), or by a visitor
entering it for the first time. All over Germany it is
customary for the reapers or threshers to lay hold of
passing strangers and bind them with a rope made of
corn-stalks, till they pay a forfeit ; and when the farmer
himself or one of his guests enters the field or the threshing-
floor for the first time, he is treated in the same way.
Sometimes the rope is only tied round his arm or his feet
or his neck.[3] But sometimes he is regularly swathed in
corn. Thus at Solör in Norway, whoever enters the field,
be he the master or a stranger, is tied up in a sheaf and
must pay a ransom. In the neighbourhood of Soest, when
the farmer visits the flax-pullers for the first time, he is
completely enveloped in flax. Passers-by are also surrounded by the women, tied up in flax, and compelled to
stand brandy.[4] At Nördlingen strangers are caught with
straw ropes and tied up in a sheaf till they pay a forfeit.[5]
Among the Germans of Haselberg, in West Bohemia, as soon
as a farmer had given the last corn to be threshed on the
threshing-floor, he was swathed in it and had to redeem

Corn-spirit represented by a stranger or a visitor to the harvest-field, who is treated accordingly.

[1] *Ibid.* pp. 50 *sq.*
[2] See above, pp. 146, 170 note [1];
Adonis, Attis, Osiris, Second Edition,
pp. 195 *sqq.*
[3] W. Mannhardt, *Mythologische For-
schunge* pp. 32 *sqq.* Compare K.
Bartsch, *Sagen, Märchen und Gebräuche
aus Meklenburg* (Vienna, 1879-1880),
ii. 296 *sq.* ; P. Drechsler, *Sitte, Brauch
und Volksglaube in Schlesien* (Leipsic,
1903-1906), ii. 62 *sq.* ; A. John,
Sitte, Brauch und Volksglaube im

deutschen Westböhmen (Prague, 1905),
p. 193 ; A. Witzschel, *Sagen, Sitten
und Gebräuche aus Thüringen* (Vienna,
1878), p. 221, § 61 ; R. Krause, *Sitten,
Gebräuche und Aberglauben in Westpreussen* (Berlin, preface dated March,
1904), p. 51 ; *Revue des Traditions
populaires,* iii. (1888) p. 598.
[4] W. Mannhardt, *Mythologische
Forschungen,* pp. 35 *sq.*
[5] *Ibid.* p. 36.

himself by a present of cakes.[1]　In Anhalt, when the proprietor or one of his family, the steward, or even a stranger
enters the harvest-field for the first time after the reaping
has begun, the wife of the chief reaper ties a rope twisted of
corn-ears, or a nosegay made of corn-ears and flowers, to
his arm, and he is obliged to ransom himself by the payment
of a fine.[2]　In the canton of Putanges, in Normandy, a
pretence of tying up the owner of the land in the last sheaf
of wheat is still practised, or at least was still practised some
quarter of a century ago.　The task falls to the women alone.
They throw themselves on the proprietor, seize him by the
arms, the legs, and the body, throw him to the ground, and
stretch him on the last sheaf.　Then a show is made of
binding him, and the conditions to be observed at the
harvest-supper are dictated to him.　When he has accepted
them, he is released and allowed to get up.[3]　At Briè, Isle
de France, when any one who does not belong to the farm
passes by the harvest-field, the reapers give chase.　If they
catch him, they bind him in a sheaf and bite him, one after
the other, in the forehead, crying, "You shall carry the key
of the field."[4]　"To have the key" is an expression used
by harvesters elsewhere in the sense of to cut or bind or
thresh the last sheaf;[5] hence, it is equivalent to the phrases
"You have the Old Man," "You are the Old Man," which
are addressed to the cutter, binder, or thresher of the last
sheaf.　Therefore, when a stranger, as at Brie, is tied up in
a sheaf and told that he will "carry the key of the field," it
is as much as to say that he is the Old Man, that is, an
embodiment of the corn-spirit.　In hop-picking, if a well-
dressed stranger passes the hop-yard, he is seized by the
women, tumbled into the bin, covered with leaves, and not
released till he has paid a fine.[6]　In some parts of Scotland,

[1] A. John, *Sitte, Brauch, und
Volksglaube im deutschen Westböhmen,*
(Prague, 1905), p. 194.

[2] O. Hartung, "Zur Volkskunde aus
Anhalt," *Zeitschrift des Vereins für
Volkskunde,* vii. (1897) p. 153.

[3] J. Lecœur, *Esquisses du Bocage
Normand* (Condé-sur-Noireau, 1883-
1887), ii. 240 *sq.*

[4] W. Mannhardt, *Mythologische
Forschungen,* p. 36.

[5] For the evidence, see *ibid.* p. 36,
note 2.　The "key" in the European
custom is probably intended to serve
the same purpose as the "knot" in
the Cingalese custom, as to which see
Taboo and the Perils of the Soul, pp.
308 *sq.*

[6] From a letter written to me by
Colonel Henry Wilson, of Farnborough
Lodge, Farnborough, Kent.　The
letter is dated 21st March, 1901.

particularly in the counties of Fife and Kinross, down to recent times the reapers used to seize and dump, as it was called, any stranger who happened to visit or pass by the harvest field. The custom was to lay hold of the stranger by his ankles and armpits, lift him up, and bring the lower part of his person into violent contact with the ground. Women as well as men were liable to be thus treated. The practice of interposing a sheaf between the sufferer and the ground is said to be a modern refinement.[1] Comparing this custom with the one practised at Putanges in Normandy, which has just been described, we may conjecture that in Scotland the " dumping " of strangers on the harvest-field was originally a preliminary to wrapping them up in sheaves of corn.

Ceremonies of a somewhat similar kind are performed by the Tarahumare Indians of Mexico not only at harvest but also at hoeing and ploughing. " When the work of hoeing and weeding is finished, the workers seize the master of the field, and, tying his arms crosswise behind him, load all the implements, that is to say, the hoes, upon his back, fastening them with ropes. Then they form two single columns, the landlord in the middle between them, and all facing the house. Thus they start homeward. Simultaneously the two men at the heads of the columns begin to run rapidly forward some thirty yards, cross each other, then turn back, run along the two columns, cross each other again at the rear and take their places each at the end of his row. As they pass each other ahead and in the rear of the columns they beat their mouths with the hollow of their hands and yell. As soon as they reach their places at the foot, the next pair in front of the columns starts off, running in the same way, and thus pair after pair performs the tour, the procession all the time advancing toward the house. A short distance in front of it they come to a halt, and are met by two young men who carry red handkerchiefs tied to sticks like flags. The father of the family, still tied up and loaded with the hoes, steps forward alone and kneels down in front of his house-door. The flag-bearers wave their banners over him, and the women of the household come out and kneel on

Ceremonies of the Tarahumare Indians at hoeing, ploughing, and harvest.

[1] "Notes on Harvest Customs," *The Folk-lore Journal*, vii. (1889) pp. 52 *sq.*

their left knees, first toward the east, and after a little while toward each of the other cardinal points, west, south, and north. In conclusion the flags are waved in front of the house. The father then rises and the people untie him, whereupon he first salutes the women with the usual greeting, '*Kwīra !*' or '*Kwirevá !*' Now they all go into the house, and the man makes a short speech thanking them all for the assistance they have given him, for how could he have gotten through his work without them? They have provided him with a year's life (that is, with the wherewithal to sustain it), and now he is going to give them tesvino. He gives a drinking-gourd full to each one in the assembly, and appoints one man among them to distribute more to all. The same ceremony is performed after the ploughing and after the harvesting. On the first occasion the tied man may be made to carry the yoke of the oxen, on the second he does not carry anything."[1] The meaning of these Mexican ceremonies is not clear. Perhaps the custom of tying up the farmer at hoeing, ploughing, and reaping is a form of expiation or apology offered to the spirits of the earth, who are naturally disturbed by agricultural operations.[2] When the Yabim of Simbang in German New Guinea see that the taro plants in their fields are putting forth leaves, they offer sacrifice of sago-broth and pork to the spirits of the former owners of the land, in order that they may be kindly disposed and not do harm but let the fruits ripen.[3] Similarly when the Alfoors or Toradjas of Central Celebes are planting a new field, they offer rice, eggs, and so forth to the souls of the former owners of the land, hoping that, mollified by these offerings, the souls will make the crops to grow and thrive.[4] However, this explanation of the Mexican ceremonies at hoeing, ploughing, and reaping is purely conjectural. In these ceremonies there is no evidence that, as in the parallel European customs, the farmer is identified

[1] C. Lumholtz, *Unknown Mexico* (London, 1903), i. 214 *sq.*

[2] Compare *Adonis, Attis, Osiris*, Second Edition, pp. 75 *sq.*

[3] K. Vetter, *Komm herüber und hilf uns !* Heft 2 (Barmen, 1898), p. 7.

[4] A. C. Kruijt, "Een en ander aangaande het geestelijk en maatschap-pelijk leven van den Poso-Alfoer," *Mededeelingen van wege het Neder-landsche Zendelinggenootschap*, xxxix. (1895) p. 137. As to the influence which the spirits of the dead are thought to exercise on the growth of the crops, see above, pp. 103 *sq.*, and below, vol. ii. pp. 109 *sqq.*

with the corn-spirit, since he is not wrapt up in the sheaves.

Be that as it may, the evidence adduced above suffices to prove that, like the ancient Lityerses, modern European reapers have been wont to lay hold of a passing stranger and tie him up in a sheaf. It is not to be expected that they should complete the parallel by cutting off his head ; but if they do not take such a strong step, their language and gestures are at least indicative of a desire to do so. For instance, in Mecklenburg on the first day of reaping, if the master or mistress or a stranger enters the field, or merely passes by it, all the mowers face towards him and sharpen their scythes, clashing their whet-stones against them in unison, as if they were making ready to mow. Then the woman who leads the mowers steps up to him and ties a band round his left arm. He must ransom himself by payment of a forfeit.[1] Near Ratzeburg, when the master or other person of mark enters the field or passes by it, all the harvesters stop work and march towards him in a body, the men with their scythes in front. On meeting him they form up in line, men and women. The men stick the poles of their scythes in the ground, as they do in whetting them ; then they take off their caps and hang them on the scythes, while their leader stands forward and makes a speech. When he has done, they all whet their scythes in measured time very loudly, after which they put on their caps. Two of the women binders then come forward ; one of them ties the master or stranger (as the case may be) with corn-ears or with a silken band ; the other delivers a rhyming address. The following are specimens of the speeches made by the reaper on these occasions. In some parts of Pomerania every passer-by is stopped, his way being barred with a corn-rope. The reapers form a circle round him and sharpen their scythes, while their leader says :—

> " *The men are ready,*
> *The scythes are bent,*
> *The corn is great and small,*
> *The gentleman must be mowed.*"

Pretence
made by
the reapers
of killing
some one
with their
scythes.

---

[1] W. Mannhardt, *Mythologische Forschungen*, p. 39.

Then the process of whetting the scythes is repeated.[1]   At
Ramin, in the district of Stettin, the stranger, standing
encircled by the reapers, is thus addressed :—

> *" We'll stroke the gentleman*
> *With our naked sword,*
> *Wherewith we shear meadows and fields.*
> *We shear princes and lords.*
> *Labourers are often athirst;*
> *If the gentleman will stand beer and brandy*
> *The joke will soon be over.*
> *But, if our prayer he does not like,*
> *The sword has a right to strike."* [2]

That in these customs the whetting of the scythes is
really meant as a preliminary to mowing appears from the
following variation of the preceding customs.   In the district
of Lüneburg, when any one enters the harvest-field, he is
asked whether he will engage a good fellow.   If he says
yes, the harvesters mow some swaths, yelling and screaming,
and then ask him for drink-money.[3]

Pretence made by threshers of choking a person with their flails.   On the threshing-floor strangers are also regarded as
embodiments of the corn-spirit, and are treated accordingly.
At Wiedingharde in Schleswig when a stranger comes to
the threshing-floor he is asked, " Shall I teach you the flail-
dance ? "   If he says yes, they put the arms of the threshing-
flail round his neck as if he were a sheaf of corn, and press
them together so tight that he is nearly choked.[4]   In some
parishes of Wermland (Sweden), when a stranger enters
the threshing-floor where the threshers are at work, they say
that " they will teach him the threshing-song."   Then they
put a flail round his neck and a straw rope about his body.
Also, as we have seen, if a stranger woman enters the
threshing-floor, the threshers put a flail round her body and
a wreath of corn-stalks round her neck, and call out, " See
the Corn-woman !   See ! that is how the Corn-maiden
looks ! " [5]

[1] W. Mannhardt, *Mythologische
Forschungen*, pp. 39 *sq.*
[2] *Ibid.* p. 40. For the speeches made
by the woman who binds the stranger
or the master, see *ibid.* p. 41 ; C.
Lemke, *Volksthümliches in Ostpreussen*
(Mohrungen, 1884-1887), i. 23 *sq.*

[3] W. Mannhardt, *Mythologische
Forschungen*, pp. 41 *sq.*
[4] W. Mannhardt, *op. cit.* p. 42. See
also above, p. 150.
[5] W. Mannhardt, *op. cit.* p. 42. See
above, p. 149. In Thüringen a being
called the Rush-cutter (*Binsenschneider*)

In these customs, observed both on the harvest-field and on the threshing-floor, a passing stranger is regarded as a personification of the corn, in other words, as the corn-spirit ; and a show is made of treating him like the corn by mowing, binding, and threshing him. If the reader still doubts whether European peasants can really regard a passing stranger in this light, the following custom should set his doubts at rest. During the madder-harvest in the Dutch province of Zealand a stranger passing by a field, where the people are digging the madder-roots, will sometimes call out to them *Koortspillers* (a term of reproach). Upon this, two of the fleetest runners make after him, and, if they catch him, they bring him back to the madder-field and bury him in the earth up to his middle at least, jeering at him the while ; then they ease nature before his face.[1]

This last act is to be explained as follows. The spirit of the corn and of other cultivated plants is sometimes conceived, not as immanent in the plant, but as its owner; hence the cutting of the corn at harvest, the digging of the roots, and the gathering of fruit from the fruit-trees are each and all of them acts of spoliation, which strip him of his property and reduce him to poverty. Hence he is often known as "the Poor Man" or "the Poor Woman." Thus in the neighbourhood of Eisenach a small sheaf is sometimes left standing on the field for "the Poor Old Woman."[2] At Marksuhl, near Eisenach, the puppet formed out of the last sheaf is itself called "the Poor Woman." At Alt Lest in Silesia the man who binds the last sheaf is called the Beggar-man.[3] In a village near Roeskilde, in Zealand (Denmark), old-fashioned peasants sometimes make up the last sheaf into a rude puppet, which is called the Rye-beggar.[4] In Southern Schonen the sheaf which is bound last is called the Beggar ;

used to be much dreaded. On the morning of St. John's Day he was wont to walk through the fields with sickles tied to his ankles cutting avenues in the corn as he walked. To detect him, seven bundles of brushwood were silently threshed with the flail on the threshing-floor, and the stranger who appeared at the door of the barn during the threshing was the Rush-cutter. See A. Witzschel, *Sagen, Sitten und*

Gebräuche aus Thüringen (Vienna, 1878), p. 221. With the *Binsenschneider* compare the *Bilschneider* and *Biberschneider* (F. Panzer, *Beitrag zur deutschen Mythologie*, Munich, 1848-1855, ii. pp. 210 *sq.*, §§ 372-378).
[1] W. Mannhardt, *Mythologische Forschungen*, pp. 47 *sq.*
[2] W. Mannhardt, *op. cit.* p. 48.
[3] W. Mannhardt, *l.c.*
[4] *Ibid.* pp. 48 *sq.*

it is made bigger than the rest and is sometimes dressed in clothes. In the district of Olmütz the last sheaf is called the Beggar; it is given to an old woman, who must carry it home, limping on one foot.[1]   Sometimes a little of the crop is left on the field for the spirit, under other names than "the Poor Old Woman." Thus at Szagmanten, a village of the Tilsit district, the last sheaf was left standing on the field "for the Old Rye-woman."[2]   In Neftenbach (Canton of Zurich) the first three ears of corn reaped are thrown away on the field "to satisfy the Corn-mother and to make the next year's crop abundant."[3]   At Kupferberg, in Bavaria, some corn is left standing on the field when the rest has been cut. Of this corn left standing they say that "it belongs to the Old Woman," to whom it is dedicated in the following words:—

Some of the corn left on the harvest-field for the corn-spirit.

> "*We give it to the Old Woman;*
> *She shall keep it.*
> *Next year may she be to us*
> *As kind as this time she has been.*"[4]

These words clearly shew that the Old Woman for whom the corn is left on the field is not a real personage, poor and hungry, but the mythical Old Woman who makes the corn to grow. At Schüttarschen, in West Bohemia, after the crop has been reaped, a few stalks are left standing and a garland is attached to them. "That belongs to the Wood-woman," they say, and offer a prayer. In this way the Wood-woman, we are told, has enough to live on through the winter and the corn will thrive the better next year. The same thing is done for all the different kinds of corn-crop.[5]   So in Thüringen, when the after-grass (*Grummet*) is being got in, a little heap is left lying on the field; it belongs to "the Little Wood-woman" in return for the blessing she has bestowed.[6]   In the Frankenwald of Bavaria three hand-fuls of flax were left on the field "for the Wood-woman."[7]

[1] W. Mannhardt, *Mythologische Forschungen*, p. 49.

[2] *Ibid.* p. 337.

[3] *Ibid.*

[4] W. Mannhardt, *Mythologische Forschungen*, pp. 337 *sq.*

[5] A. John, *Sitte, Brauch und Volks-glaube im deutschen Westböhmen* (Prague, 1905), p. 189.

[6] A. Witzschel, *Sagen, Sitten und Gebräuche aus Thüringen* (Vienna, 1878), p. 224, § 74.

[7] *Bavaria, Landes- und Volkskunde des Königreichs Bayern* (Munich, 1860-1867), iii. 343 *sq.*

At Lindau in Anhalt the reapers used to leave some stalks standing in the last corner of the last field for "the Corn-woman to eat."[1]   In some parts of Silesia it was till lately the custom to leave a few corn-stalks standing in the field, "in order that the next harvest should not fail."[2]   In Russia it is customary to leave patches of unreaped corn in the fields and to place bread and salt on the ground near them.   "These ears are eventually knotted together, and the ceremony is called 'the plaiting of the beard of Volos,' and it is supposed that after it has been performed no wizard or other evilly-disposed person will be able to hurt the produce of the fields. The unreaped patch is looked upon as tabooed ; and it is believed that if any one meddles with it he will shrivel up, and become twisted like the interwoven ears.   Similar customs are kept up in various parts of Russia.   Near Kursk and Voroneje, for instance, a patch of rye is usually left in honour of the Prophet Elijah, and in another district one of oats is consecrated to St. Nicholas.   As it is well known that both the Saint and the Prophet have succeeded to the place once held in the estimation of the Russian people by Perun, it seems probable that Volos really was, in ancient times, one of the names of the thunder-god."[3]   In the north-east of Scotland a few stalks were sometimes left unreaped on the field for the benefit of "the aul' man."[4]   Here "the aul' man " is probably the equivalent of the harvest Old Man of Germany.[5]   Among the Mohammedans of Zanzibar it is customary at sowing a field to reserve a certain portion of it for the guardian spirits, who at harvest are invited, to the tuck of drum, to come and take their share ; tiny huts are also built in which food is deposited for their use.[6]   In the island of Nias, to prevent the depredations of wandering spirits among the rice at harvest, a miniature field is dedicated

[1] *Zeitschrift des Vereins für Volks-kunde,* vii. (1897) p. 154.
[2] P. Drechsler, *Sitte, Brauch, und Volksglaube in Schlesien* (Leipsic, 1903-1906), ii. 64, § 419.
[3] W. R. S. Ralston, *Songs of the Russian People,* Second Edition (London, 1872), pp. 251 *sq.* As to Perun, the old Slavonic thunder-god, see *The Magic Art and the Evolution*

of Kings, ii. 365.
[4] Rev. Walter Gregor, *Notes on the Folk-lore of the North-east of Scotland* (London, 1881), p. 182.
[5] See above, pp. 136 *sqq.*
[6] A. Germain, "Note zur Zanzibar et la Côte Orientale d'Afrique,"*Bulletin de la Société de Géographie* (Paris), Vème Série, xvi. (1868) p. 555.

Little fields or gardens cultivated for spirits or gods. to them and in it are sown all the plants that grow in the real fields.[1] The Hos, a Ewe tribe of negroes in Togoland, observe a similar custom for a similar reason. At the entrance to their yam-fields the traveller may see on both sides of the path small mounds on which yams, stock-yams, beans, and maize are planted and appear to flourish with more than usual luxuriance. These little gardens, tended with peculiar care, are dedicated to the "guardian gods" of the owner of the land; there he cultivates for their benefit the same plants which he cultivates for his own use in the fields; and the notion is that the "guardian gods" will content themselves with eating the fruits which grow in their little private preserves and will not poach on the crops which are destined for human use.[2]

Hence perhaps we may explain the dedication of sacred fields and the offering of first-fruits to gods and spirits. These customs suggest that the little sacred rice-fields on which the Kayans of Borneo perform the various operations of husbandry in mimicry before they address themselves to the real labours of the field,[3] may be dedicated to the spirits of the rice to compensate them for the loss they sustain by allowing men to cultivate all the rest of the land for their own benefit. Perhaps the Rarian plain at Eleusis[4] was a spiritual preserve of the same kind set apart for the exclusive use of the corn-goddesses Demeter and Persephone. It may even be that the law which forbade the Hebrews to reap the corners and gather the gleanings of the harvest-fields and to strip the

---

[1] E. Modigliani, *Un Viaggio a Nías* (Milan, 1890), p. 593.

[2] J. Spieth, *Die Ewe-Stämme* (Berlin, 1906), p. 303. In the Central Provinces of India "sometimes the oldest man in the house cuts the first five bundles of the crop and they are afterwards left in the fields for the birds to eat. And at the end of harvest the last one or two sheaves are left standing in the field and any one who likes can cut and carry them away. In some localities the last sheaves are left standing in the field and are known as *barhona*, or the giver of increase. Then all the labourers rush together at this last patch of corn and tear it up by the roots; everybody seizes as much as he can [and] keeps it, the master having

no share in this patch. After the *barhona* has been torn up all the labourers fall on their faces to the ground and worship the field" (A. E. Nelson, *Central Provinces Gazetteers, Bilaspur District*, vol. A, 1910, p. 75). This quotation was kindly sent to me by Mr. W. Crooke; I have not seen the original. It seems to shew that in the Central Provinces the last corn is left standing on the field as a portion for the corn-spirit, and that he is believed to be immanent in it; hence the name of "the giver of increase" bestowed on it, and the eagerness with which other people, though not the owner of the land, seek to appropriate it.

[3] See above, pp. 93 *sq.*

[4] See above, pp. 36, 74.

vines of their last grapes [1] was originally intended for the benefit, not of the human poor, but of the poor spirits of the corn and the vine, who had just been despoiled by the reapers and the vintagers, and who, if some provision were not made for their subsistence, would naturally die of hunger before another year came round. In providing for their wants the prudent husbandman was really consulting his own interests ; for how could he expect to reap wheat and barley and to gather grapes next year if he suffered the spirits of the corn and of the vine to perish of famine in the meantime ? This train of thought may possibly explain the wide-spread custom of offering the first-fruits of the crops to gods or spirits : [2] such offerings may have been originally not so much an expression of gratitude for benefits received as a means of enabling the benefactors to continue their benefactions in time to come. Primitive man has generally a shrewd eye to the main chance : he is more prone to provide for the future than to sentimentalise over the past.

Thus when the spirit of vegetation is conceived as a being who is robbed of his store and impoverished by the harvesters, it is natural that his representative — the passing stranger — should upbraid them ; and it is equally natural that they should seek to disable him from pursuing them and recapturing the stolen property. Now, it is an old superstition that by easing nature on the spot where a robbery is committed, the robbers secure themselves, for a certain time, against interruption.[3] Hence when madder-diggers resort to this proceeding in presence of the stranger whom they have caught and buried in the field, we may infer that they consider themselves robbers and him as the person robbed. Regarded as such, he must be the natural owner of the madder-roots, that is, their spirit or demon ; and this conception is carried out by

Passing strangers treated as the spirit of the madder-roots.

---

[1] Leviticus, xix. 9 *sq.*, xxiii. 22 ; Deuteronomy, xxiv. 19-21.

[2] See above, pp. 46 *sq.*, 53 *sqq.*, and below, vol. ii. pp. 109 *sqq.*

[3] W. Mannhardt, *Mythologische Forschungen*, pp. 49 *sq.* ; A. Wuttke,

Der deutsche Volksaberglaube [2] (Berlin, 1869), p. 254, § 400 ; M. Töppen, *Aberglaube aus Masuren* [2] (Danzig, 1867), p. 57. The same belief is held and acted upon in Japan (L. Hearn, *Glimpses of Unfamiliar Japan*, London, 1904, ii. 603).

burying him, like the madder-roots, in the ground.[1] The Greeks, it may be observed, were quite familiar with the idea that a passing stranger may be a god. Homer says that the gods in the likeness of foreigners roam up and down cities.[2] Once in Poso, a district of Celebes, when a new missionary entered a house where a number of people were gathered round a sick man, one of them addressed the new-comer in these words: "Well, sir, as we had never seen you before, and you came suddenly in, while we sat here by ourselves, we thought it was a spirit."[3]

Killing of the personal representative of the corn-spirit.
Thus in these harvest-customs of modern Europe the person who cuts, binds, or threshes the last corn is treated as an embodiment of the corn-spirit by being wrapt up in sheaves, killed in mimicry by agricultural implements, and thrown into the water.[4] These coincidences with the Lityerses story seem to prove that the latter is a genuine description of an old Phrygian harvest-custom. But since in the modern parallels the killing of the personal representative of the corn-spirit is necessarily omitted or at most enacted only in mimicry, it is desirable to shew that in rude society human beings have been commonly killed as an agricultural ceremony to promote the fertility of the fields. The following examples will make this plain.

§ 3. *Human Sacrifices for the Crops*

Human sacrifices for the crops in South and Central America.
The Indians of Guayaquil, in Ecuador, used to sacrifice human blood and the hearts of men when they sowed their fields.[5] The people of Cañar (now Cuenca in Ecuador) used to sacrifice a hundred children annually at harvest. The kings of Quito, the Incas of Peru, and for a long time the Spaniards were unable to suppress the bloody rite.[6] At a

---

[1] The explanation of the custom is W. Mannhardt's (*Mythologische Forschungen*, p. 49).

[2] *Odyssey*, xvii. 485 *sqq*. Compare Plato, *Sophist*, p. 216 A.

[3] A. C. Kruijt, "Mijne eerste ervaringen te Poso," *Mededeelingen van wege het Nederlandsche Zendelinggenootschap*, xxxvi. (1892) p. 402.

[4] For throwing him into the water,

see p. 225.

[5] Cieza de Leon, *Travels*, translated by C. R. Markham, p. 203 (Hakluyt Society, London, 1864).

[6] Juan de Velasco, *Histoire du Royaume de Quito*, i. (Paris, 1840) pp. 121 *sq*. (Ternaux-Compans, *Voyages, Relations et Mémoires Originaux pour servir à l'Histoire de la Découverte de l'Amérique*, vol. xviii.).

Mexican harvest-festival, when the first-fruits of the season were offered to the sun, a criminal was placed between two immense stones, balanced opposite each other, and was crushed by them as they fell together. His remains were buried, and a feast and dance followed. This sacrifice was known as "the meeting of the stones."[1] "Tlaloc was worshipped in Mexico as the god of the thunder and the storm which precedes the fertilising rain ; elsewhere his wife Xochiquetzal, who at Tlaxcallan was called Matlalcuéyé or the Lady of the Blue Petticoats, shared these honours, and it was to her that many countries in Central America particularly paid their devotions. Every year, at the time when the cobs of the still green and milky maize are about to coagulate and ripen, they used to sacrifice to the goddess four young girls, chosen among the noblest families of the country ; they were decked out in festal attire, crowned with flowers, and conveyed in rich palanquins to the brink of the hallowed waters, where the sacrifice was to be offered. The priests, clad in long floating robes, their heads encircled with feather crowns, marched in front of the litters carrying censers with burning incense. The town of Elopango, celebrated for its temple, was near the lake of the same name, the etymology of which refers to the sheaves of tender maize (*elotl*, ' sheaf of tender maize '). It was dedicated to the goddess Xochiquetzal, to whom the young victims were offered by being hurled from the top of a rock into the abyss. At the moment of consummating this inhuman rite, the priests addressed themselves in turn to the four virgins in order to banish the fear of death from their minds. They drew for them a bright picture of the delights they were about to enjoy in the company of the gods, and advised them not to forget the earth which they had left behind, but to entreat the divinity, to whom they despatched them, to bless the forthcoming harvest."[2] We have seen that the ancient Mexicans also sacrificed human beings at all the

---

[1] Brasseur de Bourbourg, *Histoire des Nations civilisées du Mexique et de l'Amérique Centrale* (Paris, 1857-1859), i. 274 ; H. H. Bancroft, *Native Races of the Pacific States* (London, 1875-1876), ii. 340.

[2] Brasseur de Bourbourg, "Aperçus d'un voyage dans les États de San-Salvador et de Guatemala," *Bulletin de la Société de Géographie* (Paris), IVème Série, xiii. (1857) pp. 278 *sq.*

various stages in the growth of the maize, the age of the victims corresponding to the age of the corn ; for they sacrificed new-born babes at sowing, older children when the grain had sprouted, and so on till it was fully ripe, when they sacrificed old men.[1] No doubt the correspondence between the ages of the victims and the state of the corn was supposed to enhance the efficacy of the sacrifice.

Human sacrifices for the crops among the Pawnees. The Pawnees annually sacrificed a human victim in spring when they sowed their fields. The sacrifice was believed to have been enjoined on them by the Morning Star, or by a certain bird which the Morning Star had sent to them as its messenger. The bird was stuffed and preserved as a powerful talisman. They thought that an omission of this sacrifice would be followed by the total failure of the crops of maize, beans, and pumpkins. The victim was a captive of either sex. He was clad in the gayest and most costly attire, was fattened on the choicest food, and carefully kept in ignorance of his doom. When he was fat enough, they bound him to a cross in the presence of the multitude, danced a solemn dance, then cleft his head with a tomahawk and shot him with arrows. According to one trader, the squaws then cut pieces of flesh from the victim's body, with which they greased their hoes ; but this was denied by another trader who had been present at the ceremony. Immediately after the sacrifice the people proceeded to plant their fields. A particular account has been preserved of the sacrifice of a Sioux girl by the Pawnees in April 1837 or 1838. The girl was fourteen or fifteen years old and had been kept for six months and well treated. Two days before the sacrifice she was led from wigwam to wigwam, accompanied by the whole council of chiefs and warriors. At each lodge she received a small billet of wood and a little paint, which she handed to the warrior next to her. In this way she called at every wigwam, receiving at each the same present of wood and paint. On the twenty-second of April she was taken out to be sacrificed, attended by the warriors, each of whom carried two pieces of wood

---

[1] Herrera, quoted by A. Bastian, *Die Culturländer des alten Amerika* (Berlin, 1878), ii. 379 *sq.* See *Adonis, Attis, Osiris*, Second Edition, pp. 338 *sq.*

which he had received from her hands. Her body having been painted half red and half black, she was attached to a sort of gibbet and roasted for some time over a slow fire, then shot to death with arrows. The chief sacrificer next tore out her heart and devoured it. While her flesh was still warm it was cut in small pieces from the bones, put in little baskets, and taken to a neighbouring corn-field. There the head chief took a piece of the flesh from a basket and squeezed a drop of blood upon the newly-deposited grains of corn. His example was followed by the rest, till all the seed had been sprinkled with the blood; it was then covered up with earth. According to one account the body of the victim was reduced to a kind of paste, which was rubbed or sprinkled not only on the maize but also on the potatoes, the beans, and other seeds to fertilise them. By this sacrifice they hoped to obtain plentiful crops.[1]

A West African queen used to sacrifice a man and woman in the month of March. They were killed with spades and hoes, and their bodies buried in the middle of a field which had just been tilled.[2] At Lagos in Guinea it was the custom annually to impale a young girl alive soon after the spring equinox in order to secure good crops. Along with her were sacrificed sheep and goats, which, with yams, heads of maize, and plantains, were hung on stakes on each side of her. The victims were bred up for the purpose in the king's seraglio, and their minds had been so powerfully wrought upon by the fetish men that they went cheerfully to

Human sacrifices for the crops in Africa.

---

[1] E. James, *Account of an Expedition from Pittsburgh to the Rocky Mountains* (London, 1823), ii. 80 *sq.*; H. R. Schoolcraft, *Indian Tribes of the United States* (Philadelphia, 1853-1856), v. 77 *sqq.*; J. De Smet, in *Annales de la Propagation de la Foi*, xi. (1838) pp. 493 *sq.*; *id.*, in *Annales de la Propagation de la Foi*, xv. (1843) pp. 277-279; *id.*, *Voyages aux Montagnes Rocheuses*, Nouvelle Edition (Paris and Brussels, 1873), pp. 121 *sqq.* The accounts by Schoolcraft and De Smet of the sacrifice of the Sioux girl are independent and supplement each other. According to De Smet, who wrote from the descriptions of four eye-witnesses, the procession from hut to hut for the purpose of collecting wood took place on the morning of the sacrifice. Another description of the sacrifice is given by Mr. G. B. Grinnell from the recollection of an eye-witness (*Pawnee Hero Stories and Folk-tales*, New York, 1889, pp. 362 - 369). According to this last account the victim was shot with arrows and afterwards burnt. Before the body was consumed in the fire a man pulled out the arrows, cut open the breast of the victim, and having smeared his face with the blood ran away as fast as he could.

[2] J. B. Labat, *Relation historique de l'Ethiopie occidentale* (Paris, 1732), i. 380.

their fate.[1]   A similar sacrifice used to be annually offered at Benin, in Guinea.[2]   The Marimos, a Bechuana tribe, sacrifice a human being for the crops.   The victim chosen is generally a short, stout man.   He is seized by violence or intoxicated and taken to the fields, where he is killed amongst the wheat to serve as " seed " (so they phrase it). After his blood has coagulated in the sun, it is burned along with the frontal bone, the flesh attached to it, and the brain ; the ashes are then scattered over the ground to fertilise it. The rest of the body is eaten.[3]   The Wamegi of the Usagara hills in German East Africa used to offer human sacrifices of a peculiar kind once a year about the time of harvest, which was also the time of sowing ; for the Wamegi have two crops annually, one in September and one in February. The festival was usually held in September or October. The victim was a girl who had attained the age of puberty. She was taken to a hill where the festival was to be celebrated, and there she was crushed to death between two branches.[4]   The sacrifice was not performed in the fields, and my informant could not ascertain its object, but we may conjecture that it was to ensure good crops in the following year.

Human sacrifices for the crops in the Philippines.

The Bagobos of Mindanao, one of the Philippine Islands, offer a human sacrifice before they sow their rice.   The victim is a slave, who is hewn to pieces in the forest.[5]   The natives of Bontoc, a province in the interior of Luzon, one of the Philippine Islands, are passionate head-hunters. Their principal seasons for head-hunting are the times of planting and reaping the rice.   In order that the crop may turn out well, every farm must get at least one human head at planting and one at sowing.   The head-hunters go out in twos or threes, lie in wait for the victim,

[1] John Adams, *Sketches taken during Ten Voyages in Africa between the years 1786 and 1800* (London, N.D.), p. 25.
[2] P. Bouche, *La Côte des Esclaves* (Paris, 1885), p. 132.
[3] T. Arbousset et F. Daumas, *Voyage d'exploration au Nord-est de la Colonie du Cap de Bonne-Espérance* (Paris, 1842), pp. 117 *sq.*   The

custom has probably long been obsolete.
[4] From information given me by my friend the Rev. John Roscoe, who resided for some time among the Wamegi and suppressed the sacrifice in 1886.
[5] F. Blumentritt, " Das Stromgebiet des Rio Grande de Mindanao," *Petermanns Mitteilungen*, xxxvii. (1891) p. 110.

whether man or woman, cut off his or her head, hands, and feet, and bring them back in haste to the village, where they are received with great rejoicings. The skulls are at first exposed on the branches of two or three dead trees which stand in an open space of every village surrounded by large stones which serve as seats. The people then dance round them and feast and get drunk. When the flesh has decayed from the head, the man who cut it off takes it home and preserves it as a relic, while his companions do the same with the hands and the feet.[1]   Similar customs are observed by the Apoyaos, another tribe in the interior of Luzon.[2]

The Wild Wa, an agricultural tribe on the north- eastern frontier of Upper Burma, still hunt for human heads as a means of promoting the welfare of the crops. The Wa regards his skulls as a protection against the powers of evil. " Without a skull his crops would fail ; without a skull his kine might die ; without a skull the father and mother spirits would be shamed and might be enraged ; if there were no protecting skull the other spirits, who are all malignant, might gain entrance and kill the inhabitants, or drink all the liquor." The Wa country is a series of mountain ranges shelving rapidly down to narrow valleys from two to five thousand feet deep. The villages are all perched high on the slopes, some just under the crest of the ridge, some lower down on a small projecting spur of flat ground. Industrious cultivation has cleared away the jungle, and the villages stand out conspicuously in the landscape as yellowish-brown blotches on the hill- sides. Each village is fortified by an earthen rampart so thickly overgrown with cactuses and other shrubs as to be impenetrable. The only entrance is through a narrow, low, and winding tunnel, the floor of which, for additional security, is thickly studded with pegs to wound the feet of enemies who might attempt to force a way in. The Wa depend for their subsistence mainly on their crops of

Human sacrifices for the crops among the Wild Wa of Burma.

---

[1] A. Schadenberg, " Beiträge zur Kenntniss der im Innern Nordluzons lebenden Stämme," *Verhandlungen der Berliner Gesellschaft für Anthropologie, Ethnologie und Urgeschichte,* 1888, p. (39) (bound with *Zeitschrift*

für Ethnologie, xx. 1888).

[2] Schadenberg, in *Verhandlungen der Berliner Gesellschaft für Anthropologie, Ethnologie und Urgeschichte,* 1889, p. (681) (bound with *Zeitschrift für Ethnologie,* xxi. 1889).

buckwheat, beans, and maize ; rice they cultivate only to distil a strong spirituous liquor from it. They had need be industrious, for no field can be reached without a climb up or down the steep mountain-side. Sometimes the rice-fields lie three thousand feet or more below the village, and they require constant attention. But the chief crop raised by the Wa is the poppy, from which they make opium. In February and March the hill-tops for miles are white with the blossom, and you may travel for days through nothing but fields of poppies. Then, too, is the proper season for head-hunting. It opens in March and lasts through April. Parties of head-hunters at that time go forth to prowl for human prey. As a rule they will not behead people of a neighbouring village nor even of any village on the same range of hills. To find victims they go to the next range or at any rate to a distance, and the farther the better, for the heads of strangers are preferred. The reason is that the ghosts of strangers, being unfamiliar with the country, are much less likely to stray away from their skulls ; hence they make more vigilant sentinels than the ghosts of people better acquainted with the neighbourhood, who are apt to go off duty without waiting for the tedious formality of relieving guard. When head-hunters return to a village with human heads, the rejoicing is uproarious. Then the great drum is beaten frantically, and its deep hollow boom resounding far and wide through the hills announces to the neighbourhood the glad tidings of murder successfully perpetrated. Then the barrels, or rather the bamboos, of rice-spirit are tapped, and while the genial stream flows and the women and children dance and sing for glee, the men drink themselves blind and mad drunk. The ghastly head, which forms the centre of all this rejoicing, is first taken to the spirit-house, a small shed which usually stands on the highest point of the village site. There, wrapt in grass or leaves, it is hung up in a basket to ripen and bleach. When all the flesh and sinews have mouldered away and nothing remains but the blanched and grinning skull, it is put to rest in the village Golgotha. This is an avenue of huge old trees, whose inter-lacing boughs form a verdant archway overhead and, with the dense undergrowth, cast a deep shadow on the ground below. Every village has such an avenue stretching along the hillside sometimes for a long distance, or even till it meets the avenue of the neighbouring village. In the solemn gloom of this verdurous canopy is the Place of Skulls. On one side of the avenue stands a row of wooden posts, usually mere trunks of trees with the bark peeled off, but sometimes rudely carved and painted with designs in red and black. A little below the top of each post is cut a niche, and in front of the niche is a ledge. On this ledge the skull is deposited, sometimes so that it is in full view of passers-by in the avenue, sometimes so that it only grins at them through a slit. Most villages count their skulls by tens or twenties, but some of them have hundreds of these trophies, especially when the avenue forms an unbroken continuity of shade between the villages. The old skulls ensure peace to the village, but at least one new one should be taken every year, that the rice may grow green far down in the depths of the valley, that the maize may tinge with its golden hue the steep mountain-sides, and that the hilltops may be white for miles and miles with the bloom of the poppy.[1]

The Shans of Indo-China still believe in the efficacy of human sacrifice to procure a good harvest, though they act on the belief less than some other tribes of this region. Their practice now is to poison somebody at the state festival, which is generally held at some time between March and May.[2] Among the Lhota Naga, one of the many savage tribes who inhabit the deep rugged labyrinthine glens which wind into the mountains from the rich valley of Brahmapootra,[3] it used to be a common custom to chop off the heads, hands, and feet of people they met with, and then to stick up the severed extremities in their fields to ensure a good crop of grain. They bore no

Human sacrifices for the crops among the Shans of Indo-China and the Nagas and other tribes of India.

[1] (Sir) J. G. Scott and J. P. Hardiman, *Gazetteer of Upper Burma and the Shan States* (Rangoon, 1900-1901), Part i. vol. i. pp. 493-509.

[2] Col. R. G. Woodthorpe, "Some Account of the Shans and Hill Tribes of the States on the Mekong," *Journal* of the Anthropological Institute, xxvi. (1897) p. 24.

[3] For a general description of the country and the tribes see L. A. Waddell, "The Tribes of the Brahmaputra Valley," *Journal of the Asiatic Society of Bengal,* lxix. Part iii. (Calcutta, 1901), pp. 1-127.

ill-will whatever to the persons upon whom they operated
in this unceremonious fashion.   Once they flayed a
boy alive, carved him in pieces, and distributed the flesh
among all the villagers, who put it into their corn-bins to
avert bad luck and ensure plentiful crops of grain.   The
Angami, another tribe of the same region, used also to relieve
casual passers-by of their heads, hands, and feet, with the
same excellent intention.[1]   The hill tribe Kudulu, near
Vizagapatam in the Madras Presidency, offered human
sacrifices to the god Jankari for the purpose of obtaining
good crops.   The ceremony was generally performed on the
Sunday before or after the Pongal feast.   For the most part
the victim was purchased, and until the time for the sacrifice
came he was free to wander about the village, to eat and
drink what he liked, and even to lie with any woman he
met.   On the appointed day he was carried before the
idol drunk ; and when one of the villagers had cut a hole
in his stomach and smeared the blood on the idol, the
crowds from the neighbouring villages rushed upon him
and hacked him to pieces.   All who were fortunate enough
to secure morsels of his flesh carried them away and presented them to their village idols.[2]   The Gonds of India, a
Dravidian race, kidnapped Brahman boys, and kept them as
victims to be sacrificed on various occasions.   At sowing and
reaping, after a triumphal procession, one of the lads was
slain by being punctured with a poisoned arrow.   His blood
was then sprinkled over the ploughed field or the ripe crop,
and his flesh was devoured.[3]   The Oraons or Uraons of
Chota Nagpur worship a goddess called Anna Kuari, who
can give good crops and make a man rich, but to induce her
to do so it is necessary to offer human sacrifices.   In spite
of the vigilance of the British Government these sacrifices are
said to be still secretly perpetrated.   The victims are poor
waifs and strays whose disappearance attracts no notice.
April and May are the months when the catchpoles are out
on the prowl.   At that time strangers will not go about the

[1] Miss G. M. Godden, " Naga and
other Frontier Tribes of North-Eastern
India," *Journal of the Anthropological
Institute*, xxvii. (1898) pp. 9 *sq.*, 38 *sq.*

[2] *North Indian Notes and Queries*,
i. p. 4, § 15 (April 1891).
[3] *Panjab Notes and Queries*, ii. pp.
127 *sq.*, § 721 (May 1885).

country alone, and parents will not let their children enter the jungle or herd the cattle. When a catchpole has found a victim, he cuts his throat and carries away the upper part of the ring finger and the nose. The goddess takes up her abode in the house of any man who has offered her a sacrifice, and from that time his fields yield a double harvest. The form she assumes in the house is that of a small child. When the householder brings in his unhusked rice, he takes the goddess and rolls her over the heap to double its size. But she soon grows restless and can only be pacified with the blood of fresh human victims.[1]

But the best known case of human sacrifices, systematic-ally offered to ensure good crops, is supplied by the Khonds or Kandhs, another Dravidian race in Bengal. Our knowledge of them is derived from the accounts written by British officers who, about the middle of the nineteenth century, were engaged in putting them down.[2] The sacrifices were offered to the Earth Goddess, Tari Pennu or Bera Pennu, and were believed to ensure good crops and immunity from all disease and accidents. In particular, they were considered necessary in the cultivation of turmeric, the Khonds arguing that the turmeric could not have a deep red colour without the shedding of blood.[3] The victim or Meriah, as he was called, was acceptable to the goddess only if he had been purchased, or had been born a victim—that is, the son of a victim father, or had been devoted as a child by his father or guardian. Khonds in distress often sold their children for victims, "considering the beatifica-tion of their souls certain, and their death, for the benefit of mankind, the most honourable possible." A man of the Panua tribe was once seen to load a Khond with curses, and finally to spit in his face, because the Khond had sold for a victim his own child, whom the Panua had wished to

Human sacrifices for the crops among the Khonds.

[1] Rev. P. Dehon, S.J., "Religion and Customs of the Uraons," *Memoirs of the Asiatic Society of Bengal,* vol. i. No. 9 (Calcutta, 1906), pp. 141 *sq.*

[2] Major S. C. Macpherson, *Memorials of Service in India* (London, 1865), pp. 113-131 ; Major-General John Campbell, *Wild Tribes of Khondistan* (London, 1864), pp. 52-58, etc.

Compare Mgr. Neyret, Bishop of Viza-gapatam, in *Annales de la Propagation de la Foi,* xxiii. (1851) pp. 402-404 ; E. Thurston, *Ethnographic Notes on Southern India* (Madras, 1906), pp. 510-519 ; *id., Castes and Tribes of Southern India* (Madras, 1909), iii. 371-385.

[3] J. Campbell, *op. cit.* p. 56.

marry. A party of Khonds, who saw this, immediately pressed forward to comfort the seller of his child, saying, "Your child has died that all the world may live, and the Earth Goddess herself will wipe that spittle from your face."[1] The victims were often kept for years before they were sacrificed. Being regarded as consecrated beings, they were treated with extreme affection, mingled with deference, and were welcomed wherever they went. A Meriah youth, on attaining maturity, was generally given a wife, who was herself usually a Meriah or victim ; and with her he received a portion of land and farm-stock. Their offspring were also victims. Human sacrifices were offered to the Earth Goddess by tribes, branches of tribes, or villages, both at periodical festivals and on extraordinary occasions. The periodical sacrifices were generally so arranged by tribes and divisions of tribes that each head of a family was enabled, at least once a year, to procure a shred of flesh for his fields, generally about the time when his chief crop was laid down.[2]

Ceremonies preliminary to the sacrifice.

The mode of performing these tribal sacrifices was as follows. Ten or twelve days before the sacrifice, the victim was devoted by cutting off his hair, which, until then, had been kept unshorn. Crowds of men and women assembled to witness the sacrifice ; none might be excluded, since the sacrifice was declared to be for all mankind. It was preceded by several days of wild revelry and gross debauchery.[3] On the day before the sacrifice the victim, dressed in a new garment, was led forth from the village in solemn procession, with music and dancing, to the Meriah grove, a clump of high forest trees standing a little way from the village and untouched by the axe. There they tied him to a post, which was sometimes placed between two plants of the sankissar shrub. He was then anointed with oil, ghee, and turmeric, and adorned with flowers ; and "a species of reverence, which it is not easy to distinguish from adoration," was paid to him throughout the day. A great struggle now arose to obtain the smallest relic from his person ; a particle of the

[1] S. C. Macpherson, op. cit. pp. 115 sq.
[2] S. C. Macpherson, op. cit. pp. 117 sq.
[3] S. C. Macpherson, op. cit. pp. 117 sq. ; J. Campbell, op. cit. p. 112.

turmeric paste with which he was smeared, or a drop of his spittle, was esteemed of sovereign virtue, especially by the women.[1] The crowd danced round the post to music, and, addressing the earth, said, " O God, we offer this sacrifice to you ; give us good crops, seasons, and health " ; then speaking to the victim they said, " We bought you with a price, and did not seize you ; now we sacrifice you according to custom, and no sin rests with us." [2]

On the last morning the orgies, which had been scarcely interrupted during the night, were resumed, and continued till noon, when they ceased, and the assembly proceeded to consummate the sacrifice.   The victim was again anointed with oil, and each person touched the anointed part, and wiped the oil on his own head.   In some places they took the victim in procession round the village, from door to door, where some plucked hair from his head, and others begged for a drop of his spittle, with which they anointed their heads.[3]   As the victim might not be bound nor make any show of resistance, the bones of his arms and, if necessary, his legs were broken ; but often this precaution was rendered unnecessary by stupefying him with opium.[4]   The mode of putting him to death varied in different places.   One of the commonest modes seems to have been strangulation, or squeezing to death.   The branch of a green tree was cleft several feet down the middle ; the victim's neck (in other places, his chest) was inserted in the cleft, which the priest, aided by his assistants, strove with all his force to close.[5] Then he wounded the victim slightly with his axe, whereupon the crowd rushed at the wretch and hewed the flesh from the bones, leaving the head and bowels untouched.   Sometimes he was cut up alive.[6]   In Chinna Kimedy he was dragged along the fields, surrounded by the crowd, who, avoiding his head and intestines, hacked the flesh from his body with their knives till he died.[7]   Another very common mode of

Consummation of the sacrifice.

[1] S. C. Macpherson, *op. cit.* p. 118.

[2] J. Campbell, *op. cit.* pp. 54 *sq.*

[3] J. Campbell, *op. cit.* pp. 55, 112.

[4] S. C. Macpherson, *op. cit.* p. 119 ; J. Campbell, *op. cit.* p. 113.

[5] S. C. Macpherson, *op. cit.* p. 127. Instead of the branch of a green tree,

Campbell mentions two strong planks or bamboos (p. 57) or a slit bamboo (p. 182).

[6] J. Campbell, *op. cit.* pp. 56, 58, 120.

[7] E. T. Dalton, *Descriptive Ethnology of Bengal* (Calcutta, 1872), p. 288, quoting Colonel Campbell's *Report.*'

sacrifice in the same district was to fasten the victim to the proboscis of a wooden elephant, which revolved on a stout post, and, as it whirled round, the crowd cut the flesh from the victim while life remained. In some villages Major Campbell found as many as fourteen of these wooden elephants, which had been used at sacrifices.[1] In one district the victim was put to death slowly by fire. A low stage was formed, sloping on either side like a roof ; upon it they laid the victim, his limbs wound round with cords to confine his struggles. Fires were then lighted and hot brands applied, to make him roll up and down the slopes of the stage as long as possible ; for the more tears he shed the more abundant would be the supply of rain. Next day the body was cut to pieces.[2]

Flesh of the victim used to fertilise the fields.

The flesh cut from the victim was instantly taken home by the persons who had been deputed by each village to bring it. To secure its rapid arrival, it was sometimes forwarded by relays of men, and conveyed with postal fleetness fifty or sixty miles.[3] In each village all who stayed at home fasted rigidly until the flesh arrived. The bearer deposited it in the place of public assembly, where it was received by the priest and the heads of families. The priest divided it into two portions, one of which he offered to the Earth Goddess by burying it in a hole in the ground with his back turned, and without looking. Then each man added a little earth to bury it, and the priest poured water on the spot from a hill gourd. The other portion of flesh he divided into as many shares as there were heads of houses present. Each head of a house rolled his shred of flesh in leaves, and buried it in his favourite field, placing it in the earth behind his back without looking.[4] In some

---

[1] J. Campbell, *op. cit.* p. 126. The elephant represented the Earth Goddess herself, who was here conceived in elephant-form (Campbell, *op. cit.* pp. 51, 126). In the hill tracts of Goomsur she was represented in peacock-form, and the post to which the victim was bound bore the effigy of a peacock (Campbell, *op. cit.* p. 54).

[2] S. C. Macpherson, *op. cit.* p. 130. In Mexico also the tears of the human victims were sometimes regarded as an omen of rain (B. de Sahagun, *Histoire générale des Choses de la Nouvelle Espagne,* traduite par D. Jourdanet et R. Simeon, Paris, 1880, bk. ii. ch. 20, p. 86).

[3] E. T. Dalton, *Descriptive Ethnology of Bengal,* p. 288, referring to Colonel Campbell's *Report.*

[4] S. C. Macpherson, *op. cit.* p. 129. Compare J. Campbell, *op. cit.* pp. 55, 58, 113, 121, 187.

places each man carried his portion of flesh to the stream which watered his fields, and there hung it on a pole.[1]   For three days thereafter no house was swept ; and, in one district, strict silence was observed, no fire might be given out, no wood cut, and no strangers received.   The remains of the human victim (namely, the head, bowels, and bones) were watched by strong parties the night after the sacrifice ; and next morning they were burned, along with a whole sheep, on a funeral pile.   The ashes were scattered over the fields, laid as paste over the houses and granaries, or mixed with the new corn to preserve it from insects.[2] Sometimes, however, the head and bones were buried, not burnt.[3]   After the suppression of the human sacrifices, inferior victims were substituted in some places ; for instance, in the capital of Chinna Kimedy a goat took the place of a human victim.[4]   Others sacrifice a buffalo.   They tie it to a wooden post in a sacred grove, dance wildly round it with brandished knives, then, falling on the living animal, hack it to shreds and tatters in a few minutes, fighting and struggling with each other for every particle of flesh.   As soon as a man has secured a piece he makes off with it at full speed to bury it in his fields, according to ancient custom, before the sun has set, and as some of them have far to go they must run very fast.   All the women throw clods of earth at the rapidly retreating figures of the men, some of them taking very good aim.   Soon the sacred grove, so lately a scene of tumult, is silent and deserted except for a few people who remain to guard all that is left of the buffalo, to wit, the head, the bones, and the stomach, which are burned with ceremony at the foot of the stake.[5]

In these Khond sacrifices the Meriahs are represented by our authorities as victims offered to propitiate the Earth Goddess.   But from the treatment of the victims both before and after death it appears that the custom cannot be explained as merely a propitiatory sacrifice.   A part of the flesh certainly was offered to the Earth Goddess, but the

In these Khond sacrifices the human victims appear to have been regarded as divine.

[1] J. Campbell, *op. cit.* p. 182.
[2] S. C. Macpherson, *op. cit.* p. 128 ; E. T. Dalton, *Descriptive Ethnology of Bengal*, p. 288.
[3] J. Campbell, *op. cit.* pp. 55, 182.

[4] J. Campbell, *op. cit.* p. 187.

[5] E. Thurston, *Castes and Tribes of Southern India* (Madras, 1909), iii. 381-385.

rest was buried by each householder in his fields, and the ashes of the other parts of the body were scattered over the fields, laid as paste on the granaries, or mixed with the new corn.   These latter customs imply that to the body of the Meriah there was ascribed a direct or intrinsic power of making the crops to grow, quite independent of the indirect efficacy which it might have as an offering to secure the good-will of the deity.   In other words, the flesh and ashes of the victim were believed to be endowed with a magical or physical power of fertilising the land.   The same intrinsic power was ascribed to the blood and tears of the Meriah, his blood causing the redness of the turmeric and his tears producing rain ; for it can hardly be doubted that, originally at least, the tears were supposed to bring down the rain, not merely to prognosticate it.   Similarly the custom of pouring water on the buried flesh of the Meriah was no doubt a rain-charm.   Again, magical power as an attribute of the Meriah appears in the sovereign virtue believed to reside in any-thing that came from his person, as his hair or spittle.   The ascription of such power to the Meriah indicates that he was much more than a mere man sacrificed to propitiate a deity. Once more, the extreme reverence paid him points to the same conclusion.   Major Campbell speaks of the Meriah as "being regarded as something more than mortal,"[1] and Major Macpherson says, " A species of reverence, which it is not easy to distinguish from adoration, is paid to him."[2]   In short, the Meriah seems to have been regarded as divine. As such, he may originally have represented the Earth Goddess or, perhaps, a deity of vegetation ; though in later times he came to be regarded rather as a victim offered to a deity than as himself an incarnate god.   This later view of the Meriah as a victim rather than a divinity may perhaps have received undue emphasis from the European writers who have described the Khond religion.   Habituated to the later idea of sacrifice as an offering made to a god for the purpose of conciliating his favour, European observers are apt to interpret all religious slaughter in this sense, and to suppose that wherever such slaughter takes place, there must necessarily be a deity to whom the carnage is believed by

[1] J. Campbell, *op. cit.* p. 112.   [2] S. C. Macpherson, *op. cit.* p. 118.

the slayers to be acceptable. Thus their preconceived ideas may unconsciously colour and warp their descriptions of savage rites.

The same custom of killing the representative of a god, of which strong traces appear in the Khond sacrifices, may perhaps be detected in some of the other human sacrifices described above. Thus the ashes of the slaughtered Marimo were scattered over the fields; the blood of the Brahman lad was put on the crop and field; the flesh of the slain Naga was stowed in the corn-bin; and the blood of the Sioux girl was allowed to trickle on the seed.[1] Again, the identification of the victim with the corn, in other words, the view that he is an embodiment or spirit of the corn, is brought out in the pains which seem to be taken to secure a physical correspondence between him and the natural object which he embodies or represents. Thus the Mexicans killed young victims for the young corn and old ones for the ripe corn; the Marimos sacrifice, as " seed," a short, fat man, the shortness of his stature corresponding to that of the young corn, his fatness to the condition which it is desired that the crops may attain; and the Pawnees fattened their victims probably with the same view. Again, the identification of the victim with the corn comes out in the African custom of killing him with spades and hoes, and the Mexican custom of grinding him, like corn, between two stones.

One more point in these savage customs deserves to be noted. The Pawnee chief devoured the heart of the Sioux girl, and the Marimos and Gonds ate the victim's flesh. If, as we suppose, the victim was regarded as divine, it follows that in eating his flesh his worshippers believed themselves to be partaking of the body of their god.

Traces of an identification of the victim with the god in other sacrifices.

§ 4. *The Corn-spirit slain in his Human Representatives*

The barbarous rites just described offer analogies to the harvest customs of Europe. Thus the fertilising virtue ascribed to the corn-spirit is shewn equally in the savage custom of mixing the victim's blood or ashes with the seed-corn and the European custom of mixing the grain from

Analogy of these barbarous rites to the harvest customs of Europe.

[1] Above, pp. 239, 240, 244.

the last sheaf with the young corn in spring.[1]   Again, the identification of the person with the corn appears alike in the savage custom of adapting the age and stature of the victim to the age and stature, whether actual or expected, of the crop ; in the Scotch and Styrian rules that when the corn-spirit is conceived as the Maiden the last corn shall be cut by a young maiden, but when it is conceived as the Corn-mother it shall be cut by an old woman ;[2] in the Lothringian warning given to old women to save themselves when the Old Woman is being killed, that is, when the last corn is being threshed ;[3] and in the Tyrolese expectation that if the man who gives the last stroke at threshing is tall, the next year's corn will be tall also.[4]   Further, the same identification is implied in the savage custom of killing the representative of the corn-spirit with hoes or spades or by grinding him between stones, and in the European custom of pretending to kill him with the scythe or the flail.   Once more the Khond custom of pouring water on the buried flesh of the victim is parallel to the European customs of pouring water on the personal representative of the corn-spirit or plunging him into a stream.[5]   Both the Khond and the European customs are rain-charms.

Human representative of the corn-spirit slain on the harvest-field.

To return now to the Lityerses story.   It has been shewn that in rude society human beings have been commonly killed to promote the growth of the crops.   There is therefore no improbability in the supposition that they may once have been killed for a like purpose in Phrygia and Europe ; and when Phrygian legend and European folk-custom, closely agreeing with each other, point to the conclusion that men were so slain, we are bound, provisionally at least, to accept the conclusion.   Further, both the Lityerses story and European harvest-customs agree in indicating that the victim was put to death as a representative of the corn-spirit, and this indication is in harmony with the view which some savages appear to take of the victim slain to make the crops flourish.   On the whole, then, we may fairly suppose that both in Phrygia and in Europe the representative of

[1] Above, p. 134.

[2] Above, pp. 134, 157 *sqq.*

[3] Above, p. 223.

[4] Above, p. 224.

[5] Above, p. 170, with the references in note [1]; *Adonis, Attis, Osiris,* Second Edition, pp. 195-197.

the corn-spirit was annually killed upon the harvest-field. Grounds have been already shewn for believing that similarly in Europe the representative of the tree-spirit was annually slain. The proofs of these two remarkable and closely analogous customs are entirely independent of each other. Their coincidence seems to furnish fresh presumption in favour of both.

To the question, How was the representative of the corn-spirit chosen? one answer has been already given. Both the Lityerses story and European folk-custom shew that passing strangers were regarded as manifestations of the corn-spirit escaping from the cut or threshed corn, and as such were seized and slain. But this is not the only answer which the evidence suggests. According to the Phrygian legend the victims of Lityerses were not simply passing strangers, but persons whom he had vanquished in a reaping contest and afterwards wrapt up in corn-sheaves and beheaded.[1] This suggests that the representative of the corn-spirit may have been selected by means of a competition on the harvest-field, in which the vanquished competitor was compelled to accept the fatal honour. The supposition is countenanced by European harvest-customs. We have seen that in Europe there is sometimes a contest amongst the reapers to avoid being last, and that the person who is vanquished in this competition, that is, who cuts the last corn, is often roughly handled. It is true we have not found that a pretence is made of killing him; but on the other hand we have found that a pretence is made of killing the man who gives the last stroke at threshing, that is, who is vanquished in the threshing contest.[2] Now, since it is in the character of representative of the corn-spirit that the thresher of the last corn is slain in mimicry, and since the same representative character attaches (as we have seen) to the cutter and binder as well as to the thresher of the last corn, and since the same repugnance is evinced by harvesters to be last in any one of these labours, we may conjecture that a pretence has been commonly made of killing the reaper and binder as well as the thresher of the last corn, and that in ancient times this killing was actually

The victim who represented the corn-spirit may have been a passing stranger or the reaper, binder, or thresher of the last corn.

---

[1] See above, p. 217. [2] Above, p. 224.

carried out. This conjecture is corroborated by the common superstition that whoever cuts the last corn must die soon.[1] Sometimes it is thought that the person who binds the last sheaf on the field will die in the course of next year.[2] The reason for fixing on the reaper, binder, or thresher of the last corn as the representative of the corn-spirit may be this. The corn-spirit is supposed to lurk as long as he can in the corn, retreating before the reapers, the binders, and the threshers at their work. But when he is forcibly expelled from his refuge in the last corn cut or the last sheaf bound or the last grain threshed, he necessarily assumes some other form than that of the corn-stalks which had hitherto been his garment or body. And what form can the expelled corn-spirit assume more naturally than that of the person who stands nearest to the corn from which he (the corn-spirit) has just been expelled? But the person in question is necessarily the reaper, binder, or thresher of the last corn. He or she, therefore, is seized and treated as the corn-spirit himself.

Perhaps the victim annually sacrificed in the character of the corn-spirit may have been the king himself.

Thus the person who was killed on the harvest-field as the representative of the corn-spirit may have been either a passing stranger or the harvester who was last at reaping, binding, or threshing. But there is a third possibility, to which ancient legend and modern folk-custom alike point. Lityerses not only put strangers to death ; he was himself slain, and apparently in the same way as he had slain others, namely, by being wrapt in a corn-sheaf, beheaded, and cast into the river ; and it is implied that this happened to Lityerses on his own land.[3] Similarly in modern harvest-customs the pretence of killing appears to be carried out quite as often on the person of the master (farmer or squire) as on that of strangers.[4] Now when we remember that Lityerses was said to have been a son of the King of Phrygia, and that in one account he is himself called a king, and when we combine with this the tradition that he was put to death, apparently as a representative of the corn-spirit, we are led to conjecture that we have here another

[1] W. Mannhardt, *Die Korndämonen*, p. 5.
[2] H. Pfannenschmid, *Germanische Erntefeste* (Hanover, 1878), p. 98.

[3] Above, p. 217. It is not expressly said that he was wrapt in a sheaf.
[4] Above, pp. 225 *sq.*, 229 *sq.*

trace of the custom of annually slaying one of those divine or priestly kings who are known to have held ghostly sway in many parts of Western Asia and particularly in Phrygia. The custom appears, as we have seen,[1] to have been so far modified in places that the king's son was slain in the king's stead. Of the custom thus modified the story of Lityerses would be, in one version at least, a reminiscence.

Turning now to the relation of the Phrygian Lityerses to the Phrygian Attis, it may be remembered that at Pessinus —the seat of a priestly kingship—the high-priest appears to have been annually slain in the character of Attis, a god of vegetation, and that Attis was described by an ancient authority as " a reaped ear of corn." [2] Thus Attis, as an embodiment of the corn-spirit, annually slain in the person of his representative, might be thought to be ultimately identical with Lityerses, the latter being simply the rustic prototype out of which the state religion of Attis was developed. It may have been so ; but, on the other hand, the analogy of European folk-custom warns us that amongst the same people two distinct deities of vegetation may have their separate personal representatives, both of whom are slain in the character of gods at different times of the year. For in Europe, as we have seen, it appears that one man was commonly slain in the character of the tree-spirit in spring, and another in the character of the corn-spirit in autumn. It may have been so in Phrygia also. Attis was especially a tree-god, and his connexion with corn may have been only such an extension of the power of a tree-spirit as is indicated in customs like the Harvest-May.[3] Again, the representative of Attis appears to have been slain in spring ; whereas Lityerses must have been slain in summer or autumn, according to the time of the harvest in Phrygia.[4] On the whole, then, while we are not justified in regarding Lityerses as the prototype of Attis, the two may be regarded as parallel products of the same religious idea, and may have stood to each other as in Europe the Old Man of harvest

Relation of Lityerses to Attis : both may have been originally corn-spirits, or the one a corn-spirit and the other a tree-spirit.

---

[1] See *The Dying God*, pp. 160 *sqq.*
[2] See *Adonis, Attis, Osiris*, Second Edition, pp. 231 *sqq.*, 239 *sq.*
[3] See *The Magic Art and the Evolution of Kings*, ii. 47 *sqq.*

[4] I do not know when the corn is reaped in Phrygia ; but the high upland character of the country makes it likely that harvest is later there than on the coasts of the Mediterranean.

Human
representa-
tives both
of Lityerses
and Attis
annually
slain.

stands to the Wild Man, the Leaf Man, and so forth, of spring. Both were spirits or deities of vegetation, and the personal representatives of both were annually slain. But whereas the Attis worship became elevated into the dignity of a State religion and spread to Italy, the rites of Lityerses seem never to have passed the limits of their native Phrygia, and always retained their character of rustic ceremonies performed by peasants on the harvest-field. At most a few villages may have clubbed together, as amongst the Khonds, to procure a human victim to be slain as representative of the corn-spirit for their common benefit. Such victims may have been drawn from the families of priestly kings or kinglets, which would account for the legendary character of Lityerses as the son of a Phrygian king or as himself a king. When villages did not so club together, each village or farm may have procured its own representative of the corn-spirit by dooming to death either a passing stranger or the harvester who cut, bound, or threshed the last sheaf. Perhaps in the olden time the practice of head-hunting as a means of promoting the growth of the corn may have been as common among the rude inhabitants of Europe and Western Asia as it still is, or was till lately, among the primitive agricultural tribes of Assam, Burma, the Philippine Islands, and the Indian Archipelago.[1] It is hardly necessary to add that in Phrygia, as in Europe, the old barbarous custom of killing a man on the harvest-field or the threshing-floor had doubtless passed into a mere pretence long before the classical era,

[1] See above, pp. 240 *sqq.* ; and *Adonis, Attis, Osiris,* Second Edition, pp. 247-249. As to head-hunting in British Borneo see H. L. Roth, *The Natives of Sarawak and British North Borneo* (London, 1896), ii. 140 *sqq.* ; in Central Celebes, see A. C. Kruijt, "Het koppensnellen der Toradja's van Midden-Celebes, en zijne Beteekenis," *Verslagen en Mededeelingen der koninklijke Akademie van Wetenschappen,* Afdeelung Letterkunde, Vierde Reeks, iii. part 2 (Amsterdam, 1899), pp. 147-229 ; among the Igorot of Bontoc in Luzon, see A. E. Jenks, *The Bontoc Igorot* (Manilla, 1905), pp. 172 *sqq.* ; among the Naga tribes of Assam, see Miss G. M. Godden, " Naga and other Frontier Tribes of North-East India," *Journal of the Anthropological Institute,* xxvii. (1898) pp. 12-17. It must not, however, be thought that among these tribes the custom of procuring human heads is practised merely as a means to ensure the growth of the crops ; it is apparently supposed to exert a salutary influence on the whole life of the people by providing them with guardian spirits in the shape of the ghosts of the men to whom in their lifetime the heads belonged. The Scythians of Central Europe in antiquity set great store on the heads of the enemies whom they had slain in war. See Herodotus, iv. 64 *sq.*

and was probably regarded by the reapers and threshers themselves as no more than a rough jest which the license of a harvest-home permitted them to play off on a passing stranger, a comrade, or even on their master himself.[1]

I have dwelt on the Lityerses song at length because it affords so many points of comparison with European and savage folk-custom. The other harvest songs of Western Asia and Egypt, to which attention has been called above,[2] may now be dismissed much more briefly. The similarity of the Bithynian Bormus[3] to the Phrygian Lityerses helps to bear out the interpretation which has been given of the latter. Bormus, whose death or rather disappearance was annually mourned by the reapers in a plaintive song, was, like Lityerses, a king's son or at least the son of a wealthy and distinguished man. The reapers whom he watched were at work on his own fields, and he disappeared in going to fetch water for them ; according to one version of the story he was carried off by the nymphs, doubtless the nymphs of the spring or pool or river whither he went to draw water.[4] Viewed in the light of the Lityerses story and of European folk-custom, this disappearance of Bormus may be a reminiscence of the custom of binding the farmer himself in a corn-sheaf and throwing him into the water. The mournful strain which the reapers sang was probably a lamentation over the death of the corn-spirit, slain either in the cut corn or in the person of a human representative ; and the call which they addressed to him may have been a prayer that he might return in fresh vigour next year.

The Phoenician Linus song was sung at the vintage, at least in the west of Asia Minor, as we learn from Homer ; and this, combined with the legend of Syleus, suggests that in ancient times passing strangers were handled by vintagers and vine-diggers in much the same way as they are said to have been handled by the reaper Lityerses. The Lydian

[1] There are traces in Greece itself of an old custom of sacrificing human victims to promote the fertility of the earth. See Pausanias, vii. 19. 3 *sq.* compared with vii. 20. 1 ; *id.*, viii. 53. 3 ; L. R. Farnell, *The Cults of the* *Greek States,* ii. (Oxford, 1896) p. 455 ; and *The Dying God,* pp. 161 *sq.*

[2] Above, pp. 215 *sq.*

[3] Above, p. 216.

[4] Hesychius, *s.v.* Βῶρμον.

Syleus, so ran the legend, compelled passers-by to dig for him in his vineyard, till Hercules came and killed him and dug up his vines by the roots.[1] This seems to be the outline of a legend like that of Lityerses ; but neither ancient writers nor modern folk-custom enable us to fill in the details.[2] But, further, the Linus song was probably sung also by Phoenician reapers, for Herodotus compares it to the Maneros song, which, as we have seen, was a lament raised by Egyptian reapers over the cut corn. Further, Linus was identified with Adonis, and Adonis has some claims to be regarded as especially a corn-deity.[3] Thus the Linus lament, as sung at harvest, would be identical with the Adonis lament ; each would be the lamentation raised by reapers over the dead spirit of the corn. But whereas Adonis, like Attis, grew into a stately figure of mythology, adored and mourned in splendid cities far beyond the limits of his Phoenician home, Linus appears to have remained a simple ditty sung by reapers and vintagers among the corn-sheaves and the vines. The analogy of Lityerses and of folk-custom, both European and savage, suggests that in Phoenicia the slain corn-spirit—the dead Adonis—may formerly have been represented by a human victim ; and this suggestion is possibly supported by the Harran legend that Tammuz (Adonis) was slain by his cruel lord, who ground his bones in a mill and scattered them to the wind. For in Mexico, as we have seen, the human victim at harvest was crushed between two stones ; and both in Africa and India the ashes or other remains of the victim were scattered over the fields.[4] But the Harran legend may be only a mythical way of expressing the grinding of corn in the mill and the scattering of the seed. It seems worth suggesting that the mock king who was annually killed at the Babylonian festival of the Sacaea on the sixteenth day of the month Lous may have represented Tammuz himself. For the historian Berosus, who records the festival and its date, probably used the Macedonian

Marginal note: Linus identified with Adonis, who may have been annually represented by a human victim.

[1] Apollodorus, *Bibliotheca*, ii. 6. 3.

[2] The scurrilities exchanged both in ancient and modern times between vine-dressers, vintagers, and passers-by seem to belong to a different category. See W. Mannhardt, *Mythologische Forschungen*, pp. 53 *sq.*

[3] See *Adonis, Attis, Osiris*, Second Edition, pp. 188 *sqq.*

[4] Above, pp. 236 *sq.*, 240, 243, 244, 248 *sq.*

calendar, since he dedicated his history to Antiochus Soter ; and in his day the Macedonian month Lous appears to have corresponded to the Babylonian month Tammuz.[1] If this conjecture is right, the view that the mock king at the Sacaea was slain in the character of a god would be established. But to this point we shall return later on.

There is a good deal more evidence that in Egypt the slain corn-spirit—the dead Osiris—was represented by a human victim, whom the reapers slew on the harvest-field, mourning his death in a dirge, to which the Greeks, through a verbal misunderstanding, gave the name of Maneros.[2] For the legend of Busiris seems to preserve a reminiscence of human sacrifices once offered by the Egyptians in connexion with the worship of Osiris. Busiris was said to have been an Egyptian king who sacrificed all strangers on the altar of Zeus. The origin of the custom was traced to a dearth which afflicted the land of Egypt for nine years. A Cyprian seer informed Busiris that the dearth would cease if a man were annually sacrificed to Zeus. So Busiris instituted the sacrifice. But when Hercules came to Egypt, and was being dragged to the altar to be sacrificed, he burst his bonds and slew Busiris and his son.[3] Here then is a legend that in Egypt a human victim was annually sacrificed to prevent

The corn-spirit in Egypt (Osiris) annually represented by a human victim.

[1] The probable correspondence of the months, which supplies so welcome a confirmation of the conjecture in the text, was pointed out to me by my friend W. Robertson Smith, who furnished me with the following note : "In the Syro-Macedonian calendar Lous represents Ab, not Tammuz. Was it different in Babylon? I think it was, and one month different, at least in the early times of the Greek monarchy in Asia. For we know from a Babylonian observation in the Almagest (*Ideler*, i. 396) that in 229 B.C. Xanthicus began on February 26. It was therefore the month before the equinoctial moon, not Nisan but Adar, and consequently Lous answered to the lunar month Tammuz."

[2] Above, p. 215.

[3] Apollodorus, *Bibliotheca*, ii. 5. 11 ; Scholiast on Apollonius Rhodius, *Argon.* iv. 1396 ; Plutarch, *Parall.* 38.

Herodotus (ii. 45) discredits the idea that the Egyptians ever offered human sacrifices. But his authority is not to be weighed against that of Manetho (Plutarch, *Isis et Osiris*, 73), who affirms that they did. See further Dr. E. A. Wallis Budge, *Osiris and the Egyptian Resurrection* (London and New York, 1911), i. 210 *sqq.*, who says (pp. 210, 212): "There is abundant proof for the statement that the Egyptians offered up sacrifices of human beings, and that, in common with many African tribes at the present day, their customs in dealing with vanquished enemies were bloodthirsty and savage. . . . The passages from Egyptian works quoted earlier in this chapter prove that human sacrifices were offered up at Heliopolis as well as at Ṭeṭu, or Busiris, and the rumour of such sacrifices has found expression in the works of Greek writers."

the failure of the crops, and a belief is implied that an omission of the sacrifice would have entailed a recurrence of that infertility which it was the object of the sacrifice to prevent. So the Pawnees, as we have seen, believed that an omission of the human sacrifice at planting would have been followed by a total failure of their crops. The name Busiris was in reality the name of a city, *pe-Asar*, "the house of Osiris,"[1] the city being so called because it contained the grave of Osiris. Indeed some high modern authorities believe that Busiris was the original home of Osiris, from which his worship spread to other parts of Egypt.[2] The human sacrifices were said to have been offered at his grave, and the victims were red-haired men, whose ashes were scattered abroad by means of winnowing-fans.[3] This tradition of human sacrifices offered at the tomb of Osiris is confirmed by the evidence of the monuments; for "we find in the temple of Denderah a human figure with a hare's head and pierced with knives, tied to a stake before Osiris Khenti-Amentiu, and Horus is shown in a Ptolemaic sculpture at Karnak killing a bound hare-headed figure before the bier of Osiris, who is represented in the form of Harpocrates. That these figures are really human beings with the head of an animal fastened on is proved by another sculpture at Denderah, where a kneeling man has the hawk's head and wings over his head and shoulders, and in another place a priest has the jackal's head on his shoulders, his own head appearing through the disguise. Besides, Diodorus tells us that the Egyptian kings in former times had worn on their heads the fore-part of a lion, or of a bull, or of a dragon,

---

[1] E. Meyer, *Geschichte des Alter-tums*, i. (Stuttgart, 1884), § 57, p. 68.

[2] E. Meyer, *Geschichte des Alter-tums*,[2] i. 2 (Stuttgart and Berlin, 1909), p. 97; G. Maspero, *Histoire Ancienne des Peuples de l'Orient Classique, Les Origines* (Paris, 1895), pp. 129 *sqq.* Both these eminent historians have abandoned their former theory that Osiris was the Sun-god. Professor E. Meyer now speaks of Osiris as "the great vegetation god" and, on the same page, as "an earth-god" (*op. cit.*

i. 2. p. 70). I am happy to find the view of the nature of Osiris, which I advocated many years ago, supported by the authority of so distinguished an Oriental scholar. Dr. E. A. Wallis Budge holds that Busiris was the oldest shrine of Osiris in the north of Egypt, but that it was less ancient than his shrine at Abydos in the south. See E. A. Wallis Budge, *Osiris and the Egyptian Resurrection* (London and New York, 1911), ii. 1.

[3] Diodorus Siculus, i. 88; Plutarch, *Isis et Osiris*, 73, compare 30, 33.

showing that this method of disguise or transformation was a well-known custom."[1]

In the light of the foregoing discussion the Egyptian tradition of Busiris admits of a consistent and fairly probable explanation. Osiris, the corn-spirit, was annually represented at harvest by a stranger, whose red hair made him a suitable representative of the ripe corn. This man, in his representative character, was slain on the harvest-field, and mourned by the reapers, who prayed at the same time that the corn-spirit might revive and return (*mââ-ne-rha*, Maneros) with renewed vigour in the following year. Finally, the victim, or some part of him, was burned, and the ashes scattered by winnowing-fans over the fields to fertilise them. Here the choice of the victim on the ground of his resemblance to the corn which he was to represent agrees with the Mexican and African customs already described.[2] Similarly the woman who died in the character of the Corn-mother at the Mexican midsummer sacrifice had her face painted red and yellow in token of the colours of the corn, and she wore a pasteboard mitre surmounted by waving plumes in imitation of the tassel of the maize.[3] On the other hand, at the festival of the Goddess of the White Maize the Mexicans sacrificed lepers.[4] The Romans sacrificed red-haired puppies in spring to avert the supposed blighting influence of the Dog-star, believing that the crops would thus grow ripe and ruddy.[5] The heathen of Harran offered to the sun, moon, and planets human victims who were chosen on the ground of their supposed resemblance to the heavenly bodies to which they were sacrificed ; for example, the priests, clothed in red and smeared with blood, offered a red-haired, red-cheeked man to "the red planet

Assimilation of human victims to the corn which they represent.

---

[1] Margaret A. Murray, *The Osireion at Abydos* (London, 1904), p. 30, referring to Mariette, *Dendereh*, iv. plates xxxi., lvi., and lxxxi. The passage of Diodorus Siculus referred to is i. 62. 4. As to masks of animals worn by Egyptian men and women in religious rites see *The Magic Art and the Evolution of Kings*, ii. 133; *The Dying God*, p. 72.

[2] Above, pp. 237 *sq.*, 240, 251.

[3] E. J. Payne, *History of the New World called America*, i. (Oxford, 1892) p. 422.

[4] Brasseur de Bourbourg, *Histoire des Nations civilisées du Mexique et de l'Amérique Centrale* (Paris, 1857-1859), iii. 535.

[5] Festus, *s.v. Catularia*, p. 45 ed. C. O. Müller. Compare *id.*, *s.v. Rutilae canes*, p. 285 ; Columella, *De re rustica*, x. 342 *sq.* ; Ovid, *Fasti*, iv. 905 *sqq.* ; Pliny, *Nat. Hist.* xviii. 14.

Mars" in a temple which was painted red and draped with red hangings.[1] These and the like cases of assimilating the victim to the god, or to the natural phenomenon which he represents, are based ultimately on the principle of homoeopathic or imitative magic, the notion being that the object aimed at will be most readily attained by means of a sacrifice which resembles the effect that it is designed to bring about.

Remains of victims scattered over the fields to fertilise them.

Again the scattering of the Egyptian victim's ashes over the fields resembles the Marimo and Khond custom,[2] and the use of winnowing-fans for the purpose is another hint of his identification with the corn. So in Vendée a pretence is made of threshing and winnowing the farmer's wife, regarded as an embodiment of the corn-spirit ; in Mexico the victim was ground between stones ; and in Africa he was slain with spades and hoes.[3] The story that the fragments of Osiris's body were scattered up and down the land, and buried by Isis on the spots where they lay,[4] may very well be a reminiscence of a custom, like that observed by the Khonds, of dividing the human victim in pieces and burying the pieces, often at intervals of many miles from each other, in the fields.[5] However, it is possible that the story of the dismemberment of Osiris, like the similar story told of Tammuz, may have been simply a mythical expression for the scattering of the seed. Once more, the legend that the body of Osiris enclosed in a coffer was thrown by Typhon into the Nile, perhaps points to a custom of casting the body of the victim, or at least a portion of it, into the Nile as a rain-charm, or rather to make the river rise. For a similar purpose Phrygian reapers seem to have flung the headless bodies of their victims, wrapt in corn-sheaves, into a river, and the Khonds poured water on the buried flesh of the human victim. Probably when Osiris ceased to be represented by a human victim, an image of him was annually thrown into the Nile, just as the effigy of his Syrian counter-

[1] D. Chwolsohn, *Die Ssabier und der Ssabismus* (St. Petersburg, 1856), ii. 388 *sq.* Compare *ibid.*, pp. 384 *sq.*, 386 *sq.*, 391, 393, 395, 397. For other instances of the assimilation of the victim to the god, see H. Oldenberg, *Die Religion des Veda* (Berlin, 1894), pp. 77 *sq.*, 357-359.

[2] Above, pp. 240, 249.

[3] Above, pp. 149 *sq.*, 237 *sq.*, 239.

[4] Plutarch, *Isis et Osiris*, 18.

[5] See above, p. 248 ; and compare *Adonis, Attis, Osiris*, Second Edition, pp. 331 *sqq.*

part, Adonis, used to be cast into the sea at Alexandria. Or water may have been simply poured over it, as on the monument already mentioned [1] a priest is seen pouring water over the body of Osiris, from which corn-stalks are sprouting. The accompanying legend, "This is Osiris of the mysteries, who springs from the returning waters," bears out the view that at the mysteries of Osiris a charm to make rain fall or the river rise was regularly wrought by pouring water on his effigy or flinging it into the Nile.

It may be objected that the red-haired victims were slain as representatives, not of Osiris, but of his enemy Typhon; for the victims were called Typhonian, and red was the colour of Typhon, black the colour of Osiris.[2] The answer to this objection must be reserved for the present. Meantime it may be pointed out that if Osiris is often represented on the monuments as black, he is still more commonly depicted as green,[3] appropriately enough for a corn-god, who may be conceived as black while the seed is under ground, but as green after it has sprouted. So the Greeks recognised both a Green and a Black Demeter,[4] and sacrificed to the Green Demeter in spring with mirth and gladness.[5]

The black and green Osiris like the black and green Demeter.

Thus, if I am right, the key to the mysteries of Osiris is furnished by the melancholy cry of the Egyptian reapers, which down to Roman times could be heard year after year sounding across the fields, announcing the death of the corn-spirit, the rustic prototype of Osiris. Similar cries, as we have seen, were also heard on all the harvest-fields of Western Asia. By the ancients they are spoken of as songs; but to judge from the analysis of the names Linus and Maneros, they probably consisted only of a few words uttered in a prolonged musical note which could be heard for a great distance. Such sonorous and long-drawn cries, raised by a number of strong voices in concert, must have had a striking effect, and could hardly fail to arrest the attention

The key to the mysteries of Osiris furnished by the lamentations of the reapers for the annual death of the corn-spirit.

[1] See *Adonis, Attis, Osiris*, Second Edition, p. 323.
[2] Plutarch, *Isis et Osiris*, 22, 30, 31, 33, 73.
[3] Sir J. G. Wilkinson, *Manners and Customs of the Ancient Egyptians* (ed.

1878), iii. 81.
[4] Pausanias, i. 22. 3, viii. 5. 8, viii. 42. i.
[5] Cornutus, *Theologiae Graecae Compendium*, 28. See above, p. 42.

of any wayfarer who happened to be within hearing. The sounds, repeated again and again, could probably be distinguished with tolerable ease even at a distance ; but to a Greek traveller in Asia or Egypt the foreign words would commonly convey no meaning, and he might take them, not unnaturally, for the name of some one (Maneros, Linus, Lityerses, Bormus) upon whom the reapers were calling. And if his journey led him through more countries than one, as Bithynia and Phrygia, or Phoenicia and Egypt, while the corn was being reaped, he would have an opportunity of comparing the various harvest cries of the different peoples. Thus we can readily understand why these harvest cries were so often noted and compared with each other by the Greeks. Whereas, if they had been regular songs, they could not have been heard at such distances, and therefore could not have attracted the attention of so many travellers ; and, moreover, even if the wayfarer were within hearing of them, he could not so easily have picked out the words.

"Crying the neck" at harvest in Devonshire. Down to recent times Devonshire reapers uttered cries of the same sort, and performed on the field a ceremony exactly analogous to that in which, if I am not mistaken, the rites of Osiris originated. The cry and the ceremony are thus described by an observer who wrote in the first half of the nineteenth century. "After the wheat is all cut, on most farms in the north of Devon, the harvest people have a custom of 'crying the neck.' I believe that this practice is seldom omitted on any large farm in that part of the country. It is done in this way. An old man, or some one else well acquainted with the ceremonies used on the occasion (when the labourers are reaping the last field of wheat), goes round to the shocks and sheaves, and picks out a little bundle of all the best ears he can find ; this bundle he ties up very neat and trim, and plats and arranges the straws very tastefully. This is called 'the neck' of wheat, or wheaten-ears. After the field is cut out, and the pitcher once more circulated, the reapers, binders, and the women stand round in a circle. The person with 'the neck' stands in the centre, grasping it with both his hands. He first stoops and holds it near the ground, and all the men forming the ring take off their hats, stooping and holding them with both hands towards the ground. They then all begin at once in a very prolonged and harmonious tone to cry 'The neck!' at the same time slowly raising themselves upright, and elevating their arms and hats above their heads ; the person with 'the neck' also raising it on high. This is done three times. They then change their cry to 'Wee yen!'—'Way yen!'—which they sound in the same prolonged and slow manner as before, with singular harmony and effect, three times. This last cry is accompanied by the same movements of the body and arms as in crying 'the neck.' . . . After having thus repeated 'the neck' three times, and 'wee yen,' or 'way yen' as often, they all burst out into a kind of loud and joyous laugh, flinging up their hats and caps into the air, capering about and perhaps kissing the girls. One of them then gets 'the neck' and runs as hard as he can down to the farmhouse, where the dairymaid, or one of the young female domestics, stands at the door prepared with a pail of water. If he who holds 'the neck' can manage to get into the house, in any way unseen, or openly, by any other way than the door at which the girl stands with the pail of water, then he may lawfully kiss her ; but, if otherwise, he is regularly soused with the contents of the bucket. On a fine still autumn evening the 'crying of the neck' has a wonderful effect at a distance, far finer than that of the Turkish muezzin, which Lord Byron eulogises so much, and which he says is preferable to all the bells in Christendom. I have once or twice heard upwards of twenty men cry it, and sometimes joined by an equal number of female voices. About three years back, on some high grounds, where our people were harvesting, I heard six or seven 'necks' cried in one night, although I know that some of them were four miles off. They are heard through the quiet evening air at a considerable distance sometimes."[1] Again, Mrs. Bray tells how, travelling in Devonshire, "she saw a party of reapers standing in a circle on a rising ground, holding their sickles aloft. One in the middle held up some ears of corn tied together with flowers, and the party shouted three times (what she writes as) 'Arnack, arnack, arnack, we *haven*, we *haven*, we *haven*.' They went

---

[1] W. Hone, *Every-day Book* (London, N.D.), ii. coll. 1170 *sq.*

home, accompanied by women and children carrying boughs of flowers, shouting and singing. The manservant who attended Mrs. Bray said 'it was only the people making their games, as they always did, *to the spirit of harvest.*'"[1] Here, as Miss Burne remarks, "'arnack, we haven!' is obviously in the Devon dialect, 'a neck (or nack)! we have un!'" "The neck" is generally hung up in the farmhouse, where it sometimes remains for two or three years.[2] A similar custom is still observed in some parts of Cornwall, as I was told by my lamented friend J. H. Middleton. "The last sheaf is decked with ribbons. Two strong-voiced men are chosen and placed (one with the sheaf) on opposite sides of a valley. One shouts, 'I've gotten it.' The other shouts, 'What hast gotten?' The first answers, 'I'se gotten the neck.'"[3]

Other accounts of cutting and crying "the neck" in Devonshire.Another account of this old custom, written at Truro in 1839, runs thus: "Now, when all the corn was cut at Heligan, the farming men and maidens come in front of the house, and bring with them a small sheaf of corn, the last that has been cut, and this is adorned with ribbons and flowers, and one part is tied quite tight, so as to look like a neck. Then they cry out 'Our (my) side, my side,' as loud as they can; then the dairymaid gives the neck to the head farming-man. He takes it, and says, very loudly three times, 'I have him, I have him, I have him.' Then another farming-man shouts very loudly, 'What have ye? what have ye? what have ye?' Then the first says, 'A neck, a neck, a neck.' And when he has said this, all the people make a very great shouting. This they do three times, and after one famous shout go away and eat supper, and dance, and sing songs."[4] According to another account, "all went out to the field when the last corn was cut, the 'neck' was tied with ribbons and plaited, and they danced round it, and carried it to the great kitchen, where by-and-by the supper

<hr>

[1] Miss C. S. Burne and Miss G. F. Jackson, *Shropshire Folk-lore* (London, 1883), pp. 372 *sq.*, referring to Mrs. Bray's *Traditions of Devon*, i. 330.

[2] W. Hone, *op. cit.* ii. 1172.

[3] The Rev. Sydney Cooper, of 80 Gloucester Street, Cirencester, wrote to me (4th February 1893) that his wife remembers the "neck" being kept on the mantelpiece of the parlour in a Cornish farmhouse; it generally stayed there throughout the year.

[4] "Old Harvest Customs in Devon and Cornwall," *Folk-lore*, i. (1890) p. 280.

was. The words were as given in the previous account, and 'Hip, hip, hack, heck, I have 'ee, I have 'ee, I have 'ee.' It was hung up in the hall." Another account relates that one of the men rushed from the field with the last sheaf, while the rest pursued him with vessels of water, which they tried to throw over the sheaf before it could be brought into the barn.[1]

Similar customs appear to have been formerly observed in Pembrokeshire, as appears from the following account, in which, however, nothing is said of the sonorous cries raised by the reapers when their work was done: "At harvest-time, in South Pembrokeshire, the last ears of corn left standing in the field were tied together, and the harvesters then tried to cut this neck by throwing their hatchets at it. What happened afterwards appears to have varied somewhat. I have been told by one old man that the one who got possession of the neck would carry it over into some neighbouring field, leave it there, and take to his heels as fast as he could ; for, if caught, he had a rough time of it. The men who caught him would shut him up in a barn without food, or belabour him soundly, or perhaps shoe him, as it was called, beating the soles of his feet with rods—a very severe and much-dreaded punishment. On my grandfather's farm the man used to make for the house as fast as possible, and try to carry in the neck. The maids were on the look-out for him, and did their best to drench him with water. If they succeeded, they got the present of half-a-crown, which my grandfather always gave, and which was considered a very liberal present indeed. If the man was successful in dodging the maids, and getting the neck into the house without receiving the wetting, the half-crown became his. The neck was then hung up, and kept until the following year, at any rate, like the bunches of flowers or boughs gathered at the St. Jean, in the south of France. Sometimes the necks of many successive years were to be found hanging up together. In these two ways of disposing of the neck one sees the embodiment, no doubt, of the two ways of looking at the corn-spirit, as good (to be kept) or as bad (to be passed on to the neighbour)."[2]

Cutting "the neck" in Pembrokeshire.

[1] *Ibid.*
[2] Frances Hoggan, M.D., "The Neck Feast," *Folk-lore*, iv. (1893) p. 123. In Pembrokeshire the last sheaf

Cutting
"the neck"
in Shrop-
shire.
  In the foregoing customs a particular bunch of ears, generally the last left standing,[1] is conceived as the neck of the corn-spirit, who is consequently beheaded when the bunch is cut down. Similarly in Shropshire the name "neck," or "the gander's neck," used to be commonly given to the last handful of ears left standing in the middle of the field when all the rest of the corn was cut. It was plaited together, and the reapers, standing ten or twenty paces off, threw their sickles at it. Whoever cut it through was said to have cut off the gander's neck. The "neck" was taken to the farmer's wife, who was supposed to keep it in the house for good luck till the next harvest came round.[2] Near Trèves, the man who reaps the last standing corn "cuts the goat's neck off."[3] At Faslane, on the Gareloch (Dumbartonshire), the last handful of standing corn was sometimes called the "head."[4] At Aurich, in East Friesland, the man who reaps the last corn "cuts the hare's tail off."[5] In mowing down the last corner of a field French reapers sometimes call out, "We have the cat by the tail."[6] In Bresse (Bourgogne) the last sheaf represented the fox. Beside it a score of ears were left standing to form the tail, and each reaper, going back some paces, threw his sickle at it. He who succeeded in severing it "cut off the fox's tail," and a cry of " *You cou cou !* " was raised in his

Why the
last corn
cut is
called "the
neck."
honour.[7] These examples leave no room to doubt the meaning of the Devonshire and Cornish expression " the neck," as applied to the last sheaf. The corn-spirit is conceived in human or animal form, and the last standing corn is part of its body—its neck, its head, or its tail. Sometimes, as we have seen, the last corn is regarded as the navel-string.[8] Lastly, the Devonshire custom of drenching with water the person who brings in " the neck " is a rain-charm, such as we have had many examples of. Its parallel

---

of corn seems to have been commonly known as "the Hag " (*wrach*) rather than as "the Neck." See above, pp. 142-144.

[1] J. Brand, *Popular Antiquities*, ii. 20 (Bohn's edition) ; Miss C. S. Burne and Miss G. F. Jackson, *Shropshire Folk-lore*, p. 371.

[2] Burne and Jackson, *l.c.*

[3] W. Mannhardt, *Mythologische Forschungen*, p. 185.

[4] See above, p. 158.

[5] W. Mannhardt, *Mythologische Forschungen*, p. 185.

[6] *Ibid.*

[7] *Revue des Traditions populaires*, ii. (1887) p. 500.

[8] Above, p. 150.

in the mysteries of Osiris was the custom of pouring water on the image of Osiris or on the person who represented him. In Germany cries of *Waul!* or *Wol!* or *Wôld!* are sometimes raised by the reapers at cutting the last corn. Thus in some places the last patch of standing rye was called the *Waul*-rye ; a stick decked with flowers was inserted in it, and the ears were fastened to the stick. Then all the reapers took off their hats and cried thrice, " *Waul! Waul! Waul!*" Sometimes they accompanied the cry by clashing with their whetstones on their scythes.[1]

Cries of the reapers in Germany.

[1] E. Meier, in *Zeitschrift für deutsche Mythologie und Sittenkunde*, i. (1853) pp. 170-173 ; U. Jahn, *Die deutschen Opfergebräuche bei Ackerbau und Viehzucht* (Breslau, 1884), pp. 166-169 ; H. Pfannenschmid, *Germanische Erntefeste* (Hanover, 1878), pp. 104 *sq.* ; A. Kuhn, *Sagen, Gebräuche und Märchen aus Westfalen* (Leipsic, 1859), ii. pp. 177 *sq.*, §§ 491, 492 ; A. Kuhn und W. Schwartz, *Norddeutsche Sagen, Märchen und Gebräuche* (Leipsic, 1848), p. 395, § 97 ; K. Lynker, *Deutsche Sagen und Sitten in hessischen Gauen* (Cassel and Göttingen, 1860), p. 256, § 340

CHAPTER VIII

THE CORN-SPIRIT AS AN ANIMAL

§ 1. *Animal Embodiments of the Corn-spirit*

The corn-spirit as an animal.
IN some of the examples which I have cited to establish the meaning of the term "neck" as applied to the last sheaf, the corn-spirit appears in animal form as a gander, a goat, a hare, a cat, and a fox. This introduces us to a new aspect of the corn-spirit, which we must now examine. By doing so we shall not only have fresh examples of killing the god, but may hope also to clear up some points which remain obscure in the myths and worship of Adonis, Attis, Osiris, Dionysus, Demeter, and Virbius.

The corn-spirit in the form of an animal is supposed to be present in the last corn cut or threshed, and to be caught or killed by the reaper or thresher.
Amongst the many animals whose forms the corn-spirit is supposed to take are the wolf, dog, hare, fox, cock, goose, quail, cat, goat, cow (ox, bull), pig, and horse. In one or other of these shapes the corn-spirit is often believed to be present in the corn, and to be caught or killed in the last sheaf. As the corn is being cut the animal flees before the reapers, and if a reaper is taken ill on the field, he is supposed to have stumbled unwittingly on the corn-spirit, who has thus punished the profane intruder. It is said "the Rye-wolf has got hold of him," "the Harvest-goat has given him a push." The person who cuts the last corn or binds the last sheaf gets the name of the animal, as the Rye-wolf, the Rye-sow, the Oats-goat, and so forth, and retains the name sometimes for a year. Also the animal is frequently represented by a puppet made out of the last sheaf or of wood, flowers, and so on, which is carried home amid rejoicings on the last harvest-waggon. Even where the last sheaf is not made up in animal shape, it is often called the Rye-wolf, the Hare, Goat, and so forth.

Generally each kind of crop is supposed to have its special animal, which is caught in the last sheaf, and called the Rye-wolf, the Barley-wolf, the Oats-wolf, the Pea-wolf, or the Potato-wolf, according to the crop ; but sometimes the figure of the animal is only made up once for all at getting in the last crop of the whole harvest. Sometimes the creature is believed to be killed by the last stroke of the sickle or scythe. But oftener it is thought to live so long as there is corn still unthreshed, and to be caught in the last sheaf threshed. Hence the man who gives the last stroke with the flail is told that he has got the Corn-sow, the Threshing-dog, or the like. When the threshing is finished, a puppet is made in the form of the animal, and this is carried by the thresher of the last sheaf to a neighbouring farm, where the threshing is still going on. This again shews that the corn-spirit is believed to live wherever the corn is still being threshed. Sometimes the thresher of the last sheaf himself represents the animal ; and if the people of the next farm, who are still threshing, catch him, they treat him like the animal he represents, by shutting him up in the pig-sty, calling him with the cries commonly addressed to pigs, and so forth.[1]   These general statements will now be illustrated by examples.

§ 2. *The Corn-spirit as a Wolf or a Dog*

We begin with the corn-spirit conceived as a wolf or a dog. This conception is common in France, Germany, and Slavonic countries. Thus, when the wind sets the corn in wave-like motion the peasants often say, " The Wolf is going over, or through, the corn," " the Rye-wolf is rushing over the field," " the Wolf is in the corn," " the mad Dog is in the corn," " the big Dog is there."[2] When children wish to go into the corn-fields to pluck ears

The corn-spirit as a wolf or a dog, supposed to run through the corn.

---

[1] W. Mannhardt, *Die Korndämonen* (Berlin, 1868), pp. 1-6.

[2] W. Mannhardt, *Roggenwolf und Roggenhund*[2] (Danzig, 1866), pp. 6 *sqq.* ; *id.*, *Antike Wald- und Feldkulte* (Berlin, 1877), pp. 318 *sq.* ; *id.*, *Mythologische Forschungen*, p. 103 ; A. Witzchel, *Sagen, Sitten und Gebräuche aus Thüringen* (Vienna, 1878), p. 213 ;

O. Hartung, "Zur Volkskunde aus Anhalt," *Zeitschrift des Vereins für Volkskunde*, vii. (1897) p. 150 ; W. Müller, *Beiträge zur Volkskunde der Deutschen in Mähren* (Vienna and Olmutz, 1893), p. 327 ; P. Drechsler, *Sitte, Brauch und Volksglaube in Schlesien* (Leipsic, 1903-1906), ii. 60.

or gather the blue corn-flowers, they are warned not to do so, for " the big Dog sits in the corn," or " the Wolf sits in the corn, and will tear you in pieces," " the Wolf will eat you." The wolf against whom the children are warned is not a common wolf, for he is often spoken of as the Corn-wolf, Rye-wolf, or the like ; thus they say, " The Rye-wolf will come and eat you up, children," " the Rye-wolf will carry you off," and so forth.[1]   Still he has all the outward appearance of a wolf.   For in the neighbourhood of Feilenhof (East Prussia), when a wolf was seen running through a field, the peasants used to watch whether he carried his tail in the air or dragged it on the ground.   If he dragged it on the ground, they went after him, and thanked him for bringing them a blessing, and even set tit-bits before him.   But if he carried his tail high, they cursed him and tried to kill him. Here the wolf is the corn-spirit whose fertilising power is in his tail.[2]

The corn-spirit as a dog at reaping and threshing.   Both dog and wolf appear as embodiments of the corn-spirit in harvest-customs.   Thus in some parts of Silesia the person who cuts or binds the last sheaf is called the Wheat-dog or the Peas-pug.[3]   But it is in the harvest-customs of the north-east of France that the idea of the Corn-dog comes out most clearly.   Thus when a harvester, through sickness, weariness, or laziness, cannot or will not keep up with the reaper in front of him, they say, " The White Dog passed near him," " he has the White Bitch," or " the White Bitch has bitten him." [4]   In the Vosges the Harvest-May is called the " Dog of the harvest," [5] and the person who cuts the last handful of hay or wheat is said to " kill the Dog." [6]   About Lons-le-Saulnier, in the Jura, the last sheaf is called the Bitch.   In the neighbourhood of Verdun the regular expression for finishing the reaping is, " They are going to kill the Dog " ; and at Epinal they say, according to the crop, " We will kill the Wheat-dog, or the Rye-dog, or the Potato-

[1] W. Mannhardt, *Roggenwolf und Roggenhund*,[2] pp. 10 sqq. ; *id.*, *Antike Wald- und Feldkulte*, p. 319.

[2] W. Mannhardt, *Roggenwolf und Roggenhund*,[2] pp. 14 sq.

[3] W. Mannhardt, *Mythologische Forschungen*, p. 104 ; P. Drechsler, *Sitte, Brauch und Volksglaube in Schlesien*, ii. 64.

[4] W. Mannhardt, *Mythologische Forschungen*, p. 104.

[5] *Ibid.* pp. 104 sq.   On the Harvest-May, see *The Magic Art and the Evolution of Kings*, ii. 47 sq.

[6] L. F. Sauvé, *Folk-lore des Hautes-Vosges* (Paris, 1889), p. 191.

VIII   *THE CORN-SPIRIT AS A WOLF OR A DOG*   273

dog." [1]   In Lorraine it is said of the man who cuts the last corn, " He is killing the Dog of the harvest." [2]   At Dux, in the Tyrol, the man who gives the last stroke at threshing is said to " strike down the Dog " ; [3] and at Ahne-bergen, near Stade, he is called, according to the crop, Corn-pug, Rye-pug, Wheat-pug. [4]

So with the wolf.   In Silesia, when the reapers gather round the last patch of standing corn to reap it they are said to be about " to catch the Wolf." [5]   In various parts of Mecklenburg, where the belief in the Corn-wolf is particularly prevalent, every one fears to cut the last corn, because they say that the Wolf is sitting in it ; hence every reaper exerts himself to the utmost in order not to be the last, and every woman similarly fears to bind the last sheaf because "the Wolf is in it."   So both among the reapers and the binders there is a competition not to be the last to finish. [6]   And in Germany generally it appears to be a common saying that "the Wolf sits in the last sheaf." [7]   In some places they call out to the reaper, " Beware of the Wolf " ; or they say, " He is chasing the Wolf out of the corn." [8]   In Mecklenburg the last bunch of standing corn is itself commonly called the Wolf, and the man who reaps it " has the Wolf," the animal being described as the Rye-wolf, the Wheat-wolf, the Barley-wolf, and so on according to the particular crop.   The reaper of the last corn is himself called Wolf or the Rye-wolf, if the crop is rye, and in many parts of Mecklenburg he has to support the character by pretending to bite the other harvesters or by howling like a wolf. [9]   The last sheaf of corn is also called the Wolf or the Rye-wolf or the Oats-wolf according to the crop, and of the woman who binds it they say, " The Wolf is biting her," " She has the Wolf," " She must fetch the Wolf " (out of the corn).   Moreover, she

The corn-spirit as a wolf at reaping.

[1] W. Mannhardt, *Mythologische Forschungen*, p. 105.
[2] *Ibid.* p. 30.
[3] *Ibid.* pp. 30, 105.
[4] *Ibid.* pp. 105 *sq.*
[5] P. Drechsler, *Sitte, Brauch und Volksglaube in Schlesien* (Leipsic, 1903-1906), ii. 64.
[6] W. Mannhardt, *Roggenwolf und Roggenhund,*[2] pp. 33, 39 ; K. Bartsch, *Sagen, Märchen und Gebräuche aus*

Meklenburg (Vienna, 1879-1880), ii. p. 309, § 1496, p. 310, §§ 1497, 1498.
[7] W. Mannhardt, *Antike Wald- und Feldkulte*, p. 320.
[8] W. Mannhardt, *Roggenwolf und Roggenhund,*[2] p. 33.
[9] W. Mannhardt, *Roggenwolf und Roggenhund,*[2] pp. 33 *sq.* ; K. Bartsch, *op. cit.* ii. p. 309, § 1496, p. 310, §§ 1497, 1500, 1501.

PT. V. VOL. I   T

herself is called Wolf; they cry out to her, "Thou art the Wolf," and she has to bear the name for a whole year; sometimes, according to the crop, she is called the Rye-wolf or the Potato-wolf.[1]   In the island of Rügen not only is the woman who binds the last sheaf called Wolf, but when she comes home she bites the lady of the house and the stewardess, for which she receives a large piece of meat. Yet nobody likes to be the Wolf.   The same woman may be Rye-wolf, Wheat-wolf, and Oats-wolf, if she happens to bind the last sheaf of rye, wheat, and oats.[2]   At Buir, in the district of Cologne, it was formerly the custom to give to the last sheaf the shape of a wolf.   It was kept in the barn till all the corn was threshed.   Then it was brought to the farmer and he had to sprinkle it with beer or brandy.[3]   At Brunshaupten in Mecklenburg the young woman who bound the last sheaf of wheat used to take a handful of stalks out of it and make "the Wheat-wolf" with them; it was the figure of a wolf about two feet long and half a foot high, the legs of the animal being represented by stiff stalks and its tail and mane by wheat-ears.   This Wheat-wolf she carried back at the head of the harvesters to the village, where it was set up on a high place in the parlour of the farm and remained there for a long time.[4]   In many places the sheaf called the Wolf is made up in human form and dressed in clothes.   This indicates a confusion of ideas between the corn-spirit conceived in human and in animal form.   Generally the Wolf is brought home on the last waggon with joyful cries.   Hence the last waggon-load itself receives the name of the Wolf.[5]

Again, the Wolf is supposed to hide himself amongst the cut corn in the granary, until he is driven out of the last bundle by the strokes of the flail.   Hence at Wanzleben, near Magdeburg, after the threshing the peasants go in procession, leading by a chain a man who is enveloped in the

[1] W. Mannhardt, *Roggenwolf und Roggenhund*,[2] pp. 33, 34.

[2] W. Mannhardt, *Roggenwolf und Roggenhund*,[2] p. 38; *id., Antike Wald- und Feldkulte*, p. 320.

[3] W. Mannhardt, *Roggenwolf und Roggenhund*,[2] pp. 34 *sq.*

[4] K. Bartsch, *op. cit.* ii. p. 311, § 1505.

[5] W. Mannhardt, *Roggenwolf und Roggenhund*,[2] pp. 35-37; K. Bartsch, *op. cit.* ii. p. 309, § 1496, p. 310, §§ 1499, 1501, p. 311, §§ 1506, 1507.

threshed-out straw and is called the Wolf.[1]   He represents The corn-
the corn-spirit who has been caught escaping from the spirit as
a wolf
threshed corn.   In the district of Treves it is believed that killed at
the Corn-wolf is killed at threshing.   The men thresh the threshing.
last sheaf till it is reduced to chopped straw.   In this way
they think that the Corn-wolf, who was lurking in the last
sheaf, has been certainly killed.[2]

In France also the Corn-wolf appears at harvest.   Thus The corn-
they call out to the reaper of the last corn, "You will wolf at
harvest in
catch the Wolf."   Near Chambéry they form a ring round France.
the last standing corn, and cry, "The Wolf is in there."
In Finisterre, when the reaping draws near an end, the
harvesters cry, "There is the Wolf; we will catch him."
Each takes a swath to reap, and he who finishes first calls
out, "I've caught the Wolf."[3]   In Guyenne, when the last The corn-
corn has been reaped, they lead a wether all round the field. wolf killed
on the
It is called "the Wolf of the field."   Its horns are decked with harvest-
a wreath of flowers and corn-ears, and its neck and body are field.
also encircled with garlands and ribbons.   All the reapers
march, singing, behind it.   Then it is killed on the field.   In this
part of France the last sheaf is called the *coujoulage*, which, in
the patois, means a wether.   Hence the killing of the wether
represents the death of the corn-spirit, considered as present
in the last sheaf; but two different conceptions of the corn-
spirit—as a wolf and as a wether—are mixed up together.[4]

Sometimes it appears to be thought that the Wolf, The corn-
caught in the last corn, lives during the winter in the farm- wolf at
midwinter.
house, ready to renew his activity as corn-spirit in the spring.
Hence at midwinter, when the lengthening days begin to
herald the approach of spring, the Wolf makes his appearance once more.   In Poland a man, with a wolf's skin
thrown over his head, is led about at Christmas; or a
stuffed wolf is carried about by persons who collect money.[5]
There are facts which point to an old custom of leading
about a man enveloped in leaves and called the Wolf, while
his conductors collected money.[6]

---

[1] W. Mannhardt, *Antike Wald- und Feldkulte*, p. 321.
[2] *Ibid.* pp. 321 *sq.*
[3] *Ibid.* p. 320.

[4] *Ibid.* pp. 320 *sq.*
[5] *Ibid.* p. 322.
[6] *Ibid.* p. 323.

§ 3. *The Corn-spirit as a Cock*

The corn-spirit as a cock at harvest.

Another form which the corn-spirit often assumes is that of a cock. In Austria children are warned against straying in the corn-fields, because the Corn-cock sits there, and will peck their eyes out.[1] In North Germany they say that "the Cock sits in the last sheaf"; and at cutting the last corn the reapers cry, "Now we will chase out the Cock." When it is cut they say, "We have caught the Cock."[2] At Braller, in Transylvania, when the reapers come to the last patch of corn, they cry, "Here we shall catch the Cock."[3] At Fürstenwalde, when the last sheaf is about to be bound, the master releases a cock, which he has brought in a basket, and lets it run over the field. All the harvesters chase it till they catch it. Elsewhere the harvesters all try to seize the last corn cut; he who succeeds in grasping it must crow, and is called Cock.[4] Among the Wends it is or used to be customary for the farmer to hide a live cock under the last sheaf as it lay on the field; and when the corn was being gathered up, the harvester who lighted upon this sheaf had a right to keep the cock, provided he could catch it. This formed the close of the harvest-festival and was known as "the Cock-catching," and the beer which was served out to the reapers at this time went by the name of "Cock-beer."[5] The last sheaf is called Cock, Cock-sheaf, Harvest-cock, Harvest-hen, Autumn-hen. A distinction is made between a Wheat-cock, Bean-cock, and so on, according to the crop.[6] At Wünschensuhl, in Thüringen, the last sheaf is made into the shape of a cock, and called the Harvest-cock.[7] A figure of a cock, made of wood, pasteboard, ears of corn,

---

[1] W. Mannhardt, *Die Korndämonen,* p. 13.

[2] W. Mannhardt, *l.c.*; J. H. Schmitz, *Sitten und Sagen, Lieder, Sprüchwörter und Rathsel des Eifler Volkes* (Treves, 1856-1858), i. 95 ; A. Kuhn und W. Schwartz, *Norddeutsche Sagen, Märchen und Gebräuche* (Leipsic, 1848), p. 398.

[3] G. A. Heinrich, *Agrarische Sitten und Gebräuche unter den Sachsen Siebenbürgens* (Hermannstadt, 1880), p. 21.

[4] W. Mannhardt, *Die Korndämonen,* p. 13. Compare A. Kuhn and W. Schwartz, *l.c.*

[5] K. Haupt, *Sagenbuch der Lausitz* (Leipsic, 1862-1863), i. p. 232, No. 277 note.

[6] W. Mannhardt, *Die Korndämonen,* p. 13.

[7] A. Witzschel, *Sagen, Sitten und Gebräuche aus Thüringen* (Vienna, 1878), p. 220.

or flowers, is borne in front of the harvest-waggon, especially in Westphalia, where the cock carries in his beak fruits of the earth of all kinds. Sometimes the image of the cock is fastened to the top of a May-tree on the last harvest-waggon. Elsewhere a live cock, or a figure of one, is attached to a harvest-crown and carried on a pole. In Galicia and elsewhere this live cock is fastened to the garland of corn-ears or flowers, which the leader of the women-reapers carries on her head as she marches in front of the harvest procession.[1] In Silesia a live cock is presented to the master on a plate. The harvest-supper is called Harvest-cock, Stubble-cock, etc., and a chief dish at it, at least in some places, is a cock.[2] If a waggoner upsets a harvest-waggon, it is said that "he has spilt the Harvest cock," and he loses the cock, that is, the harvest-supper.[3] The harvest-waggon, with the figure of the cock on it, is driven round the farmhouse before it is taken to the barn. Then the cock is nailed over or at the side of the house-door, or on the gable, and remains there till next harvest.[4] In East Friesland the person who gives the last stroke at threshing is called the Clucking-hen, and grain is strewed before him as if he were a hen.[5]

Again, the corn-spirit is killed in the form of a cock. In parts of Germany, Hungary, Poland, and Picardy the reapers place a live cock in the corn which is to be cut last, and chase it over the field, or bury it up to the neck in the ground; afterwards they strike off its head with a sickle or scythe.[6] In many parts of Westphalia, when the harvesters bring the wooden cock to the farmer, he gives them a live

The corn-spirit killed in the form of a live cock.

---

[1] W. Mannhardt, *Die Korndämonen*, pp. 13 *sq.*; J. H. Schmitz, *Sitten und Sagen, Lieder, Sprüchwörter und Räthsel des Eifler Volkes* (Treves, 1856-1858), i. 95; A. Kuhn, *Sagen, Gebräuche und Märchen aus Westfalen* (Leipsic, 1859), ii. 180 *sq.*; H. Pfannenschmid, *Germanische Erntefeste* (Hanover, 1878), p. 110.

[2] W. Mannhardt, *Die Korndämonen*, p. 14; H. Pfannenschmid, *op. cit.* pp. 111, 419 *sq.*

[3] W. Mannhardt, *Die Korndämonen*, p. 15. So in Shropshire, where the corn-spirit is conceived in the form of a gander (see above, p. 268), the

expression for overthrowing a load at harvest is "to lose the goose," and the penalty used to be the loss of the goose at the harvest-supper (C. S. Burne and G. F. Jackson, *Shropshire Folk-lore*, London, 1883, p. 375); and in some parts of England the harvest-supper was called the Harvest Gosling, or the Inning Goose (J. Brand, *Popular Antiquities*, ii. 23, 26, Bohn's edition).

[4] W. Mannhardt, *Die Korndämonen*, p. 14.

[5] *Ibid.* p. 15.

[6] W. Mannhardt, *Mythologische Forschungen*, p. 30.

cock, which they kill with whips or sticks, or behead with an old sword, or throw into the barn to the girls, or give to the mistress to cook.   If the harvest-cock has not been spilt—that is, if no waggon has been upset—the harvesters have the right to kill the farmyard cock by throwing stones at it or beheading it.   Where this custom has fallen into disuse, it is still common for the farmer's wife to make cockie-leekie for the harvesters, and to shew them the head of the cock which has been killed for the soup.[1]   In the neighbourhood of Klausenburg, Transylvania, a cock is buried on the harvest-field in the earth, so that only its head appears.   A young man then takes a scythe and cuts off the cock's head at a single sweep.   If he fails to do this, he is called the Red Cock for a whole year, and people fear that next year's crop will be bad.[2]   Near Udvarhely, in Transylvania, a live cock is bound up in the last sheaf and killed with a spit.   It is then skinned.   The flesh is thrown away, but the skin and feathers are kept till next year ; and in spring the grain from the last sheaf is mixed with the feathers of the cock and scattered on the field which is to be tilled.[3]   Nothing could set in a clearer light the identification of the cock with the spirit of the corn.   By being tied up in the last sheaf and killed, the cock is identi-fied with the corn, and its death with the cutting of the corn.   By keeping its feathers till spring, then mixing them with the seed-corn taken from the very sheaf in which the bird had been bound, and scattering the feathers together with the seed over the field, the identity of the bird with the corn is again emphasised, and its quickening and fertilising power, as an embodiment of the corn-spirit, is intimated in the plainest manner.   Thus the corn-spirit, in the form of a cock, is killed at harvest, but rises to fresh life and activity in spring.   Again, the equivalence of the cock to the corn is expressed, hardly less plainly, in the custom of burying the bird in the ground, and cutting off its head (like the ears of corn) with the scythe.

---

[1] W. Mannhardt, *Die Korndämonen*, p. 15.

[2] *Ibid.* pp. 15 *sq.*

[3] W. Mannhardt, *Die Korndämonen*, p. 15 ; *id., Mythologische Forschungen*, p. 30.

§ 4. *The Corn-spirit as a Hare*

Another common embodiment of the corn-spirit is the hare.[1] In Galloway the reaping of the last standing corn is called " cutting the Hare." The mode of cutting it is as follows. When the rest of the corn has been reaped, a handful is left standing to form the Hare. It is divided into three parts and plaited, and the ears are tied in a knot. The reapers then retire a few yards and each throws his or her sickle in turn at the Hare to cut it down. It must be cut below the knot, and the reapers continue to throw their sickles at it, one after the other, until one of them succeeds in severing the stalks below the knot. The Hare is then carried home and given to a maidservant in the kitchen, who places it over the kitchen-door on the inside. Sometimes the Hare used to be thus kept till the next harvest. In the parish of Minnigaff, when the Hare was cut, the unmarried reapers ran home with all speed, and the one who arrived first was the first to be married.[2] In Southern Ayrshire the last corn cut is also called the Hare, and the mode of cutting it seems to be the same as in Galloway ; at least in the neighbourhood of Kilmarnock the last corn left standing in the middle of the field is plaited, and the reapers used to try to cut it by throwing their sickles at it. When cut, it was carried home and hung up over the door.[3] In the Vosges Mountains the person who cuts the last handful of hay or wheat is sometimes said to have caught the Hare ; he is congratulated by his comrades and has the honour of carrying the nosegay or the small fir-tree decorated with ribbons which marks the conclusion of the harvest.[4] In Germany also one of the names for the last sheaf is the Hare.[5] Thus in some parts of Anhalt, when the corn has been reaped and only a few stalks are left standing, they say, " The Hare will soon come," or the reapers cry to each other, " Look how the Hare comes

The corn-spirit as a hare at harvest.

---

[1] W. Mannhardt, *Die Korndämonen*, p. 1.

[2] W. Gregor, " Preliminary Report on Folklore in Galloway, Scotland," *Report of the British Association for 1896*, p. 623.

[3] *Folk-lore Journal*, vii. (1889) pp. 47 *sq.*

[4] L. F. Sauvé, *Folk-lore des Hautes-Vosges* (Paris, 1889), p. 191.

[5] W. Mannhardt, *Die Korndämonen*, p. 3.

jumping out."[1]   In East Prussia they say that the Hare sits in
the last patch of standing corn, and must be chased out by the
last reaper.   The reapers hurry with their work, each being
anxious not to have " to chase out the Hare " ; for the man
who does so, that is, who cuts the last corn, is much laughed
at.[2]   At Birk, in Transylvania, when the reapers come to the
last patch, they cry out, " We have the Hare."[3]   At Aurich,
as we have seen,[4] an expression for cutting the last corn in
"to cut off the Hare's tail."   " He is killing the Hare " is
commonly said of the man who cuts the last corn in Germany, Sweden, Holland, France, and Italy.[5]   In Norway
the man who is thus said to " kill the Hare " must give
" hare's blood " in the form of brandy, to his fellows to
drink.[6]   In Lesbos, when the reapers are at work in two
neighbouring fields, each party tries to finish first in order
to drive the Hare into their neighbour's field ; the reapers
who succeed in doing so believe that next year the crop
will be better.   A small sheaf of corn is made up and kept
beside the holy picture till next harvest.[7]

The corn-
spirit as a
hare killed
in the last
corn cut.

§ 5. The Corn-spirit as a Cat

The corn-
spirit as
a cat
sitting in
the corn.

Again, the corn-spirit sometimes takes the form of a cat.
Near Kiel children are warned not to go into the corn-fields
because " the Cat sits there."   In the Eisenach Oberland they
are told " the Corn-cat will come and fetch you," " the Corn-
cat goes in the corn."   In some parts of Silesia at mowing
the last corn they say, " The Cat is caught " ; and at threshing,
the man who gives the last stroke is called the Cat.   In
the neighbourhood of Lyons the last sheaf and the harvest-
supper are both called the Cat.   About Vesoul when they
cut the last corn they say, " We have the Cat by the tail."
At Briançon, in Dauphiné, at the beginning of reaping, a

The corn-
spirit as a
cat at reap-
ing and
threshing.

[1] O. Hartung, "Zur Volkskunde
aus Anhalt," Zeitschrift des Vereins für
Volkskunde, vii. (1897) p. 154.
[2] C. Lemke, Volksthümliches in Ostpreussen (Mohrungen, 1884-1887), i.
24.
[3] G. A. Heinrich, Agrarische Sitten
und Gebräuche unter den Sachsen Siebenbürgens (Hermannstadt, 1880), p. 21.

[4] Above, p. 268.
[5] W. Mannhardt,   Mythologische
Forschungen, p. 29.
[6] W.   Mannhardt,   Mythologische
Forschungen, pp. 29 sq. ; id., Die
Korndämonen, p. 5.
[7] Georgeakis et Pineau, Folk-lore de
Lesbos (Paris, 1894), p. 310.

cat is decked out with ribbons, flowers, and ears of corn. It is called the Cat of the ball-skin (*le chat de peau de balle*). If a reaper is wounded at his work, they make the cat lick the wound. At the close of the reaping the cat is again decked out with ribbons and ears of corn ; then they dance and make merry. When the dance is over the girls solemnly strip the cat of its finery. At Grüneberg, in Silesia, the reaper who cuts the last corn goes by the name of the Tom-cat. He is enveloped in rye-stalks and green withes, and is furnished with a long plaited tail. Sometimes as a companion he has a man similarly dressed, who is called the (female) Cat. Their duty is to run after people whom they see and to beat them with a long stick. Near Amiens the expression for finishing the harvest is, "They are going to kill the Cat"; and when the last corn is cut they kill a cat in the farmyard. At threshing, in some parts of France, a live cat is placed under the last bundle of corn to be threshed, and is struck dead with the flails. Then on Sunday it is roasted and eaten as a holiday dish.[1] In the Vosges Mountains the close of haymaking or harvest is called "catching the cat," "killing the dog," or more rarely "catching the hare." The cat, the dog, or the hare is said to be fat or lean according as the crop is good or bad. The man who cuts the last handful of hay or of wheat is said to catch the cat or the hare or to kill the dog. He is congratulated by his comrades and has the honour of carrying the nosegay or rather the small fir-tree decked with ribbons which marks the end of the haymaking or of the harvest.[2] In Franche-Comté also the close of harvest is called "catching or killing the cat."[3]

The corn-spirit as a cat killed at reaping and threshing.

§ 6. *The Corn-spirit as a Goat*

Further, the corn-spirit often appears in the form of a goat. In some parts of Prussia, when the corn bends before

[1] W. Mannhardt, *Antike Wald- und Feldkulte*, pp. 172-174 ; *id.*, *Mythologische Forschungen*, p. 30 ; P. Drechsler, *Sitte, Brauch und Volksglaube in Schlesien* (Leipsic, 1903-1906), ii. 64, 65.
[2] L. F. Sauvé, *Le Folk-lore des Hautes-Vosges* (Paris, 1889), p. 191.
[3] Ch. Beauquier, *Les Mois en Franch-Comté* (Paris, 1900), p. 102.

The corn-
spirit as
a goat
running
through
the corn
or sitting
in it.
the wind, they say, "The Goats are chasing each other,"
"the wind is driving the Goats through the corn," "the
Goats are browsing there," and they expect a very good
harvest.   Again they say, "The Oats-goat is sitting in the
oats-field," "the Corn-goat is sitting in the rye-field."[1]
Children are warned not to go into the corn-fields to pluck
the blue corn-flowers, or amongst the beans to pluck pods,
because the Rye-goat, the Corn-goat, the Oats-goat, or the
Bean-goat is sitting or lying there, and will carry them away

The corn-
goat at
reaping
and
binding
the corn.
or kill them.[2]   When a harvester is taken sick or lags
behind his fellows at their work, they call out, "The Harvest-
goat has pushed him," "he has been pushed by the Corn-
goat."[3]   In the neighbourhood of Braunsberg (East Prussia)
at binding the oats every harvester makes haste "lest the
Corn-goat push him."   At Oefoten, in Norway, each reaper
has his allotted patch to reap.   When a reaper in the middle
has not finished reaping his piece after his neighbours have
finished theirs, they say of him, "He remains on the island."
And if the laggard is a man, they imitate the cry with which
they call a he-goat ; if a woman, the cry with which they
call a she-goat.[4]   Near Straubing, in Lower Bavaria, it is said
of the man who cuts the last corn that "he has the Corn-
goat, or the Wheat-goat, or the Oats-goat," according to
the crop.   Moreover, two horns are set up on the last heap
of corn, and it is called "the horned Goat."   At Kreutzburg,
East Prussia, they call out to the woman who is binding the
last sheaf, "The Goat is sitting in the sheaf."[5]   At Gab-
lingen, in Swabia, when the last field of oats upon a farm is
being reaped, the reapers carve a goat out of wood.   Ears
of oats are inserted in its nostrils and mouth, and it is
adorned with garlands of flowers.   It is set up on the field
and called the Oats-goat.   When the reaping approaches an
end, each reaper hastens to finish his piece first ; he who is
the last to finish gets the Oats-goat.[6]   Again, the last sheaf
is itself called the Goat.   Thus, in the valley of the Wiesent,
Bavaria, the last sheaf bound on the field is called the Goat,

[1] W. Mannhardt, *Antike Wald- und
Feldkulte*, pp. 155 sq.
[2] *Ibid.* pp. 157 sq.
[3] *Ibid.* p. 159.
[4] *Ibid.* pp. 161 sq.

[5] *Ibid.* p. 162.
[6] F. Panzer, *Beitrag zur deutschen
Mythologie* (Munich, 1848-1855), ii.
pp. 232 sq., § 426 ; W. Mannhardt,
Antike Wald- und Feldkulte, p. 162.

and they have a proverb, " The field must bear a goat." [1]   At
Spachbrücken, in Hesse, the last handful of corn which is
cut is called the Goat, and the man who cuts it is much
ridiculed. [2] At Dürrenbüchig and about Mosbach in Baden the
last sheaf is also called the Goat. [3] Sometimes the last sheaf
is made up in the form of a goat, and they say, " The Goat
is sitting in it." [4]   Again, the person who cuts or binds the
last sheaf is called the Goat.   Thus, in parts of Mecklenburg
they call out to the woman who binds the last sheaf, " You
are the Harvest-goat."   Near Uelzen, in Hanover, the harvest
festival begins with " the bringing of the Harvest-goat ";
that is, the woman who bound the last sheaf is wrapt in
straw, crowned with a harvest-wreath, and brought in a wheelbarrow to the village, where a round dance takes place.
About Luneburg, also, the woman who binds the last corn is
decked with a crown of corn-ears and is called the Corn-
goat. [5] At Münzesheim in Baden the reaper who cuts the
last handful of corn or oats is called the Corn-goat or the
Oats-goat. [6] In the Canton St. Gall, Switzerland, the person
who cuts the last handful of corn on the field, or drives the
last harvest-waggon to the barn, is called the Corn-goat or the
Rye-goat, or simply the Goat. [7] In the Canton Thurgau he
is called Corn-goat ; like a goat he has a bell hung round his
neck, is led in triumph, and drenched with liquor.   In parts
of Styria, also, the man who cuts the last corn is called
Corn-goat, Oats-goat, or the like.   As a rule, the man who
thus gets the name of Corn-goat has to bear it a whole year
till the next harvest. [8]

According to one view, the corn-spirit, who has been   The corn-
caught in the form of a goat or otherwise, lives in the farm-   spirit as the
house or barn over winter.   Thus, each farm has its own   Goat in
embodiment of the corn-spirit.   But, according to another   Skye.
view, the corn-spirit is the genius or deity, not of the corn

[1] F. Panzer, *op. cit.* ii. pp. 228 *sq.*,
§ 422 ; W. Mannhardt, *Antike Wald-
und Feldkulte,* p. 163 ; *Bavaria,
Landes- und Volkskunde des Königreichs
Bayern,* iii. (Munich, 1865) p. 344.
[2] W. Mannhardt, *Antike Wald- und
Feldkulte,* p. 163.
[3] E. H. Meyer, *Badisches Volksleben*
(Strasburg, 1900), p. 428.

[4] W. Mannhardt, *Antike Wald- und
Feldkulte,* p. 164.
[5] *Ibid.* p. 164.
[6] E. H. Meyer, *Badisches Volksleben*
(Strasburg, 1900), p. 428.
[7] W. Mannhardt, *Antike Wald- und
Feldkulte,* pp. 164 *sq.*
[8] *Ibid.* p. 165.

of one farm only, but of all the corn. Hence when the corn on one farm is all cut, he flees to another where there is still corn left standing. This idea is brought out in a harvest-custom which was formerly observed in Skye. The farmer who first finished reaping sent a man or woman with a sheaf to a neighbouring farmer who had not finished; the latter in his turn, when he had finished, sent on the sheaf to his neighbour who was still reaping; and so the sheaf made the round of the farms till all the corn was cut. The sheaf was called the *goabbir bhacagh*, that is, the Cripple Goat.[1] The custom appears not to be extinct at the present day, for it was reported from Skye only a few years ago. We are told that when the crofters and small farmers are cutting down their corn, each tries his best to finish before his neighbour. The first to finish goes to his neighbour's field and makes up at one end of it a bundle of sheaves in a fanciful shape which goes by the name of the *gobhar bhacach* or Lame Goat. As each man in succession finishes reaping his field, he proceeds to set up a lame goat of this sort in his neighbour's field where there is still corn standing. No one likes to have the Lame Goat put in his field, " not from any ill-luck it brings, but because it is humiliating to have it standing there visible to all neighbours and passers-by, and of course he cannot retaliate."[2] The corn-spirit was prob-ably thus represented as lame because he had been crippled by the cutting of the corn. We have seen that sometimes the old woman who brings home the last sheaf must limp on one foot.[3] In the Böhmer Wald mountains, between Bohemia and Bavaria, when two peasants are driving home their corn together, they race against each other to see who shall get home first. The village boys mark the loser in the race, and at night they come and erect on the roof of his house the Oats-goat, which is a colossal figure of a goat made of straw.[4]

But sometimes the corn-spirit, in the form of a goat, is

[1] J. Brand, *Popular Antiquities*, ii. 24, Bohn's edition, quoting *The Gentleman's Magazine* for February, 1795, p. 124; W. Mannhardt, *op. cit.* p. 165.

[2] R. C. Maclagan, "Notes on folk-lore objects collected in Argyleshire," *Folk-lore*, vi. (1895) p. 151, from in-formation given by Mrs. C. Nicholson.

[3] Above, p. 232.

[4] W. Mannhardt, *Antike Wald- und Feldkulte*, p. 165.

believed to be slain on the harvest-field by the sickle or The corn-spirit killed as a goat on the harvest-field.
scythe. Thus, in the neighbourhood of Bernkastel, on the
Moselle, the reapers determine by lot the order in which they
shall follow each other. The first is called the fore-reaper,
the last the tail-bearer. If a reaper overtakes the man in
front he reaps past him, bending round so as to leave the
slower reaper in a patch by himself. This patch is called
the Goat; and the man for whom "the Goat is cut" in this
way, is laughed and jeered at by his fellows for the rest of
the day. When the tail-bearer cuts the last ears of corn, it
is said, " He is cutting the Goat's neck off." [1]   In the neighbourhood of Grenoble, before the end of the reaping, a live
goat is adorned with flowers and ribbons and allowed to run
about the field. The reapers chase it and try to catch it.
When it is caught, the farmer's wife holds it fast while the
farmer cuts off its head. The goat's flesh serves to furnish
the harvest-supper. A piece of the flesh is pickled and kept
till the next harvest, when another goat is killed. Then all
the harvesters eat of the flesh. On the same day the skin of
the goat is made into a cloak, which the farmer, who works
with his men, must always wear at harvest-time if rain or
bad weather sets in. But if a reaper gets pains in his back,
the farmer gives him the goat-skin to wear. [2]   The reason
for this seems to be that the pains in the back, being inflicted
by the corn-spirit, can also be healed by it. Similarly, we
saw that elsewhere, when a reaper is wounded at reaping, a
cat, as the representative of the corn-spirit, is made to lick
the wound. [3]   Esthonian reapers in the island of Mon think
that the man who cuts the first ears of corn at harvest will
get pains in his back, [4] probably because the corn-spirit is
believed to resent especially the first wound ; and, in order to
escape pains in the back, Saxon reapers in Transylvania gird
their loins with the first handful of ears which they cut. [5]
Here, again, the corn-spirit is applied to for healing or pro-

[1] W. Mannhardt, *op. cit.* p. 166 ;
id., Mythologische Forschungen, p. 185.
  [2] W. Mannhardt, *Antike Wald- und
Feldkulte*, p. 166.
  [3] Above, p. 281.
  [4] J. B. Holzmayer, "Osiliana," *Verhandlungen der gelehrten Estnischen*

Gesellschaft zu Dorpat, vii. Heft 2
(Dorpat, 1872), p. 107.
  [5] G. A. Heinrich, *Agrarische Sitten
und Gebräuche unter den Sachsen Siebenbürgens* (Hermannstadt, 1880), p. 19.
Compare W. Mannhardt, *Baumkultus*,
pp. 482 *sqq.*

tection, but in his original vegetable form, not in the form of a goat or a cat.

The corn-spirit in the form of a goat supposed to lurk among the corn in the barn, till he is expelled by the flail at threshing.

Further, the corn-spirit under the form of a goat is sometimes conceived as lurking among the cut corn in the barn, till he is driven from it by the threshing-flail. Thus in Baden the last sheaf to be threshed is called the Corn-goat, the Spelt-goat, or the Oats-goat according to the kind of grain.[1] Again, near Marktl, in Upper Bavaria, the sheaves are called Straw-goats or simply Goats. They are laid in a great heap on the open field and threshed by two rows of men standing opposite each other, who, as they ply their flails, sing a song in which they say that they see the Straw-goat amongst the corn-stalks. The last Goat, that is, the last sheaf, is adorned with a wreath of violets and other flowers and with cakes strung together. It is placed right in the middle of the heap. Some of the threshers rush at it and tear the best of it out ; others lay on with their flails so recklessly that heads are sometimes broken. In threshing this last sheaf, each man casts up to the man opposite him the misdeeds of which he has been guilty throughout the year.[2] At Oberinntal, in the Tyrol, the last thresher is called Goat.[3] So at Haselberg, in West Bohemia, the man who gives the last stroke at threshing oats is called the Oats-goat.[4] At Tettnang, in Würtemburg, the thresher who gives the last stroke to the last bundle of corn before it is turned goes by the name of the He-goat, and it is said, " He has driven the He-goat away." The person who, after the bundle has been turned, gives the last stroke of all, is called the She-goat.[5] In this custom it is implied that the corn is inhabited by a pair of corn-spirits, male and female.

The corn-spirit in the form of a goat passed on to a neighbour

Further, the corn-spirit, captured in the form of a goat at threshing, is passed on to a neighbour whose threshing is not yet finished. In Franche Comté, as soon as the threshing is over, the young people set up a straw figure of a goat on the

[1] E. L. Meyer, *Badisches Volksleben* (Strasburg, 1900), p. 436.

[2] F. Panzer, *Beitrag zur deutschen Mythologie*, ii. pp. 225 *sqq.*, § 421 ; W. Mannhardt, *Antike Wald- und Feldkulte*, pp. 167 *sq.*

[3] W. Mannhardt, *Antike Wald- und Feldkulte*, p. 168.

[4] A. John, *Sitte, Brauch und Volksglaube im deutschen Westböhmen* (Prague, 1905), p. 194.

[5] E. Meier, *Deutsche Sagen, Sitten und Gebräuche aus Schwaben* (Stuttgart, 1852), p. 445, § 162 ; W. Mannhardt, *Antike Wald- und Feldkulte*, p. 168.

farmyard of a neighbour who is still threshing. He must
give them wine or money in return. At Ellwangen, in
Würtemburg, the effigy of a goat is made out of the last
bundle of corn at threshing ; four sticks form its legs, and
two its horns. The man who gives the last stroke with
the flail must carry the Goat to the barn of a neighbour
who is still threshing and throw it down on the floor ; if he
is caught in the act, they tie the goat on his back.[1] A
similar custom is observed at Indersdorf, in Upper Bavaria ;
the man who throws the straw Goat into the neighbour's
barn imitates the bleating of a goat ; if they catch him, they
blacken his face and tie the Goat on his back.[2] At Zabern,
in Elsace, when a farmer is a week or more behind his neighbours with his threshing, they set a real stuffed goat or fox
before his door.[3]

Sometimes the spirit of the corn in goat form is believed
to be killed at threshing. In the district of Traunstein,
Upper Bavaria, they think that the Oats-goat is in the last
sheaf of oats. He is represented by an old rake set up on
end, with an old pot for a head. The children are then told
to kill the Oats-goat.[4] Elsewhere, however, the corn-spirit
in the form of a goat is apparently thought to live in the
field throughout the winter. Hence at Wannefeld near
Gardelegen, and also between Calbe and Salzwedel, in the
Altmark, the last stalks used to be left uncut on the harvest-
field with the words, " That shall the He-goat keep ! "
Evidently the last corn was here left as a provision for the
corn-spirit, lest, robbed of all his substance, he should die of
hunger. A stranger passing a harvest-field is sometimes
taken for the Corn-goat escaping in human shape from the
cut or threshed grain. Thus, when a stranger passes a
harvest-field, all the labourers stop and shout as with one
voice, " He-goat ! He-goat ! " At rape-seed threshing in
Schleswig, which is generally done on the field, the same
cry is raised if the stranger does not take off his hat.[5]

---

[1] W. Mannhardt, *op. cit.* p. 169.
[2] F. Panzer, *Beitrag zur deutschen
Mythologie*, ii. pp. 224 *sq.*, § 420 ;
W. Mannhardt, *Antike Wald- und Feldkulte*, p. 169.
[3] W. Mannhardt, *op. cit.* p. 169.

[4] *Ibid.* p. 170.

[5] *Ibid.* p. 170. As to the custom
of leaving a little corn on the field for
the subsistence of the corn-spirit, see
above, pp. 231 *sqq.*

Old Prussian custom of killing a goat at sowing.

At sowing their winter corn the old Prussians used to kill a goat, consume its flesh with many superstitious ceremonies, and hang the skin on a high pole near an oak and a large stone. There it remained till harvest, when a great bunch of corn and herbs was fastened to the pole above the goat-skin. Then, after a prayer had been offered by a peasant who acted as priest (*Weidulut*), the young folks joined hands and danced round the oak and the pole. Afterwards they scrambled for the bunch of corn, and the priest distributed the herbs with a sparing hand. Then he placed the goat-skin on the large stone, sat down on it, and preached to the people about the history of their forefathers and their old heathen customs and beliefs.[1] The goat-skin thus suspended on the field from sowing time to harvest perhaps represents the corn-spirit superintending the growth of the corn. The Tomori of Central Celebes imagine that the spirits which cause rice to grow have the form of great goats with long hair and long lips.[2]

§ 7. *The Corn-spirit as a Bull, Cow, or Ox*

The corn-spirit in the form of a bull running through the corn or lying in it.

Another form which the corn-spirit often assumes is that of a bull, cow, or ox. When the wind sweeps over the corn they say at Conitz, in West Prussia, "The Steer is running in the corn";[3] when the corn is thick and strong in one spot, they say in some parts of East Prussia, "The Bull is lying in the corn." When a harvester has overstrained and lamed himself, they say in the Graudenz district of West Prussia, "The Bull pushed him"; in Lothringen they say, "He has the Bull." The meaning of both expressions is that he has unwittingly lighted upon the divine corn-spirit, who has punished the profane intruder with lameness.[4] So near Chambéry when a reaper wounds himself with his sickle, it is said that he has "the wound of the Ox."[5] In

The corn-spirit as a bull, ox, or cow at harvest.

[1] M. Praetorius, *Deliciae Prussicae* (Berlin, 1871), pp. 23 *sq.* ; W. Mannhardt, *Baumkultus*, pp. 394 *sq.*
[2] A. C. Kruijt, "Eenige ethnografische aanteekeningen omtrent de Toboengkoe en de Tomori," *Mededeelingen van wege het Nederlandsche Zendelinggenootschap*, xliv. (1900) p. 241.
[3] W. Mannhardt, *Mythologische Forschungen*, p. 58.
[4] *Ibid.*
[5] *Ibid.* p. 62.

the district of Bunzlau (Silesia) the last sheaf is sometimes made into the shape of a horned ox, stuffed with tow and wrapt in corn-ears. This figure is called the Old Man. In some parts of Bohemia the last sheaf is made up in human form and called the Buffalo-bull.[1] These cases shew a confusion of the human with the animal shape of the corn-spirit. The confusion is like that of killing a wether under the name of a wolf.[2] In the Canton of Thurgau, Switzerland, the last sheaf, if it is a large one, is called the Cow.[3] All over Swabia the last bundle of corn on the field is called the Cow; the man who cuts the last ears "has the Cow," and is himself called Cow or Barley-cow or Oats-cow, according to the crop; at the harvest-supper he gets a nosegay of flowers and corn-ears and a more liberal allowance of drink than the rest. But he is teased and laughed at; so no one likes to be the Cow.[4] The Cow was sometimes represented by the figure of a woman made out of ears of corn and corn-flowers. It was carried to the farmhouse by the man who had cut the last handful of corn. The children ran after him and the neighbours turned out to laugh at him, till the farmer took the Cow from him.[5] Here again the confusion between the human and the animal form of the corn-spirit is apparent. In various parts of Switzerland the reaper who cuts the last ears of corn is called Wheat-cow, Corn-cow, Oats-cow, or Corn-steer, and is the butt of many a joke.[6] In some parts of East Prussia, when a few ears of corn have been left standing by inadvertence on the last swath, the foremost reaper seizes them and cries, "Bull! Bull!"[7] On the other hand, in the district of Rosenheim, Upper Bavaria, when a farmer is later of getting in his harvest than his neighbours, they set up on his land a Straw-bull, as it is called. This is a gigantic figure of a bull made of stubble on a framework of wood and adorned with flowers and leaves. Attached to it is a label on which are scrawled

---

[1] W. Mannhardt, *Mythologische Forschungen*, p. 59.

[2] Above, p. 275.

[3] W. Mannhardt, *op. cit.* p. 59.

[4] E. Meier, *Deutsche Sagen, Sitten und Gebräuche aus Schwaben* (Stuttgart, 1852), pp. 440 *sq.*, §§ 151, 152, 153; F. Panzer, *Beitrag zur deutschen*

Mythologie, ii. p. 234, § 428; W. Mannhardt, *Mythologische Forschungen*, p. 59.

[5] F. Panzer, *op. cit.* ii. p. 233, § 427; W. Mannhardt, *Mythologische Forschungen*, p. 59.

[6] W. Mannhardt, *op. cit.* pp. 59 *sq.*

[7] *Ibid.* p. 58.

doggerel verses in ridicule of the man on whose land the Straw-bull is set up.[1]

The corn-spirit in the form of a bull or ox killed at the close of the reaping. Again, the corn-spirit in the form of a bull or ox is killed on the harvest-field at the close of the reaping. At Pouilly, near Dijon, when the last ears of corn are about to be cut, an ox adorned with ribbons, flowers, and ears of corn is led all round the field, followed by the whole troop of reapers dancing. Then a man disguised as the Devil cuts the last ears of corn and immediately slaughters the ox. Part of the flesh of the animal is eaten at the harvest-supper ; part is pickled and kept till the first day of sowing in spring. At Pont à Mousson and elsewhere on the evening of the last day of reaping, a calf adorned with flowers and ears of corn is led thrice round the farmyard, being allured by a bait or driven by men with sticks, or conducted by the farmer's wife with a rope. The calf chosen for this ceremony is the calf which was born first on the farm in the spring of the year. It is followed by all the reapers with their tools. Then it is allowed to run free ; the reapers chase it, and whoever catches it is called King of the Calf. Lastly, it is solemnly killed ; at Lunéville the man who acts as butcher is the Jewish merchant of the village.[2]

The corn-spirit as a bull or cow at threshing. Sometimes again the corn-spirit hides himself amongst the cut corn in the barn to reappear in bull or cow form at threshing. Thus at Wurmlingen, in Thüringen, the man who gives the last stroke at threshing is called the Cow, or rather the Barley-cow, Oats-cow, Peas-cow, or the like, according to the crop. He is entirely enveloped in straw ; his head is surmounted by sticks in imitation of horns, and two lads lead him by ropes to the well to drink. On the way thither he must low like a cow, and for a long time afterwards he goes by the name of the Cow.[3] At Obermedlingen, in Swabia, when the threshing draws near an end, each man is careful to avoid giving the last stroke. He who does give it "gets the Cow," which is a straw figure dressed in an old ragged petticoat, hood, and stockings. It is tied on his back

---

[1] W. Mannhardt, *Mythologische Forschungen*, pp. 58 sq.

[2] *Ibid.* p. 60.

[3] E. Meier, *Deutsche Sagen, Sitten und Gebräuche aus Schwaben*, pp. 444 sq., § 162 ; W. Mannhardt, *Mythologische Forschungen*, p. 61.

with a straw-rope; his face is blackened, and being bound with straw-ropes to a wheelbarrow he is wheeled round the village.[1]   Here, again, we meet with that confusion between the human and animal shape of the corn-spirit which we have noted in other customs.   In Canton Schaffhausen the man who threshes the last corn is called the Cow; in Canton Thurgau, the Corn-bull; in Canton Zurich, the Thresher-cow.   In the last-mentioned district he is wrapt in straw and bound to one of the trees in the orchard.[2]   At Arad, in Hungary, the man who gives the last stroke at threshing is enveloped in straw and a cow's hide with the horns attached to it.[3]   At Pessnitz, in the district of Dresden, the man who gives the last stroke with the flail is called Bull.   He must make a straw-man and set it up before a neighbour's window.[4]   Here, apparently, as in so many cases, the corn-spirit is passed on to a neighbour who has not finished threshing.   So at Herbrechtingen, in Thüringen, the effigy of a ragged old woman is flung into the barn of the farmer who is last with his threshing.   The man who throws it in cries, " There is the Cow for you."   If the threshers catch him they detain him over night and punish him by keeping him from the harvest-supper.[5]   In these latter customs the confusion between the human and the animal shape of the corn-spirit meets us again.

Further, the corn-spirit in bull form is sometimes believed to be killed at threshing.   At Auxerre, in threshing the last bundle of corn, they call out twelve times, " We are killing the Bull."   In the neighbourhood of Bordeaux, where a butcher kills an ox on the field immediately after the close of the reaping, it is said of the man who gives the last stroke at threshing that " he has killed the Bull."[6]   At Chambéry the last sheaf is called the sheaf of the Young Ox, and a race takes place to it in which all the reapers join.   When the last stroke is given at threshing they say that " the Ox is killed "; and immediately thereupon

The corn-spirit in the form of a bull supposed to be killed at threshing.

---

[1] F. Panzer, *Beitrag zur deutschen Mythologie*, ii. p. 233, § 427.
[2] W. Mannhardt, *Mythologische Forschungen*, pp. 61 *sq.*
[3] *Ibid.* p. 62.
[4] *Ibid.* p. 62.

[5] E. Meier, *Deutsche Sagen, Sitten und Gebräuche aus Schwaben*, pp. 445 *sq.*, § 163.

[6] W. Mannhardt, *Mythologische Forschungen*, p. 60.

a real ox is slaughtered by the reaper who cut the last corn. The flesh of the ox is eaten by the threshers at supper.[1]

The corn-spirit as a calf at harvest or in spring.

We have seen that sometimes the young corn-spirit, whose task it is to quicken the corn of the coming year, is believed to be born as a Corn-baby on the harvest-field.[2] Similarly in Berry the young corn-spirit is sometimes supposed to be born on the field in calf form ; for when a binder has not rope enough to bind all the corn in sheaves, he puts aside the wheat that remains over and imitates the lowing of a cow. The meaning is that " the sheaf has given birth to a calf."[3] In Puy-de-Dôme when a binder cannot keep up with the reaper whom he or she follows, they say " He (or she) is giving birth to the Calf."[4] In some parts of Prussia, in similar circumstances, they call out to the woman, " The Bull is coming," and imitate the bellowing of a bull.[5] In these cases the woman is conceived as the Corn-cow or old corn-spirit, while the supposed calf is the Corn-calf or young corn-spirit. In some parts of Austria a mythical calf (*Muhkälbchen*) is believed to be seen amongst the sprouting corn in spring and to push the children ; when the corn waves in the wind they say, " The Calf is going about." Clearly, as Mannhardt observes, this calf of the spring-time is the same animal which is afterwards believed to be killed at reaping.[6]

§ 8. *The Corn-spirit as a Horse or Mare*

The corn-spirit as a horse or mare running through the corn.

Sometimes the corn-spirit appears in the shape of a horse or mare. Between Kalw and Stuttgart, when the corn bends before the wind, they say, " There runs the Horse."[7] At Bohlingen, near Radolfzell in Baden, the last sheaf of oats is called the Oats-stallion.[8] In Hertfordshire, at the end of the reaping, there is or used to be observed a ceremony called " crying the Mare." The last blades of corn left standing on the field are tied together and called the Mare.

"Crying the Mare" in Hertfordshire and Shropshire.

[1] W. Mannhardt, *op. cit.* p. 62.
[2] Above, pp. 150 *sq.*
[3] Laisnel de la Salle, *Croyances et Légendes du Centre de la France* (Paris, 1875), ii. 135.
[4] W. Mannhardt, *Mythologische*

Forschungen, p. 62 : " *Il fait le veau.*"
[5] *Ibid.*
[6] *Ibid.* p. 63.
[7] *Ibid.* p. 167.
[8] E. H. Meyer, *Badisches Volksleben* (Strasburg, 1900), p. 428.

The reapers stand at a distance and throw their sickles at it; he who cuts it through " has the prize, with acclamations and good cheer." After it is cut the reapers cry thrice with a loud voice, " I have her! " Others answer thrice, " What have you ? "—" A Mare! a Mare! a Mare! "—" Whose is she ? " is next asked thrice. " A. B.'s," naming the owner thrice. " Whither will you send her ? "—" To C. D.," naming some neighbour who has not reaped all his corn.[1] In this custom the corn-spirit in the form of a mare is passed on from a farm where the corn is all cut to another farm where it is still standing, and where therefore the corn-spirit may be supposed naturally to take refuge. In Shropshire the custom is similar. " Crying, calling, or shouting the mare is a ceremony performed by the men of that farm which is the first in any parish or district to finish the harvest. The object of it is to make known their own prowess, and to taunt the laggards by a pretended offer of the 'owd mar'' [old mare] to help out their 'chem' [team]. All the men assemble (the wooden harvest-bottle being of course one of the company) in the stackyard, or, better, on the highest ground on the farm, and there shout the following dialogue, preceding it by a grand ' Hip, hip, hip, hurrah ! '

" ' I 'ave 'er, I 'ave 'er, I 'ave 'er ! '

" ' Whad 'ast thee, whad 'ast thee, whad 'ast thee ? '

" ' A mar'! a mar'! a mar'! '

" ' Whose is 'er, whose is 'er, whose is 'er ? '

" ' Maister A.'s, Maister A.'s, Maister A.'s ! ' (naming the farmer whose harvest is finished).

" ' W'eer sha't the' send 'er ? w'eer sha't the' send 'er ? w'eer sha't the' send 'er ? '

" ' To Maister B.'s, to Maister B.'s, to Maister B.'s ' (naming one whose harvest is *not* finished).

" ' 'Uth a hip, hip, hip, hurrah ! ' (in chorus)."

The farmer who finishes his harvest last, and who therefore cannot send the Mare to any one else, is said " to keep her all winter." The mocking offer of the Mare was sometimes responded to by a mocking acceptance of her help. Thus an old man told an enquirer, " While we wun at supper, a mon cumm'd wi' a autar [halter] to fatch

1 J. Brand, *Popular Antiquities*, ii. 24, Bohn's edition.

her away." But at one place (Longnor, near Leebotwood), down to about 1850, the Mare used really to be sent. "The head man of the farmer who had finished harvest first was mounted on the best horse of the team—the leader—both horse and man being adorned with ribbons, streamers, etc. Thus arrayed, a boy on foot led the pair in triumph to the neighbouring farmhouses. Sometimes the man who took the 'mare' received, as well as plenty of harvest-ale, some rather rough, though good-humoured, treatment, coming back minus his decorations, and so on." [1]

The corn-spirit as a horse in France.

In the neighbourhood of Lille the idea of the corn-spirit in horse form is clearly preserved. When a harvester grows weary at his work, it is said, "He has the fatigue of the Horse." The first sheaf, called the "Cross of the Horse," is placed on a cross of boxwood in the barn, and the youngest horse on the farm must tread on it. The reapers dance round the last blades of corn, crying, "See the remains of the Horse." The sheaf made out of these last blades is given to the youngest horse of the parish (*commune*) to eat. This youngest horse of the parish clearly represents, as Mannhardt says, the corn-spirit of the following year, the Corn-foal, which absorbs the spirit of the old Corn-horse by eating the last corn cut; for, as usual, the old corn-spirit takes his final refuge in the last sheaf. The thresher of the last sheaf is said to "beat the Horse." [2] Again, a trace of the horse-shaped corn-spirit is reported from Berry. The harvesters there are accustomed to take a noonday nap in the field. This is called "seeing the Horse." The leader or "King" of the harvesters gives the signal for going to sleep. If he delays giving the signal, one of the harvesters will begin to neigh like a horse, the rest imitate him, and then they all go "to see the Horse." [3]

[1] C. F. Burne and G. F. Jackson, *Shropshire Folk-lore* (London, 1883), pp. 373 *sq.*

[2] W. Mannhardt, *Mythologische Forschungen*, p. 167. We may compare the Scotch custom of giving the last sheaf to a horse or mare to eat. See above, pp. 141, 156, 158, 160 *sq.*, 162.

[3] Laisnel de la Salle, *Croyances et*

Légendes du Centre de la France (Paris, 1875), ii. 133; W. Mannhardt, *Mythologische Forschungen*, pp. 167 *sq.* We have seen (above, p. 267) that in South Pembrokeshire the man who cut the "Neck" used to be "shod," that is, to have the soles of his feet severely beaten with sods. Perhaps he was thus treated as representing the corn-spirit in the form of a horse.

§ 9. *The Corn-spirit as a Bird*

Sometimes the corn-spirit assumes the form of a bird.   The corn-
Thus among the Saxons of the Bistritz district in Transyl-   spirit as
a quail.
vania there is a saying that the quail is sitting in the last
standing stalks on the harvest-field, and all the reapers rush
at these stalks in order, as they say, to catch the quail.[1]
Exactly the same expression is used by reapers in Austrian
Silesia when they are about to cut the last standing corn,
whatever the kind of grain may be.[2]   In the Bocage of
Normandy, when the reapers have come to the last ears of
the last rig, they surround them for the purpose of catching
the quail, which is supposed to have taken refuge there.   They
run about the corn crying, " Mind the Quail ! " and make
believe to grab at the bird amid shouts and laughter.[3]
Connected with this identification of the corn-spirit with a
quail is probably the belief that the cry of the bird in spring
is prophetic of the price of corn in the autumn ; in Germany
they say that corn will sell at as many gulden a bushel as
the quail uttered its cry over the fields in spring.   Similar
prognostications are drawn from the note of the bird in
central and western France, in Switzerland and in Tuscany.[4]
Perhaps one reason for identifying the quail with the corn-
spirit is that the bird lays its eggs on the ground, without
making much of a nest.[5]   Similarly the Toradjas of Central   The rice-
spirit as a
Celebes think that the soul of the rice is embodied in a   blue bird.
pretty little blue bird which builds its nest in the rice-field
at the time when the rice is beginning to germinate, and
which disappears again after the harvest.   Thus both the
place and the time of the appearance of the bird suggest to
the natives the notion that the blue bird is the rice incarnate.
And like the note of the quail in Europe the note of this

[1] G. A. Heinrich, *Agrarische Sitten und Gebräuche unter den Sachsen Siebenbürgens* (Hermannstadt, 1880), p. 21.

[2] A. Peter, *Völksthumliches aus Österreichisch - Schlesien* (Troppau, 1865-1867), ii. 268.

[3] J. Lecoeur, *Esquisses du Bocage Normand* (Condé-sur-Noireau, 1883-1887), ii. 240.

[4] A. Wuttke, *Der deutsche Volks aberglaube*[2] (Berlin, 1869), p. 189, § 277 ; Chr. Schneller, *Märchen und Sagen aus Wälschtirol* (Innsbruck; 1867), p. 238 ; Rev. Ch. Swainson, *The Folk Lore and Provincial Names of British Birds* (London, 1886), p. 173.

[5] Alfred Newton, *Dictionary of Birds*, New Edition (London, 1893-1896), p. 755.

little bird in Celebes is believed to prognosticate the state of the harvest, foretelling whether the rice will be abundant or scarce. Nobody may drive the bird away; to do so would not merely injure the rice, it would hurt the eyes of the sacrilegious person and might even strike him blind.

The rice-spirit as a quail.

In Minahassa, a district in the north of Celebes, a similar though less definite belief attaches to a sort of small quail which loves to haunt the rice-fields before the rice is reaped; and when the Galelareeze of Halmahera hear a certain kind of bird, which they call *togè*, croaking among the rice in ear, they say that the bird is putting the grain into the rice, so they will not kill it.[1]

§ 10. *The Corn-spirit as a Fox*

The corn-spirit as a fox running through the corn or sitting in it.

Another animal whose shape the corn-spirit is sometimes thought to assume is the fox. The conception is recorded at various places in Germany and France. Thus at Nördlingen in Bavaria, when the corn waves to and fro in the wind, they say, "The fox goes through the corn," and at Usingen in Nassau they say, "The foxes are marching through the corn." At Ravensberg, in Westphalia, and at Steinau, in Kurhessen, children are warned against straying in the corn, "because the Fox is there."

The corn-spirit as a fox at reaping the last corn.

At Campe, near Stade, when they are about to cut the last corn, they call out to the reaper, "The Fox is sitting there, hold him fast!" In the Department of the Moselle they say, "Watch whether the Fox comes out." In Bourbonnais the expression is, 'You will catch the Fox.' When a reaper wounds himself or is sick at reaping, they say in the Lower Loire that "He has the Fox." In Côte-d'or they say, "He has killed the Fox." At Louhans, in Saône-et-Loire, when the reapers are cutting the last corn they leave a handful standing and throw their sickles at it. He who hits it is called the Fox, and two girls deck his bonnet with flowers.

---

[1] A. C. Kruijt, "Eenige ethnografische aanteekeningen omtrent de Toboengkoe en de Tomori," *Mededeelingen van wege het Nederlandsche Zendelinggenootschap*, xliv. (1900) pp. 228, 229; *id.*, "De rijstmoeder in den Indischen Archipel," *Verslagen en Mededeelingen van der koninklijke Akademie van Wetenschappen*, Afdeeling Letterkunde, Vierde Reeks, v., part 3 (Amsterdam, 1903), pp. 374 *sq.*

In the evening there is a dance, at which the Fox dances with all the girls. The supper which follows is also called the Fox ; they say, " We have eaten the Fox," meaning that they have partaken of the harvest-supper. In the Canton of Zurich the last sheaf is called the Fox. At Bourgogne, in Ain, they cry out, " The Fox is sitting in the last sheaf," and having made the figure of an animal out of white cloth and some ears of the last corn, they dub it the Fox and throw it into the house of a neighbour who has not yet got in all his harvest.[1] In Poitou, when the corn is being reaped in a district, all the reapers strive to finish as quickly as possible in order that they may send " the Fox " to the fields of a farmer who has not yet garnered his sheaves. The man who cuts the last handful of standing corn is said to " have the Fox." This last handful is carried to the farmer's house and occupies a place on the table during the harvest-supper ; and the custom is to drench it with water. After that it is set up on the chimney-piece and remains there the whole year.[2] At threshing, also, in Sâone-et-Loire, the last sheaf is called the Fox ; in Lot they say, "We are going to beat the Fox " ; and at Zabern in Alsace they set a stuffed fox before the door of the threshing-floor of a neighbour who has not finished his threshing.[3] With this conception of the fox as an embodiment of the corn-spirit may possibly be connected an old custom, observed in Holstein and Westphalia, of carrying a dead or living fox from house to house in spring ; the intention of the custom was perhaps to diffuse the refreshing and invigorating influence of the reawakened spirit of vegetation.[4] In Japan the rice-god Inari is represented as an elderly man with a long beard riding on a white fox, and the fox is always associated with this deity. In front of his shrines may usually be seen a pair of foxes carved in wood or stone.[5]

The corn-spirit as a fox at threshing.

The Japanese rice-god associated with the fox.

[1] W. Mannhardt, *Mythologische Forschungen*, p. 109 note [2].

[2] L. Pineau, *Folk-lore du Poitou* (Paris, 1892), pp. 500 sq.

[3] W. Mannhardt, *Mythologische Forschungen*, pp. 109 sq., note [2].

[4] J. F. L. Woeste, *Volksüberlieferungen in der Grafschaft Mark* (Iserlohn, 1848), p. 27 ; W. Mannhardt,

Mythologische Forschungen, p. 110 note.

[5] Lafcadio Hearn, *Glimpses of Unfamiliar Japan* (London, 1894), ii. 312 sqq. ; W. G. Aston, *Shinto* (London, 1905), p̣. 162 sq. At the festival of the Roman corn-goddess Ceres, celebrated on the nineteenth of April, foxes were allowed to run about with burning torches tied to their tails,

§ 11. *The Corn-spirit as a Pig (Boar or Sow)*

The corn-spirit as a boar rushing through the corn.

The last animal embodiment of the corn-spirit which we shall notice is the pig (boar or sow). In Thüringen, when the wind sets the young corn in motion, they sometimes say, "The Boar is rushing through the corn."[1] Amongst the Esthonians of the island of Oesel the last sheaf is called the

The corn-spirit as a boar or sow at reaping.

Rye-boar, and the man who gets it is saluted with a cry of "You have the Rye-boar on your back!" In reply he strikes up a song, in which he prays for plenty.[2] At Kohlerwinkel, near Augsburg, at the close of the harvest, the last bunch of standing corn is cut down, stalk by stalk, by all the reapers in turn. He who cuts the last stalk "gets the Sow," and is laughed at.[3] In other Swabian villages also the man who cuts the last corn "has the Sow," or "has the Rye-sow."[4] In the Traunstein district, Upper Bavaria, the man who cuts the last handful of rye or wheat "has the Sow," and is called Sow-driver.[5] At Bohlingen, near Radolfzell in Baden, the last sheaf is called the Rye-sow or the Wheat-sow, according to the crop; and at Röhrenbach

The corn-spirit as a sow at threshing.

in Baden the person who brings the last armful for the last sheaf is called the Corn-sow or the Oats-sow. And in the south-east of Baden the thresher who gives the last stroke at threshing, or is the last to hang up his flail on the wall, is called the Sow or the Rye-sow.[6] At Friedingen, in Swabia, the thresher who gives the last stroke is called Sow— Barley-sow, Corn-sow, or the like, according to the crop.

and the custom was explained as a punishment inflicted on foxes because a fox had once in this way burned down the crops (Ovid, *Fasti,* iv. 679 *sqq.*). Samson is said to have burned the crops of the Philistines in a similar fashion (Judges xv. 4 *sq.*). Whether the custom and the tradition are connected with the idea of the fox as an embodiment of the corn-spirit is doubtful. Compare W. Mannhardt, *Mythologische Forschungen,* pp. 108 *sq.*; W. Warde Fowler, *Roman Festivals of the Period of the Republic* (London, 1899), pp. 77-79.

[1] A. Witzschel, *Sagen, Sitten und Gebräuche aus Thüringen* (Vienna,

1878), p. 213, § 4. So at Klepzig, in Anhalt (*Zeitschrift des Vereins für Volkskunde,* vii. (1897) p. 150).

[2] J. B. Holzmayer, "Osiliana," *Verhandlungen der gelehrten Estnischen Gesellschaft zu Dorpat,* vii. Heft 2 (Dorpat, 1872), p. 107; W. Mannhardt, *Mythologische Forschungen,* p. 187.

[3] A. Birlinger, *Aus Schwaben* (Wiesbaden, 1874), ii. 328.

[4] F. Panzer, *Beitrag zur deutschen Mythologie* (Munich, 1848-1855), ii. pp. 223, 224, §§ 417, 419.

[5] W. Mannhardt, *Mythologische Forschungen,* p. 112.

[6] E. L. Meyer, *Badisches Volksleben* (Strasburg, 1900), pp. 428, 436.

At Onstmettingen the man who gives the last stroke at threshing "has the Sow"; he is often bound up in a sheaf and dragged by a rope along the ground.[1] And, generally, in Swabia the man who gives the last stroke with the flail is called Sow. He may, however, rid himself of this invidious distinction by passing on to a neighbour the straw-rope, which is the badge of his position as Sow. So he goes to a house and throws the straw-rope into it, crying, "There, I bring you the Sow." All the inmates give chase; and if they catch him they beat him, shut him up for several hours in the pig-sty, and oblige him to take the "Sow" away again.[2] In various parts of Upper Bavaria the man who gives the last stroke at threshing must "carry the Pig"—that is, either a straw effigy of a pig or merely a bundle of straw-ropes. This he carries to a neighbouring farm where the threshing is not finished, and throws it into the barn. If the threshers catch him they handle him roughly, beating him, blackening or dirtying his face, throwing him into filth, binding the Sow on his back, and so on; if the bearer of the Sow is a woman they cut off her hair. At the harvest supper or dinner the man who "carried the Pig" gets one or more dumplings made in the form of pigs; sometimes he gets a large dumpling and a number of small ones, all in pig form, the large one being called the sow and the small ones the sucking-pigs. Sometimes he has the right to be the first to put his hand into the dish and take out as many small dumplings (" sucking-pigs ") as he can, while the other threshers strike at his hand with spoons or sticks. When the dumplings are served up by the maid-servant, all the people at table cry "Süz, süz, süz!" that being the cry used in calling pigs. Sometimes after dinner the man who "carried the Pig" has his face blackened, and is set on a cart and drawn round the village by his fellows, followed by a crowd crying "Süz, süz, süz!" as if they were calling swine. Sometimes, after being wheeled round the village, he is flung on the dunghill.[3]

[1] E. Meier, *Deutsche Sagen, Sitten und Gebräuche aus Schwaben* (Stuttgart, 1852), p. 445, § 162.

[2] A. Birlinger, *Volksthümliches aus Schwaben* (Freiburg im Breisgau, 1861-1862), ii. p. 425, § 379.

[3] F. Panzer, *Beitrag zur deutschen Mythologie*, ii. pp. 221-224, §§ 409, 410, 411, 412, 413, 414, 415, 418.

The corn-
spirit as
a pig at
sowing. Again, the corn-spirit in the form of a pig plays his part at sowing-time as well as at harvest. At Neuautz, in Courland, when barley is sown for the first time in the year, the farmer's wife boils the chine of a pig along with the tail, and brings it to the sower on the field. He eats of it, but cuts off the tail and sticks it in the field ; it is believed that the ears of corn will then grow as long as the tail.[1] Here the pig is the corn-spirit, whose fertilising power is sometimes supposed to lie especially in his tail.[2] As a pig he is put in the ground at sowing-time, and as a pig he reappears amongst the ripe corn at harvest. For amongst the neighbouring Esthonians, as we have seen,[3] the last sheaf is called the Rye-boar. Somewhat similar customs are observed in Germany. In the Salza district, near Meiningen, a certain bone in the pig is called " the Jew on the winnowing-fan." The flesh of this bone is boiled on Shrove Tuesday, but the bone is put amongst the ashes which the neighbours exchange as presents on St. Peter's Day (the twenty-second of February), and then mix with the seed-corn.[4] In the whole of Hesse, Meiningen, and other districts, people eat pea-soup with dried pig-ribs on Ash Wednesday or Candlemas. The ribs are then collected and hung in the room till sowing-time, when they are inserted in the sown field or in the seed-bag amongst the flax seed. This is thought to be an infallible specific against earth-fleas and moles, and to cause the flax to grow well and tall.[5] In many parts of White Russia people eat a roast lamb or sucking-pig at Easter, and then throw the bones backwards upon the fields, to preserve the corn from hail.[6]

The corn-
spirit em-
bodied in
the Yule
Boar of
Scandi-
navia. But the idea of the corn-spirit as embodied in pig form is nowhere more clearly expressed than in the Scandinavian custom of the Yule Boar. In Sweden and Denmark at Yule (Christmas) it is the custom to bake a loaf in the form of a boar-pig. This is called the Yule Boar. The corn of

---

[1] W. Mannhardt, *Mythologische Forschungen*, pp. 186 sq.

[2] Above, p. 272 ; compare 268.

[3] Above, p. 298.

[4] W. Mannhardt, *op. cit.* p. 187.

[5] W. Mannhardt, *op. cit.* pp. 187 sq. ; A. Witzschel, *Sagen, Sitten und Gebräuche aus Thüringen*, pp. 189,

218 ; W. Kolbe, *Hessische VolksSitten und Gebräuche* (Marburg, 1888), p. 35.

[6] W. Mannhardt, *Mythologische Forschungen*, p. 188 ; W. R. S. Ralston, *Songs of the Russian People* (London, 1872), p. 220.

the last sheaf is often used to make it. All through Yule
the Yule Boar stands on the table. Often it is kept till the
sowing-time in spring, when part of it is mixed with the
seed-corn and part given to the ploughmen and plough-
horses or plough-oxen to eat, in the expectation of a good
harvest.[1] In this custom the corn-spirit, immanent in the
last sheaf, appears at midwinter in the form of a boar made
from the corn of the last sheaf; and his quickening influence
on the corn is shewn by mixing part of the Yule Boar with
the seed-corn, and giving part of it to the ploughman and
his cattle to eat. Similarly we saw that the Corn-wolf
makes his appearance at midwinter, the time when the year
begins to verge towards spring.[2] We may conjecture that
the Yule straw, which Swedish peasants turn to various
superstitious uses, comes, in part at least, from the sheaf out
of which the Yule Boar is made. The Yule straw is long
rye-straw, a portion of which is always set apart for this
season. It is strewn over the floor at Christmas, and the
peasants attribute many virtues to it. For example, they
think that some of it scattered on the ground will make a
barren field productive. Again, the peasant at Christmas
seats himself on a log ; and his eldest son or daughter, or the
mother herself, if the children are not old enough, places a
wisp of the Yule straw on his knee. From this he draws
out single straws, and throws them, one by one, up to the
ceiling ; and as many as lodge in the rafters, so many will
be the sheaves of rye he will have to thresh at harvest.[3]
Again, it is only the Yule straw which may be used in binding the fruit-trees as a charm to fertilise them.[4] These uses
of the Yule straw shew that it is believed to possess fertilising virtues analogous to those ascribed to the Yule Boar ;
we may therefore fairly conjecture that the Yule straw is

The Yule straw in Sweden.

[1] W. Mannhardt, *Antike Wald- und
Feldkulte*, pp. 197 *sq.* ; F. Panzer,
Beitrag zur deutschen Mythologie, ii.
491 ; J. Jamieson, *Etymological
Dictionary of the Scottish Language*,
New Edition (Paisley, 1879-1882),
vol. iii. pp. 206 *sq.*, *s.v.* " Maiden " ;
Arv. Aug. Afzelius, *Volkssagen und
Volkslieder aus Schwedens älterer und
neuerer Zeit*, übersetzt von F. H.

Ungewitter (Leipsic, 1842), i. 9.
[2] Above, p. 275.
[3] L. Lloyd, *Peasant Life in Sweden*
(London, 1870), pp. 169 *sq.*, 182.
On Christmas night children sleep on
a bed of the Yule straw (*ibid.* p. 177).
[4] U. Jahn, *Die deutschen Opfergebräuche* (Breslau, 1884), p. 215.
Compare *The Magic Art and the
Evolution of Kings*, ii. 17, 27 *sq.*

made from the same sheaf as the Yule Boar. Formerly a real boar was sacrificed at Christmas,[1] and apparently also a man in the character of the Yule Boar. This, at least, may perhaps be inferred from a Christmas custom still observed in Sweden. A man is wrapt up in a skin, and carries a wisp of straw in his mouth, so that the projecting straws look like the bristles of a boar. A knife is brought, and an old woman, with her face blackened, pretends to sacrifice him.[2]

The Christmas Boar among the Esthonians

On Christmas Eve in some parts of the Esthonian island of Oesel they bake a long cake with the two ends turned up. It is called the Christmas Boar, and stands on the table till the morning of New Year's Day, when it is distributed among the cattle. In other parts of the island the Christmas Boar is not a cake but a little pig born in March, which the housewife fattens secretly, often without the knowledge of the other members of the family. On Christmas Eve the little pig is secretly killed, then roasted in the oven, and set on the table standing on all fours, where it remains in this posture for several days. In other parts of the island, again, though the Christmas cake has neither the name nor the shape of a boar, it is kept till the New Year, when half of it is divided among all the members and all the quadrupeds of the family. The other half of the cake is kept till sowing-time comes round, when it is similarly distributed in the morning among human beings and beasts.[3] In other parts of Esthonia, again, the Christmas Boar, as it is called, is baked of the first rye cut at harvest; it has a conical shape and a cross is impressed on it with a pig's bone or a key, or three dints are made in it with a buckle or a piece of charcoal. It stands with a light beside it on the table all through the festal season. On New Year's Day and Epiphany, before sunrise, a little of the cake is crumbled with salt and given to the cattle. The rest is kept till the day when the cattle are driven out to pasture for the first time in spring. It is then put in the

[1] A. A. Afzelius, *op. cit.* i. 31.

[2] A. A. Afzelius, *op. cit.* i. 9; L. Lloyd, *Peasant Life in Sweden*, pp. 181, 185.

[3] J. B. Holzmayer, "Osiliana," *Verhandlungen der gelehrten Estnischen Gesellschaft zu Dorpat*, vii. Heft 2 (Dorpat, 1872), pp. 55 *sq.*

herdsman's bag, and at evening is divided among the cattle to guard them from magic and harm.   In some places the Christmas Boar is partaken of by farm-servants and cattle at the time of the barley sowing, for the purpose of thereby producing a heavier crop.[1]

§ 12. *On the Animal Embodiments of the Corn-spirit*

So much for the animal embodiments of the corn-spirit as they are presented to us in the folk-customs of Northern Europe.   These customs bring out clearly the sacramental character of the harvest-supper.   The corn-spirit is conceived as embodied in an animal ; this divine animal is slain, and its flesh and blood are partaken off by the harvesters.   Thus, the cock, the goose, the hare, the cat, the goat, and the ox are eaten sacramentally by the harvesters, and the pig is eaten sacramentally by ploughmen in spring.[2]   Again, as a substitute for the real flesh of the divine being, bread or dumplings are made in his image and eaten sacramentally ; thus, pig-shaped dumplings are eaten by the harvesters, and loaves made in boar-shape (the Yule Boar) are eaten in spring by the ploughman and his cattle.

Sacramental character of the harvest-supper.

The reader has probably remarked the complete parallelism between the conceptions of the corn-spirit in human and in animal form.   The parallel may be here briefly resumed.   When the corn waves in the wind it is said either that the Corn-mother or that the Corn-wolf, etc., is passing through the corn.   Children are warned against straying in corn-fields either because the Corn-mother or because the Corn-wolf, etc., is there.   In the last corn cut or the last sheaf threshed either the Corn-mother or the Corn-wolf, etc., is supposed to be present.   The last sheaf is itself called either the Corn-mother or the Corn-wolf, etc., and is made up in the shape either of a woman or of a wolf, etc. The person who cuts, binds, or threshes the last sheaf is called either the Old Woman or the Wolf, etc., according to

Parallelism between the conceptions of the corn-spirit in human and animal forms.

---

[1] F. J. Wiedemann, *Aus dem inneren und äussern Leben der Ehsten* (St. Petersburg, 1876), pp. 344, 485.
[2] Above, pp. 277 *sq.*, 280, 281, 285, 290, 300, 301.   In regard to the hare, the substitution of brandy for hare's blood is probably modern.

the name bestowed on the sheaf itself. As in some places a sheaf made in human form and called the Maiden, the Mother of the Maize, etc., is kept from one harvest to the next in order to secure a continuance of the corn-spirit's blessing ; so in some places the Harvest-cock and in others the flesh of the goat is kept for a similar purpose from one harvest to the next. As in some places the grain taken from the Corn-mother is mixed with the seed-corn in spring to make the crop abundant ; so in some places the feathers of the cock, and in Sweden the Yule Boar, are kept till spring and mixed with the seed-corn for a like purpose. As part of the Corn-mother or Maiden is given to the cattle at Christmas or to the horses at the first ploughing, so part of the Yule Boar is given to the ploughing horses or oxen in spring. Lastly, the death of the corn-spirit is represented by killing or pretending to kill either his human or his animal representative ; and the worshippers partake sacramentally either of the actual body and blood of the representative of the divinity, or of bread made in his likeness.

The reason why the corn-spirit is thought to take the forms of so many animals may be that wild creatures are commonly penned by the advance of the reapers into the last patch of standing corn, which is usually regarded as the last refuge of the corn-spirit.   Other animal forms assumed by the corn-spirit are the stag, roe, sheep, bear, ass, mouse, stork, swan, and kite.[1] If it is asked why the corn-spirit should be thought to appear in the form of an animal and of so many different animals, we may reply that to primitive man the simple appearance of an animal or bird among the corn is probably enough to suggest a mysterious link between the creature and the corn ; and when we remember that in the old days, before fields were fenced in, all kinds of animals must have been free to roam over them, we need not wonder that the corn-spirit should have been identified even with large animals like the horse and cow, which nowadays could not, except by a rare accident, be found straying in an English corn-field. This explanation applies with peculiar force to the very common case in which the animal embodiment of the corn-spirit is believed to lurk in the last standing corn. For at harvest a number of wild animals, such as hares, rabbits, and partridges, are commonly driven by the progress of the reaping into the last patch of standing corn, and make their escape from it as it is being cut down. So

1 W. Mannhardt, *Die Korndämonen* (Berlin, 1868), p. 1.

regularly does this happen that reapers and others often stand round the last patch of corn armed with sticks or guns, with which they kill the animals as they dart out of their last refuge among the stalks. Now, primitive man, to whom magical changes of shape seem perfectly credible, finds it most natural that the spirit of the corn, driven from his home in the ripe grain, should make his escape in the form of the animal which is seen to rush out of the last patch of corn as it falls under the scythe of the reaper. Thus the identification of the corn-spirit with an animal is analogous to the identification of him with a passing stranger. As the sudden appearance of a stranger near the harvest-field or threshing-floor is, to the primitive mind, enough to identify him as the spirit of the corn escaping from the cut or threshed corn, so the sudden appearance of an animal issuing from the cut corn is enough to identify it with the corn-spirit escaping from his ruined home. The two identifications are so analogous that they can hardly be dissociated in any attempt to explain them. Those who look to some other principle than the one here suggested for the explanation of the latter identification are bound to shew that their theory covers the former identification also.

NOTE

THE PLEIADES IN PRIMITIVE CALENDARS

THE constellation of the Pleiades plays an important part in the Import-
calendar of primitive peoples, both in the northern and in the ance of the
southern hemisphere; indeed for reasons which at first sight are primitive
not obvious savages appear to have paid more attention to this calendars.
constellation than to any other group of stars in the sky, and in
particular they have commonly timed the various operations of the
agricultural year by observation of its heliacal rising or setting.
Some evidence on the subject was adduced by the late Dr. Richard
Andree,[1] but much more exists, and it may be worth while to put
certain of the facts together.

In the first place it deserves to be noticed that great attention Attention
has been paid to the Pleiades by savages in the southern hemisphere paid to the
who do not till the ground, and who therefore lack that incentive to by the
observe the stars which is possessed by peoples in the agricultural Australian
stage of society; for we can scarcely doubt that in early ages the aborigines.
practical need of ascertaining the proper seasons for sowing and
planting has done more than mere speculative curiosity to foster
a knowledge of astronomy by compelling savages to scrutinise the
great celestial clock for indications of the time of year. Now
amongst the rudest of savages known to us are the Australian
aborigines, none of whom in their native state ever practised
agriculture. Yet we are told that "they do, according to their
manner, worship the hosts of heaven, and believe particular constellations rule natural causes. For such they have names, and
sing and dance to gain the favour of the Pleiades (*Mormodellick*),
the constellation worshipped by one body as the giver of rain; but
if it should be deferred, instead of blessings curses are apt to be
bestowed upon it." [2] According to a writer, whose evidence on

---

[1] R. Andree, "Die Pleiaden im
Mythus und in ihrer Beziehung zum
Jahresbeginn und Landbau," *Globus*,
lxiv. (1893) pp. 362-366.
[2] Mr. McKellar, quoted by the Rev.

W. Ridley, "Report on Australian
Languages and Traditions," *Journal of
the Anthropological Institute*, ii. (1873)
p. 279; *id.*, *Kamilaroi* (Sydney, 1875),
p. 138. Mr. McKellar's evidence was

other matters of Australian beliefs is open to grave doubt, some of the aborigines of New South Wales denied that the sun is the source of heat, because he shines also in winter when the weather is cold ; the real cause of warm weather they held to be the Pleiades, because as the summer heat increases, that constellation rises higher and higher in the sky, reaching its greatest elevation in the height of summer, and gradually sinking again in autumn as the days grow cooler, till in winter it is either barely visible or lost to view altogether.[1]   Another writer, who was well acquainted with the natives of Victoria in the early days of the colony and whose testimony can be relied upon, tells us that an old chief of the Spring Creek tribe "taught the young people the names of the favourite planets and constellations, as indications of the seasons.   For example, when Canopus is a very little above the horizon in the east at daybreak, the season for emu eggs has come ; when the Pleiades are visible in the east an hour before sunrise, the time for visiting friends and neighbouring tribes is at hand."[2]

Attention paid to the Pleiades by the Indians of Paraguay and Brazil.

Again, the Abipones of Paraguay, who neither sowed nor reaped,[3] nevertheless regarded the Pleiades as an image of their ancestor. As that constellation is invisible in the sky of South America for several months every year, the Abipones believed that their ancestor was then sick, and they were dreadfully afraid that he would die.   But when the constellation reappeared in the month of May, they saluted the return of their ancestor with joyous shouts and the glad music of flutes and horns, and they congratulated him on his recovery from sickness.   Next day they all went out to collect wild honey, from which they brewed a favourite beverage. Then at sunset they feasted and kept up the revelry all night by the

given before a Select Committee of the Legislative Council of Victoria in 1858 ; from which we may perhaps infer that his statement refers especially to the tribes of Victoria or at all events to be a common belief among the aborigines of central and south-eastern Australia that the Pleiades are women who once lived on earth but afterwards went up into the sky. See W. E. Stanbridge, in *Transactions of the Ethnological Society of London*, N.S. i. (1861) p. 302 ; P. Beveridge, "Of the Aborigines inhabiting the great Lacustrine and Riverine Depression of the Lower Murray," etc., *Journal and Proceedings of the Royal Society of New South Wales*, xvii. (Sydney, 1884) p. 61 ; Baldwin Spencer and F. J. Gillen, *Native Tribes of Central Australia* (London, 1899), p. 566 ; *id.*, *Northern Tribes*

of Central Australia (London, 1904), p. 628; A. W. Howitt, *Native Tribes of South-East Australia* (London, 1904), pp. 429 *sq.*   Some tribes of Victoria believed that the Pleiades were originally a queen and six of her attendants, but that the Crow (Waa) fell in love with the queen and ran away with her, and that since then the Pleiades have been only six in number. See James Dawson, *Australian Aborigines* (Melbourne, Sydney, and Adelaide, 1881), p. 100.

[1] J. Manning, "Notes on the Aborigines of New Holland," *Journal and Proceedings of the Royal Society of New South Wales*, xvi. (Sydney, 1883) p. 168.

[2] James Dawson, *Australian Aborigines*, p. 75.

[3] M. Dobrizhoffer, *Historia de Abiponibus* (Vienna, 1784), ii. 118.

light of torches, while a sorceress, who presided at the festivity, shook her rattle and danced. But the proceedings were perfectly decorous ; the sexes did not mix with each other.[1] The Mocobis of Paraguay also looked upon the Pleiades as their father and creator.[2] The Guaycurus of the Gran Chaco used to rejoice greatly at the reappearance of the Pleiades. On this occasion they held a festival at which men and women, boys and girls all beat each other soundly, believing that this brought them health, abundance, and victory over their enemies.[3] Amongst the Lengua Indians of Paraguay at the present day the rising of the Pleiades is connected with the beginning of spring, and feasts are held at this time, generally of a markedly immoral character.[4] The Guaranis of Paraguay knew the time of sowing by observation of the Pleiades ;[5] they are said to have revered the constellation and to have dated the beginning of their year from the rising of the constellation in May.[6] The Tapuiyas, formerly a numerous and warlike tribe of Brazil, hailed the rising of the Pleiades with great respect, and worshipped the constellation with songs and dances.[7] The Indians of north-western Brazil, an agricultural people who subsist mainly by the cultivation of manioc, determine the time for their various field labours by the position of certain constellations, especially the Pleiades ; when that constellation has sunk beneath the horizon, the regular, heavy rains set in.[8] The Omagua Indians of Brazil ascribe to the Pleiades a special influence on human destiny.[9] A Brazilian name for the Pleiades is *Cyiuce*, that is, " Mother of those who are thirsty." The constellation, we are told, " is known to the Indians of the whole of Brasil and appears to be even worshipped by some tribes in Matto Grosso. In the valley of the Amazon a number of popular sayings are current about it. Thus they say that in the first days of its appearance in the firmament, while it is still low, the birds and especially the fowls sleep on the lower branches or perches, and that just as it rises so do they ; that it brings much cold and rain ; that when the constellation vanishes, the serpents lose their venom ; that the reeds

[1] M. Dobrizhoffer, *op. cit.* ii. 77 *sq.*, 101-105.

[2] Pedro de Angelis, *Coleccion de Obras y Documentos relativos a la Historia antigua y moderna de las Provincias del Rio de la Plata* (Buenos Ayres, 1836-1837), iv. 15.

[3] P. Lozano, *Descripcion chorographico del terreno, rios, arboles, y animales del Gran Chaco* (Cordova, 1733), p. 67.

[4] W. Barbrooke Grubb, *An Unknown People in an Unknown Land* (London, 1911), p. 139.

[5] Pedro de Angelis, *op. cit.* iv. 14.

[6] Th. Waitz, *Anthropologie der Naturvölker*, iii. (Leipsic, 1862) p. 418, referring to Marcgrav de Liebstadt, *Hist. rerum naturalium Brasil.* (Amsterdam, 1648), viii. 5 and 12.

[7] M. Dobrizhoffer, *Historia de Abiponibus*, ii. 104.

[8] Th. Koch-Grünberg, *Zwei Jahre unter den Indianern* (Berlin, 1909-1910), ii. 203.

[9] C. F. Phil. v. Martius, *Zur Ethnographie Amerika's, zumal Brasiliens* (Leipsic, 1867), p. 441.

used in making arrows must be cut before the appearance of the Pleiades, else they will be worm-eaten. According to the legend the Pleiades disappear in May and reappear in June. Their reappearance coincides with the renewal of vegetation and of animal life. Hence the legend relates that everything which appears before the constellation is renewed, that is, the appearance of the Pleiades, marks the beginning of spring."[1] The Indians of the Orinoco called the Pleiades *Ucasu* or *Cacasau*, according to their dialect, and they dated the beginning of their year from the time when these stars are visible in the east after sunset.[2]

Attention paid to the Pleiades by the Indians of Peru and Mexico.

By the Indians of Peru "the Pleiades were called *Collca* (the maize-heap): in this constellation the Peruvians both of the sierra and the coast beheld the prototype of their cherished stores of corn. It made their maize to grow, and was worshipped accordingly."[3] When the Pleiades appeared above the horizon on or about Corpus Christi Day, these Indians celebrated their chief festival of the year and adored the constellation "in order that the maize might not dry up."[4] Adjoining the great temple of the Sun at Cuzco there was a cloister with halls opening off it. One of these halls was dedicated to the Moon, and another to the planet Venus, the Pleiades, and all the other stars. The Incas venerated the Pleiades because of their curious position and the symmetry of their shape.[5] The tribes of Vera Cruz, on the coast of Mexico, dated the beginning of their year from the heliacal setting of the Pleiades, which in the latitude of Vera Cruz (19° N.) in the year 1519 fell on the first of May of the Gregorian calendar.[6] The Aztecs appear to have attached great importance to the Pleiades, for they timed the most solemn and impressive of all their religious ceremonies so as to coincide with the moment when that constellation was in the middle of the sky at midnight. The ceremony consisted in kindling a sacred new fire on the breast of a human victim on the last night of a great period of fifty-two years. They expected that at the close of one of these periods the stars would cease to revolve and the world itself would come to an end. Hence, when the critical moment approached,

[1] Carl Teschauer, S.J., "Mythen und alte Volkssagen aus Brasilien," *Anthropos*, i. (1906) p. 736.
[2] J. Gumilla, *Histoire Naturelle et Civile et Géographique de l'Orenoque* (Avignon, 1758), iii. 254 *sq.*
[3] E. J. Payne, *History of the New World called America*, i. (Oxford, 1892) p. 492.
[4] P. J. de Arriaga, *Extirpacion de la Idolatria del Piru* (Lima, 1621), pp. 11, 29 *sq.* According to Arriaga, the Peruvian name for the Pleiades is *Oncoy*.

[5] Garcilasso de la Vega, *First Part of the Royal Commentaries of the Yncas*, translated by (Sir) Clements R. Markham (London, 1869-1871, Hakluyt Society), i. 275. Compare J. de Acosta, *Natural and Moral History of the Indies* (London, 1880, Hakluyt Society), ii. 304.

[6] E. Seler, *Alt-Mexikanische Studien*, ii. (Berlin, 1899) pp. 166 *sq.*, referring to Petrus Martyr, *De nuper sub D. Carolo repertis insulis* (Basileae, 1521), p. 15.

the priests watched from the top of a mountain the movement of the stars, and especially of the Pleiades, with the utmost anxiety. When that constellation was seen to cross the meridian, great was the joy; for they knew that the world was respited for another fifty-two years. Immediately the bravest and handsomest of the captives was thrown down on his back; a board of dry wood was placed on his breast, and one of the priests made fire by twirling a stick between his hands on the board. As soon as the flame burst forth, the breast of the victim was cut open, his heart was torn out, and together with the rest of his body was thrown into the fire. Runners carried the new fire at full speed to all parts of the kingdom to rekindle the cold hearths; for every fire throughout the country had been extinguished as a preparation for this solemn rite.[1]

The Blackfeet Indians of North America "know and observe the Pleiades, and regulate their most important feast by those stars. About the first and the last days of the occultation of the Pleiades there is a sacred feast among the Blackfeet. The mode of observance is national, the whole of the tribe turning out for the celebration of its rites, which include two sacred vigils, the solemn blessing and planting of the seed. It is the opening of the agricultural season. . . . In all highly religious feasts the calumet, or pipe, is always presented towards the Pleiades, with invocation for life-giving goods. The women swear by the Pleiades as the men do by the sun or the morning star." At the general meeting of the nation there is a dance of warriors, which is supposed to represent the dance of the seven young men who are identified with the Pleiades. For the Indians say that the seven stars of the constellation were seven brothers, who guarded by night the field of sacred seed and danced round it to keep themselves awake during the long hours of darkness.[2] According to another legend told by the Blackfeet, the Pleiades are six children, who were so ashamed because they had no little yellow hides of buffalo calves that they wandered away on the plains and were at last taken up into the sky. "They are not seen during the moon, when the buffalo calves are yellow (spring, the time of their shame), but, every year, when the calves turn brown (autumn), the lost children can be seen in the sky every night."[3] This version of the myth, it will be observed, recognises

Attention paid to the Pleiades by the North American Indians.

[1] B. de Sahagun, *Histoire Générale des choses de la Nouvelle Espagne* (Paris, 1880), pp. 288 *sq.*, 489 *sqq.*; A. de Herrera, *General History of the Vast Continent and Islands of America*, translated by Capt. J. Stevens (London, 1725-1726), iii. 222; F. S. Clavigero, *History of Mexico*, translated by C. Cullen (London, 1807), i. 315 *sq.*; J. G. Müller, *Geschichte der amerikanischen Urreligionen* (Bâle, 1867), pp. 519 *sq.*;

H. H. Bancroft, *The Native Races of the Pacific States of North America* (London, 1875-1876), iii. 393-395.
[2] Jean l'Heureux, " Ethnological Notes on the Astronomical Customs and Religious Ideas of the Chokitapia or Blackfeet Indians," *Journal of the Anthropological Institute*, xv. (1886) pp. 301-303.
[3] Walter McClintock, *The Old North Trail* (London, 1910), p. 490.

only six stars in the constellation, and many savages apparently see no more, which speaks ill for the keenness of their vision; since among ourselves persons endowed with unusually good sight are able, I understand, to discern seven. Among the Pueblo Indians of Tusayan, an ancient province of Arizona, the culmination of the Pleiades is often used to determine the proper time for beginning a sacred nocturnal rite, especially an invocation addressed to the six deities who are believed to rule the six quarters of the world. The writer who records this fact adds : " I cannot explain its significance, and why of all stellar objects this minute cluster of stars of a low magnitude is more important than other stellar groups is not clear to me." [1] If the Pueblo Indians see only six stars in the cluster, as to which I cannot speak, it might seem to them a reason for assigning one of the stars to each of the six quarters, namely, north, south, east, west, above, and below.

Attention paid to the Pleiades by the Polynesians. The Society Islanders in the South Pacific divided the year into two seasons, which they determined by observation of the Pleiades. " The first they called *Matarii i nia*, Pleiades above. It commenced when, in the evening, these stars appeared on or near the horizon ; and the half year, during which, immediately after sunset, they were seen above the horizon, was called *Matarii i nia*. The other season commenced when, at sunset, the stars were invisible, and continued until at that hour they appeared again above the horizon. This season was called *Matarii i raro*, Pleiades below." [2] In the Hervey Islands of the South Pacific it is said that the constellation was originally a single star, which was shattered into six fragments by the god Tane. " This cluster of little stars is appropriately named Mata-riki or *little-eyes*, on account of their brightness. It is also designated Tau-ono, or *the-six*, on account of the apparent number of the fragments ; the presence of the seventh star not having been detected by the unassisted native eye." [3] Among these islanders the arrival of the new year was indicated by the appearance of the constellation on the eastern horizon just after sunset, that is, about the middle of December. " Hence the idolatrous worship paid to this beautiful cluster of stars in many of the South Sea Islands. The Pleiades were worshipped at Danger Island, and at the Penrhyns, down to the introduction of Christianity in 1857. In many islands extravagant joy is still manifested at the rising of this constellation out of the ocean." [4] For example, in Manahiki or Humphrey's Island, South Pacific, " when the constellation Pleiades was seen there was unusual joy all over the month, and expressed by singing, dancing,

[1] J. Walter Fewkes, "The Tusayan New Fire Ceremony," *Proceedings of the Boston Society of Natural History*, xxvi. (1895) p. 453.

[2] Rev. W. Ellis, *Polynesian Researches*, Second Edition (London,

1832-1836), i. 87.

[3] Rev. W. W. Gill, *Myths and Songs from the South Pacific* (London, 1876), p. 43.

[4] Rev. W. W. Gill, *op. cit.* p. 317, compare p. 44.

and blowing-shell trumpets."¹ So the Maoris of New Zealand, another Polynesian people of the South Pacific, divided the year into moons and determined the first moon by the rising of the Pleiades, which they called *Matariki*.² Indeed throughout Polynesia the rising of the Pleiades (variously known as Matariki, Mataliki, Matalii, Makalii, etc.) seems to have marked the beginning of the year.³

Among some of the Melanesians also the Pleiades occupy an important position in the calendar. "The Banks' islanders and Northern New Hebrides people content themselves with distinguishing the Pleiades, by which the approach of yam harvest is marked."⁴ Attention paid to the Pleiades by the Melanesians.

" Amongst the constellations, the Pleiades and Orion's belt seem to be those which are most familiar to the natives of Bougainville Straits. The former, which they speak of as possessing six stars, they name *Vuhu* ; the latter *Matatala*. They have also names for a few other stars. As in the case of many other savage races, the Pleiades is a constellation of great significance with the inhabitants of these straits. The Treasury Islanders hold a great feast towards the end of October, to celebrate, as far as I could learn, the approaching appearance of the constellation above the eastern horizon soon after sunset. Probably, as in many of the Pacific Islands, this event marks the beginning of their year. I learned from Mr. Stephens that, in Ugi, where of all the constellations the Pleiades alone receives a name, the natives are guided by it in selecting the times for planting and taking up the yams."⁵

The natives of the Torres Straits islands observe the appearance of the Pleiades (*Usiam*) on the horizon at sunset ; and when they see it, they say that the new yam time has come.⁶ The Kai and the Bukaua, two agricultural tribes of German New Guinea, also determine the season of their labour in the fields by observation of the Pleiades : the Kai say that the time for such labours is when the Pleiades are visible above the horizon at night.⁷ In some districts of northern Celebes the rice-fields are similarly prepared for cultivation when the Pleiades are seen at a certain height above the Attention paid to the Pleiades by the natives of New Guinea and the Indian Archipelago.

¹ G. Turner, *Samoa* (London, 1884), p. 279.
² E. Shortland, *Traditions and Superstitions of the New Zealanders*, Second Edition (London, 1856), p. 219.
³ *The United States Exploring Expedition, Ethnography and Philology*, by Horatio Hale (Philadelphia, 1846), p. 170 ; E. Tregear, *Maori-Polynesian Comparative Dictionary* (Wellington, N.Z., 1891), p. 226.
⁴ Rev. R. H. Codrington, *The Melanesians* (Oxford, 1891), p. 348.

In the island of Florida the Pleiades are called *togo ni samu*, "the company of maidens" (*op. cit.* p. 349).
⁵ H. B. Guppy, *The Solomon Islands and their Natives* (London, 1887), p. 56.
⁶ A. C. Haddon, "Legends from Torres Straits," *Folk-lore*, i. (1890) p. 195. We may conjecture that the " new yam time " means the time for planting yams.
⁷ R. Neuhauss, *Deutsch Neu-Guinea* (Berlin, 1911), pp. 159, 431 *sq.*

horizon.[1]   As to the Dyaks of Sarawak we read that "the Pleiades themselves tell them when to farm; and according to their position in the heavens, morning and evening, do they cut down the forest, burn, plant, and reap. The Malays are obliged to follow their example, or their lunar year would soon render their farming operations unprofitable."[2]   When the season for clearing fresh land in the forest approaches, a wise man is appointed to go out before dawn and watch for the Pleiades. As soon as the constellation is seen to rise while it is yet dark, they know that the time has come to begin. But not until the Pleiades are at the zenith before dawn do the Dyaks think it desirable to burn the fallen timber and to sow the rice.[3]   However, the Kenyahs and Kayans, two other tribes of Sarawak, determine the agricultural seasons by observation of the sun rather than of the stars; and for this purpose they have devised certain simple but ingenious mechanisms. The Kenyahs measure the length of the shadow cast by an upright pole at noon; and the Kayans let in a beam of light through a hole in the roof and measure the distance from the point immediately below the hole to the place where the light reaches the floor.[4]   But the Kayans of the Mahakam river, in Dutch Borneo, determine the time for sowing by observing when the sun sets in a line with two upright stones.[5]   In Bali, an island to the east of Java, the appearance of the Pleiades at sunset in March marks the end of the year.[6]   The Pleiades and

[1] A. F. van Spreeuwenberg, "Een blik op de Minahassa," *Tijdschrift voor Neerlands Indië*, Vierde Deel (Batavia, 1845), p. 316; J. G. F. Riedel, "De landschappen Holontalo, Limoeto, Bone, Boalemo, et Kattingola, of Andagile," *Tijdschrift voor Indische Taal- Land- en Volkenkunde*, xix. (1869) p. 140; *id.*, in *Zeitschrift für Ethnologie*, iii. (1871) p. 404.

[2] Spenser St. John, *Life in the Forests of the Far East*, Second Edition (London, 1863), i. 214. Compare H. Low, *Sarawak* (London, 1848), p. 251.

[3] Dr. Charles Hose, "Various Modes of computing the Time for Planting among the Races of Borneo," *Journal of the Straits Branch of the Royal Asiatic Society*, No. 42 (Singapore, 1905), pp. 1 *sq.* Compare Charles Brooke, *Ten Years in Sarawak* (London, 1866), i. 59; Rev. J. Perham, "Sea Dyak Religion," *Journal of the Straits Branch of the Royal Asiatic Society*, No. 10 (Singapore, 1883), p. 229.

[4] Dr. Charles Hose, *op. cit.* p. 4.

Compare *id.*, "The Natives of Borneo," *Journal of the Anthropological Institute*, xxiii. (1894) pp. 168 *sq.*, where the writer tells us that the Kayans and many other races in Borneo sow the rice when the Pleiades appear just above the horizon at daybreak, though the Kayans more usually determine the time for sowing by observation of the sun. As to the Kayan mode of determining the time for sowing by the length of shadow cast by an upright pole, see also W. Kükenthal, *Forschungsreise in den Molukken und in Borneo* (Frankfort, 1896), pp. 292 *sq.* Some Dyaks employ a species of sun-dial for dating the twelve months of the year. See H. E. D. Engelhaard, "Aanteekeningen betreffende de Kindjin Dajaks in het Landschap Baloengan," *Tijdschrift voor Indische Taal- Land- en Volkenkunde*, xxxix. (1897) pp. 484-486.

[5] A. W. Nieuwenhuis, *Quer durch Borneo* (Leyden, 1904-1907), i. 160.

[6] F. K. Ginzel, *Handbuch der mathematischen und technischen Chronologie*, i. (Leipsic, 1906) p. 424.

Orion are the only constellations which the people of Bali observe for the purpose of correcting their lunar calendar by intercalation. For example, they bring the lunar year into harmony with the solar by prolonging the month Asada until the Pleiades are visible at sunset.[1] The natives of Nias, an island to the south of Sumatra, pay little heed to the stars, but they have names for the Morning Star and for the Pleiades; and when the Pleiades appear in the sky, the people assemble to till their fields, for they think that to do so before the rising of the constellation would be useless.[2] In some districts of Sumatra "much confusion in regard to the period of sowing is said to have arisen from a very extraordinary cause. Anciently, say the natives, it was regulated by the stars, and particularly by the appearance (heliacal rising) of the *bintang baniak* or Pleiades; but after the introduction of the Mahometan religion, they were induced to follow the returns of the *puāsa* or great annual fast, and forgot their old rules. The consequence of this was obvious; for the lunar year of the *hejrah* being eleven days short of the sidereal or solar year, the order of the seasons was soon inverted; and it is only astonishing that its inaptness to the purposes of agriculture should not have been immediately discovered."[3] The Battas or Bataks of central Sumatra date the various operations of the agricultural year by the positions of Orion and the Pleiades. When the Pleiades rise before the sun at the beginning of July, the Achinese of northern Sumatra know that the time has come to sow the rice.[4]

Scattered and fragmentary as these notices are, they suffice to shew that the Pleiades have received much attention from savages in the tropical regions of the world from Brasil in the east to Sumatra in the west. Far to the north of the tropics the rude Kamchatkans are said to know only three constellations, the Great Bear, the Pleiades, and three stars in Orion.[5] When we pass to Africa we again find the Pleiades employed by tribes in various parts of the continent to mark the seasons of the agricultural year. We have seen that the Caffres of South Africa date their new year from the rising of the Pleiades just before sunrise and fix the time for sowing by observation of that constellation.[6] "They calculate

Attention paid to the Pleiades by the natives of Africa.

[1] R. Friederich, "Voorloopig Verslag van het eiland Bali," *Verhandelingen van het Bataviaasch Genootschap van Kunsten en Wettenschappen*, xxiii. (1849) p. 49.

[2] J. T. Nieuwenhuisen en H. C. B. von Rosenberg, "Verslag omtrent het eiland Nias en deszelfs Bewoners," *Verhandelingen van het Bataviaasch Genootschap van Kunsten en Wetenschappen*, xxx. (Batavia, 1863) p. 119.

[3] W. Marsden, *History of Sumatra*, Third Edition (London, 1811), p. 71.

[4] F. K. Ginzel, *Handbuch der mathematischen und technischen Chronologie*, i. (Leipsic, 1906) p. 428.

[5] S. Krascheninnikow, *Beschreibung des Landes Kamtschatka* (Lemgo, 1766), p. 217. The three stars are probably the Belt.

[6] See above, vol. i. p. 116.

only twelve lunar months for the year, for which they have descriptive names, and this results in frequent confusion and difference of opinion as to which month it really is.   The confusion is always rectified by the first appearance of Pleiades just before sunrise, and a fresh start is made and things go on smoothly till once more the moons get out of place, and reference has again to be made to the stars." [1]   According to another authority on the Bantu tribes of South Africa, "the rising of the Pleiades shortly after sunset was regarded as indicating the planting season.   To this constellation, as well as to several of the prominent stars and planets, they gave expressive names.   They formed no theories concerning the nature of the heavenly bodies and their motions, and were not given to thinking of such things." [2]   The Amazulu call the Pleiades *Isilimela*, which means "The digging-for (stars),'' because when the Pleiades appear the people begin to dig.   They say that "*Isilimela* (the Pleiades) dies, and is not seen.   It is not seen in winter; and at last, when the winter is coming to an end, it begins to appear— one of its stars first, and then three, until going on increasing it becomes a cluster of stars, and is perfectly clear when the sun is about to rise.   And we say *Isilimela* is renewed, and the year is renewed, and so we begin to dig." [3]   The Bechuanas "are directed by the position of certain stars in the heavens, that the time has arrived, in the revolving year, when particular roots can be dug up for use, or when they may commence their labours of the field.   This is their *likhakologo* (turnings or revolvings), or what we should call the spring time of the year.   The Pleiades they call *seleméla*, which may be translated 'cultivator,' or the precursor of agriculture, from *leméla*, the relative verb to cultivate *for*; and *se*, a pronominal prefix, distinguishing them as the actors.   Thus, when this constellation assumes a certain position in the heavens, it is the signal to commence cultivating their fields and gardens." [4]   Among some of these South African tribes the period of seclusion observed by lads after circumcision comes to an end with the appearance of the Pleiades, and accordingly the youths are said to long as ardently for the rising of the constellation as Mohammedans for the rising of the moon which will put an end to the fast of Ramadan. [5]   The Hottentots date the seasons of the

[1] Rev. J. Macdonald, *Light in Africa*, Second Edition (London, 1890), pp. 194 *sq.*   Compare J. Sechefo, "The Twelve Lunar Months among the Basuto," *Anthropos*, iv. (1909) p. 931.

[2] G. McCall Theal, *Records of South-Eastern Africa*, vii. (1901) p. 418.   Compare G. Thompson, *Travels and Adventures in Southern Africa*

(London, 1827), ii. 359.

[3] Rev. H. Callaway, *The Religious System of the Amazulu*, Part iii. (London, etc., 1870), p. 397.

[4] R. Moffat, *Missionary Labours and Scenes in Southern Africa* (London, 1842), pp. 337 *sq.*

[5] Stephen Kay, *Travels and Researches in Caffraria* (London, 1833), p. 273.

year by the rising and setting of the Pleiades.[1] An early Moravian missionary settled among the Hottentots, reports that "at the return of the Pleiades these natives celebrate an anniversary; as soon as these stars appear above the eastern horizon mothers will lift their little ones on their arms, and running up to elevated spots, will show to them those friendly stars, and teach them to stretch their little hands towards them. The people of a kraal will assemble to dance and to sing according to the old custom of their ancestors. The chorus always sings : 'O Tiqua, our Father above our heads, give rain to us, that the fruits (bulbs, etc.), *uientjes,* may ripen, and that we may have plenty of food, send us a good year.'"[2] With some tribes of British Central Africa the rising of the Pleiades early in the evening is the signal for the hoeing to begin.[3] To the Masai of East Africa the appearance of the Pleiades in the west is the sign of the beginning of the rainy season, which takes its name from the constellation.[4] In Masailand the Pleiades are above the horizon from September till about the seventeenth of May; and the people, as they express it themselves, "know whether it will rain or not according to the appearance or non-appearance of the six stars, called The Pleiades, which follow after one another like cattle. When the month which the Masai call 'Of the Pleiades'[5] arrives, and the Pleiades are no longer visible, they know that the rains are over. For the Pleiades set in that month and are not seen again until the season of showers has come to an end :[6] it is then that they reappear."[7] The only other groups of stars for which the Masai appear to have names are Orion's sword and Orion's belt.[8] The Nandi of British East Africa have a special name (*Koremerik*) for the Pleiades, " and it is by the appearance or non-appearance of these stars that the Nandi know whether they may expect a good or a bad harvest."[9] The Kikuyu of the same region say that "the Pleiades is the mark in the heavens to show the people when to plant their crops; they plant when this constellation is in a certain position early in the night."[10] In Sierra Leone "the proper time

[1] Gustav Fritsch, *Die Eingeborenen Süd-Afrika's* (Breslau, 1872), p. 340.

[2] Theophilus Hahn, *Tsuni-Goam, the Supreme Being of the Khoi-Khoi* (London, 1881), p. 43, quoting the Moravian missionary George Schmidt, who was sent out to the Cape of Good Hope in 1737.

[3] H. S. Stannus, "Notes on some Tribes of British Central Africa," *Journal of the R. Anthropological Institute,* xl. (1910) p. 289.

[4] M. Merker, *Die Masai* (Berlin, 1894), pp. 155, 198.

[5] May.   [6] June-August.

[7] A. C. Hollis, *The Masai* (Oxford, 1905), p. 275, compare p. 333. The " season of showers " seems to be a name for the dry season (June, July, August), when rain falls only occasionally ; it is thus distinguished from the rainy season of winter, which begins after the reappearance of the Pleiades in September.

[8] A. C. Hollis, *The Masai,* pp. 275 *sq.*

[9] A. C. Hollis, *The Nandi* (Oxford, 1909), p. 100.

[10] C. W. Hobley, "Further Researches into Kikuyu and Kamba

for preparing the plantations is shewn by the particular situation in which the Pleiades, called by the Bulloms *a-warrang*, the only stars which they observe or distinguish by peculiar names, are to be seen at sunset."[1] We have seen that ancient Greek farmers reaped their corn when the Pleiades rose at sunrise in May, and that they ploughed their fields when the constellation set at sunrise in November.[2] The interval between the two dates is about six months. Both the Greeks and the Romans dated the beginning of summer from the heliacal rising of the Pleiades and the beginning of winter from their heliacal setting.[3] Pliny regarded the autumnal setting of the Pleiades as the proper season for sowing the corn, particularly the wheat and the barley, and he tells us that in Greece and Asia all the crops were sown at the setting of that constellation.[4]

So widespread over the world has been and is the association of the Pleiades with agriculture, especially with the sowing or planting of the crops. The reason for the association seems to be the coincidence of the rising or setting of the constellation with the commencement of the rainy season; since men must very soon have learned that the best, if not the only, season to sow and plant is the time of year when the newly-planted seeds or roots will be quickened by abundant showers. The same association of the Pleiades with rain seems sufficient to explain their importance even for savages who do not till the ground; for ignorant though such races are, they yet can hardly fail to observe that wild fruits grow more plentifully, and therefore that they themselves have more to eat after a heavy fall of rain than after a long drought. In point of fact we saw that some of the Australian aborigines, who are wholly ignorant of agriculture, look on the Pleiades as the givers of rain, and curse the constellation if its appearance is not followed by the expected showers.[5] On the other side of the world, and at the opposite end of the scale of culture, the civilised Greeks similarly supposed that the autumnal setting of the Pleiades was the cause of the rains which followed it; and the astronomical writer Geminus thought it worth while to argue against the supposition, pointing out that the vicissitudes of the weather and of the seasons, though they may coincide with the risings and settings of the constellations, are not produced by them,

Marginal notes: Attention paid to the Pleiades by the Greeks and Romans.

The widespread association of the Pleiades with agriculture seems to be based on the coincidence of their rising or setting with the commencement of the rainy season.

Religious Beliefs and Customs," *Journal of the Royal Anthropological Institute,* xli. (1911) p. 442.

[1] Thomas Winterbottom, *An Account of the Native Africans in the Neighbourhood of Sierra Leone* (London, 1803), p. 48.

[2] Hesiod, *Works and Days,* 383 *sq.,* 615 *sqq.* See above, pp. 45, 48.

[3] Aratus, *Phaenomena,* 264-267; Pliny, *Nat. Hist.* ii. 123, 125, xviii. 280, " *Vergiliae privatim attinent ad*

fructus, ut quarum exortu aestas incipiat, occasu hiems, semenstri spatio intra se messes vindemiasque et omnium maturitatem conplexae." Compare L. Ideler, *Handbuch der mathematischen und technischen Chronologie* (Berlin, 1825-1826), i. 241 *sq.* Pliny dated the rising of the Pleiades on the 10th of May and their setting on the 11th of November (*Nat. Hist.* ii. 123, 125).

[4] Pliny, *Nat. Hist.* xviii. 49 and 223.

[5] See above, p. 307.

the stars being too distant from the earth to exercise any appreciable influence on our atmosphere.   Hence, he says, though the constellations serve as the signals, they must not be regarded as the causes, of atmospheric changes ; and he aptly illustrates the distinction by a reference to beacon-fires, which are the signals, but not the causes, of war.[1]

[1] Geminus, *Elementa Astronomiae*, xvii. 10 *sqq*.   If " the sweet influences of the Pleiades " in the Authorised Version of the English Bible were an exact translation of the corresponding Hebrew words in Job xxxviii. 31, we should naturally explain the " sweet influences " by the belief that the autumnal setting of the constellation is the cause of rain.   But the rendering of the words is doubtful ; it is not even certain that the constellation referred to is the Pleiades.   See the commentaries of A. B. Davidson and Professor A. S. Peak on the passage.   The Revised English Version translates the words in question " the cluster of the Pleiades."   Compare H. Grimme, *Das israelitische Pfingstfest und der Plejadenkult* (Paderborn, 1907), pp. 61 *sqq*.

END OF VOL. I